ARGUMENT STRUCTURE:
A PRAGMATIC THEORY

The current difficulty with using argument diagramming as a teaching tool in courses designed to help students think more critically and criticize arguments more effectively is that the students are not able to carry out these tasks in a confident and definitive way, so that they are sure they have the right answer. The reason for this is that the various tests used in logic textbooks to carry out these tasks are often highly variable and contradictory. In many cases, either no real criteria at all are given, or else those given do not yield clear answers. For example, the same argument might be identified as linked according to the test advocated in one textbook, but as convergent according to another. Some textbook tests even give results that appear intuitively wrong to students.

Douglas Walton provides a systematic survey, clarification, and assessment of the different tests currently being used to carry out the tasks involved in argument identification. He tests the tests themselves, and develops new methods for determining missing premises, for determining whether an argument is linked or convergent, and for deciding whether a given test of discourse contains an argument or not. The result is a clearly expressed theory of argument structure that yields a precise and consistent method of argument diagramming, making the technique much more useful and easily applicable.

Suitable for courses in informal logic, critical thinking, argumentation, and logical reasoning, the book will also be of interest to those in the fields of speech communication, rhetoric, discourse analysis, and education.

DOUGLAS WALTON is Professor of Philosophy at the University of Winnipeg.

Argument Structure: A Pragmatic Theory

DOUGLAS WALTON

UNIVERSITY OF TORONTO PRESS
Toronto Buffalo London

© University of Toronto Press Incorporated 1996
Toronto Buffalo London
Printed in Canada
Reprinted in 2018
ISBN 0-8020-0768-6 (cloth)
ISBN 978-0-8020-7137-8 (paper)

Printed on acid-free paper

Toronto Studies in Philosophy
Editors: James R. Brown and Calvin Normore

Canadian Cataloguing in Publication Data

Walton, Douglas N. (Douglas Neil), 1942–
   Argument structure : a pragmatic theory

(Toronto studies in philosophy)
ISBN 0-8020-0768-6 (bound)   ISBN 978-0-8020-7137-8 (paper)

1. Reasoning. 2. Logic. I. Title. II. Series.

BC177.W35 1996   160   C96-930107-3

University of Toronto Press acknowledges the financial assistance to its publishing program of the Canada Council and Ontario Arts Council.

For Karen, with love

Contents

Preface xi

Chapter One: What Is an Argument? 3

1. Textbook Definitions 4
2. Reasoning in Argument 9
3. Hypothetical Arguments 11
4. *Reductio ad Absurdum* 15
5. The Probative Function 20
6. The Dialectical Context 22
7. The Concepts of Argument and Explanation 26
8. The *Ad Populum* Fallacy 31
9. The Fallacy of Begging the Question 33
10. Towards a Pragmatic Concept of Argument 37

Chapter Two: Arguments and Explanations 42

1. Argument and Explanation Combined 42
2. Arguments That Are Not Explanations 46
3. Indicator-Words 49
4. Insufficiency of Indicator-Words 52

Contents

- 5. The Pedagogical Problem   56
- 6. The Textbook Test Revised   59
- 7. Reasoning in Argument and Explanation   63
- 8. The 'Risks for Managers' Case   67
- 9. The 'Foundations of Philosophy' Case   71
- 10. Reorienting the Task as Dialectical   74

Chapter Three: The Art of Diagramming   78

- 1. The State of the Art   78
- 2. Elements of Diagramming   83
- 3. Linked and Convergent Arguments   85
- 4. Serial and Divergent Arguments   89
- 5. Combined Structures in Diagrams   92
- 6. Some Problem Cases Introduced   95
- 7. The 'Study in Scarlet' Case   99
- 8. Arguments and Explanations   103
- 9. Enthymemes Introduced   105
- 10. The Pedagogical Problem Revisited   107

Chapter Four: Linked and Convergent Arguments   109

- 1. Standard Tests Used in Logic Texts   109
- 2. Tests Used in Speech Communication   114
- 3. The Variety of Tests   118
- 4. Problems in Applying the Tests   122
- 5. Degrees of Support Tests   125
- 6. Evidence-Accumulating Arguments   130
- 7. Key Counter-Examples   134

8. Valid Arguments   137

9. Bad Arguments   139

10. Initial Conditions of Use   143

Chapter Five: Rethinking the Linked–Convergent Distinction   151

1. Problems with the *Susp./No Supp.* and *Fals./No Supp.* Tests   152

2. Problems with the *Susp./Insuf. Prf.* Test   154

3. Argument from Sign   158

4. Cases Lacking Known Structure   161

5. Precision of the Tests   165

6. Concepts behind the Test   168

7. Defining Necessity and Sufficiency   171

8. The Purpose of the Distinction   174

9. The Functional Perspective   176

10. Recommendation on the Best Test   179

Chapter Six: The New Method of Diagramming   183

1. Use of Digraphs to Model Argumentation   184

2. Reasoning Structure   187

3. Circular Reasoning   191

4. Diagramming Incompleteness   196

5. Abstraction Distorts Diagramming   198

6. Vague Concepts Are a Problem   201

7. Interpretation of Discourse Is Subjective   204

8. Distortion and Commitment   208

9. The Principle of Charity   211

10. Outline of the New Method   216

Chapter Seven: Enthymemes 220

1. The Tradition of the Textbooks 221
2. The Aristotelian Enthymeme 226
3. The Question of Terminology 230
4. Types of Basis for the Enthymeme 233
5. Innuendo and Implicature 235
6. The Dangers of Deductivism 237
7. The 'Straw Man' Fallacy 241
8. Argumentation Schemes 245
9. The Two Levels: Need and Use 248
10. Incompleteness 252

Chapter Eight: Abductive Inference 256

1. Peirce on Abduction 256
2. Abduction in Computer Science 260
3. Affirming the Consequent 264
4. Aristotle on the Fallacy of Consequent 266
5. Ancient Views of Argument from Sign 268
6. What Is a Sign? 270
7. Form of Argument from Sign 272
8. How Argument from Sign Works 274
9. Sign versus Best Explanation 277
10. Tentative Conclusions 278

Notes 283

References 289

Index 297

Preface

The genesis of this book was my awareness that I was often repeating to the students in my logic course (especially during our discussion of informal fallacies) that identifying an argument – asking 'What is the argument?' – is a very important part of logic. I found I was frequently pointing out to the students that a particular example could be judged to be an instance of this or that fallacy only if some prior agreement had been reached on exactly what the premises and conclusion of the argument were supposed to be.

I didn't think about this idea very much when I first started teaching logic. But, over the years, I observed that these applied aspects of logic were gaining importance. It occurred to me that, since many people were saying that logic ought to be applied to realistic cases of conversational argumentation, some systematic method of improving skills, or existing techniques, of argument identification should be developed, and the identification of argument ought to be taken much more seriously, as an important branch of logic.

The second stage in the development of this book was a year I spent as a fellow-in-residence at the Netherlands Institute for Advanced Study in the Humanities and Social Sciences (NIAS) as part of a research group on the topic 'Fallacies as Violations of Rules for Argumentative Discourse.' This period of working with some of the leading theorists in the field of argumentation showed me (among other things) the importance of the basic concepts and structures of argument that are used in argument diagramming.

At the same time, this work also demonstrated an interesting divergence of points of view on the concept of argument itself. The NIAS research group was composed of European (Dutch) and North American fellows in roughly equal numbers. The members of our nucleus group were Frans van Eemeren, Rob Grootendorst, Sally Jackson, Scott Jacobs, Agnes van Haft Rees, Agnes Verbiest, Charles Willard, and John Woods. Interestingly, the European theorists tended (generally) to think of an argument as constructive, as a social and verbal process of reasoning together collaboratively to arrive at agreement or resolve a difference. In contrast, the North American scholars tended to think of an argument as a more adversarial type of exchange.

This year at NIAS was to lead me towards a more pragmatic approach to the evaluation of argumentation, resulting in two research projects that were the basis of two books on argument evaluation, *A Pragmatic Theory of Fallacy* (1995) and *Argumentation Schemes for Presumptive Reasoning* (1996). In neither of these books did I attempt to tackle the prior problem of identifying arguments through argument diagramming, the technique most commonly used in logic textbooks to model the identification of an argument. However, in an earlier journal article (Walton, 1990b), I had raised the question 'What is an argument?,' and in several works (Walton 1980 and 1991; Walton and Batten, 1984) on the fallacy of begging the question, I had made some systematic proposals regarding the method of argument diagramming but had focused on the use of the method only in relation to the problem of analysing circular reasoning.

The third stage was my attending the Summer Institute on Argumentation at McMaster University in June 1991. This institute brought together a number of researchers whose work reflects an understanding of argumentation as primarily a kind of conversational interaction. Surprisingly, however, a remarkable preponderance of the material turned out to be on argument diagramming.

Although there was basic agreement among institute participants on how the technique works in broad perspective, and good unanimity on most of the notation and some of the general concepts, there was striking disagreement on some key particulars.

One significant area of disagreement was the nature of the criteria and tests used to distinguish between linked and convergent arguments. Different participants advocated different tests, each appearing to conflict with the others. Some of the participants even argued for the point of view that *none* of the tests worked!

Another key area of disagreement was the question of exactly how to distinguish between an argument and an explanation. Many of the participants despaired that this could even be done at all, and remarked on how often and persistently their students tried to analyse 'arguments' that were not really arguments at all (or not clearly so), but explanations, descriptions, narrations, or other forms of speech.

A third area of concern was that of identifying missing (non-explicit) premises and conclusions. Everyone frankly admitted this to be a major, unsolved problem, even though a traditional method of analysis of enthymemes has been taught throughout the history of logic.

Among the participants in the McMaster summer institute whose lectures or discussions were especially helpful in shaping my views on argument diagramming, I would like to thank J. Anthony Blair, George Bowles, Frans van Eemeren, James Freeman, Rob Grootendorst, Hans Hansen, David Hitchcock, Sally Jackson, Scott Jacobs, Ralph Johnson, Erik Krabbe, Christopher Tindale, Mark Vorobej, and John Woods.

The fourth stage was the teaching of my second-year logic course in 1991–2. I had chosen a textbook that dealt with argument diagramming in its first chapter. When I began the first part of the course, I found this section on argument diagramming surprisingly hard to teach. The students found the exercises not only difficult, but very confusing. Their confidence in logic seemed to be undermined at the outset, and they needed a lot of carefully detailed reassurances and explanations in order that the course could continue smoothly. This experience convinced me that there was something wrong with the technique of argument diagramming, at least in the way it is currently presented in introductory courses on logic and critical thinking (or other courses designed to teach the use of techniques of logical reasoning). I wasn't exactly sure what was wrong, but this feeling of uneasiness was confirmed when I looked more carefully at other logic textbooks, and the literature on argumentation, and saw how flatly many of these texts contradicted one another, even in terms of the basic tests used to identify the component argument structures!

The fifth stage was the assembling and presenting of some lecture notes on these different tests, which provided me an opportunity to discuss questions and problems of argument diagramming with my third-year argumentation class. Three of my students in particular, Paulino Majok, Stephen Morse, and Kevin Paradis, raised a lot of critical questions concerning the usefulness of these tests, and pointed out difficulties in applying them to various problematic cases. During this same period, while visiting the University of Groningen to work on a collaborative research project (Walton and Krabbe, 1995), I had some discussions with Erik Krabbe on the topic of argument diagramming. During these discussions, some useful thoughts came forward on how the subject could be approached generally, in order to make it useful for those of us working and teaching in the area of argumentation. As a result, I was encouraged to develop my ideas on argument diagramming; our findings on the issue of commitment (ibid.) actually pointed the way towards solving the most intractable problems posed by diagramming.

During all these stages, I had been making notes on my own problems with argument diagramming, especially on some of the central concepts that, to me at least, did not appear to make coherent sense in any precise way which could be expressed as clear criteria for use by students learning the technique. But it was during the last stage that I came to the conclusion that, even with all the uncertainties and gaps that seemed so characteristic of the subject, something could be done about it as a research project, by developing a pragmatic theory that gives a unified grasp of the subject, while solving the three central problems in a particular manner. It is clear that we are far from knowing all the answers. But, after all, since the subject was and is being taught widely at the introductory level, clearly a serious research effort is appropriate, to examine the basic gaps, contradictions, and problems in the subject, and to propose clearly worked-out objective methods that can be applied to the solution of these problems. Other work has also begun to appear in the field, notably by Freeman (1991) and Snoeck Henkemans (1992). This book uses similar methods, taking a pragma-dialectical approach, but proposes different solutions.

To accomplish the goal of providing practical methods as well as a theory, I used a case-study approach, taking ordinary, mainly quite simple examples of arguments that occurred in everyday conversations, and trying to apply to them the different tests advocated in the textbooks and other literature. Often, the results were unexpectedly problematic and puzzling, leading to more questions instead of giving definite answers. However, my goal was not to drown the technique of argument diagramming in a sea of counter-examples, puzzles, and problems, but to rescue it, refine it, define its core structure precisely, and to work towards making it a better method that is of practical use for bringing some order to the apparent chaos of everyday argumentation. You, the reader, will have to be the judge of the outcome. The theory presented here will have to compete with other existing theories; however, the theory in this book has two advantages: it is based on a central account of argument structure that can be automated in a computer program, and it is based on a body of evidence consisting of detailed analysis of numerous case-studies of argumentation of a kind that are common in everyday conversation.

The work in this research was supported by a fellowship from NIAS, and a research grant from the Social Sciences and Humanities Research Council of Canada. I am very grateful to Amy Merrett for word-processing the manuscript, including the figures. I would like to thank Harry Simpson for help with the proof-reading, and Rita Campbell for preparing the index.

Argument Structure

1

What Is an Argument?

In this book, we will be concerned with problems in attempting to determine whether a given text of discourse contains an argument, and if so, what the components of the argument are – that is, its premises and conclusion.

These problems are essentially practical in that they involve taking the techniques used in logic to evaluate arguments and applying them to the real world of argumentation as it occurs in everyday speech. But they are also connected to the theoretical level, in so far as the logic textbooks, and the scholarly authorities in the field of argumentation and logic generally, do not agree on (exactly) what an argument is. So, if we don't know exactly what it is we are identifying, how can we devise practical techniques or criteria for identifying it (or subclassifying it as linked, convergent, or whatever)? The problem then is: what is an argument?

In this chapter, we will see that the conventional definitions of 'argument' given in the logic textbooks and in other sources such as reference works and academic theories are too confining to be suitable for informal logic, exhibit considerable disagreements and confusion, or are otherwise inappropriate or non-useful for our purposes. These accounts generally define an argument as a set of propositions, one of which is 'designated' as the 'conclusion,' and the remainder as the 'premises.' But no reference is made to the purpose of putting these propositions forward, or indeed to their having been put forward at all. The general criticism of these textbook definitions made in this chapter is that they are too narrow. More specifically, the following criticisms are advanced:

1 The textbook definitions generally ignore the fact that arguments are often used to refute or question (rather than support) a claimed opinion.
2 The leading textbook definitions define an argument (or its premises) as

giving support (evidence, reasons) for the conclusion, conflicting with a minority view that sees arguments as hypothetical.
3. The textbook definitions do not accommodate indirect proofs.
4. The textbook definitions adopt a localized viewpoint that does not do justice to the context in which an argument was used and to the part the locally designated argument plays in a broader argument.
5. The textbook accounts tend to use words like 'inference,' 'reasoning,' and 'argument' interchangeably, and fail to make clear or generally accepted distinctions among these concepts.
6. Textbook definitions typically exclude the quarrel (eristic exchange) as part of the meaning of 'argument' in logic.

What is needed in logic – especially if logic is to be applied to realistic cases of natural language discourse – is a less restricted and artificial definition of 'argument.' We need a concept of argument that is natural and robust enough to deal with the questions of argument identification, analysis, and evaluation posed by the various informal fallacies, and by related problems in the evaluation of natural language argumentation. Taking several examples of everyday arguments as cases in point, it is shown here how their analysis requires a new, broader definition of the concept of argument put forward in a new theory of argumentation.

The new concept of argument advanced below defines 'argument' in a pragmatic way – an 'argument' is a sequence of propositions, called 'reasoning,' used in different contexts of dialogue in various characteristic ways. Acceptance of this new definition will mean a radical change in the way that textbooks define an 'argument.' But, as is reasoned here, this change is the only way to obtain a workable solution to practical problems of argument identification, analysis, and evaluation.

1. Textbook Definitions

Typically, in everyday conversations and discussions, arguments are used in such a fashion that the proponent of the argument is advocating or claiming the conclusion on the basis of premises put forward as evidence to support the conclusion. Hence, in leading logic textbooks, an 'argument' is defined as a claim for the truth of the conclusion, justified by premises that are regarded as providing support for the conclusion.

Copi and Cohen (1990, p. 6) define an 'argument,' in the logician's sense, as a 'group of propositions of which one is claimed to follow from the others, which are regarded as providing support or grounds for the truth of that one.'

Later (p. 26) they redefine an 'argument' as 'a group of propositions of which one, the conclusion, is claimed to be true on the basis of other propositions, the premisses, that are asserted as providing grounds or reasons for accepting the conclusion.' Copi and Cohen give a test (p. 30) for distinguishing between explanations and arguments (the 'Copi-Cohen test,' discussed in chapter 2, below) which says that, in an argument (as opposed to an explanation), we are interested in establishing the truth of the conclusion, and the premises are offered as evidence for it.

To try to grasp the essentials of this definition a little better, we need to ask what is meant by a 'claim.' A 'claim' that a proposition is true seems to imply a burden of proof to defend it as true, that is, as something that one 'holds' or is committed to. But does this leave enough room for hypothetical arguments, in which a conclusion is accepted provisionally, or 'for the sake of argument'? Such provisional acceptance of a conclusion does not necessarily involve acceptance of it as a claim on the part of the accepting participant in argumentation; that is, she might not take on a burden of proof for it.

Also, if an 'argument' is defined in terms of the premises in it 'providing grounds or reasons for accepting the conclusion,' then we have to ask what 'grounds' or 'reasons' are, other than being good or reasonable arguments. Moreover, a bad or failed argument in which the premises might not provide grounds or reasons for accepting the conclusion would still be an argument.

A similar definition is given by Govier (1992, pp. 2–3):

> An argument is a set of claims that a person puts forward in an attempt to show that some further claim is rationally acceptable. Typically, people present arguments to try to persuade others to accept claims. The evidence or reasons put forward in defense of a claim are called the *premises* of an argument. An argument may have several premises, or it may have only one. The claim being defended in the argument is called *its conclusion*. An argument, then, is composed of one or more premises and a conclusion.

In this definition, it is said that people typically present arguments 'to try to persuade others to accept claims.' This seems like a very good suggestion that does bring out something characteristic of the nature of an argument. But it also brings in a personal element: seemingly, in an argument one party would persuade a second party (the respondent or audience) to come to accept the conclusion that is being advocated or 'claimed' by the first party. It seems, then, that connected to the concept of an argument is that of an arguer, an advocate, presenter, or claimant.

The notion of a claim is very important to both the Govier and the Copi–

Cohen accounts. But neither tells us what a claim is, nor whether a claim implies the existence of a claimant or arguer. It seems to be characteristic of the Copi–Cohen definition that the person making the claim is kept very much in the background. In that definition, the conclusion is a claim, but it is not said that the premises actually support the conclusion. The key notion is that of support, but it is said only that the premises are 'regarded as providing support' for the conclusion. Regarded by whom? Presumably the proponent of the argument. But the concept of a proponent is not, at least explicitly, a part of the definition.

Casullo (1992) defines argument in terms of purported support for a conclusion:

> **argument** A group of statements, some of which purportedly provide support for another. The statements which purportedly provide the support are the *premises* while the statement purportedly supported is the *conclusion*. Arguments are typically divided into two categories depending on the *degree* of support they purportedly provide. *Deductive* arguments purportedly provide *conclusive* support for their conclusions while *inductive* arguments purportedly provide only *probable* support. Some, but not all, arguments succeed in providing support for their conclusions.

The word 'purportedly' is important here, where it means that not every argument has to be a case in which the premises actually support the conclusion. This word suggests some sort of act of putting forward the argument by a purporting agency, but we are not told exactly what 'purportedly' means.

Freeman (1988, p. 20) offers quite a broad definition that includes evidence and justification, as well as support, as characteristics. He also includes as part of it the concept of a claim:

> When we use the word *argument* in this book, we mean a message which attempts to establish a statement as true or worthy of belief on the basis of other statements. Persons putting forward arguments present certain claims, make certain assertions, which they expect or hope their audience will simply accept. They also put forward some further statement as being supported by these accepted claims. There is, thus, a further claim that because we accept the first statements, we should accept the latter. The former give evidence, justification, support for the latter. There are thus two radically different roles which a statement may play in an argument. A reason for some other statement is a *premise*. A statement defended by some other statement or statements is a *conclusion*. Arguments, then, involve these three factors: premises, conclusions, and a claim that the premises support the conclusions.

Here, for the first time, we have 'persons putting forward arguments' as an explicit part of the definition. The focus is still on the statements that make up the argument. But, even so, the acknowledged role of the person presenting the claim, in the hope of getting an audience to accept it, reveals that more is involved in an argument than just this set of propositions. The propositions are said to be part of a relationship between two parties or persons, one of whom makes a claim in order to try to get the other to accept it.

An aspect of all the definitions quoted so far is that the party presenting the argument is using the premises as claims that will be accepted by the other party. In all these definitions, not only the conclusion, but also the premises, are claimed to be true or acceptable.

Hence, we could say that the conception of argument put forward in these definitions is non-hypothetical. Not only is the conclusion claimed to follow from the premises, but the premises themselves are claimed to be true or acceptable. Because we accept the premises, they may be regarded as providing support, justification, or evidence for the conclusion.

According to another definition (Soccio and Barry, 1992, p. 5), the key defining characteristic of an argument is *the claim of following logically from*, whereby one proposition is claimed to follow logically from some others:

> As used in the study of logic, *an argument is any group of propositions* (truth claims), *one of which is claimed to follow logically from the others*. The key phrase here is 'follow logically from.' For a group of propositions to be an argument, one of them must be claimed to *follow logically from* the others.

This definition certainly allows hypothetical arguments to be included. Indeed, it seems tailor-made for hypothetical arguments. This definition does not require that the premises be given to support the conclusion, or as a reason for the conclusion. Rather, a conclusion may be claimed to follow from some premises even though they give no support for it at all, or any reason to accept it.

On this definition, it may be a little hard to distinguish between an argument and an inference (or, at least, a claimed inference). That may be a disadvantage, when compared with the definitions quoted previously. But this definition has the apparent advantage of being able to include a hypothetical argument as an argument.

Carney and Scheer (1974, p. 3) give a very simple definition of an argument as a set of statements offered as a reason for a conclusion:

> Logic is primarily concerned with arguments; it attempts to provide methods to distinguish between correct and incorrect arguments. An *argument* consists of a set

of statements offered as reasons for another statement. The set of statements offered as reasons is called the *premises* of the argument. The statement for which the reasons are offered is called the *conclusion* of the argument.

Some might say this defines 'reasoning' or 'giving a reason' rather than 'argument.' Also, this definition does not distinguish very well between explanation and argument. An explanation can also be a set of statements offered as reasons for another statement (presumably). At any rate, the basic characteristic of this definition of an argument is that of offering a reason. But no account is given of what this amounts to, in general terms.

A different kind of definition is given by Gustason and Ulrich (1973, p. 1): 'For our purposes an *argument* may be characterized as a sequence of sentences of which one – the *conclusion* of the argument – is marked off as following from the others – which are the *premises* of the argument.' This definition appears to be much less substantial than the others. Any set of propositions can be an argument where one is 'marked off as following from the others.' But 'marked off' by whom? By anybody, perhaps? Here, the definition of 'argument' comes close to 'any arbitrarily designated set of propositions.' The premises do not need to be offered as reasons for the conclusion, or as propositions that support the conclusion.

Another very minimal definition, offered by Packard and Faulconer (1980, p. 3), also does not require that the premises actually support, or give reasons for, the conclusion. An 'argument' (in 'standard form') is defined as 'a sequence of statements, called assumptions, followed by the word *so* and a statement called the conclusion.' A sequence containing such words as 'therefore' or 'since' would be an 'argument' if it 'means the same as the standard form.' This definition is clearly hypothetical in nature, contrasting with many of the definitions quoted above, and with the definition given by Kahane (1978, p. 2): 'An *argument* consists of one or more sentences, called *premises* of the argument, offered in support of another sentence, called the argument's *conclusion*.' According to Hurley (1991, p. 1), 'an *argument*, as it occurs in logic, is a group of statements, one or more of which (the premises) are claimed to provide support for, or reasons to believe, one of the others (the conclusion).'

The definitions presented here are fairly typical of what one finds in logic textbooks, both current and traditional. There are differences of phrasing, and highly significant contradictions, but generally they have quite a lot in common.

In one respect, they are all too narrow. In all of these accounts, the premises are meant to support, or provide evidence for, the conclusion, or the conclusion is meant to follow from the premises. But, in many arguments, the premises are meant to refute the conclusion.

2. Reasoning in Argument

The textbook definitions quoted above fail to capture any broad meaning of the term 'argument' in ordinary discourse, in at least one important sense: they focus exclusively on the justification or support of a claimed opinion, ignoring the reality that arguments are often used to refute or to question a claimed opinion.

Of course, all these definitions are taken from logic textbooks, where the intent is to define 'argument' only in 'a logical sense.' The aim is not to give a general lexical definition but, instead, a technical or special definition appropriate for the discipline of logic. And traditionally, the primary concern of the textbooks has been to distinguish between (deductively) valid and invalid arguments.[1]

However, given that many textbooks are also concerned with fallacies and with other factors that have to do with the evaluation of arguments, it could be more appropriate to look to a broader definition of the concept of an argument.

Aristotle, at the beginning of the *De Sophisticis Elenchis* (165 a 3), took his subject-matter as including not only reasoning (*syllogismos*), but also refutation (*elenchos*), defined as 'reasoning accompanied by a contradiction of the conclusion.' The definition of argumentation given by van Eemeren and Grootendorst (1984) takes both these aspects into account.

According to van Eemeren, Grootendorst, and Kruiger (1987, p. 5), the purposes of argumentation are the justification and refutation of opinions. Of course, refutation presents no special problem in terms of defining it: it is the negative counterpart of justification. But it is important that it be included as part of the concept of an argument.

Van Eemeren and Grootendorst (1984, pp. 43–4) put forward five conditions defining *pro-argumentation*:

(1) The speaker has advanced an opinion O.
(2) The speaker has put forward a series of assertions, $S_1, S_2, \ldots, S_n$.
(3) Advancing $S_1, S_2, \ldots, S_n$ counts as an attempt by the speaker to convince the hearer O is acceptable.
(4) The speaker believes the hearer does not already accept O, but will accept $S_1, S_2, \ldots, S_n$ as justification for O.
(5) The speaker believes that O and $S_1, S_2, \ldots, S_n$ are acceptable, and that $S_1, S_2, \ldots, S_n$ justify O.

A comparable, negative set of conditions is given (p. 45) for *contra-argumentation*. The duality of this set of conditions reflects the view of the Amsterdam School – namely, that the purpose of argumentation is both the justification and the refutation of opinions, as noted above. The set of conditions for contra-argumentation is identical to the set quoted above, except that the speaker believes that O is unacceptable (as opposed to acceptable) and she is advancing $S_1, S_2, ..., S_n$ to refute O to the listener's satisfaction (instead of using them to justify O).

The account of the concept of argument put forward by the Amsterdam School is, to some extent, very similar to that given by most of the logic textbooks. The account of pro-argumentation is very similar to what many of the textbooks (by Copi and Cohen, Govier, and so on) say – namely, that the conclusion is a claim, and that the premises are regarded as support, justification, and so on, for that claim.

One key difference, though, is that the Amsterdam definition is more explicitly dialectical, in the sense that it more explicitly takes the context of dialogue into account. Instead of just a 'claim,' we have a 'speaker' and a 'hearer,' and the argument is viewed as an exchange between these two parties. For the first time, explicit mention of persons, speakers, or arguers is made. This idea was brought out, to some extent, by some of the textbook accounts. For example, Govier (1992, p. 2) mentioned that typically arguments are used by people to 'try to persuade others to accept claims.' But, in most of these accounts, the idea of a 'claim' stands by itself, and no explicit mention is made of the claimant, or the disputant or questioner of the claim.

Notice that all the definitions surveyed up to this point take the conclusion of an argument as a claim made that the proposition expressed as the conclusion is true, and take the premises as propositions offered to support, justify, or give evidence that the conclusion is true – except one, Soccio and Barry's. This definition requires only that the conclusion is claimed to 'follow logically from' the premises. In other words, Soccio and Barry's definition is weaker than all the others. It does not require that the premises are claimed to be true, or that they function as reasons or justification offered to support the conclusion. According to the Soccio and Barry definition, an argument can be purely hypothetical.

But are arguments ever purely hypothetical? Or is it better to speak of 'hypothetical reasoning' in such a case? These questions bring us to a prior question. Is there a difference between reasoning and argument? If so, what is it?

Govier (1989b, p. 117) has made a highly plausible characterization of the difference between reasoning and argument:

> An argument is a publicly expressed tool of persuasion. Typically it takes thinking to construct an argument. Reasoning is distinguished from arguing along these lines: reasoning is what you may do before you argue, and your argument expresses some of your (best) reasoning. But much reasoning is done before and outside the context of argument.

Following along these lines of thinking, 'reasoning' is defined by Walton (1990b, p. 403) as 'the making or granting of assumptions called *premises* (starting points) and the process of moving toward conclusions (end points) from these assumptions by means of warrants.' According to this definition, reasoning is often purely hypothetical, and can even be aimless. In contrast, argument (as viewed by van Eemeren and Grootendorst, and also the author in this text) is goal-directed.

According to the account given by Walton (1990b), reasoning is essentially a sequence of inferences joined together – the conclusion of one inference becomes a premise in the next inference. By this account (ibid., p. 404), reasoning normally has a direction, and proceeds backwards as well as forwards. Also, reasoning is used in argument. And, in fact, 'argument' is best defined as 'reasoning used in various types of dialogue.' Eight of these types of dialogue are defined by Walton (ibid., p. 413). One of them is the critical discussion–type dialogue featured in the definition of argument given by van Eemeren and Grootendorst. However, the types of dialogue outlined by Walton elsewhere (1995) include not only persuasion dialogue (of which critical discussion is a subtype), but five other basic subtypes as well. (See also the framework given by Walton and Krabbe [1995].)

3. Hypothetical Arguments

A central difficulty with all (but one) of the definitions of 'argument' outlined above is their failure to take into account the existence of *hypothetical (suppositional)* arguments, where the premises are (mere) assumptions, of the kind recognized by Jacobs (1989). In this kind of argument, the premises are not being asserted, or claimed to be true. They are merely assumptions, from which a conclusion is inferred. In such arguments, the premises are not being used to justify the claim that the conclusion is true, or to support or give evidence for that claim. Certainly it is possible to have hypothetical reasoning. But is it also possible to have hypothetical arguments?

Hypothetical reasoning is very important in science (one famous example is given in section 4, below). Fisher (1988) has noted that, although suppositional reasoning is 'elegant, powerful, and extremely common,' it is not discussed in most texts on informal logic. Fisher thinks that suppositional reasoning is a genuine species of argumentation, and that it ought to be included in argument diagrams that are used to represent arguments in logic textbooks.

Hypothetical arguments have also been recognized by Jacobs (1989) as an important species of argumentation. His criticism of the five conditions for pro-argumentation given by van Eemeren and Grootendorst would apply to all the other definitions of argument in sections 1 and 2, above, as well. Jacobs (p. 353) has argued that the set of conditions (1) through (5), above, is too narrow to define the concept of an argument. He suggests that, in hypothetical and 'devil's advocacy' arguments, the speaker is not necessarily trying to get the hearer to accept an opinion O that she (the speaker) accepts but that he (the hearer) did not initially accept. A *devil's advocacy* argument is one in which the proponent's argument does not support her own claim or the conclusion she advocates, but instead supports the conclusion of the opposing side. This is a hypothetical type of argumentation, used when one wants to see the justification for the other position, that is, the one opposed to one's conclusion, to assess the weight of arguments on both sides of an issue.

A related type of hypothetical argument, in which one argues from a conclusion that is the opposite of one's own, is the *reductio ad absurdum* argument, taken up in section 4, below.

Let us begin consideration of this general problem by taking a simple case of hypothetical reasoning, and seeing whether, or in what sense, it can be called a 'hypothetical argument.'

Consider the following case of hypothetical reasoning, which includes a premise and a conclusion. The premise is a supposition, and an inference is made from this premise to the conclusion.

Case 1.1
Suppose Bob is the murderer.
It follows that Bob would have been in Chicago on the third of May.

This case certainly appears to contain an argument. For sure, it contains an inference, because the speaker makes a supposition, and then says that a proposition 'follows' from this supposition, a prior proposition. The case contains reasoning, then. But is it the sort of inference or reasoning that properly qualifies as an argument?

According to the tests surveyed in sections 1 and 2, it would seem that case 1.1 should not be classified as an argument. The reasons are that: (i) the 'conclusion' that Bob was not in Chicago on the third of May is not a claim being made by the speaker; (ii) the 'premise' that Bob is the murderer is not an assertion being made by the speaker; and (iii) the speaker is not justifying, supporting, or establishing the truth of the conclusion that Bob was in Chicago on the third of May by offering the proposition that Bob is the murderer as evidence for it. At least, none of these is definitely, or necessarily, the case here.

One way out of this apparent difficulty for the definitions of sections 1 and 2 is to say that case 1.1 does contain an argument, but only when filled out with some further context that shows how the inference in it is being used in respect to some contested claim. For example, it could be that the argument is really a kind of *reductio ad falsum*, where a detective is arguing that Bob is not the murderer on the grounds that he couldn't have been in Chicago on the third of May. So interpreted, case 1.1 does contain an argument, complete with claim and asserted premises.

This interpretation can be put in a form that recasts the part explicitly stated in case 1.1 as a hypothetical (conditional) proposition. When the rest is added, the result is an argument having the form of *modus tollens*.

Case 1.2
If Bob is the murderer, then Bob was in Chicago on the third of May.
Bob was not in Chicago on the third of May.
Therefore, Bob is not the murderer.

Here, then, we have a case that seems to be an argument, because the conclusion is a claim backed up by premises, where the form of argument is *modus tollens*.

But is 1.2 the same case as 1.1? The answer is: not necessarily. Case 1.2 is only one possible interpretation or extension of case 1.1. This question raises the problem of enthymemes – arguments with non-explicit premises. The context of case 1.1 is probably that of some sort of investigation of a murder that took place in Chicago. The non-explicit premise seems to be that, in order to commit the murder, the murderer would have to have been in Chicago on that day.

However, notice now that we are starting to 'read in' contextual assumptions so that the inference in case 1.1 is being plausibly portrayed as an argument. This process is difficult to resist. Given any inference, or sequence of reasoning, we naturally want to place it in some sort of context of use as an argument.

We could, in fact, do this explicitly. We could say that the context of case 1.1 is that of a discussion between two detectives who are trying to investigate Bob's murder in Chicago. Now what we have surely is an argument, but the added information makes it (quite possibly) a different case from 1.1. And so we have to revert back to our discussion of case 1.1. Is *that* case an argument? Never mind that it has possible extensions or enrichments.

Suppose, then, that all we know by way of context is what is given in the text of discourse of case 1.1. Is that, by itself, an argument? Or is it better to say that it is an inference, or an instance of reasoning, but not (as the case stands) an argument?

Copi and Cohen are on the right track when they say that the difference between arguments and non-arguments is one of 'purpose or interest.' In our extension of case 1.1, we were given the information that the speaker is a detective who is working on a murder case (once a fuller context of the case was filled in). We know, then, that his ultimate purpose in reasoning is to find evidence to show that someone is the murderer. This gives us enough of a context to surmise that this extension of case 1.1 appears to be some sort of argument, simply because it has to do with some sort of potential evidence that either Bob was the murderer or he was not. But regardless of how plausible this extension is, can we go further and say it shows that case 1.1 definitely is an argument, on the Copi–Cohen definition, and the other definitions given in sections 1 and 2? It appears not, since some more definite context (thus changing case 1.1 to a different or enriched case) is required in order to get to that conclusion.

Another way out of the difficulty is to say that case 1.1 is an instance of inference, and reasoning, but is not an argument. This solution appears plausible, because a genuine and important distinction can be made between inference and argument. Reasoning and inference are used in argument, but neither is the same thing as argument, according to Bitzer (1992) as well as Walton (1990b).

This solution is part of one way out of the problem. But it is still not the whole solution, in so far as many may still want to say that case 1.1 is an argument – a hypothetical argument. For everyone who takes this point of view, the definitions from sections 1 and 2 need to be broadened to take hypothetical arguments of this sort explicitly into account.

To broaden the definition, we need to recognize that arguments can occur in other forms, as well as in the pattern 'Q because P.' Moreover, we need to say that inferences can be parts of arguments, and hence themselves subarguments, where they are linked in a chain of reasoning to some conclusion that is in doubt or dispute or is a proposition that parties are interested in as something to offer evidence for or against.

These modifications would make the previous definitions of argument more complicated. And it would make the criteria for identifying an argument more difficult to apply. But the point could be made that it would constitute a better definition by doing better justice to suppositional (hypothetical) arguments.

There is room for two schools of thought here, however. Some will likely still want to say that hypothetical inferences such as case 1.1 are not really arguments as such. Instead, advocates of this point of view will say that such inferences are cases of reasoning that have a potential for use in arguments but, as long as they are purely hypothetical, are not really arguments *per se*.

The subtlety here is that there are really both possibilities. In some instances, an inference such as that of case 1.1 could be simply that, an inference. However, in other instances (as suggested by our extension of case 1.1), the same

What Is an Argument?   15

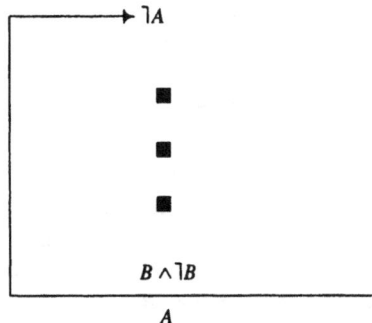

Figure 1.1 An Indirect Proof

inference, in a different context, could be used as part of an argument. If this is right, then surely it is appropriate to say that, at least in some cases, a hypothetical inference or chain of reasoning is itself an argument (a hypothetical argument) because it is part of an argument (a subargument).

4. Reductio Ad Absurdum

If you adopt the point of view of sections 1 and 2 that, in an argument, the premises must be used as evidence to support (or refute) the conclusion, then the type of argumentation called '*reductio ad absurdum*,' which involves hypothetical reasoning, may be a problem. In a *reductio ad absurdum* argument (sometimes also called an 'indirect proof') the opposite (negation) of the conclusion is assumed, and then shown to imply a contradiction. Where the original conclusion to be proved is the proposition A, a *reductio* proof takes the form shown in figure 1.1. (The bent arrow marks the scope of the assumption.)

The *reductio* proof works, provided that each step in the argument from '$\neg A$' to '$B \wedge \neg B$' is valid. Then, since '$B \wedge \neg B$' must be false – being a contradiction – it follows by *modus tollens* that $\neg A$ must be false, as well. Then, by double negation, it follows that A must be true.

Indirect proof is a common type of argumentation in science. It was often used, for example, in Euclidean geometry. A famous case of *reductio ad absurdum* argumentation is the thought-experiment argument used by Galileo in the form of a dialogue, in *Dialogues Concerning Two New Sciences* (quoted in Hamblin, 1970, p. 134):

Case 1.3
SALVIATI: If then we take two bodies whose natural speeds are different, it is

16 Argument Structure

> clear that on uniting the two, the more rapid one will be partly retarded by the slower, and the slower will be somewhat hastened by the swifter. Do you not agree with me in this opinion?
> SIMPLICIO: You are unquestionably right.
> SALVIATI: But if this is true, and if a large stone moves with a speed of, say, eight while a smaller moves with a speed of four, then when they are united, the system will move with a speed less than eight; but the two stones when tied together make a stone larger than that which before moved with a speed of eight. Hence the heavier body moves with less speed than the lighter; an effect which is contrary to your supposition.

The original conclusion that Galileo set out to prove was that the speed of a body as it falls towards the earth is independent of its size. To do this, he began by assuming that a larger body would move faster towards the earth than would a smaller one (contrary to what he intended to prove). As the dialogue shows, however, this assumption leads to an absurdity, or contradiction, as we can see if we imagine the two objects tied together. By indirect proof, then, we can conclude that the natural speed of a body must be independent of its size.

This thought-experiment of Galileo's is definitely an argument, used to prove a conclusion. But it is not an ordinary argument, of the kind we are normally familiar with, in which the premises are used as evidence to support the conclusion. Indeed, it is not a straightforward matter to specify exactly which propositions are the premises of the argument. The conclusion is the proposition that the speed of a body is independent of its size, but what premises are being used to prove that conclusion in Galileo's argument?

Is the premise the negation of the conclusion to be proved? In terms of figure 1.1, is the premise '$\neg A$'? Or is the premise the whole operation of deriving the contradiction from the negation of the conclusion? In terms of figure 1.1, is it the whole part within the boundaries of the bent arrow? Or is there really no premise at all in this kind of argument?

If we think of the premises as the 'set of statements offered as reasons' for the conclusion (Carney and Scheer, 1974, p. 3), then the whole part inside the bent arrow in figure 1.1 should be called 'the premises.' If, however, we think of the premises as what is 'laid down' to prove the conclusion, then the assumption ($\neg A$ in figure 1.1) would seem to be the premise of the argument.

No matter how we reconstruct the argument contained in case 1.3, it proves to be a problem for the definitions of argument given in sections 1 and 2, above. Whatever the premises are (if there are any), they do not seem to claim to be true as a basis for supporting the conclusion.

It might be added here that, normally, in formal logic, indirect proofs have given premises, and there seems to be no special problem about them as arguments. Indirect proof can, in fact, easily be shown to be just a special type of conditional proof. Consider a typical example, from Hurley (1991, p. 415):

Case 1.4
1. $(\exists x) Ax \lor (\exists x) Fx$
2. $(x)(Ax \supset Fx)$ / $(\exists x) Fx$
   3. $\lnot(\exists x) Fx$ AIP
   4. $(\exists x) Ax$ 1, 3, Com, DS
   5. Ac 4, EI
   6. $Ac \supset Fc$ 2, UI
   7. Fc 5, 6, MP
   8. $(x) \lnot Fx$ 3, CQ
   9. $\lnot Fc$ 8, UI
   10. $Fc \land \lnot Fc$ 7, 9, Conj
11. $(\exists x) Fx$ 3–10, IP, DN

Here, the statements (1) and (2) are the given premises. In such cases, there are often other ways to deduce the conclusion from the premises. Indirect proof is just one method among many.

Indeed, once we can prove a contradiction of the form '$B \land \lnot B$' from a set of given premises, in classical logic we can prove any conclusion C, whatever. This is easily shown, supposing that we have reached '$B \land \lnot B$' at step n of a deduction.

n : $B \land \lnot B$
$n + 1 : B$ n, Simp
$n + 2 : B \lor C$ $n + 1$, Add
$n + 3 : \lnot B$ n, Simp
$n + 4 : C$ $n + 2, n + 3$, DS

What is shown, in effect, is that, in classical logic, we can deduce any proposition whatever from a contradiction.

At any rate, in case 1.4, we do have two premises explicitly stated (nos. 1 and 2), and they do appear to be put forward as a basis upon which the conclusion is proved. But what about the part within the assumption (steps 3 through 10)? This is a hypothetical sequence of inferences that is part of the larger argument in which it appears (steps 1 through 11). Shouldn't we then properly call it an argument (a subargument) as well?

If so, then the definitions of argument given in sections 1 and 2 need to be

18 Argument Structure

expanded. To do this, we put forward a new definition of the concept of argument. This definition has three parts, and defines an argument as having three essential characteristics.

1. An argument is a sequence of reasoning, that is, a set of propositions, in which some propositions (conclusions) are inferred from others (premises). (The concept of reasoning is defined precisely in chapter 6, using the theory of directed graphs to define reasoning structures.)
2. There is an issue (determined by the context of dialogue in which the argument was used) to be settled.
3. The reasoning is being used (or can later be used, in the case of hypothetical arguments) to contribute to a settling of that issue.

The purpose of an argument is to resolve some uncertainty, instability, or conflict that attaches to a particular proposition. There is a kind of unsettledness about this particular proposition, so to speak, and the purpose of the argument is to remove this unsettledness if possible, or at least to deal with it.

This unsettledness can take six basic forms. First, it could be a conflict of opinions, that is, where one party thinks a particular proposition is true and the other thinks it is not true. Or it could take the form of a milder kind of conflict of opinions, where one party accepts a proposition as true, but the other party doubts whether it is true. Second, it could be a conflict of interests. What is unsettled here is how the involved parties are going to reach some kind of compromise concerning the uncertainty of how particular goods or interests are going to be divided up. The third kind of unsettledness is the lack of a decisive or definitive proof of some claim that is alleged as true or has been contested as true, but has not been definitively established as true. The fourth kind of unsettledness concerns a situation that has arisen which requires some sort of choice regarding what would be a prudent course of action, where the existing knowledge is insufficient for one to determine clearly whether one should proceed this way or that. The fifth kind of unsettledness involves a lack of information; thus, one wants or needs to get that information. The sixth kind of unsettledness involves a conflict or antagonism between two parties who have some kind of perceived grudge or grievance against each other that is felt but has not been articulated in words. This unsettledness means that there is a lack of agreement between two parties, or that one party sees a problem or a situation from two different points of view, and is uncertain about which is the best to adopt. This is the way the situation is viewed, so that the assumption is that a particular proposition is an issue, and is not settled.

A proposition's not being settled in a dialogue situation means that this proposition is or has become an issue for the participants in the dialogue. In such a case, a need or concern to settle the issue has arisen.

In the third type of unsettledness, above, the uncertainty, instability, or conflict need not attach to whether or not the claim is true. Instead, the concern is to show that it can be known to be true, based on facts that are well established, and that anyone who has access to these facts would agree to it. Or if it can't be known to be true, then the concern is to establish that fact. The uncertainty or unsettledness here is about how the proposition in question can be proved so that there will no longer be doubts attached to it by anyone who examines the evidence and reasoning used in the proof.

We can see, then, how argument contrasts with explanation. In an explanation, the assumption is that the proposition or event to be explained is settled. It is not an issue. All parties to the explanation agree, or make the presumption, that this proposition is a fact. The purpose is not to settle the issue of whether or not the proposition is true, or to prove it, but to throw some light on the proposition to show why it is true, or how it came to be so.

It is this very element of fixity that is lacking in an argument. An argument is based on an initial lack of agreement about what may be taken as true or settled. A particular proposition is perceived as an issue that can be, or needs to be, settled by weighing the considerations on both sides. There is an issue that is open to contention on two sides, and this is what makes argument appropriate or useful.

We may have a text of discourse containing a set of propositions, and the propositions may be connected by some indicator-word such as 'because' or 'so.' But how do we decide whether it is an argument, an explanation, a description, or some other type of speech act? We have to ask what the purpose of the reasoning is. If the text contains a sequence of propositions, and indicator-words showing that an inference, or chain of inferences, is being made, we can definitely say that the passage contains reasoning. And we can identify that sequence of reasoning. But, is the reasoning being used to put forward an argument or an explanation? We may not know, in some cases. But, in other cases, we may be able to make this determination by asking what the purpose of the reasoning is. How is it being used for a certain purpose as a type of discourse or conversational exchange? If it is being used to give reasons or considerations in favour of, or against, a particular proposition that is unsettled, and is at issue, then it is an argument. If it is being used to throw light on a proposition that is being taken for granted by both parties in the conversation as a settled fact, then it is an explanation.

A sequence of hypothetical reasoning, like the inference steps 3 through 10 within the assumption in case 1.4, is an argument because it is used as part of a

20   Argument Structure

larger sequence of argumentation that settles an issue, or contributes to the settling of an issue (as part of a *reductio* argument, in case 1.4). In so far as the whole sequence of reasoning in case 1.4 is an argument, then the part in the scope of the bent arrow is an argument too. The situation in case 1.4 is therefore comparable to the one in case 1.1. There, too, the inference, the sequence of reasoning, became an argument when it was used as part of an argument.

The function of a single argument with a given set of premises and a conclusion is to be part of a sequence of reasoning that moves the unsettled issue towards the one side or the other. It will not do this, at least immediately, if the single argument is purely hypothetical. But it can do it if the argument is valid (or inductively strong or presumptively strong) and the premises are better supported (less doubtful) than the conclusion. Then the probative function pushes the weight of evidence forward from the premises to the conclusion. But, then, given its link with other arguments in a connected sequence of reasoning, the probative function can push forward and pullulate through a whole line of argumentation that has some outcome in supporting or lessening support for the proposition at issue in the dialogue.

5. The Probative Function

The key problem with the textbook definitions of the concept of argument outlined in sections 1 and 2, above, is that they, with one or two exceptions, focused exclusively on a typical – but not, it seems, universal – use of arguments whereby the conclusion is a claim that is held to be true, and to be supported or justified by the premises. This is a narrow or localized view and is not general enough for the purposes of argument identification and evaluation required for argument diagramming and the study of fallacies.

The concept of argument we need to move towards is broader, meaning that an argument should be viewed as reasoning used in a verbal, social interaction, a dialogue between two parties who are trying to settle an issue on which they take different sides. However, when logicians approach an argument in order to apply traditional textbook methods of logic, they take a much more narrow, localized view – namely, that an argument is some very specific, typically small, set of propositions, one of which is designated as 'the conclusion.' They concentrate on the reasoning aspect of arguments and try to minimize or eliminate the dialectical aspect. Their goal is to evaluate such an argument (often by deductive logic). To do this, they focus down to deal with what they perceive as a manageable chunk of given discourse.

This localized viewpoint is not a bad thing, in itself. But the problem is that it tends to overlook the factors of context in which the argument has been used for some purpose. This, too, may not always be a bad thing, if these contextual factors are not important in evaluating the argument as correct, valid, and so on, or in meeting some criterion of adequacy.

However, when it comes to evaluating enthymemes, or evaluating arguments to say whether certain informal fallacies have been committed or not, it may be crucial to view the argument as being used for some purpose in a context of dialogue. One of the most important uses or functions of an argument is the *probative function*, whereby the premises are used to give evidence that will shift forward and transfer to the conclusion, making the conclusion evident or acceptable to the respondent, in a way or to a level that it was not before. Not all arguments are used probatively. Some are used hypothetically, in the sense that the premises are mere assumptions, and are not put forward as based on evidence that supports them as being true.

Sextus Empiricus, presumably presenting the Stoic principles of logic, summarized this probative function of argument concept very well, in the *Outlines of Pyrrhonism* (Book II, 140–1):

> Of true arguments, again, some are 'probative' (*apodeiktikoi*), some 'nonprobative'; and the probative are those which deduce something non-evident by means of pre-evident premises, the nonprobative those not of this sort. For example, an argument such as this – 'If it is day it is light; but in fact it is day; therefore it is light' is not probative; for its conclusion, that 'it is light,' is pre-evident. But an argument like this – 'If sweat pours through the surface, there are insensible pores; but in fact sweat does pour through the surface; therefore there are insensible pores' – is a probative one, as its conclusion ('there are therefore insensible pores') is non-evident.[2]

A probative argument, by this account, is one that deduces a non-evident conclusion from pre-evident premises. Thus, the argument that proves that there are insensible pores is probative, because this conclusion is not evident in itself, but it becomes evident when inferred from the two premises Sextus cites, using *modus ponens* to link the premises together.

This concept of the probative use of an argument (see section 9, below) was used by Walton (1991) as the key basis for distinguishing between non-fallacious circular arguments and arguments in which the fallacy of begging the question is committed.

This probative function can manifest itself in different ways in different contexts of dialogue.[3] In a persuasion dialogue, the probative argument is one in which the respondent is initially uncommitted to the conclusion, but then the proponent brings forward an argument in which the respondent is commit-

22   Argument Structure

ted to the premises, and in which the structure of the argument is such that there is a transfer of commitment from the premises to the conclusion.[4] In an inquiry, the probative argument is one in which the conclusion was initially not yet established as known to be true, but is then deduced from premises that are established, by rules of inference appropriate for the inquiry. Accordingly, the conclusion then becomes established as a proposition verified by the inquiry.

The probative function does not always have to be positive. In some cases, it can take the negative form of *refutation*, where a set of premises is being used to show that a conclusion is not true. Here, an argument is used to disprove a proposition. There are two forms of refutation. In *strong refutation*, a proposition is disproved, or shown to be false. In *weak refutation*, a proposition is shown to be open to doubt; that is, it is shown that the proposition has not been shown to be true.

In contrast to the probative use of argument, in the *hypothetical* use, the premises are mere assumptions (as opposed to assertions), and the conclusion is held to follow from the premises by inferences. However, in the hypothetical use of argument, the conclusion is not claimed to be true, as justified by the premises. The only 'claim' made is that, if the premises *were* true, then the conclusion would be true too.

6. The Dialectical Context

How do we identify an argument? Well, certainly one mark of an argument is reasoning, that is, a connected sequence of propositions, some of which are inferred from others. Thus, generally the logic textbooks have strongly emphasized that an argument is a set of propositions, called 'premises' and 'conclusions.'

But this mark, by itself, is not sufficient to identify arguments, because explanations (and perhaps other species of non-arguments) can contain reasoning as well, as we will see in chapter 2. It seems, then, that what is distinctive about an argument is that reasoning is being used in a particular way, or for a particular purpose. Often, as we saw in section 5 above, this purpose is to 'prove' something, that is, to fulfil the probative function.

We also saw in section 5, however, that the probative function can be fulfilled in different ways in different contexts of dialogue. But the purpose of argumentation is different in each different context. What common mark of an argument should we look for?

What we should be looking for, when we are seeking to identify an arguments, is a proposition that is unsettled, that is, open to contention or discussion, so that considerations can be brought for or against it in a dialogue. But different types of dialogue can be involved.[5] In logic, we often tend to look at an argument in a localized way, as a set of specific propositions singled out for attention – a set of premises and a conclusion. But every argument is used in a context of dialogue. The argument, in the broad sense of the term, also includes this context of use. An argument can also be viewed in a more global way, as a lengthy sequence of exchanges in a dialogue over some unsettled issue.

Several of these types of dialogue or normative structures of conversation have already been described by van Eemeren and Grootendorst (1984; 1992) and Walton (1989; 1992; 1993; 1995) in some detail. There is no need to define at length the essential characteristics of each of these types of dialogue here. But, below, we briefly indicate how each of them functions as a goal-directed, conventional framework of conversation in which arguments occur. Each type of dialogue has its various stages, and the Gricean Cooperative Conversational Principle applies (Grice, 1975, p. 67): 'Make your conversational contribution such as is required, at the stage at which it occurs, by the accepted purpose or direction of the talk exchange in which you are engaged.'

In a critical-discussion, or persuasion, type of dialogue, the unsettled issue is a conflict of opinions over some particular proposition. One side is convinced that the proposition is true; the other is not. The aim of this type of dialogue is to present reasons or arguments on both sides, to determine which side has the best case.

Arguments also occur in negotiation dialogue as well, but there the goal is not to make a case to show that a proposition is true (or false) by presenting reasons or evidence for (or against) it. In negotiation, the unsettled issue is the division or exchange of some goods or services. The aim is to reach a settlement that is satisfactory to both (or all) parties. Here is where the Copi–Cohen criterion (1990, p. 30) of an argument – as a case in which we are interested in establishing the truth of a proposition, and another proposition is offered as evidence for it – is too narrow. Truth is not the (primary) issue in a negotiation.

When arguments that have the goal of presenting evidence to show that a proposition is true (or false) occur in negotiation dialogue, they do so because there has been a shift from one type of dialogue to another, or because there is a mixed dialogue. These mixed dialogues and dialectical shifts have been studied in detail by Walton and Krabbe (1995). For example, if a buyer and a contractor are negotiating the cost of a basement, and they are discussing how much cement is needed, the issue may shift to the question of what the normal standards are for thickness of concrete for basements in this area, according to city engineers. This issue is not itself a negotiation, but involves an information-seeking type of dialogue. So, truth is involved here, within the negotiation, but that is because one type of dialogue is joined to another.

The issue in a negotiation is to bargain, to make trade-offs and compromises in order to 'get the best deal.' Such an activity does not have the goal of finding or presenting evidence to establish the truth of something. Yet, it is nevertheless rightly described as 'argument' of an important kind.

Arguments also occur in an inquiry type of dialogue, where the purpose is to prove some proposition, or, alternatively, to show that it cannot be proved, at the present state of knowledge. In persuasion dialogue, retraction is commonplace and is generally allowed under certain conditions. But the aim of the inquiry is to argue only on the basis of premises that are well established so that (at least ideally) there will be no need for retractions in the future. The philosophy behind the inquiry is often called 'foundationalism,' and it corresponds to the type of argument Aristotle called a 'demonstration.'

Another context of dialogue in which arguments occur is the deliberation. Here, the aim is to decide what to do, what course of action to take, in a particular situation in which several courses of action are open. Practical reasoning characteristically takes the form of much of the argumentation in a deliberation. An agent (or group) has a goal, or is formulating a goal, and has several alternative courses of action open that represent means to achieve this goal. These are the premises. The conclusion takes the form of an imperative, to the effect that the agent should go forward with one particular line of action as 'prudent' or practically reasonable in the circumstances.

Case 1.5 presents an example.

Case 1.5
LOLA: Do you think we should go to Florida this year, as usual, for our vacation?
BRAD: I think we ought to go to Hawaii instead this year, because you are virtually guaranteed of getting sunny weather in February in Hawaii.

In this case, Lola and Brad are deliberating on the question of where to take their winter holidays this year. Brad puts forward an argument for the conclusion of going to Hawaii. Here, there is not necessarily a conflict of opinions, but there is a decision to be made between two possible courses of action.

In some cases, a dialogue may involve only one person. Deliberation is often a dialogue framework of this kind. A person may deliberate in a solitary fashion, using argument, for example, by looking at the possible consequences of taking or not taking a contemplated course of action. In such a single-person process of argumentation, the same person plays both roles, proponent and

What Is an Argument? 25

respondent, by taking a 'devil's advocate' point of view on one side. This familiar kind of case of solitary deliberation can still be viewed as an argument, even though the same person is, in effect, playing two roles in the argumentation.

It is not necessarily the case that all deliberation must be in the form of argument that has a dialogue structure. But, generally, it is the case that a person can argue with herself, by expressing doubts while also bringing forward lines of reasoning that would answer these doubts.

Another context of dialogue is the *eristic* type of dialogue, or quarrel, where the aim is to air hidden grievances. Each party hits out at the other party verbally, using *ad hominem* arguments and 'counterblaming' for perceived wrongs committed in the past. The quarrel has the valuable function of airing these private grievances, and can be a good type of dialogue if the participants learn increased sensitivity to the feelings of the other. Quite a few textbooks exclude the quarrel as part of what is meant by the term 'argument' in logic. Rescher (1964, p. 59) writes that the 'specialized' use of the term 'argument' appropriate for logic 'is to be distinguished from its ordinary meaning of a quarrel, a heated controversy, or the like.' Freeman (1988, p. 20) also excludes the quarrel type of argument.[6]

> Our discussion [of the concept of argument] has already ruled out one popular understanding of this term. By argument, we do not mean the sort of behavior that goes on in barroom brawls or locker room fights. Arguments are not the heated exchange of words.

Similarly, Govier (1992, p. 3) excludes the verbal fight.

> Sometimes the word *argument* is used to mean dispute or fight as in the sentence 'The parents got into so many arguments over the child's problems that finally they got a divorce.' In ordinary speech, this use of the word *argument* is quite common. But this is not the way we use the word *argument* in this book. In our sense, arguments have to do not with fights but with rational persuasion. An argument is a reasoned attempt to justify a conclusion.

This exclusion of eristic dialogue is understandable, because the critical discussion is often the context of dialogue with which we are chiefly concerned in argument evaluation. But, in order to understand and evaluate fallacies, it is frequently necessary to view the argument in question as occurring in the context of a shift from some other type of dialogue (like a critical discussion) to a quarrel. Hence, the quarrel does represent a species of dialogue we need to recognize.

Another type of dialogue in which arguments occur is the information-seeking type, where the purpose is to impart information from one party to another. Case 1.6 provides an example.

Case 1.6
MOTORIST: How do I get to Main Street?
PEDESTRIAN: Turn left at the next light, and turn right after you go over the bridge. Don't go straight after the bridge, because the construction will slow you down, that way.

The pedestrian's argument here is a species of practical reasoning used to give advice to the motorist on how to reach his stated goal.

Interviews of various kinds and expert-consultation dialogues are subspecies of this type of dialogue. Pedagogical dialogue also fits in here (see cases 2.13 and 2.14, below).

What is characteristic of an argument generally, in all these contexts, is the existence of a proposition that is unsettled, that is, open to questioning or doubt, and open to being settled by a dialogue exchange between (typically) two parties. So, when we are looking to identify an argument, yes, we are looking for a set of propositions – premises and a conclusion, locally. But also what we are looking for primarily is a particular proposition that is unsettled, and occurs in the context of a dialogue exchange that could potentially settle it, one way or the other. That is an argument.

This analysis of the concept of argument provides the setting in which we can place the dialectical test to distinguish between arguments and explanations formulated in chapter 2, section 6. When we are examining a given text of discourse, we can judge it to be an explanation if the key proposition that is the focus of the discourse is a settled proposition; that is, that it is being presumed for the purposes of the dialogue that both parties are prepared to accept this proposition as true, or at least tentatively true. By contrast, the discourse contains an argument if the parties are taking a stance of questioning or disputing the truth of this proposition, the issue that needs to be settled, or at least discussed, in a dialogue exchange.

7. The Concepts of Argument and Explanation

The focus of this book is directed to the practical task of devising techniques to enable us to identify arguments and analyse their structure. Part of this task is that of being able to have a clear-enough idea of what an argument is so that we can avoid the trap of evaluating non-arguments, such as descriptions or explanations, as though they were arguments. Clearly, in order to do this, we need to have some definition, some target concept of what it is we are supposed to be identifying, that is, an argument. But does that mean we also need to determine what an explanation is? That task would certainly pose a problem of formidable dimensions. How far do we need to go in providing or presuming underlying theories of argument and explanation?

Given the disagreements and uncertainties in the literature (see Walton, 1990b, pp. 399–402), and even in the textbooks, about how to define the concept of argument and the associated concept of reasoning, it seems difficult to know how to proceed. Declaring absolutely for one point of view or theory would be too exclusive to help with developing a method of argument identification that is not tied too closely to a not widely accepted theory. On the other hand, if we are supposed to be identifying arguments, and distinguishing between arguments and explanations, we surely have to have some prior idea of what an argument is supposed to be.

To deal with this problem, we will take a soft approach and try not to declare for our own special theory too rigidly. That theory has already been developed and advocated by Walton (1992b) and in other works on argumentation theory, and this is not the place to push for it too heavy-handedly as the only possible approach. On the other hand, we must have some sketch or target concept, at least in broad strokes, of what an argument is. In section 5 above, a summary of our new definition of the concept of an argument was given – but it is a sketch that tries not to close too many doors at this initial stage. Below, in section 10, the sketch is filled in somewhat, and a functional concept (so-called) of argument is presented, as the target for argument identification.

Basically, our problem with the concept of an argument is posed by a clash of points of view of disciplines in different fields. Logicians are used to looking at an argument from a semantic point of view that sees an argument as a set of propositions. Each proposition has a truth-value (truth or falsity) or it has an assigned probability-value. Logic is perceived as the study of various formal relations on the truth-values (or probabilities) like validity (or conditional probability). From this point of view, the context of the argument (how it was used in relation to the purpose of the kind of discourse in which it occurred) is regarded as beyond the scope of logic (at least, for the most part). Or, at any rate, as noted in section 1, above, the textbooks typically keep these matters in the background when treating the concept of an argument.

In the field of speech communication, however, an argument is regarded as a social and verbal activity governed by rules of politeness appropriate for a particular type of conversation (context of dialogue). Here, context is extremely important, and whether the argument is evaluated positively or negatively depends on the goal of dialogue that the participants in the argument are supposed to be engaged in. Van Eemeren and Grootendorst (1984), for example, see an argument (or, as they prefer to call it, 'argumentation') as a rule-governed discussion (called a 'critical discussion') in which two parties reason together in an orderly manner, in order to resolve a conflict of opinions.

Following the outline of the proposal by Walton (1990b), a functional view of reasoning in argument is advocated here that does justice to both viewpoints, but leans, more than the traditional textbook treatment has in the past, towards the pragmatic concept of an argument as a social and verbal interaction between participants who are engaged in one of several conventionalized types of dialogue. According to this view, *reasoning* is a sequence of steps of inference whereby propositions are joined together by warrants or argumentation schemes. *Argument* (in the sense appropriate for logic) is defined as the use of reasoning in order to fulfil a conventionalized conversational purpose when two parties interact in one of various types of dialogue. Clearly, the central type of dialogue in evaluating argumentation generally from a logical point of view is the critical discussion (or 'persuasion dialogue,' as it was called in Walton, 1984). But in order to evaluate arguments containing traditional informal fallacies (see sections 8 and 9, below), other types of arguments have to be taken into account as well.

As if it isn't bad enough that there is little agreement on how to define what an argument is, we are in even worse shape with regard to the concept of explanation. There is a huge, unwieldy literature in philosophy on this subject (especially in the philosophy of science), and it appears to be rife with fundamental disagreements. Although explanation is an interesting and important concept for informal logic, clearly this book is not the place to attempt to give a theory of scientific explanation, or to define, in general terms, what requirements something should meet in order to qualify as an explanation in science, or to be a successful explanation in any particular science.

A main problem here, as noted by Kasachkoff (1988), is the widespread conception among analytical philosophers that explanations in daily life do, or ought to, conform to a certain model of how the logic of scientific explanation has been portrayed. According to the Hempelian deductive–nomological model (DN model) of explanation, an explanation is a statement (or proposition) that is logically deduced (by deductive or inductive logic) from statements of universal natural laws (often equated with scientific laws or general principles).[7] Two informal logic textbooks that explicitly advocate this point of view on explanation are Beardsley's (1950, see p. 219) and Fogelin's (1987, see p. 111). Kasachkoff (1988, p. 24) quite rightly points out, however, that explanations in everyday conversations in natural language are not like the DN model at all, and thinking of them in this way 'subverts any attempts we might make to get our students to think critically and deeply about explanations generally, and particularly about explanations as they apply to human conduct, intentions, desires, aspirations, and the like.' The kinds of explanations most commonly encountered in using the method of argument diagramming are based on practical reasoning (Walton, 1990a) and are inherently different from the kind of scientific explanation portrayed by the DN model. An early exponent of this practical approach to explanation is von Wright (1971).

Cawsey (1992) provides a computational model of explanation which takes account of its interactive (dialogue) nature as an exchange between two parties. The kinds of examples of explanations studied are practical in nature. For example, one case consists of what is called a 'cooperative informing dialogue' between two parties, one of whom is trying to explain to the other how a burglar-alarm system works (ibid., p. 44). Characteristic of these kinds of cases is an attempt by the explaining party to guess what the other party (the user) already knows and to respond to the user's questions in a cooperative way, to add new knowledge that will be helpful. In these cases, the model of explanation does not seem to be like a deductive inference, or deductive chain of reasoning, from scientific laws or generalizations.

Typical cases of scientific explanation cited as instances of the DN model in the literature on philosophy of science are, in fact, discourses that have been 'cleaned up' and formulated to meet disciplinary standards of a science, and then to be presented to 'outsiders' (students, the public) and to 'insiders' (one's colleagues) in a particular way.

The majority of cases of explanations encountered in everyday conversation are quite different from those of scientific discourse precisely because the context is not that of a scientific inquiry, or the presentation of the results of a scientific investigation. However, it is difficult to make this point to those immersed in the philosophy of science and traditional approaches to logic, because they tend to equate explanation with scientific explanation, and in particular with the DN model.

We do not want to get dragged into the problem of trying to say, in both precise and general terms, what a scientific explanation is.[8] Nevertheless, we have to say enough about it to be able to look at a given passage of discourse and arrive at some decision as to whether it ought to be treated as an argument, or as some species of non-argument, of which the leading contender is usually an explanation. Moreover, as we will see subsequently, arguments in everyday conversation are frequently connected to explanations in an intimate way. In fact, we will shortly argue that the most common kinds of arguments in everyday conversations can be identified as 'inferences to the best explanation,' meaning that the argument is a sort of reverse explanation. As we will see in chapter 8, arguments of a sort recognized in computer science involve a backwards sequence of reasoning, from conclusions to premises. The philosopher C.S. Peirce called this type of argument 'abductive inference.' It turns out, then, that arguments and explanations are more closely connected in practice than one might initially have been inclined to think.

Hence, to some degree, to solve the problem of building up a practically useful method of argument diagramming, we will have to identify, in broad terms, criteria to distinguish arguments from explanations. This, in turn, means that some concept of what an argument is, and what an explanation is, have to be put forward (if only provisionally).

In this book, we argue that both explanation and argument contain reasoning, but that the key to the distinction lies in how that reasoning is used for a purpose. The purpose of an argument is to settle an open issue with another arguer with whom one is engaged in dialogue. This partner does not have to be a specific person. But it is a respondent (sometimes called an 'opponent') in the sense that it represents an opposed point of view on an issue. Basically, the goal of an argument is to use reasoning to get this partner in dialogue to become committed to a proposition to which he was not committed at the beginning of the dialogue. The purpose of an explanation is to take something unfamiliar to this co-participant in dialogue and make it make sense to him by relating it to something with which he is familiar (or, at least, that makes some sense to him already).[9] This is really the crux of the difference between argument and explanation, and the key to identifying each of them in a given case of discourse.

Of course, in some cases it will be much easier to make this distinction than in others. In cases of arguments in which a probative function is clearly present, this distinction will indicate the presence of an argument, as opposed to an explanation, very markedly. Also, in some cases, a lot of contextual information is given to indicate precisely what the particular global issue to be settled is. Here again, it may be quite clear what the purpose of the discourse is meant to be. However, in many cases, even though an indicator-word such as 'thus' or 'because' is used, it may be simply unclear whether the sequence of reasoning is an argument or an explanation.

It is possible to have a case in which two people give different, or even conflicting, explanations of the same proposition or event. In such a case, there is an unsettledness, and some may think, therefore, that what each party is doing must be described as argument, and not explanation. In such a case, indeed, the two parties may be arguing that each has the better explanation, or may get into such an argument. It is, of course, possible to argue about an explanation (or to explain an argument, for that matter) by moving to a metalevel discourse.

In a case like this, there can be a kind of unsettledness present. But in so far as

What Is an Argument?   31

the parties, at the outset, were both giving explanations of some event or proposition they were taking for granted as factual or true, their dialogue presumed a settledness, *in this respect*, which is characteristic of the act of explanation, as opposed to argument. Admittedly, however, explanation and argument could coexist in a case like this.

Some readers may begin to baulk at this point, and reply that, now that we have seen all the complications inherent in identifying arguments and distinguishing them from explanations (and the difficulties, borderline cases, and so on), do we need to import all these problems into logic? Couldn't we just assume that something can be conditionally 'designated' as an argument or not, and then evaluated on that basis? This seems a tempting way out of all the problems we have encountered in building a method of argument identification. But it won't work, if part of our goal is to evaluate arguments of a kind corresponding to traditional fallacies. To show why, we turn to a consideration of two of these traditional informal fallacies, the *ad populum* and the *petitio principii*.

8. The *Ad Populum* Fallacy

In some cases, students may be quick to identify a passage of discourse as containing one of the traditional informal fallacies, based on the presumption that what has been identified is an argument. However, in some of these cases, when we think twice about whether the case really is an argument, the judgment appears questionable.

The following case concerned looters smashing store windows and running off with goods, after the announcement of the verdict in the Rodney King trial. Just after the Los Angeles riots, a news interviewer put the following question to a young man who was just coming out of a vandalized store with some stolen goods:

Case 1.7
QUESTION: What are you doing that for?
REPLY: Everybody's doing it.[10]

Was the reply a justification (argument) or an explanation? The problem with this type of case is that most students of informal logic will quickly identify it as an instance of the *ad populum* fallacy.[11] But the presumption of this classification is that the reply is an argument – an argument that, in this instance, is fallacious. But is it an argument? Or is it really an explanation of why the young man did what he did? It seems hard to say.

The problem with this case, and with cases of this type generally, is that, if the reply is not an argument, it is not appropriate or helpful to convict the speaker of having committed an *ad populum* fallacy. A fallacy is a deceptive, erroneous, or otherwise incorrect move in argumentation. If a person is not arguing, but doing something else, it could be inappropriate and misleading to accuse him or her of committing a fallacy, or of arguing wrongly.

Was the young man in this case trying to justify his actions, saying, in effect: 'I know that this act seems wrong, from your point of view. But everyone is doing it. That makes it right.' This type of argument could be identified as a species of *ad populum* fallacy.

Or was he only trying to explain, not justify his actions, saying, in effect: 'Well, as you see, everyone else is doing it. That's what led me to do it too.' Here, he could have been explaining, or trying to explain, his motives in engaging in a kind of conduct that he perhaps would not be inclined towards in normal circumstances.

One problem here is the uncertainty of putting the case in the one category or the other. If we are not certain that it is an argument, is it not somehow premature or inappropriate to classify the case as an instance of a fallacy? This really does seem to be a genuine problem in identifying and evaluating fallacies, and it is worth being aware of the problem, and thinking twice about such cases.

Perhaps there is a way to resolve the problem, however. You could say that, whether the young man's reply in case 1.7 is an explanation or an argument, it involves reasoning of a kind that is questionable. On this basis, if the young man could conditionally be interpreted as trying to give a sufficient justification of his conduct based only on the premise 'Everybody's doing it,' then his argument could be called an instance of the *ad populum* fallacy. This kind of response was neatly summed up in the form of a question expressed by a young woman as a reaction to the often-expressed 'Everybody's doing it.'

Case 1.8
If everyone were jumping off a cliff, would you do it too?[12]

What this reply expresses is the idea that the *argumentum ad populum*, 'Everybody in this situation, as far as I can see, is doing action *a*, therefore it is prudentially appropriate or acceptable for me to do *a*' is a defeasible kind of reasoning that should default in the looting case; that is, that the *ad populum* may work in some cases, but we should have the good sense (or judgment) to recognize a case in which it does not work.

In other words, the response in case 1.7 can be interpreted as saying that the reply in case 1.7 may be acceptable as an explanation, but, if it is meant to be a justification (sufficient reason or argument) that the conduct defended was

What Is an Argument? 33

acceptable, it is a failure. It fails because an *ad populum* may carry some weight in some cases, but it is not a sufficient reason, and it is definitely not a good argument, in some cases.

Thus, it seems we can handle this kind of case if we are clearly aware that making a charge that someone has committed a fallacy may involve a conditional presumption that the person is engaging in a speech act of argumentation, as opposed to explanation, description, and so on. The charge, then, is to the effect: 'If you are trying to argue, or to give a sufficient reason (justification) for your conclusion, then the argumentation scheme you are using is not sufficient (because of such-and-such a counter-case or critical question).' This type of criticism is *conditional*, in the sense that it says that, *if* you are presenting an argument, your argument is open to critical questioning or refutation of the following kind.

In the author's experience, there are a lot of cases like this, in which evaluation of the argument as fallacious, or as committing some sort of logical error or lapse, depends on a prior answer to the question 'What is the argument?' In many cases, an even more basic question needs to be asked – 'Is it really an argument?' In such cases, the evaluation of the argument rests on the prior stage of processing that could be called the stage of 'identification' or 'recognition' of an argument. The study of fallacies increasingly shows the importance of argument-identification questions that are prior to questions of evaluation of the (presumed) argument.

9. The Fallacy of Begging the Question

One kind of case in which a problem of argument identification can arise concerns the fallacy of begging the question. In cases where the sequence of reasoning shows a circular structure, it is easy to leap to the conclusion that the fallacy of begging the question has been committed. But, according to the analysis of this fallacy presented by Walton (1991), identification of circular reasoning is not, by itself, sufficient to determine that a fallacy of begging the question has been committed in a given case.

Consider the following case from Walton (ibid., p. 29):

Case 1.9
When asking why the economy in a certain state is in a recession, an economist replies: 'A lot of people are leaving the state. Things are very poor in the housing industry, for example, because there is no need for new housing.' As the dialogue continues, the economist is asked why people are leaving this state in such large numbers, and he answers, 'The condition of the economy

in this state is poor. People don't seem to be able to get jobs, because of the recession in this state.'

As we look through the reasoning in the dialogue, we see that the economist's replies have taken us in a circle. The economy is in a recession, we are told at first, because people are leaving. But, at the end of the sequence, the reason why people are leaving, we are told, is because the economy is in a recession. The diagram of this chain of reasoning is clearly circular. Shouldn't we therefore say that here we have an instance of the fallacy of begging the question, or, as it is sometimes known, the fallacy of arguing in a circle?

In case 1.9, the immediate problem is whether it is an argument at all. For if we can't be sure that it really is an argument, how can we be sure that it is a case of arguing in a circle? Perhaps what the economist is doing is attempting to give an explanation, as opposed to an argument. If she were accused of having committed the fallacy of arguing in a circle, she might reply as follows (quoted from ibid., p. 30):

Case 1.9a
'The relationship of housing, jobs, recessions, and so forth, is a cyclical type of feedback process, and is therefore inherently circular in itself. But my explanation, linking these variables, and drawing attention to their circular relationship is not fallacious. For I was only explaining how the structure of the economy works.' The economist might imply, for one thing, that her remarks were not meant to be taken as an *argument*, as such, but more as an explanation of a situation. And since it is arguments that are fallacious, not explanations, the charge of begging the question could be inappropriate in this case.

Such a defence against the charge of having committed a fallacy could be quite reasonable. And, if so, a genuine problem of argument identification is posed. How can we determine that a speaker's utterance is truly an argument, or should be so interpreted?

Of course, a circular explanation could be some sort of error, or inadequate explanation, as well.[13] But, even so, the economist could perhaps defend herself against such a charge by saying that the circularity is inherent in the situation, and that her explanation merely reflected this feedback (mutual causal process). She might say that she is describing (or explaining) the situation correctly and accurately. The economy being what it is, there is a feedback at work connecting recessions and migrations in a given area. It's comparable to the case of a diabetic who, as he gains more weight, builds up more insulin in his blood, which makes him eat more and store up more fat. The process is circular, but there is no fallacy in that *per se*. Reality is sometimes circular in feedback, and explaining the circular process should not, in itself, be regarded as fallacious.[14]

The economist's circular sequence is a chain of reasoning, and it could even possibly be an argument. She could be trying to present evidence to her interviewer, to argue for the conclusion that people are leaving the state. The key question, then, is whether a probative function exists in the use of the argument in this case.

But there is another option open. It could be that the economist is only explaining economic behaviour, and is not really arguing, in the sense of trying to justify the one proposition by appealing to the other as a premise that supports it (probative function).

Thus, here we have a problem of distinguishing between argument and explanation that could be the basis of a serious error at a later stage, when the presumed argument is evaluated as correct or fallacious, if the identification stage is mismanaged.

In addition to this problem, another related to diagramming arguments is worth mentioning that affects the evaluation of the fallacy of begging the question. This problem has to do with determining whether an argument is linked (in the sense defined in chapter 3, meaning that the premises function together to support the conclusion) or convergent (meaning that the premises function independently of each other). In a variant on the previous case, let us suppose that the economist puts forward the argument in case 1.10 to the interviewer. And let's assume that, in this new case, we definitely know that what is put forward is an argument (as opposed to an explanation). The argument has two premises and a conclusion:

Case 1.10
The economy in this state is in a recession.
Things look better elsewhere (to the people in this state).
Therefore, a lot of people are leaving the state.

Now, let's suppose that the dialogue continues, and the interviewer asks: 'Well, how can you prove that the economy in this state is in a recession? How can you tell that?' The economist then gives the following reply.

Case 1.10a
People are leaving in large numbers.

This last statement (case 1.10a) is virtually identical to the conclusion of the

36   Argument Structure

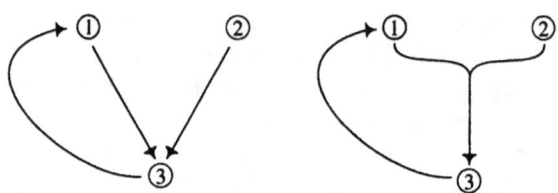

Figure 1.2 The Argument in Case 1.10

argument in case 1.10. So, it seems that here we have a case of arguing in a circle. But is the original argument, in case 1.10, linked or convergent? We have to answer this question before we can construct an argument diagram and exhibit the circular argument that supposedly contains the fallacy.

Let us number the two premises and the conclusion in case 1.10 as ①, ②, and ③, respectively. Now we have a choice of how to draw the argument diagram. In figure 1.2, the argument is diagrammed on the left as being convergent, and on the right as being linked, using the standard method of diagramming that will be explained more fully in chapter 3. Whether the circle in the argument diagram in figure 1.2 is evidence that a fallacy of arguing in a circle has been committed is very much influenced by which diagram we choose to represent the argument structure. In the convergent figure, on the left, the circle may not be too damaging, because the proponent has an alternative line of argument open (premise ②), which, by itself, could function as sufficient proof for ③. In the diagram on the right, however, the circle is much more serious, as things stand. The premise ① depends on the conclusion. But also, we need both ① and ② to get ③. So, ③ has to depend on ①, as things stand. Mutual dependency of this sort is serious evidence of a circle that destroys the argument.

So the problem is how to interpret the original argument in case 1.10. Is it convergent or linked? It seems hard to say. Yet, key aspects of evaluating whether a fallacy of arguing in a circle has been committed depend on this analysis of the structure of the argument. Here, the linked–convergent distinction is a real problem. Identifying the argument as linked or convergent is an important piece of argument-structure information needed to evaluate whether or not the argument is committing the fallacy of *petitio*.

If the economist really meant the argument in case 1.10 as convergent, then she could defend herself much more easily against the charge that she has committed the fallacy of begging the question. For example, suppose she continued the dialogue by rephrasing her argument in exactly these words (presuming that we know it is an argument, as opposed to an explanation):

What Is an Argument? 37

Case 1.11
Independently of whether the economy in this state is really in a recession, that is the way it appears to these people. Things look better elsewhere to them. That is why, I think, they are leaving this state.

Here, it is clear that the argument is convergent. Here, ② functions as an independent line of support for ③. So, the admission of the circle between ① and ② is not very damaging. Even despite the circle, ② stands as an independent line of argument for ③ that is not on any circle (as things stand, to this point in the dialogue). The economist can say, with some justification: 'I have not committed the fallacy of begging the question. Although there is a circle in my argument, that just reflects the feedback at work in human economic behaviour. My argument is not refuted by the circle.' To the extent that this rejoinder has some legitimate basis, it is crucial that the importance of the difference between diagramming the original argument as linked or convergent be appreciated. Our evaluation of the argument, with regard to its alleged fallaciousness, depends crucially on whether it is linked or convergent.

Circular reasoning is not itself fallacious, unless the circular reasoning is used in an argument that fails to, yet is supposed to, fulfil the probative function in a context of dialogue. Thus, the fallacy of *petitio principii* is a pragmatic failure relating to how an argument is used, and its evaluation depends on what structure the argument is supposed to have.

10. Towards a Pragmatic Concept of Argument

As we noted in sections 1 and 2, above, many logic textbooks emphasize as basic the semantic concept of an argument as a set of propositions with truth-values, stressing tests and criteria that are concerned with truth-functional relations on these truth-values (like first-order deductive validity) or with conditional probability-values on these propositions.

This semantic orientation systematically encourages students to think that logic is a precise mathematical calculus that can be applied to propositions, in abstraction from the context of an argument, with its subtleties of interpretation and presumptions of background knowledge. For purposes of teaching deductive logic, syllogisms, or the probability calculus, this may be a very useful way to view an argument (and has proved to be of some worth in the past). But the problem is that it abstracts too much from the context of use of arguments, and gives a false sense of precision, when the real need is to deal with questions of identifying, analysing, and evaluating arguments as they occur in realistic cases in natural language discourse.

It has been borne out that, when dealing with argument identification and diagramming, this semantic conception is a narrow way to view the concept of an argument, and it leads to an exacerbation of practical problems in evaluating arguments – problems that are necessary for logic to deal with as an applied discipline. To improve the situation, it is necessary to move to the pragmatic definition of argument presented above. Below, a summary of this new point of view is given.

An argument is, from a pragmatic point of view, a tool that has various uses. The primary use of argument is to steer commitment towards a specific proposition, called the 'conclusion' of the argument. The study of the different uses of arguments is the pragmatic account of argument. The pragmatic use of argument takes the semantic structure of an argument and deploys it, most often by putting individual links of argument together in an argumentation sequence directed towards a final conclusion, that is, by linking chains of premises and conclusions.

The user of the argument, called the 'proponent,' attempts to steer the commitment of the 'respondent' (the one to whom the argument is directed) towards the conclusion aimed at by the argument. Accordingly, there are two sides to every argument, the proponent's side and the respondent's side.[15]

Each participant has her or his own conclusion in the argument, and this pair of propositions is the *issue* to be decided. An *open issue* is one in which neither proposition has definitely been proven, according to the standards of proof appropriate for the context of dialogue for the argument.

Generally, any argument presupposes an issue, and for the argument to be applicable, the issue should be open. The most typical function of an argument is to drive the respondent towards one side of the issue, called the 'conclusion' of the argument, presuming that the respondent is committed to the other propositions in the argument, called 'premises.' The sequence of inferences from premises to conclusions is the reasoning used in the argument. But, in many cases, as shown subsequently, in order to even identify that sequence of reasoning in a given case, it is necessary to figure out how the argument is being used in that case.

An argument can have different kinds of uses. Sometimes an argument is used in a hypothetical fashion. Sometimes an argument is used to refute a proposition, that is, to drive the respondent towards the rejection of a proposition. The kind of argument called '*reductio ad absurdum*' involves both of these uses. By showing that a proposition which must be rejected (like a contradiction) follows from a set of premises, the proponent's strategy in this type of argument is to get the respondent to reject at least one of the premises. By using this type of argument, the proponent may be trying to argue positively for some

What Is an Argument? 39

ultimate conclusion, perhaps the opposite of the rejected premise. However, the use of an argument does not have to be for positive acceptance of a proposition. It can be for rejection. Or, as noted in case 1.4, above, an argument can begin with a given set of premises, and then contain a hypothetical indirect proof as a subargument. Here, the function of the argument in altering commitment may be more oblique and subtle, containing both a positive and a negative probative function, one inside the other.

There are commonly said to be three kinds of arguments: deductive, inductive, and abductive. This triadic method of classification will be supported in subsequent chapters, and, particularly in chapter 8, it will be shown how the abductive and plausibilistic type of argument is the most fundamental and common kind used in everyday argumentation. Yet, at the same time, it is the abductive type – which rests on presumption and has a tentative nature, making it a species of hypothetical (suppositional) reasoning used to shift a weight of presumption in a dialogue exchange – that has been most neglected in the history of logic. Perhaps because of its tentative and fallible nature as a species of argument best employed in balance-of-consideration issues, and because of its susceptibility to fallacies, the abductive type of reasoning has been neglected in the past by the majority of logicians, who have traditionally emphasized deductive and inductive arguments. But we recognize three types. Each type of argument, as is shown in chapter 8, has its standard of proof (which defines a burden of proof in a context of dialogue).

Interesting issues remain, on whether a question can be an argument, or whether an argument can be a question. Although questions are not arguments *per se*, questions are often part of an argument, and often contain an argument. However, in some cases, questions can be open to criticism precisely because they implicitly contain arguments. In such instances, the question is said to be unduly argumentative, in virtue of its presumptions.[16]

We have raised interesting questions about how argument is related to persuasion. Argument is often the vehicle of persuasion in everyday discourse. However, there are instances of argument that are not necessarily instances of persuasion. We can have argument in a scientific inquiry, like proof of a mathematical theorem, that is not necessarily an instance of persuasion. Argument in negotiation is different from argument in persuasion, but both are attempts to extract commitments. Much depends on how 'persuasion' is defined here, however. Distinctions need to be made among 'persuasion,' 'rational persuasion,' and 'reasoned conviction.' Generally, although *argument* and *persuasion* are closely related, the two concepts are not identical, in our view.

Pragmatically speaking, argument is a form of goal-directed action in which one participant steers the position of the other towards a specific proposition.

40 Argument Structure

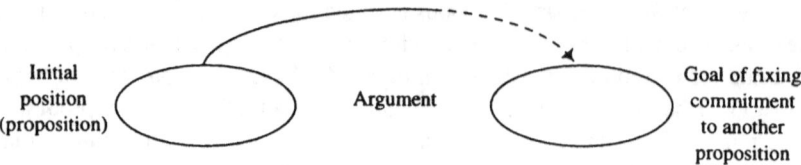

Figure 1.3 Argument as a Pragmatic Concept

Argument moves from an initial position, where the respondent has a certain commitment or is uncommitted, towards a goal position of fixing commitment to another proposition, the conclusion (see figure 1.3). The argument is the link or relation of reasoning that is used by the proponent to shift the respondent's commitment in a direction towards her conclusion.

There is an important distinction to be made between an argument and a successful (good, correct, reasonable) argument. Not all arguments are correct (good, valid). Burden of proof in a context of dialogue implements a standard for success of an argument in realizing its goal. There is also an important distinction to be made between an argument that is *effective* in persuading the respondent successfully, and an argument that is *correct*, meaning that it is valid or sound (normative criterion of correctness) or that it meets the appropriate burden of proof in context (pragmatic criterion of correctness).

Is an argument a 'claim' that a conclusion is true or acceptable? The problem here is to know what 'claim' means. But an argument does not necessarily have to have premises and a conclusion that are *advocated* in every instance – hypothetical arguments are a case in point. Also, an argument can be *questioned* or *rejected*. Are these 'claims'? As noted in section 4, above, there can be *reductio* arguments, and there are questions about whether such arguments can straightforwardly be described as claims. They may not be claims that the conclusion of the immediate argument of the discussion is true or acceptable. Also, it should be noted that you can discuss, reject, advocate, or question somebody else's argument. To handle these types of cases, we may need to make an important distinction among advocating an argument, putting it forward hypothetically in a dialogue, and discussing or evaluating it at the level of *meta-argument*.

An argument, according to the pragmatic theory advocated here, is typically a sequence of subarguments used in a larger goal-oriented unit of dialogue. Although arguments occur in dialogue, often a dialogue can best be seen as one large argument. The core of an argument is always a set of inferences or propositions, but the argument is determined by how those inferences are used in a

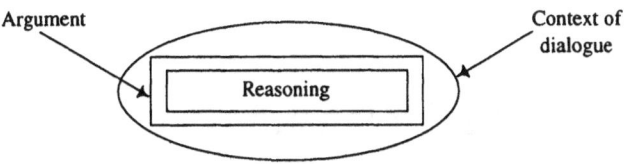

Figure 1.4 Nesting of Components of an Argument

context of dialogue. The nature of the relationship of this containment of reasoning in argumentation is very important in understanding, evaluating, or criticizing arguments. For example, questions often contain propositions in such a way that an argument can be discerned or extrapolated by detecting non-explicit conclusions inferred contextually.

Another important factor about arguments we have emphasized is that, in a given case, they always occur as used in a context of dialogue. Hence, in any argument, there is a triadic containment relation of nested components (see figure 1.4). The first step in the analysis or critical evaluation of any argument is the identification of the proposition which is the (ultimate) conclusion. The next step is the identification of the premises. The premises and the conclusions, connected together as a sequence of inferences, define the reasoning in the argument. The argument is defined by how that reasoning is used. It will be shown in subsequent chapters that evidence for these attributions must always be highly sensitive to both the textual evidence in a given case and the context of dialogue involved.

What is often called an 'argument' is in fact only the tip of the iceberg. The actual text of discourse given or explicitly presented by the proponent may make sense only because of background knowledge or assumptions shared by the speaker and her audience. Therefore, interpreting an argument from a given text in order to answer the question 'What is the argument?' demands skills and techniques of 'reading off' the argument from the discourse. An argument is typically much more than would appear in a transcript of what was said or overtly recorded as the text of discourse.

These new pragmatic ways of looking at the concept of an argument may at first appear radical to those raised in traditional logic. However, chapters 2 through 6, below, provide evidence of the usefulness of such a pragmatic point of view, when it comes to solving the various practical problems posed by argument identification and analysis of argument structure.

2

Arguments and Explanations

In this chapter, the problem of how to distinguish between arguments and explanations is addressed. When using the methods of logic to evaluate reasoning, one grows accustomed to presuming that a given passage of discourse contains an argument. This is especially true where the passage includes a sequence of propositions, shows an orderly progression towards some particular end – point proposition, and contains an indicator-word such as 'because' or 'since' in the sequence. However, explanations also show these characteristics. So, it becomes easy to make a mistake by assuming that a given passage contains an argument when, in fact, it does not, but really contains an explanation.

As noted in chapter 1, this kind of error can be serious when it comes to evaluating the 'argument.' It could be a bad argument, but a good explanation. Mistakenly taking it to be an argument could be the key step in evaluating the case incorrectly.

But how can we avoid this error if, as one critic (Thomas, 1981) has especially pointed out, it is very hard, in many everyday cases, to distinguish clearly and definitively between arguments and explanations?

Many of the textbooks and other writings on the subject have adopted various tests for this purpose. But do the tests really work, and how reliable are they? These questions are addressed in this chapter. They are hard questions, and this chapter does not purport to give the final answers, or to perfect the techniques developed and advocated in it. However, a particular version of this type of test is formulated and advocated below. And not only its uses, but also its limitations, are explored.

1. Argument and Explanation Combined

Among those textbooks that use the method of argument diagramming, the preponderance of the recent ones attempt to teach students how to distinguish between passages of discourse that contain an argument and those that contain an explanation. An exception to this general rule is Thomas's (1981), a textbook that claims that it is not possible to distinguish cleanly between arguments and explanations in so many cases that the textbooks have taken on an impossible task.

The following case is one of several used by Thomas (ibid., p. 13) to support his contention.

Case 2.1
One of the fundamental axioms of physics, embodied in what is known as Fourier's law of heat conduction, is that heat flows from the warmer parts of a body to the cooler ones. It can therefore be inferred that since the temperature increases with depth in the earth's crust, there is a flow of heat outward from the earth's interior. (Henry N. Pollack and David S. Chapman, 'The Flow of Heat from the Earth's Interior,' *Scientific American* 237/2 [1965], p. 60)

In this case, Thomas says that the authors justify their claim, that there is a flow of heat outward in the earth, by explaining it. So, according to Thomas (p. 13), it is quite common to justify something by explaining it, as in the sentence 'This mixture will explode because it has reached the critical mass.' In such a case, a claim is justified by explaining why it is true, or how it came to be true. Hence, according to Thomas, in this as in a lot of cases – see sections 8 and 9, below – the same passage contains both an explanation and an argument.

Much depends on how 'argument' and 'explanation' are defined, as we see below, in evaluating this issue. But it is not hard to see how the claim made by Thomas could possibly be defended. On some views of what an explanation is – for example, the deductive–nomological view that an explanation is a proposition deduced from general laws[1] – an explanation does indeed seem much like an argument, or is perhaps even a species of argument. And in chapter 6, we will show that a very common species of argument can be described as inference to the best explanation. Clearly, then, argument and explanation are closely connected as concepts, in various ways. Thomas could be justified in being sceptical about our ability to distinguish between them. Although Thomas's is the minority viewpoint, it is far from evident that it can be rejected out of hand.

If Thomas is right about these kinds of cases, the implications for argumentation and discourse analysis are striking and radically disturbing. We can no longer teach students to classify explanations as non-arguments; on the contrary, we should expect explanations, in general, to be species of arguments, if Thomas is right. The best we could still hope to do in our pedagogical practice is to find *some* cases of explanations that are not justifications (arguments). But our ability and pedagogical motivation to do even this much will be hampered by the expectation of finding plenty of cases in which a passage of discourse can be correctly interpreted as both an explanation and an argument.

However, if we look to textbook accounts that advocate techniques of distinguishing between arguments and explanations, we see that they are generally prepared to live with some ambiguous or mixed cases in which a passage of discourse contains primarily one thing (argument or explanation) but also the other.

Copi and Cohen (1990, p. 31) present the following example in an exercise asking the student to distinguish between passages that contain arguments and those that contain explanations:

Case 2.2
... a decaying satellite can look like an incoming warhead to a sensor. That is the reason we have a man in the loop. (General James Hartinger, Chief, Air Force Space Command, 'Nuclear War by Accident – Is It Impossible?,' interview in *U.S. News & World Report*, 19 December 1983, p. 27)

The answer given by Copi and Cohen (p. 506) is that their example (case 2.2) contains an explanation. However, they add that it could also be interpreted as a kind of argument.

Here we have an explanation for our having a man in the loop, not an argument intended to prove that we do. However, the fact that a decaying satellite can look like an incoming warhead may also serve as the premise of an argument of which the conclusion is that a human being *ought* to be involved in the system used for detecting approaching warheads.

The interpretation of this passage as an argument involves practical reasoning. We could interpret the speaker as justifying the prudential rationality of having a man in the loop on the grounds that the defence system was set up this way for safety. Because the sensor could make a 'wrong decision' that could trigger a nuclear response, a man is in the system to prevent this kind of error from occurring and having harmful consequences. The speaker is then justifying the conclusion, saying, in effect: 'the way it was done is the right way, or is prudentially reasonable on practical grounds.'

The conclusion, on this interpretation, is not the claim that a man is in the

Arguments and Explanations   45

loop, but rather the defence of the action of having a man in the loop on prudential grounds.

But, at the same time, it seems plausible that case 2.2 can be interpreted as an explanation of why 'we have a man in the loop.' It could be an explanation of how the group responsible for this decision arrived at the conclusion to have a man in the loop. Such an explanation would involve practical reasoning. The group presumably has certain goals, such as safety, and defending against nuclear attack in particular. Having a man in the loop is presumably a means they judged appropriate to contribute to these goals. Going into all these prior deliberations of the group, therefore, constitutes a kind of explanation of why they decided to have a man in the loop. But the explanation, in effect, outlines the steps of practical reasoning that the group undertook in deciding in favour of having a man in the loop. Thus, the explanation contains reasoning. Does it also contain argument? It might, for example, give an account of the argumentation that the group advanced as their reasons for deciding to have a man in the loop. Here, therefore, it is hard to avoid the conclusion that the explanation excludes argument altogether, at least as a component part.

How problematic is this potential ambiguity? It is the author's experience of using Copi and Cohen's textbook that students do find it disturbing (perhaps especially because it occurs in the first chapter). However, other textbooks have developed a strategy for dealing with the problem.

In their textbook (1984, p. 48), van Eemeren, Grootendorst, and Kruiger give an example that would normally, and could quite reasonably, be interpreted as an explanation, as opposed to an argument.

Case 2.3
Because I noticed that my songtexts get to individuals only and never reached the masses, I gradually dropped my political commitment. (Translated from quotation from Nona Hendrix in an interview in *Humo,* 28 July 1983)

This case naturally seems to be an explanation. But perhaps it could be interpreted as an argument in some contexts, for example, if the preceding question had been: 'How could you defend your gradual dropping of political commitment in your songs?' Here, what at first seemed like an explanation could be an argument, used as a justification of the respondent's position.

To deal with such cases, van Eemeren, Grootendorst, and Kruiger (p. 49) formulate a principle called the 'strategy of maximally argumentative argumentation' – in case of doubt, interpret statements as argumentative. As applied to case 2.3, this policy would advocate treating the apparent explanation (in the absence of any more definitive textual evidence) as an argument. In an exercise (pp. 63–4), van Eemeren, Grootendorst, and Kruiger ask the student to spot ('explicitize') the hidden premise in their example (case 2.3), indicating its interpretation as an argument.

2. Arguments That Are Not Explanations

Even if some passages of discourse can be classified as being simultaneously both an argument and an explanation, are there cases where there is only the one thing and not the other? First, are there arguments that are not explanations?

Govier (1987, p. 164) gives the following example of an argument that is not an explanation:

Case 2.4
(1) Jones is a Liberal.
(2) Jones is fat.
(3) Jones is a bachelor.
Therefore,
(4) Jones is a fat, Liberal bachelor.
Therefore,
(5) There are fat Liberal bachelors.

This sequence of inferences can rightly be called an argument. Indeed, it is a deductively valid argument that proves its conclusion, (5) – and its subconclusion (4) – from its premises, (1), (2), and (3). The conclusion, (5), is 'proved,' given the assumptions of the premises. However, (5) is not explained by the premises, (1), (2), and (3). It is hard, or perhaps even impossible, to think of a context in which (1), (2), and (3) would explain (5). For the last is simply an existential generalization, a kind of limited summing-up of the particular facts expressed by (1), (2), and (3). As Govier (p. 165) points out, typically explanations put something in a broader context by subsuming it under a law, 'showing how it fits a pattern,' 'indicating one or more of its causes,' or showing 'how or why it came to be.' Many arguments, like the one in case 2.4, above, do not perform any of these functions. Instead, they perform a different function – namely, providing evidence that a conclusion is acceptable, based on given premises.

Presumptive arguments based on appeals to expert opinion also provide a type of case that does not seem to be appropriately described as an explanation.

Consider a case where a little girl, Melissa, comes down with a fever and appears very ill. Taken by her mother to a physician, Melissa is examined. Later, Melissa's father asks her mother, 'How do you know she has the measles?' The mother replies: 'Dr Smith said so and assures me it is true.' This reply can be paraphrased as an argument.

Case 2.5
(1) Dr Smith assures me Melissa has the measles.
(2) Dr Smith has examined Melissa.
(3) Dr Smith is a medical expert who knows how to diagnose measles.
(4) Melissa has the measles.[2]

Here, we have a presumptive type of argument based on an appeal to expert opinion, based on medical knowledge.

But it is hard to see how (1), (2), and (3) in case 2.5 could serve as an explanation of (4). An explanation of why Melissa has the measles would, by contrast, probably refer to events prior to her catching the measles, for example, her coming into contact with other children who had the measles, or her not being vaccinated against this strain of measles.

Another type of case of presumptive reasoning involving argumentation from sign also exhibits instances that are arguments but not explanations. In questioning whether there were dinosaurs in Manitoba, the following argument might be put forward:

Case 2.6
(1) Dinosaur skeletons have been found in Manitoba.
(2) There were dinosaurs in Manitoba.[3]

In this case, it is easily seen that (1) can function as a premise in an argument where (2) is the conclusion. But is (1) an explanation of (2)? Here, once again, (1) does not seem to function appropriately that way.

What seems to interfere with (1) functioning as a good explanation of (2) in this case is the temporal factor. Generally, an explanation goes into the past events or circumstances leading up to the event to be explained. However, in case 2.6, the temporal relation is backwards. The event to be explained, or *explanandum*, (2), predates the event supposedly doing the explaining (the *explanans*), (1). So, as an explanation of (2), (1) does not really seem to perform the right sort of function.

Even in simpler cases of argumentation from sign, it appears that there are instances of arguments that are not explanations.

Case 2.7
(1) Melissa has red spots.
(2) Typically, in this type of case, having red spots is a sign of the measles.
(3) Melissa has the measles.

The sequence in case 2.7 can be quite naturally treated as an argument. It is an argument from sign, based on presumptive reasoning to a conclusion that is subject to retraction if the case turns out to be atypical, that is, if information comes in indicating that, in this case, the spots are not a sign of measles after all.

But case 2.7 is not a very good explanation of why Melissa has the measles, of how she came to get them, or of the fact that she has the measles. Propositions (1) and (2) do not seem to function in this way, and it would not be natural to treat them as furnishing an explanation of (3).

Some critics would say, however, with respect to case 2.7, that even if it is not an explanation *per se*, it contains an explanation. These critics would say that case 2.7 can naturally be treated as an inference to the best explanation.[4] According to this interpretation, (3) is the best explanation of (1), and that is why we infer (3) from (1) instead of some other conclusion that would explain the red spots.

But, according to this analysis of case 2.7, the inference goes from (3) as *explanans* to (1) as *explanandum*. The direction of the reasoning in the explanation is from (3), taken together with (2) and perhaps some additional assumptions about the circumstances, to the outcome or thing to be explained, – namely, (1), the proposition that Melissa has red spots. Construed as an argument, the line of reasoning in case 2.7 goes in one direction. Construed as an explanation, the line of reasoning goes in the opposite direction. So, while this case shows that there is a connection between argument and explanation in that they both use the same general line of reasoning in the same set of propositions, it also reveals an important difference in how that reasoning is used in an explanation versus an argument.

The same sort of analysis could be applied quite naturally to case 2.5. But it would not seem to work on cases 2.6 and 2.7 in any straightforward way. Of the kinds of cases like 2.6 and 2.7, then, we can say that they are arguments that are not explanations, as such. But some would say that they are a kind of argument that involves explanation, or contains an explanation within it. From this point of view, you could say that these cases are both arguments and explanations (or, at least, partly the latter). If so, we can't exclude them from being explanations altogether, or, at least, from containing explanations. But the direction of the argument is different from that of the explanation. We return to this general problem of inference to the best explanation in chapter 6.

To sum up, then, it has been shown that there are definitely some cases that are arguments and not explanations. But it is hard to resist the claim that many arguments in everyday conversations are either explanations as well as arguments, or at least contain explanations as well as arguments, or at least involve explanation somehow being woven into the thread of the argument (perhaps indirectly, or in the background). It seems though that, in many such instances, the case is primarily an argument, and involves explanation only in a secondary or supportive way.

In section 1, above, we saw that many explanations are also partly justifications, and therefore are also arguments, or can be interpreted as containing argumentation as well as explanation. Such cases can legitimately and straightforwardly be interpreted, with the reasoning going in the same direction, either as explanations or as arguments.

This poses our problem, then. How can we be confident when we are about to diagram an argument, that it is really an argument and not an explanation (or some other type of discourse that is not an argument)? Virtually all the textbooks and other sources that attempt to distinguish between arguments and explanations agree that there are contextual criteria (or at least clues) to be found in the text of discourse of a given case.

3. Indicator-Words

According to the typical accounts provided in the logic textbooks, the first step in the process of recognizing an argument is to look for certain key indicator-words. *Conclusion-indicators*, such as the word 'therefore,' tend to signal that the proposition which follows is the conclusion of an argument. *Premise-indicators*, such as the word 'since,' may signal that the proposition which follows is the premise of an argument.

No list of premise- or conclusion-indicators is complete, because there are any number of ways an arguer can indicate the putting-forward of a conclusion in argumentation in natural language. Even so, the partial lists provided by several of the leading textbooks give the reader a pretty good idea of what to look for. Copi and Cohen (1990, p. 9) list the following conclusion-indicators:

therefore ...	for these reasons ...
hence ...	it follows that ...
thus ...	we may infer ...
so ...	I conclude that ...

accordingly ...	which shows that ...
in consequence ...	which means that ...
consequently ...	which entails that ...
prove that ...	which implies that ...
as a result ...	which allows us to infer ...
for this reason ...	which points to the conclusion that ...

According to Copi and Cohen, these words typically serve to introduce a conclusion, while the premise-indicators below are typical signs of a premise (p. 10):

since ...	as indicated by ...
because ...	the reason is that ...
for ...	for the reason that ...
as ...	may be inferred from ...
follows from ...	may be derived from ...
as shown by ...	may be deduced from ...
inasmuch as ...	in view of the fact that ...

Copi and Cohen make it clear, however, that not every passage of discourse that contains an argument also contains these indicator-words. They cite the following example (p. 10):

Case 2.8
In 20 years' time the only maple leaf left in Canada might be on the national flag. Acid rain is killing the maple trees of central and eastern Canada, as well as in New England. ('Maple Syrup,' *The Economist*, 4 April 1987, p. 63)

According to Copi and Cohen (p. 10), their example, case 2.8, is an argument in which the conclusion is stated first, followed by a premise put forward in support of it. Yet, in this case, no indicator-words are present. Here already, then, is the first limitation of the use of indicator-words to identify arguments. The presence of an indicator-word is not necessary in a particular case to have the occurrence of an argument.

Thomas (1981, p. 10) gives the following list of premise-indicators:

as ... *(many exceptions)*	seeing that ...
since ... *(many exceptions)*	for the reasons that ...
for ... *(many exceptions)*	in view of the fact that ...
because ...	on the correct supposition that ...

Arguments and Explanations   51

as shown by ...	assuming, as we may, that ...
as indicated by ...	may be inferred from ...
follows from ...	may be deduced from ...
being that ...	may be derived from ...
being as ...	whereas ... *(in legal documents)*
inasmuch as ...	in the second place ...
in the first place ...	secondly ...
firstly ...	

According to Thomas, the presence of one of these terms 'generally, but not always,' indicates that the proposition following is the premise of an argument.

The following list of conclusion-indicators is given by Thomas (p. 11):

consequently ...	points to the conclusion that ...
therefore ...	allows us to infer that ...
which shows that ...	suggests very strongly that ...
proves that ...	leads me to believe that ...
hence ...	bears out the point that ...
so ...	thus ... *(frequent exceptions)*
you see that ...	demonstrates that ...
implies that ...	it follows that ...
entails that ...	in this way one sees that ...
accordingly ...	then ... *(without preceding 'if';*
I conclude that ...	*has exceptions)*

Comparable lists are given by Freeman (1988, p. 22), who adds a few other conclusion-indicators, such as 'the point I am trying to make is that ...' and 'bears out my point that ...' According to Freeman (p. 22), giving a complete list would be 'impossible and impracticable.' The list is best seen as a signal or suggestion-indicator that builds on the native speaker's intuitions by supplying terms that are typically or commonly used to indicate premises or conclusions.

There is another very important limitation to the use of indicator-words to identify arguments – namely, some indicator-words have other functions as well. For example, according to Copi and Cohen (p. 29), the word 'since' indicates a premise in 'Since Kleo graduated from medical school her income is probably very high,' whereas, in the proposition 'Since Kleo graduated from medical school there have been many changes in medical techniques,' the word does not indicate a premise. In the latter sentence, the word 'since' has a temporal, as opposed to a logical, meaning.

This fact, that the indicator-words do not always indicate the presence of an argument, is highly significant. It means that we cannot use the indicator-words automatically or unreflectively to identify the presence of an argument in a given case. They are only an initial clue or signal, and each case has to be interpreted carefully in relation to its own special circumstances.

This point about the limitation of indicator-words becomes especially acute when it comes to distinguishing between arguments and non-arguments. The term 'because,' for example, signals the premise of an argument in some cases. But, in other cases, it signals an explanation being offered, as opposed to an argument being put forward (see cases 2.9 and 2.10, below).

Thus, the indicator-words are neither necessary nor sufficient to mark the presence of an argument in a given case. Not only do arguments occur without their presence, but, even if an indicator-word is present, that in itself is not sufficient to determine the existence of an argument. Indicator-words are best seen as signals or clues – warning indicators that are very important in identifying arguments, but not conclusive determiners that can be taken for granted as marking an argument in every case.

4. Insufficiency of Indicator-Words

The pair of contrasting examples (cases 2.9 and 2.10, below) offered by Copi and Cohen (1990, p. 29) to illustrate the difference between an argument and an explanation are good ones to reflect on. The point Copi and Cohen make is that we can't always go, at least literally, by the indicator-words. The indicator-word 'because,' for example, sometimes indicates an argument, but at other times may indicate the presence of an explanation.

Case 2.9
Encryption and decryption keys must be protected more securely than any other secret message, because these are the keys that allow either the intended recipient of a cipher message or a spy to decipher it. ('Most Ferocious Math Problem Is Tamed,' *New York Times*, 12 October 1988, p. 11)

Case 2.10
We have decided to write this article together because of our deep belief that the security of free peoples and the growth of freedom both demand a restoration of bipartisan consensus in American foreign policy. (Henry Kissinger and Cyrus Vance, 'An Agenda for 1989,' *Newsweek*, 6 June 1988, p. 31)

Case 2.9 is an argument in which the word 'because' marks the premise that

Arguments and Explanations 53

functions as a reason or grounds for accepting the conclusion. What follows the 'because' in their second example (case 2.10), however, is a proposition 'we already know to be true,' according to Copi and Cohen (p. 29):

> The first passage is plainly an argument. Its conclusion is that encryption and decryption keys must be protected more securely than any other secret message; its premiss (that these are the keys that allow either the intended recipient of a cipher message or a spy to decipher it) is marked by the word 'because.' But in the second passage there is no argument at all. That the authors chose to write their article together is not a conclusion; it is not inferred; it is a fact that they are here explaining. The word 'because' does not mark a premiss in this passage; what follows it is not evidence, or grounds, or reasons for believing what we already know to be true from looking at the first page of the article. 'Because' is here an indication of an *explanation* of the decision by these two authors – one a prominent Republican, the other a prominent Democrat – to write about American foreign policy jointly.

According to Copi and Cohen's analysis, then, we know that case 2.10 is an explanation, as opposed to an argument, because we know from the context, that is, 'from looking at the first page of the article,' that the proposition before the 'because' is 'already,' that is, given as, true. Presumably, then, it is clear from the *Newsweek* story that Kissinger and Vance's decision to write this article is a *fait accompli*. Thus, there is no need to argue for it, in the sense of attempting to convince the readers that this proposition is true. The function of the part after the 'because' must be something else.

Copi and Cohen write that the proposition that the authors decided to write the article together is 'not inferred.' This is right, but inference could be involved. What the authors are presumably doing is reporting that they (at some earlier stage in their joint deliberations) drew the practical inference that they ought to write this article together. The reason, or, at least, a key part of it, is their 'deep belief' reported by the proposition after the 'because.' Thus, inference could be involved in the explanation, but it plays a different role from that of the inference in the argument in case 2.9.

The explanation in case 2.10 is based on a report of a sequence of practical reasoning allegedly carried out jointly by Kissinger and Vance in their deliberations together. They are telling us that they are both committed to the goal of the security of free peoples and the growth of freedom. According to their reasoning, a necessary means to achieve this goal is the 'restoration of bipartisan consensus in American foreign policy.' The conclusion drawn, they are telling us, was their decision 'to write this article together.' This was a conclusion, presumably, because it represented to them a possible way to contribute to carrying-out the restoration of bipartisan consensus cited in the means-premise. We know from the context that Kissinger and Vance are important representatives of both the leading political points of view in American politics.

Clearly, then, case 2.10 does involve inference. It is, in fact, a reporting by the proponents of a sequence of practical reasoning that explains their decision, a citing of the reasons and goals that went into the decision in the course of their deliberations together. But the inference in case 2.10 is used in a different way from that in case 2.9. Case 2.9 is not a reporting of how a conclusion was arrived at by inference in the past, but of the direct use of an inference to arrive at a conclusion now.

Case 2.9 is also based on practical reasoning. The argument here gives practical grounds or reasons why encryption and decryption keys must be especially protected. Presumably, the big danger that needs to be protected against is the deciphering of a message by a spy. But these keys have to be used – they are indispensable if the message is to be sent at all – because they are what allows the intended recipient to decipher the message. Hence, we reach the practical conclusion that, to achieve these twin goals of transmission and security, these special keys need to be better protected than any other secret message. Here, once again, the reasoning is a goal-directed practical inference that leads to a conclusion stipulating a course of action required as a practical 'ought' or 'must.'[5] The prudent action is protection of these special keys if one has the aim of getting one's message through, undetected by spies.

Case 2.10 can also be compared very nicely with another case used by Copi and Cohen (1990, p. 30) as an exercise:

Case 2.11
Because the best physicists were not zealous for weapons, because they made uncorrected mistakes, because Hitler was Hitler, and because men like Speer always had more urgent production priorities, the Germans never really tried to make an atomic bomb. ('Hitler and the Bomb,' *New York Times Magazine*, 13 November 1988, p. 64)

This case comes out as an explanation, as opposed to an argument, according to the Copi–Cohen test (see section 5, below), because it can be taken for granted as a historical fact known to the readers that the Germans did not really try to make an atomic bomb. This claim is not in dispute, presumably. Case 2.11, then, is a historical explanation of a known fact, or item of historical knowledge.

Case 2.11 is different from case 2.10 because, in the latter, the principals are explaining the reasoning or deliberations that led up to their own decision to act in a certain way. In case 2.11, the author of the *New York Times Magazine* article is attempting to explain why someone else (the Germans prior to 1945) failed to take a certain line of possible action. He or she does so by citing the goals, characteristics, and priorities of the principal persons involved in not carrying out this possible action.

In other words, the author could be sketching out some key elements in what he or she takes to be the practical reasoning of these principals. For various reasons, none of them thought that the project of making an atomic bomb was important. The account given is very sketchy, however. 'Hitler was Hitler,' for example, doesn't really tell us much. It is a tautology, but presumably appeals to our historical knowledge that Hitler was irrational and anti-intellectual, and did not have a good grasp or appreciation of the potential of scientific research.

The scientists, it is said, were not zealous for weapons. Their goals, interests, and priorities were elsewhere. Hence, the conclusion, of working on nuclear science as a means to invent weapons for war use, was not one they arrived at as a practical course of action for them.

Thus, the three propositions given after the three occurrences of 'because' in case 2.11 could be interpreted or reconstructed as parts of practical inferences attributable to third parties retrospectively by the author of the article.

We could say, then, that the explanation in case 2.10 was a first-person reconstruction of deliberations that went into a practical decision. In case 2.11, the explanation reports on the presumed deliberations, goals, or priorities of other parties who (in the past) arrived at certain conclusions which can be inferred or conjectured by implicature from their actions, known goals, priorities, personal traits, and so on. Here, too, practical reasoning is involved, but in a more removed, second-party, conjectural, and sketchy way.

Cases 2.10 and 2.11 are reminiscent of case 2.2, where the conclusion was: 'That is the reason we have a man in the loop.' Case 2.2 was judged to be primarily an explanation, but it also contained practical reasoning used to justify the prudential wisdom of a past decision (as the situation appeared to the participants, who were also the speakers in case 2.2). Thus, we concluded, case 2.2 also involved reasoning, suggesting, too, somehow, that it contained argumentation of some kind (perhaps indirectly).

Cases like this appear to be quite common in everyday conversation, and are highly problematic, because the theoretical question of how to distinguish between 'argument' and 'reasoning' is fundamental. These two terms are often used interchangeably in the textbooks, and there appears to be no consistency in how they are defined in the textbook accounts.[6] We return to this problem in section 7, below.

First, however, it is appropriate to state the nature of the pedagogical problem

56 Argument Structure

posed by the difficulty of distinguishing between arguments and explanations, as indicated so far. Then we go on to pose a specific test designed to supplement the indicator-words for this purpose.

5. The Pedagogical Problem

The pedagogical problem of distinguishing between arguments and explanations is exacerbated by the fact that the indicator-words are not generally sufficient to identify arguments. Some of the indicator-words, such as 'because,' mark the presence of an argument in some cases. But, in other cases, the same word may indicate the presence of an explanation. Hence, students need some guidelines to distinguish between cases of argument and cases of explanation.

This problem appears to be a difficult one, for several reasons. One is that students, in the author's experience, find it difficult to distinguish between arguments and explanations. They appear to be discouraged that there is no clear answer, when they find cases that could legitimately be interpreted as either an explanation or an argument. Govier (1987, p. 160) states this observation succinctly from pedagogical experience:

> As many informal logic teachers have observed to their displeasure, it is very difficult to teach students the distinction between explanation and argument. They find it hard to grasp in theory and still more difficult to apply in practice. In a culture which does not generally emphasize the importance of rational evidence for disputed views, questions 'why?' are often taken as requesting explanations for how people came to hold their beliefs. Such crucial terms as 'why,' 'reasons,' and 'because' fit naturally into both explanations and arguments. Many students are so unused to rational argument that they find it hard to appreciate any contrast.

This pedagogical problem is no doubt partly caused by what could be called the 'indeterminacy problem' – namely, that in many instances, it is hard, or even impossible, to determine whether the case in question was meant by the speaker to be an argument or an explanation (or perhaps even both).

As an indication of the nature of the pedagogical problem, an example from the author's teaching experiences in a second-year logic course may be instructive. In a term test in this course, given in October 1994, students were asked to apply the test in Hurley (quoted below, in section 6) to determine whether an argument or an explanation is expressed in the following two texts of discourse (cases 2.12 and 2.13, below; student exercises in Hurley, 1994, p. 27). According to the Hurley test, one must ask whether the conclusion proposition (or thing to be explained, in the case of an explanation) describes something that is an 'accepted fact.' If so, the passage is an explanation. If not, it is an argument. The other question is whether the remainder of the passage is intended to shed light on this event. If so, it is an explanation. If not, it is an argument.

Case 2.12
A person never becomes truly self-reliant. Even though he deals effectively with things, he is necessarily dependent upon those who have taught him to do so. They have selected the things he is dependent upon and determined the kinds and degrees of dependencies. (B.F. Skinner, *Beyond Freedom and Dignity*)

Case 2.13
Silver, mercury, and all the other metals except iron and zinc, are insoluble in diluted sulfuric acid, because they have not sufficient affinity with oxygen to draw it off from its combination either with the sulfur, the sulfurous acid, or the hydrogen. (Antoine Lavoisier, *Elements of Chemistry*)

The answers, supplied in the back of Hurley's text (p. 564), are that the first passage (case 2.12) is an argument, the conclusion being: 'A person never becomes truly self-reliant,' and that the second (case 2.13) is a non-argument (explanation). The second outcome is produced, on the Hurley test, because the proposition 'A person never becomes truly self-reliant' is not an 'accepted fact.' Clearly, the conclusion is meant by Skinner to be controversial and to provoke a sceptical reaction. Hence, the premises are being used to try to justify this conclusion. By contrast, in case 2.13, the first proposition is meant by Lavoisier to be an 'accepted fact' in chemistry, and so the sequence of propositions in case 2.13 is not an argument but an explanation.

However, on the test, the students were equally divided, in that about the same number who got both answers right (according to the answers supplied in the back of Hurley's text) had the order reversed. A smaller number guessed that both were explanations or that both were arguments. Although the Hurley test was strongly emphasized in the class, and quite a few sample exercises were taken up in class discussions, it seemed that the students were not very successful at all in being able to distinguish between argument and explanation in these two cases, both of which seem relatively straightforward. When the test was taken up, despite a review of the Hurley test and the application of it to case 2.12, one student insisted doggedly that he still saw this case as an explanation and refused to concede that it was an argument.

The pedagogical problem is compounded by a theoretical problem. There is a large literature on the topic of explanation, and in it fundamental differences occur on what an explanation is. There appears to be no consensus of opinion on how to define the concept of explanation. Moreover, this concept does appear difficult to pin down – it may well vary with different contexts of discourse. This is a real problem for teachers of informal logic who take on the job of trying to instruct students to distinguish between cases that are arguments and cases that are explanations. How does one identify something in practice if one is not really sure what it is?

When we put all these things together, it suggests aiming towards a more modest goal. While it is true that explanation is a concept of intrinsic interest for informal logic, nevertheless the primary focus should be on argument. At this stage, it would be a worthwhile and worthy-enough goal to give students the means of identifying arguments, taking care that they are alert to those instances in which what appears to be an argument may really be an explanation. As far as the present pedagogical task is concerned, then, the job with respect to explanations is the negative one of excluding them from inadvertently, and incorrectly, being processed by the methods of argument analysis and diagramming. The job is one of recognizing when something is *not* an argument. The presumption can generally be that a sequence of reasoning is used to convey an argument, but we need to be alert to realize that this interpretation is not altogether routine.

For this purpose, it is not necessary to provide a theory that will solve all the problems of explanation in the philosophy of science. However, it is necessary to give students a general or rough idea of what an explanation is or looks like, at least enough to be able to recognize that, in some cases, something is not an argument but, rather, an explanation because the reasoning is being used in a different way and has a different conventional purpose of communication.

The practical requirement amounts to the following. In teaching students to recognize arguments, we have to warn them to be alert to the possibility that, in some cases, non-arguments will contain argument indicator-words. Explanations are a common case in point. Hence, students need to be alert to this possibility of error. A warning signal should be ready. If a passage of discourse is clearly an explanation only, and not an argument, then no further attempts should be made to diagram its 'premises' and 'conclusion.'

Passages that legitimately contain both an explanation and an argument need not be excluded. The only cases we have to worry about are those that can be interpreted only as an explanation, and not as an argument. The negative-exclusion test needs to screen out only these cases and reject them as things to be analysed by argument diagramming.

The aim of such a negative test is more limited than a positive test that would identify every explanation. It needs to screen out only cases that are clearly (and only) explanations, and are therefore non-arguments. However, even this type of test involves contextual interpretation of a passage of discourse.

6. The Textbook Test Revised

The textbook accounts see the distinction between an argument and an explanation as one of purpose or interest. Their way of drawing the distinction enables the construction of a test.

According to Hughes (1992, p. 76), the way to avoid confusing arguments and explanations is to understand the difference in purposes:

> The purpose of an explanation is to show *why* or *how* some phenomenon occurred or some event happened; the purpose of an argument is to show *that* some view or statement is correct or true. Explanations are appropriate when the event in question is taken for granted, and we are seeking to understand why it occurred. Arguments are appropriate when we want to show that something is true, usually when there is some possibility of disagreement about its correctness.

This way of making the distinction gives us a criterion or test to distinguish between arguments and explanations. Hughes adds (p. 77), however, that the context in a given case, usually, but not always, makes it clear whether the passage in question is an explanation or an argument.

There are different kinds of explanations, depending on the kind of question asked. A how-explanation asks for an account of how something works, for example, or how something happened. A why-explanation asks for some basis that will enable the questioner to understand why something is the way it is. In still other cases, a questioner will simply ask a respondent to 'explain' something that the questioner does not understand.

Hinderer (1992, p. 16) defines an 'argument' as a 'reason offered to influence a person's belief about something.' Then the distinction between an argument and an explanation is expressed as follows (p. 6):

> There's a difference between explaining and giving reasons. When you explain something, your purpose is to help people understand your point. When you give reasons for your belief, your purpose is to get people to accept your point. You sometimes hear people say, 'I don't think you are really hearing what I'm saying' or 'I'm not sure you really understand,' when they mean 'You should agree with me.' But understanding what someone is saying and believing that person is right are two different things.

Once again, the distinction is drawn as one of purpose. The way to tell the difference between an explanation and an argument is to determine (as well as one can) the purpose of the conventional activity the speaker is engaged in. Copi and Cohen (1990, p. 30) see the distinction as 'primarily one of purpose or interest,' and offer the following test:

> The difference between these arguments and nonarguments is primarily one of purpose or interest. Either can be formulated in the pattern
>
> *Q because P.*
>
> If we are interested in establishing the *truth of Q* and *P* is offered as evidence for it, then '*Q because P*' formulates an argument. However, if we regard the truth of *Q* as being unproblematic, as being at least as well established as the truth of *P*, but are interested in explaining *why Q is the case*, then '*Q because P*' is not an argument but an explanation.

At least in general outline, this Copi–Cohen test seems basically to be along the right lines. The key indicator is the purpose of putting *P* forward, and part of the test is whether the truth of *Q* is problematic, or whether some interest other than establishing *Q* as true is behind the *because*-locution.

The test proposed by Hurley (1994, p. 23) explicitly breaks down into two tasks, once the target proposition (the conclusion or *explanandum*) is identified.

> To distinguish explanations from arguments, first identify the statement that is either the conclusion or the explanandum (this is often the statement that occurs before the word 'because'). Then ask the question: Is the event described in this statement something that is an accepted fact? If the answer is 'yes,' then ask: Is the remainder of the passage intended to shed light on this event? If the answer is again 'yes,' the passage in question is an explanation.

In this test, the two questions are whether the target proposition being put forward is an accepted fact, and what the purpose of the discourse is. This way of posing the test fits in quite well with the theory of argument advocated in chapter 1, above. What is characteristic of an argument is an unsettled issue on which some line of reasoning is supposed to bear. In contrast, the purpose of an explanation is to 'shed light on' some proposition that is supposedly settled as an 'accepted fact.'

But all four of these accounts of how to distinguish between an argument and an explanation fall somewhat short of identifying the real nature of the former, as expressed in the theory of argument outlined in chapter 1. According to the

Copi-Cohen definition (p. 26), 'an argument is a group of propositions of which one, the conclusion, is claimed to be true on the basis of the other propositions, the premises, that are asserted as providing grounds or reasons for accepting the conclusion.'

Hurley (1994, p. 1) defines an 'argument' as 'a group of statements, one or more of which (the premises) are claimed to provide support for, or reasons to believe, one of the others (the conclusion).' This type of definition is too narrow, because it does not take into account hypothetical and/or presumptive arguments, where the premises are not asserted but only presumed or assumed to be true. Such arguments do not always make a claim that the conclusion is true, or a claim to support the conclusion, in the sense of giving a reason to believe it is true. But they are, none the less, arguments.

Copi and Cohen do, properly and usefully, point out (p. 27) that certain hypothetical propositions (conditionals of the 'if ... then' form) are not arguments. Hurley (pp. 18-21) also explains this distinction carefully. But, even so, these authors fail to note that there exist hypothetical arguments (where not all the premises are asserted) which are genuine arguments, and are not just propositions which are not arguments.

Ignoring the existence of hypothetical arguments makes it much easier for the textbook test plausibly to do its job of distinguishing between arguments and explanations. The textbook test focuses on those cases of argument in which the conclusion is a claim, and the premises are assertions made to back up that claim. Such cases more sharply contrast with those that are explanations and not arguments. Whereas this does tend to serve a pedagogical purpose, unfortunately it does overlook the cases of genuine arguments in which the premises are not asserted to be true, and the conclusion is not a proposition that is claimed to be true by the arguer.

The textbook tests are focusing on the kind of argumentation for an expressed opinion called 'pro-argumentation' and 'contra-argumentation' by van Eemeren and Grootendorst (1984, pp. 43-6). Roughly, this means that two parties are engaged in a critical discussion based on a conflict of opinions between them, and one party is giving reasons to the other party (premises, and inferences based on these premises) that she thinks he will find acceptable (as a justification or refutation of the proposition at issue). This concept does, indeed, capture a central notion of argument. But it also fails to capture many cases in natural language that we would commonly call 'arguments' in everyday conversation.[7]

It omits cases of negotiation dialogue and eristic dialogue (quarrelling) that we would normally call 'arguments,' in so far as it narrows the concept of argument to the critical discussion. That may not be too bad, however, as far as the test is concerned, because the critical discussion is a central type of dialogue for argument to occur in. And also, it is often evident from the textbook treatments that the critical discussion is the primary type of dialogue that the text is trying to instruct the student to manage, and learn to cope with.

As mentioned above, the other omission is hypothetical argumentation. These omissions make the textbook test somewhat artificially narrow in terms of its ability to capture the real basis of the distinction between argument and explanation. Even though it may be narrow, and may misfire in some cases, or not perform well, that does not mean the test is completely useless.

To improve the test, it can be phrased in a dialectical way that focuses on the respondent's attitude, as expressed in the text of discourse in a given case. In judging whether a given text of discourse contains an argument or an explanation, we have to look at the context of dialogue, and at the proposition at issue – namely, the proposition that is the putative conclusion or *explanandum*. Then we have to ask what the dialogue was meant to accomplish. Was it meant to resolve some unsettled issue between the proponent and respondent, for example, to persuade the respondent that this proposition is true? Or was it meant to help the respondent come to a better understanding of why this proposition is true, or how it came to be true? The question is the dialectical one of what purpose the discourse has for the proponent with respect to the respondent. How was it meant to be used by the proponent to affect the respondent's point of view or understanding? Examining the text of discourse in a particular case, we need to ask what the dialogue expressed was meant to do, with respect to the respondent. Two key questions should be asked, with respect to the proposition at issue.

1. Does the respondent doubt it or disagree with it, implying an obligation on the part of the proponent to support it with premises that provide reasons why the respondent should come to accept it as a commitment?
2. Is the proposition one the respondent is prepared to accept (or, at least, not to dispute), but desires more understanding of why it is so, or lacks clarification about it?

This dialectical test is to examine the context of dialogue, and then look at the speech act from what is evidently presumed to be the point of view of the respondent (reader, audience). If there is an implied disagreement, conflict of opinion, doubt, or other initial situation characteristic of the notion of unsettledness described in chapter 1, section 4, then the speech act is an argument. Otherwise, it is not, or, at any rate, there is not evidence of the kind required to categorize it as an argument. In such a case, it may be an explanation, or even simply a report or observation that is neither an argument nor an explanation.

Arguments and Explanations 63

Of course, the respondent, for the purposes of this dialectical test, is not the actual person who is reading the text of discourse at any particular time. The test is based on the purpose of the discourse as a type of dialogue in which the proponent or speaker is attempting to communicate with an audience or readership. In some cases, this audience could be a specific person; however, in many cases, the purpose of the discourse is to persuade anyone who reads the argument to accept its conclusion, to help anyone who reads the discourse to understand something. What is important is how the discourse in the given case is being used as conventional type of dialogue that has a communicative goal.

Although this dialectical test focuses on the presumed attitude of the respondent (according to the evidence of the text of discourse in the given case), what is basic is the underlying type of conventionalized speech act and type of dialogue both participants are supposed to be engaged in. It is not the proponent's, or the respondent's, purpose that is the key to the argument–explanation distinction. It is the goal of the type of dialogue they are supposed to be engaged in, as a conventional type of social activity which has normative maxims and principles.

Explanation is one type of activity, argument another. But the key to testing in a given case is to look for the element of unsettledness reflected in the respondent's presumed doubts or sceptical attitudes, as indicated by the context of the given discourse.

Argumentation can occur in different contexts of dialogue. The purpose of argumentation in a critical discussion is to resolve a conflict of opinions (van Eemeren and Grootendorst, 1984). The textbook tests seem oriented towards, or even designed to distinguish between, an argument, as used in a critical discussion, and an explanation.

However, there are other cases where argumentation is used, but the context is not that of a critical discussion. For example, in sections 8 and 9, below, we see cases where the context is that of a pedagogical dialogue. Here, the goal is not to resolve a conflict of opinions, but to impart knowledge to someone who is trying to learn a subject or domain of knowledge. In these cases, it is harder to apply the test described here in order to get a definitive outcome.

7. Reasoning in Argument and Explanation

It is very important to notice that, in some cases, the same reasoning can be used in an argument and an explanation. An example provided by Little, Groarke, and Tindale (1989, p. 10) illustrates this point very well.

Case 2.14
Suppose, for example, Bill gets out of bed, goes to the window, and sees a

blizzard raging outside. Rather than getting dressed and setting off for school, he goes back to bed. Bill apparently reasoned:

There is a blizzard, and if there is a blizzard the school will be closed. Therefore, the school will be closed.

The *argument* he presents to himself convinces him of the truth of his conclusion. Then, when his mother comes into his room and asks Bill why he isn't getting ready for school, he replies with the same reasoning in a slightly different form: 'Because there's a blizzard and whenever there's a blizzard, the school is closed.' Thus he provides the same reasoning as an *explanation* for his staying in bed.

This is an important type of case to reflect on, because it shows that explanations and arguments are much closer in terms of their components than one might have thought. Bill's explanation of why he didn't go to school seems almost the same as the argument he presented to himself. Perhaps we could even say that the explanation itself contained or recapitulated the argument.

Notice also that the argument cited in case 2.14 contains the same steps of reasoning as the explanation, but the steps go backwards. When Bill uses practical reasoning in his argument, he reasons from two premises: 'There is a blizzard' and 'If there is a blizzard, the school will be closed.' He concludes: 'The school will be closed.' And then he concludes to a new subargument:

If the school is closed, I don't need to go to school.
The school is closed [previous conclusion].
Therefore, I don't need to go to school.

Finally, he adds a further subargument to the chain of reasoning in the form of the additional premise 'If I don't need to go to school, I don't need to get ready.' Basing his decision on this sequence of practical reasoning, Bill takes the course of action, or inaction, of not getting ready.

Seeing Bill's behaviour, his mother asks why he is not getting ready. This why-question is a request for an explanation. In giving his explanation, Bill goes backwards up the same chain of reasoning that was, earlier, his argument. He doesn't need to go to school. Why? Because the school is closed. Why? Because there is a blizzard.

Thus, in case 2.14, the same line of reasoning functions as both an explanation and an argument. Used in one direction, the sequence of propositions is an argument. Used the other way, the same sequence serves as an explanation.

Later, in chapter 6, more is revealed on how arguments and explanations can use the same reasoning but in reverse sequence.

Little, Groarke, and Tindale express a key fact about this relationship very well when they say that the argument and the explanation contain the same reasoning. The idea here is that reasoning is something contained in arguments, and it is also something that can be contained in an explanation. The difference between the argument and the explanation, then, is not to be sought in the set of propositions contained in both of them, for these are essentially the same (the same line of reasoning, generally). The difference is to be sought in the use made of this reasoning in the different contexts of dialogue in which they occur. The argument was used by Bill in his personal deliberations on what to do (or not do) on that day. It involved practical reasoning, based on Bill's goals and particular circumstances, as he saw them that day. The explanation was used by Bill to recapitulate this to tell his mother what reasons had led him to follow this line of action (or inaction). Essentially, the same line of reasoning was involved or contained in both instances, but it was used in a different way.

Case 2.14 is similar to cases 2.2, 2.10, and 2.11 in that the explanation seems to recapitulate a line of practical reasoning that is, or can also be, used to function as an argument. It seems like the same line of reasoning is used two different ways in the same case, because there is a shift in the context of dialogue. Looked at in one way, the line of reasoning functions as an argument. But then the same line of reasoning also serves to fulfil a different purpose when the type of dialogue the speaker and hearer are (supposedly) engaged in is interpreted in a different way.

This brings us back to the general problem of how to make a distinction – if one should be made – between reasoning and argument.[8] It seems that practical reasoning may be a structure that underlies both argumentation and explanation.

Thomas (1981, p. 14) puts forward a radical thesis that argument and explanation tend to overlap in many cases. According to Thomas, the same passage of discourse can be (legitimately and correctly) both an argument and an explanation at the same time.

Actually, the view represented by Thomas is a little more complicated than this, because of the way the key terms 'argument,' 'explanation,' and 'justification' are defined. As Thomas sees it, both explanations and justifications come under the category of arguments. According to Thomas (p. 10), an *argument* is 'any discourse in which some statement is given as a reason for some conclusion.' A *justification* (p. 11) is the giving of 'grounds, evidence, or reasons of any other sort designed to convince others (or persuade ourselves) of the "truth" of a "claim or assertion."' An *explanation* (p. 11) is a making clear or telling why a state of affairs exists or happened.[9] Thomas sees argument as a broad concept of 'giving reasons' which can encompass both explanations and justifications.

In part, Thomas's broad approach turns on the way he sees another key concept – reasoning. According to Thomas (p. 10), *reasoning* is 'to accept some claim as true on the basis of reasons, or to offer or consider reasons in support or explanation of some claim or fact ...' From this definition, he draws the conclusion (p. 10) that 'an argument is any discourse that expresses reasoning.' Since both explanations and justifications express reasoning, according to Thomas, it follows that both are species of arguments.

This seems like quite a strong and non-standard point of view that conflicts with the more usual approach of the logic textbooks, where argument and explanation are treated as distinct entities that do not overlap, at least in clear cases. Thomas himself saw this opposition when he castigated 'a few introductory logic textbooks' (citing the fourth edition of Copi's *Introduction to Logic* specifically) for the supposed error of refusing to count explanatory discourses as arguments (p. 12). For Thomas, this exclusiveness is a mistake, primarily because of the way he sees the concept of reasoning as being involved in both argument and explanation.

> Certainly much reasoning involves giving evidence, grounds, or reasons with the intention of proving a claim that someone did not formerly believe. But we also often engage in reasoning in order to explain the occurrence of some state of affairs that we already know exists. And since we are interested in all kinds of *reasoning*, we will avoid linguistic narrowness, and taking a deeper view of the matter, apply the word 'argument' to *any* kind of *reasoning* done for *any* purpose. There is ample precedent for this application of the word 'argument' in the philosophy of science, where writers explicitly refer to explanatory discourses such as we have quoted earlier as 'causal arguments.' (p. 12)

Clearly, then, Thomas sees himself as taking a non-standard but 'broad' and 'deep' view of the matter by defining the concept of argument in a special way that has significant implications for logic as a subject. He goes so far as to say that the word 'argument' should apply to '*any* kind of *reasoning* done for *any* purpose.' This is obviously a much broader definition than many in the field of logic would likely be prepared to accept.

In chapter 1, the theoretical claim was put forward that Thomas's definition of argument is too broad and decontextualized, with the result that Thomas is unable to distinguish (as clearly as he should) in a given case between arguments and explanations. Chapter 5, below, posits that, instead of seeing argument as *any* kind of reasoning done for *any* purpose, argument is reasoning used in a conventionalized, goal-directed, interactive context of dialogue (conversation).

Putting these theoretical questions aside for the moment, however, we should not despair too soon or too much over our apparent inabilities and difficulties in clearly defining argument and explanation in a way that enables us to determine sharply whether the reasoning used in a given case is definitely the one thing or the other.

Now we have begun to adopt a dialectical point of view, which allows that there may not be enough information given, in a particular case, to pin down exactly what the purpose of the conversation is supposed to be. From this point of view, it is quite possible that many cases should be judged conditionally – that is, depending on the type of dialogue that the participants are supposed to be engaged in.

From a practical point of view, it may not matter that we cannot give a decisive test that will absolutely exclude all cases of explanations when we are diagramming arguments. One reason is that explanations may often share the same kind of underlying sequential structure with arguments. A theoretical reason behind this could be that both arguments and explanations contain reasoning. And if the argument diagram models the sequence of reasoning, it may well represent the structure of reasons given equally well in both an argument and an explanation.

For example, suppose we have a case that appears to be a linked argument, with two premises and a conclusion. But then, on reflection, we realize that this same discourse could also possibly be interpreted as an explanation, with two reasons combined to support the proposition being explained. Couldn't the linked-argument diagram equally well be used to represent the structure of the explanation? Or, perhaps more accurately, we could say that the diagram represents the structure of the reasoning used in the explanation.

If this is so, it may be unnecessary to fret unduly about the failure to provide a decisive test that will absolutely exclude all explanations from argument diagramming. It may be enough to say that we can interpret a given case (conditionally) from the point of view of its being an argument. This point of view for analysis need not absolutely exclude the point of view of the case's being an explanation.

8. The 'Risks for Managers' Case

To support his contention that explanation should be viewed as a species of argument, Thomas (1981) presented two special test cases as skill-testing experiments. We are supposed to look at them and judge whether they are

68   Argument Structure

explanations or justifications. In the first case (p. 13), the indicator-word 'thus' appears to mark the conclusion of an argument.

Case 2.15
Managers who at an early stage showed much promise, career growth, and mobility may find themselves classified as nonpromotable for any of a dozen reasons ... Once labeled nonpromotable, a person is frequently put on a shelf and only tolerated within an organization. Thus, there is a great potential for the development of insecurity and fear in a manager in an organization, since he has few legal rights for his protection and must develop himself so that the organization continually views him as a valuable asset. (Joseph L. Massie and John Douglas, *Managing: A Contemporary Introduction*, 2d ed. [Englewood Cliffs, NJ: Prentice-Hall, 1977], p. 16)

Thomas judges this case to be both an explanation and a justification, because the authors justify their statement that there is great potential for insecurity, and so on, by explaining how and why this potential exists. As Thomas puts it (p. 13), 'the authors justify their statement that this situation exists by showing the factors that lead to, or cause, its existence.' Thus, the discourse both explains and justifies this statement.

To get a better idea of what is going on in this case, it is helpful to look at it in light of the context of dialogue in which it was put forward. Case 2.15 comes from a textbook that is an introduction to the fundamentals of managing, designed to answer a reader's questions, such as 'How do you manage an organization when all its parts seem to have different participants and separate objectives?' (p. 8). The book's introduction (p. 8) makes it clear that the purpose of the text is to extend the reader's already existing knowledge of managing by depicting management in a broad context.

> We intend to answer many of the questions you have about managing. For example, we'll offer you the opportunity to learn some of the language of management – a language that will enable you to converse with practicing managers of organizations. You'll also have the opportunity to add to what you already know about managers. You may know something about managers of manufacturing plants but not managers of service institutions. You may have knowledge of management in small firms but not large firms; in profit-making organizations but not nonprofit organizations. By depicting management in a very broad context, we intend the coverage to be as complete and real as possible.

The first two chapters of the book, in which Thomas's first test case (case 2.15) occurs, are specifically designed, according to the authors (p. 8), to give the reader an 'overview of the manager's world.'

The particular passage quoted by Thomas (case 2.15) comes from a section of Massie and Douglas's text (p. 16) entitled 'Opportunities and Risks.' The purpose of the passage that includes the text quoted by Thomas is to show the reader that the manager's world is more full of risks than the reader might have anticipated. People accustomed to the protection of a union might not realize how vulnerable the job situation of a manager can be. To add to what the reader is already likely to know or think about this aspect of the manager's situation, Massie and Douglas show how these risks come about.

To get a good grasp of the context, it is useful to read the prior paragraph, as well as part of a sentence Thomas left out in his test case. The version quoted below, in case 2.15a, is taken directly from Massie and Douglas's text (1977, p. 16).

Case 2.15a
The manager's world is filled with both opportunities and risks. Most managers are not members of any union. They do not bargain collectively for wages, nor are they guaranteed any rights through the power group of large numbers of organized workers. It is uncommon for managers to have legally binding contracts. This means that a manager may be released on a Friday and find he is unemployed and looking for a job on the weekend. Individual-to-organization relationships in the managerial world are very, very different from those in the work world of the organized employee.

Managers who at an early stage showed much promise, career growth, and mobility may find themselves classified as nonpromotable for any of a dozen reasons – when they have a bad performance year, or when their boss suddenly changes jobs. Once labeled nonpromotable, a person is frequently put on a shelf and only tolerated within an organization. Thus, there is great potential for the development of insecurity and fear in a manager in an organization, since he has few legal rights for his protection and must develop himself so that the organization continually views him as a valuable asset.

Now we can get a better idea of what is going on in this passage. The passage is part of a pedagogical dialogue that occurs in a textbook. The authors are trying to portray 'the manager's world' for the reader. Of course, there will be different readers, with different backgrounds. Some of them may have experiences of being organized workers. To put them 'in a manager's world,' the authors show how managers have risks, because they do not have the kind of job protection that organized workers have come to expect.

Pedagogical dialogue can be of different types. It can be an expert-consultation type of dialogue, or an information-conveying type of dialogue. It can be meant to convey skills or information, and it can take place on different levels. It can, and typically does, contain explanation and argumentation.

In case 2.15a, is the proposition that appears after the indicator-word 'thus,' and before the word 'since,' the conclusion of an argument, or the *explanandum* of an explanation? To get at this question, we have to see what the passage quoted in case 2.15a does, how it functions in the larger context of the textbook.

The passage in case 2.15a enumerates all the various risks of the manager's job situation: the manager does not belong to a union, the manager may be 'classified as unpromotable,' and so forth. An inference drawn from all those risks constitutes yet another risk: 'there is great potential for the development of insecurity and fear in a manager in an organization.' This is a new risk, drawn to the attention of the reader, but it is drawn by inference, rather than reported or described directly from the depiction of 'the manager's world,' as the other risks are.

The purpose of the inference is to point out to the reader another risk, and thereby to bring him or her more 'into the manager's world,' or to teach him or her about the manager's job situation. Case 2.15a is not an explanation of why there is potential for insecurity and fear in a manager, because this proposition is not something that is already agreed upon by the writers and readers as a fact in the manager's world. The writers are, instead, inferring it as something new from the facts already presented – that managers do not have the protection of unions, that managers can be labelled unpromotable, and so forth. These facts could serve as an explanation of why there is great potential for the development of insecurity and fear in a manager. But, once we look at the whole passage in context, we can see that this potential is being pointed out, as opposed to being explained, to the reader.

The proposition that there is great potential for the development of insecurity and fear in a manager is not the conclusion of an argument, either, in the sense that the authors and the reader are resolving a conflict of opinions on this issue. It is not that the authors are trying to persuade or convince the reader to accept this proposition because they think the reader opposes it, or already has doubts about it. It is not a critical discussion between the authors and the reader that is taking place.

It is a pedagogical dialogue. The authors are informing the reader about the risks of managers in an organization. They describe some risks, and then infer a new risk, thereby adding to the reader's knowledge of the risks for a manager. In this context, the proposition that there is great potential for fear and insecurity in a manager can be described as the conclusion of an argument, but the purpose of the argument is to inform and educate the reader.

According to this interpretation, the prior listing of risks are premises that describe facts that are, or would be, generally accepted in the field of management studies. Then an inference is drawn from these facts to point out a new risk to the reader.

9. The 'Foundations of Philosophy' Case

Many of the examples chosen by Thomas to illustrate his contention that the passage is both an argument and an explanation are cases of pedagogical dialogue. And, indeed, this is the type of dialogue in which we would expect argument and explanation to come very close together. For the purpose of an argument in a pedagogical dialogue is normally for the teacher to educate the student by showing the student that a new proposition can rightly be inferred from some other propositions that are accepted as belonging to a domain of knowledge. In such a case, the teacher is not 'arguing' in the sense of having a dispute or conflict of opinions with the student, at least in the usual case, although this may be so. Rather, the teacher is presenting an argument in the sense of drawing out a conclusion by inference, a conclusion that is (presumably) new to the student. The argument is designed to inform or enlighten the student in such a case. This is why an argument, in such a pedagogical context, seems very similar to an explanation. It does have partly the same function as an explanation – to enlighten the student, to contribute to her knowledge or understanding of a field.

According to Govier (1987, p. 170), the following example is one of the most persuasive cases Thomas chose, in his set of exercises, to prove his claim that some discourses constitute both argument and explanation, on the same interpretation. This passage is quoted from a brief introduction that appears in all the books in the Foundations of Philosophy series:

Case 2.16
Many of the problems of philosophy are of such broad relevance to human concerns, and so complex in their ramifications, that they are, in one form or another, perennially present. Though in the course of time they yield in part to philosophical inquiry, they may need to be rethought by each age in the light of its broader scientific knowledge and deepened ethical and religious experience. Better solutions are found by more refined and rigorous methods. Thus, one who approaches the study of philosophy in the hope of understanding the best of what it affords will look for both fundamental issues and con-

temporary achievements. (Elizabeth Beardsley and Monroe Beardsley, Introduction, Foundations of Philosophy series published by Prentice-Hall)

The writers in this case are both senior professors of philosophy. The book series is intended for the introductory level – presumably many of the intended readers are students who have not previously taken a philosophy course. The authors are writing this introduction with the purpose of telling these readers what they can expect from studying this subject. The type of dialogue is pedagogical.

Is this passage an argument or an explanation? Although the pedagogical context would give any argument in such a case a function similar to that of an explanation, still it is possible to tell the difference, in general. An explanation of why a proposition is true is put forward on the presumption that the audience already knows or accepts that it is true. An argument is put forward on the opposite presumption, that the conclusion inferred will be something new for the students – something they don't know or accept yet as part of the field being presented to them.

Govier's comments (1987, p. 171) on this case are very interesting. She interprets the passage as an argument, not an explanation. The reasons she gives are essentially pragmatic – that is, they relate to the context of dialogue in which the text in case 2.16 was put forth. The intended audience, according to Govier (p. 171), is students who, presumably, do not know very much about philosophy as a field.

> The authors wrote to tell them what to expect from studies of the subject. To take the passage as an explanation is to presume that the students already know or believe that those looking for the best in philosophy will look at both fundamental issues and historical achievements. Pragmatically, this seems incorrect. It makes more sense to regard the passage as an argument. The authors, who have the authority of established philosophers writing an introduction to a series of texts, make statements about the time-significant aspects of philosophical problems and students accept their premises, in part because of their authority. The conclusion follows from these; it is almost a summary of what has been said before.

Once we look at the passage in case 2.16 in its context of dialogue pragmatically, it 'makes more sense' to interpret it as an argument rather than as an explanation. Why? Because the conclusion is a more general re-statement or 'summary' of the premises that describe various facts about philosophy for the student. Based on these facts, the conclusion tells the student what to look for in coming to the study of philosophy. It makes less sense, in this pedagogical context, as a message to explain something to the students that they have already encountered.

It is also interesting to note, however, that Govier (p. 171) is subtle and careful about her interpretation of this case. She admits that one could also look at the passage as an explanation. But she still feels that this interpretation would not be as plausible, because of the function of the reasoning of the case in its given context of dialogue. Her reason for this conclusion is revealing. In order to see the passage as an explanation, one would have to see it in such a way that the audience would 'have to be convinced of the truth of the conclusion before an explanation as to why it was true would seem necessary' (p. 171). And, given the pedagogical context of dialogue in case 2.16, this interpretation, pragmatically speaking, does not make sense.

Context of dialogue aside, the sequence of propositions in case 2.16 can be interpreted as either an argument or an explanation. According to Govier (p. 171), the sequence can function as an explanation because 'the justifying premises are also statements that are appropriate to explain the fact that is in the conclusion.' Not taking the context into account, one can interpret the sequence of propositions in the passage as fulfilling this function, to some extent.

But the bottom line is that we do not just need to look at how a sequence of propositions could function, whether they could be used to contribute to the function of an explanation or an argument. We need to go beyond this – to the extent that such information is available – and look at how the sequence of propositions actually does function in the given context of dialogue.

In a pedagogical context of dialogue, it is hard to differentiate argument from explanation because the function of argument is not, in every respect, altogether disjoint or different from that of an explanation. Both have the aim of enlightening the student, or contributing to the student's knowledge of a subject.

But, even so, there is a basic difference in the two functions that can be clearly apparent in many cases, provided enough is known about the context of the dialogue that is supposed to be taking place. We have to ask the normative question: what type of dialogue are the participants rightly supposed to be engaging in? If it is a pedagogical dialogue, then the function of an argument is different from that of an explanation. We need to ask: is the audience already convinced of the truth of the conclusion, or aware of its truth? Or is the speaker drawing out an inference from a set of premises that are taken to represent facts or items of knowledge in the field being taught to the student, and then moving to a conclusion that is a summary, generalization, or recapitulation of these facts that presents a new item of knowledge to the student? The one function is different, in certain key respects, from the other.

Thus, after careful analysis, one of Thomas's most persuasive cases for his conclusion that the same passage is both argument and explanation falls apart. The case illustrates the subtlety, the difficulty, and the context-dependence of distinguishing explanation from argument in a given case. But it fails to demonstrate his thesis that there is an important class of cases where the same passage can be legitimately and correctly interpreted as either an argument or an explanation.

What Thomas has shown, however, is that the textbook test (see section 6, above) would not work in such cases as 2.15 and 2.16, because the context of dialogue is not that of a critical discussion.

10. Reorienting the Task as Dialectical

We might initially be inclined to think that the task of identifying arguments is one of identifying some particular entity, an 'argument' that either exists in a given passage of discourse or does not. If this is the way we view the task, then finding vague cases, in which we are not sure whether something is an argument or not, tends to be very discouraging. It makes one wonder whether the task is worthwhile, or even possible to accomplish with any objectivity or precision.

However, if we can reorient our view of the task of argument identification, it begins to seem less discouraging and more feasible. In attempting to see whether a given passage contains an argument, what we are really trying to do is to determine whether the speaker or writer of the passage is making, and can rightly be held to, a commitment to having put forward a particular proposition in a particular way. The way he should correctly have been interpreted to have put it forward, if it is an argument, is as a conclusion held out to us, the hearer or reader, which should make a rational claim on our commitment to accept it on the basis of some premises that can also be found in the passage. In other words, whether there is an argument, in a given case, is a function of the speaker's speech act in the kind of conversation he is supposedly engaging in with the hearer. It is a question of the purpose of the dialogue the two are supposed to be engaging in together.

Whether there is an argument does not exactly depend on the speaker's intentions, but it comes close to that. It depends on what type of speech act the speaker can rightly be said to have shown himself to be engaged in, given the evidence from the passage in question and what we know of the larger context of dialogue surrounding the passage. Thus, the task of argument identification is somewhat like the process in archaeology whereby a discovered fragment must be identified as having some function as an artefact within the context of a civilization.

Within this perspective on the task of argument identification, it should not be too surprising that, in some instances, there is no way to tell whether a passage of discourse is an argument or not.

Govier (1987, pp. 194–5) gives the case of a sentence on a billboard, seen near Salem, Ontario: 'Jesus Christ died for our sins. Trust him.' Is it an argument? Is the first sentence a premise and the second a conclusion, perhaps linked by the missing premise 'Anyone who died for our sins should be trusted'? Or is it really just two separate sentences, one an assertion and the other an imperative, not connected by any link that makes the pair an argument?

Govier (p. 195) concludes that, in this case, the discourse could legitimately be taken in the one way or the other. We could interpret the two sentences as an argument, even an argument based on appeal to pity. Or we could interpret it as two distinct statements, with no inferential relationship between them.

In this case, there is not enough context given for us to know, based on textual evidence, whether the discourse on the billboard expresses an argument or not. This may seem discouraging at first, but perhaps all it shows is that we simply aren't given enough information, in this case, about the function of the given two sentences in relation to what the writer of the passage was trying to convey or engage the reader to think. Quite possibly, as in the case in many advertisements, the strategy was simply one of catching the reader's attention with some arresting or memorable phrases. And any ambiguity or uncertainty about what was meant would, by prompting some readers to be puzzled, contribute to, more than hinder, such an aim.

Having adopted the dialectical point of view of the task, we should no longer be surprised or disappointed that there are lots of cases in which we can't make a definitive judgment whether the passage of discourse contains an argument or an explanation. In such cases, we need to be prepared to give a conditional evaluation of the form 'If such-and-such is meant to be the context of dialogue, then we can adopt the interpretation (subject to default if more context becomes known) that this sequence of reasoning is an argument (or an explanation).' We might even come to distinguish primary and secondary uses of reasoning; for example, a case might be evaluated as primarily an explanation but secondarily an argument (or justification).

Hamblin (1970, p. 273) commented on the ambiguity of 'Why?' that needs to be taken into account in formal dialectic.[10] In one sense, 'Why A?' is a request for proof or argument to back up A. In another sense, 'Why A?' is a request for a causal or teleological explanation (p. 274). Hamblin mentions a third sense, as well, but our focus here is on these two basic senses.

There are two basic types of why-questions that commonly occur in conversational dialogue that forms the context of argumentation. One type of why-question asks the respondent to provide proof, support, or justification for a proposition that he (the respondent) is committed to. Although it is not an absolute requirement, it is a general presumption that the questioner is not committed to this proposition. The questioner need not be opposed to the proposition, but it is a normal presumption that he is sceptical about it. The other type of why-question asks the respondent to clarify a proposition for the proponent (question-asker). Such a clarification typically takes the form of showing how the proposition at issue came to be true. For example, if the proposition describes an event that presumably happened, the respondent might describe the causal or teleological sequence leading up to that event.

The key to the distinction between an explanation and an argument lies in understanding the difference in function between these two types of why-questions. An argument is the right kind of reply to the first type of why-question. An explanation is the right type of response to the second type of why-question. Both types of responses involve reasoning, so it is generally not very easy to distinguish, in a particular case, whether a reply to a why-question is best taken as an argument or as an explanation. To make the distinction, we have to look at the function of the reply.

When the why-question is a request for an argument, the function of the reply should be to take some propositions the proponent is already committed to, and use these as premises to reason to a conclusion. The idea is that, because of this sequence of reasoning, the proponent will become committed to the conclusion, the very proposition he queried in his why-question. An argument has a particular kind of dynamic or movement. At first, the asker of the why-question was not committed to the proposition he questioned. But then, through the respondent's furnishing of a successful argument in response, the proponent was led to incur commitment to this proposition. Of course, arguments are not always successful, but, when they are, this is the function they are meant to perform.

When the why-question is a request for an explanation, the function of the reply should be to take the proposition queried, the *explanandum*, and link it to some other propositions that will throw light on it for the questioner. But, in contrast to the other type of why-question, the proposition at issue is already a commitment of both parties. Neither party disputes it, or is sceptical about its acceptability as a proposition that is true, or an event that has happened. That is not the object of concern. The concern is for the respondent to clarify the proposition by relating it to something more familiar to the proponent.

Thus, the dynamic for explanation is different from that characteristic of argument. In explanation, the aim is not for the one party to secure the commitment of the other party for a proposition which was previously in doubt. The aim is, given the commitment of both parties to a proposition, for the one party to throw light on the proposition for the other party, by linking it to something else that other party is familiar with.

Whether the one aim or the other should express the purpose of a passage of discourse in a given case can be judged only by arriving at some interpretation of that discourse as being some conventionalized and familiar type of dialogue we can recognize. Of course, in making such judgments, we could be wrong, or there may not be even enough textual or contextual evidence for us to decide (other than conditionally – based on assumptions).

What kind of evidence is needed to make such a decision? As this chapter has shown, the indicator-words are the place to start. In general, when applying the method of diagramming, the given assumption is that the passage contains an argument. But it is always good to check and think twice about a case. Could it be an explanation, as opposed to an argument? At this stage, the dialectical test can be applied. In applying the dialectical test, some investigations or assumptions will have to be made about the broader context of dialogue. This involves a contextual judgment of the purpose of the discourse, as fitting in with the goals and maxims of a type of conversation.

3

The Art of Diagramming

Most of the readers of this book will already be familiar with argument diagramming, a method widely in use in current courses in logic, critical thinking, and argumentation. For those who are not, this chapter presents an introduction to the method. For those who are, this chapter outlines the standard approach to the subject, as it is treated in most of the textbooks – or, at any rate, typically. If the account given in this chapter deviates from what is typical of the textbook treatments, it is in virtue of trying to give a relatively simple exposition of the main techniques used.

Later, a detailed treatment of the refinements and problems in the method is undertaken.

1. The State of the Art

Traditionally, the main task of logic has been taken to be the evaluation of arguments as valid, invalid, fallacious, and so on. But, in recent years, this orientation has moved more towards the applying of logic to argumentation used in everyday conversation. As a result, it is becoming more apparent that there is a problem of identification of arguments and their basic structure as sequences of reasoning. More and more, experience is telling us that, in order to do an adequate job of judging a given argument as correct or incorrect by some logical standard, we first must determine what the argument is.[1]

This book is devoted to argument structure, to systematizing and improving the techniques widely used in informal logic to identify premises and conclusions in an extended sequence of argumentation in a text of discourse. The focus here is on the techniques used for argument structure in the textbooks, and on the three key problems inherent in the use of these techniques – the problem of linked versus convergent arguments, the problem of distinguishing

The Art of Diagramming 79

between arguments and explanations, and the problem of non-explicit premises and conclusions in arguments. The second problem has already been analysed in chapter 2. The remaining two problems will be dealt with in subsequent chapters.

The primary tool currently in use to give an account of argument structure is the argument diagram. An argument diagram is a set of points (nodes) used to represent propositions, the premises and conclusions in the argument, and a set of lines (arrows) joining the points together to represent steps of inference. A typical argument diagram gives a map of the overall structure of an extended argument. The primary function of the argument diagram is to answer the question 'What is the argument?,' to identify the argument, prior to undertaking the tasks of analysing and evaluating it.

Most logic textbooks emphasize the use of logic as a tool for evaluating arguments, showing that a given argument is valid, invalid, supported by good reasons, fallacious, and so on. However, in practice, if logic is to apply to 'real world' cases, where a given text of discourse is to be evaluated, the stage of argument evaluation presumes a prior stage of argument identification and analysis of argument structure. First, we must identify what the argument is (or what it is supposed to be, at any rate); otherwise our evaluation could be faulty and misleading. It has already been shown, in chapter 1, section 9, in attempting to evaluate a case alleged to be an instance of the fallacy of begging the question, how the evaluation depended on the prior outcome of identification and analysis of structure. The evaluation of case 1.9 as containing a fallacious argument depended on: (a) the determination that the line of reasoning in this case was an argument, as opposed to an explanation; and (b) the analysis of the structure of the argument, as being linked or convergent.

This process of argument identification is, in fact, non-trivial in many cases, as we will see abundantly in this book. Often people get their premises and conclusions mixed up, and it is hard to tell what they are really committing themselves to as something they are advocating, if anything at all. In some cases, it is unclear whether a speaker is really putting forward an argument at all, as opposed to explaining or describing something, as noted in chapter 2.

The one problem is that of determining whether a given passage of discourse contains an argument, as opposed to an explanation, for example, or some kind of discourse other than an argument. This problem, as we saw in chapter 2, section 5, is often a severe obstacle in teaching logic courses, because the students quickly come to see that, in some cases, there can be a legitimate basis for interpreting a text of discourse either way. Another serious pedagogical difficulty with the current logic textbooks is the problem of distinguishing between linked arguments, where the premises go together to support the conclusion, and convergent arguments, where each premise is an independent line of evidence to support the conclusion. Here, too, students often exhibit divided opinions, and this apparent inability of logic to make a clean and decisive distinction (a discovery that typically occurs at the beginning of the course) shakes their confidence in the subject. Similarly, when confronted with cases of arguments with non-explicit premises or conclusions – called 'enthymemes' – students are greatly discouraged when they perceive that there are two (or maybe even more) plausible candidates for the missing part, and that there is no clear and conclusive basis for deciding between them.

The current difficulty with using argument diagramming as a teaching tool in courses designed to help students think more critically and criticize arguments more effectively is that the students are not able to carry out these tasks in a clear and definite way, so that they can be sure they have the right answer. The reason for this is that the tests used in the logic textbooks to carry out these tasks are highly variable and contradict one another. In many cases, no real criteria at all are given, or the ones given do not yield a clear answer. For example, the same argument might be linked according to the test advocated in one textbook, but convergent according to the test advocated in another. Some of the textbook tests even give results that appear intuitively wrong to students.

These difficulties, along with the conflicts in the textbook treatments of argument identification as a method, give some justification to the critics who would say that you can 'deconstruct' a text any way you like, and that no objective method of argument identification is possible. Willard (1976, p. 313), for example, criticized argument diagramming by an argumentation analyst as 'nothing more significant than drawing lines on sheets of paper' because it is merely a subjective abstraction from an event.

In part, this book will support such a critical assessment by concluding that the best methods of argument identification are inherently pragmatic, in the sense that they depend on the speaker's purpose within the context of dialogue he or she is engaging in. Thus, according to the analysis put forward in this book, argument identification does depend on an interpretation of a text of natural language discourse in a given case. According to our pragmatic theory of how to interpret a case, we must judge how the speaker or writer of a text of discourse is engaging in a reasoned dialogue with a respondent, and with the critic who is proposing an evaluation of the argumentation (supposedly) put forward by that speaker or writer.

However, one of the main theses of the book is that the interpretation expressed or modelled by an argument diagram can (if properly done) be based on objective, reproducible evidence that is open to inspection and verification by anyone (including the speaker whose argument is analysed). By tying the

The Art of Diagramming 81

method of argument diagramming to the theory of argument put forward in chapter 1 of this book, it will be argued later, in chapter 8, below, that the method can be justified as a valid tool for determining argument structures in the practical or applied part of logic.

In fact, it is clear that informal logic could not get along, or perform its job of evaluating arguments adequately, without this method, or some comparable technique of argument-structure identification.

Consider the fallacy of begging the question, or 'arguing in a circle,' as it is sometimes called. This fallacy is one of the traditional errors or types of shortcomings criticized in informal logic. But it is fairly clear, as shown by our remarks on case 1.9 just above, that if there is confusion or uncertainty about what is the premise or what is the conclusion of a given argument, we can hardly say whether or not the argument commits the fallacy of arguing in a circle.

In short, to do the job of argument evaluation required for informal logic, we really must presuppose that we already have a method of argument identification that will tell us what the premises and conclusions are in a given case.

The basic problem, however, is that there has been very little scholarly material (aside from textbook treatments) written in the past on argument structure as such (the possible exceptions are Shoesmith and Smiley, 1980, and Thomas, 1981, but the former is a book on logical theory, the latter is a textbook, and both books are more concerned with evaluating than identifying arguments). Moreover, the differences in the methods of argument identification used in both the specific techniques and the basic concepts found in the logic textbooks are awesomely wide. So the job has to be partly a foundational one of asking the philosophical question of what an argument is, as well as the practical job of finding useful methods of identifying arguments in a particular given case.

Interest in this subject is now increasing, however, and two books have recently appeared – Freeman, 1991, and Snoeck Henkemans, 1992. Both of these books are directed to the linked-convergent distinction as their central focus, or problem to be dealt with in giving an account of argument structure. Both of them (like the present book) take a pragmatic and dialectical approach to the problem.

However, both of these books, as we will see subsequently, provide solutions that are different from the one we will propose. These differences are no doubt partly attributable to the theories of argument presumed by both approaches, which are somewhat different from each other, and also different from the theory expressed in chapter 1, above.

Before the advent of these two books, however, the method of diagramming was developed in textbooks. The tests and criteria used for argument identification by many of the current logic textbooks are dissected and critically tested out in the chapters that follow. Many readers will interpret this analysis as an indictment of the textbooks, showing that they are 'full of errors' or engaged in superficial treatment. However, this is far from the right attitude to take. The problem with the subject of argument structure has been that the textbooks have been in the 'front lines,' so to speak, without any generals guiding the battle from the rear, and they have to use whatever tools or techniques are at hand, even if those tools were not very well developed and the instructions for their use were not clear. Despite this liability, the textbooks are an excellent source of problem cases, and have all kinds of innovative and useful things to say, when they attempt to deal with these cases (even, or perhaps especially, when they are unsuccessful). Thus, our own book is not condemning the textbook authors who have used the technique of argument diagramming. Rather it attempts to bring them closer together by developing a unified method of argument identification that not only is practically useful, but also has a sound theoretical basis that is, at least, open to inspection and critical evaluation.

The textbook by Copi and Cohen (1991) is the eighth edition of the book originally written by Irving Copi in 1953. This book has long been the leading logic textbook, much appreciated by instructors and students for its clear, user-friendly presentation, and abundance of helpful exercises and examples. In the critical analysis of argument-identification techniques given in the following chapters, the text by Copi and Cohen (1991) very often seems to be the target. However, this attention is not meant as a victimization of this fine textbook (the author has paid it the ultimate compliment by often using it in his own logic class). If Copi and Cohen often seem to be the target of critical remarks, it is because they so often give the best and clearest exposition of how to use the technique of argument diagramming in the classroom.

Our way of improving the method of diagramming is (in rough outline) to identify as problems the weakest points, or gaps in the basic technique, and then to solve these individual problems, or at least to present recommendations, based on what we have found or think to be the best solutions. Our conclusion is that the method of diagramming is salvageable, in broad outline. But, in chapter 8, we will recommend several key changes and new features, so that, in the end, we will speak of a new method.

The work in this project has both a theoretical and a practical aspect. The theoretical aspect is that it is interesting in its own right to ask what an argument is, and to inquire into the relationships between the concept of argument and the related concepts of inference, reasoning, explanation, and so forth. The method of argument diagramming, and, along with it, the distinctions between linked and convergent, and other types of arguments, are intrinsically interesting as foundational problems of informal logic in their own right.

The practical aspect is the task of developing methods and curriculum materials that are useful for helping students to learn to recognize and analyse arguments in courses that aim to improve reasoning skills. One goal here, for example, is to give students some useful tests and techniques that would help them distinguish between arguments and non-arguments. These tests and techniques are useful in practice because they enable students to avoid the pitfall of attempting to analyse and evaluate arguments in passages of discourse that do not really contain arguments at all. This species of error is significant enough in practice to be worth taking some care to avoid, as noted above.

The basic motivation for the inquiry is practical and pedagogical, but, in this instance, theoretical questions have to be raised as well that are necessary to address in solving the practical problem. By necessity, the project must arrive at some clear, even if provisional, definition of what an argument is. And part of that job is to try to give some clear-enough analysis of the concept of argument to distinguish between cases of argument and cases of non-argument, that is, explanations, inferences, and so on, that are hard to distinguish from arguments in some instances.

However, the intent was to resist the temptation to go in for purely abstract theorizing, and instead to balance the theory with work towards a practical result – namely, devising criteria and tests that would be useful to logic students, or to anyone who ventures a criticism of some text of discourse on the grounds that there is some gap or error in the argument. Our conclusion will be that the method of argument diagramming is, at least potentially, useful for this purpose, once some of the admittedly serious basic problems in it are solved. On the other hand, the various gaps and severe foundational problems we will encounter suggest that the method of argument-structure analysis needs more research and, in general, needs to be taken more seriously as a legitimate subject for research in applied logic.

2. Elements of Diagramming

Many of the current textbooks have adopted the practice of including a section, or several sections, usually at the beginning of the book, on how to 'reconstruct' arguments. This process is usually taken to be one of breaking an argument down into its component parts – namely, its premises and conclusions.

The method used predominantly in these textbooks is called 'argument diagramming.' Johnson (1992, p. 14) gives a typical description of how the method works. One begins by numbering all the component propositions (premises and conclusions) in an argument, using the indicator-words like 'thus' or 'therefore' to mark the premises and conclusions.

84   Argument Structure

Those who are familiar with the method of argument diagramming know that it is the main tool we have in argumentation and informal logic for analysing the structure of an argument. In the analysis of any argument expressed in a given passage of discourse, the first step is to locate the premises and the conclusion. This first step of argument identification (recognition) becomes especially important when the passage to be analysed involves a long sequence of reasoning, an interlocking sequence of premises and conclusions spread over a larger passage of discourse.

Those who are new to argument diagramming can easily get a grasp of how it is used, and its basic concepts, by looking at how it is used with the examples of arguments presented in this chapter. These readers can see that argument diagramming is a familiar type of technique – a process diagram or 'flow chart' of the steps in a sequence – in this instance, as applied to an argument. Many textbooks on introduction to logical reasoning, critical thinking, and so on, use this technique to help students think more clearly and critically evaluate argumentation of the kind they encounter in everyday life, academic pursuits, or wherever they must judge arguments critically.

The technique of argument diagramming has clearly established itself as a useful, working tool of informal logic. It is the method widely used in logic to identify an argument by picking out its premises and conclusions, as well as the chain of 'steps' or inferential 'links' that join these propositions together as something we can recognize as an argument.

In the simplest kind of case, the *single argument*, there is only one premise and one conclusion. Johnson (1992, p. 14) cites the following example:

Case 3.1
Webb was promoted to vice-president.
Therefore, she will move to Pittsburgh.

Here, we number the component propositions ① and ②, respectively. Then, using the word 'therefore' as an indicator of which is the conclusion, we diagram the argument as shown in figure 3.1. Not all arguments are this simple. With multiple premises and conclusions, the component propositions are joined together in four types of structures explained below – linked, convergent, serial, and divergent.

For any given argument in a text of discourse, the job is to identify the ultimate conclusion first, and then to judge how the other conclusions and premises are ordered in a sequence that supports that ultimate conclusion. When each proposition in the argument is numbered, and lines drawn in, connecting the numbers to show which premises support which conclusions, the diagram reconstructs or identifies the line of argumentation in a given case.

Figure 3.1 Single Argument

The resulting argument diagram gives you a map or snapshot of the overall flow and structure of an extended chain of reasoning in a given passage of discourse containing argumentation. Hence, the technique of argument diagramming is not only very useful, but is widely adopted in current informal-logic textbooks. It is a method of argument recognition (or identification) to be used prior to the analysis and evaluation of an argument.

The use of this method appears very straightforward and natural. It seems to represent the natural kind of move anyone would make when trying to recapitulate, or make sense of, a complex argument.

However, as we have indicated already to some extent, and will find out more extensively later, this technique suffers from three major, basic problems – determining in a particular case whether something is an explanation or an argument, determining whether an argument is linked or convergent, and determining what the non-explicit premises of an argument are. Together, these three problems impair the effectiveness of using the method, thereby interfering with the proper evaluation of an argument, and with the use of the method of diagramming as a way of identifying the structure of the argument.

3. Linked and Convergent Arguments

A *linked argument* has more than one premise, where the premises function together to give support to the conclusion. Linked arguments can have any number of premises, but the simplest type has two premises, and each requires or relies upon the other in order to support the conclusion.

The phrase 'linked argument' is not used by Beardsley (1950); the first known use of it is by Thomas (1981; first edition 1973).[2] According to Thomas (1981, p. 52), 'an argument is *linked* when it involves several reasons, each of which is helped by the others to support the conclusion.' Amplifying a bit more, Thomas (pp. 51–2) adds that, in a linked argument, 'each reason needs the other in order to support the conclusion.' Such an argument is said to 'combine' two or more reasons (pp. 52 and 53).

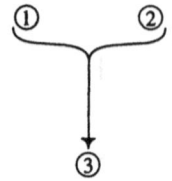

Figure 3.2 Linked Argument

According to Copi and Cohen (1990, p. 20), in a linked argument each premise supports the conclusion through the mediation of the other premise. Both are needed, and neither supports the conclusion independently – the two premises work 'cooperatively' rather than 'independently.' According to Hurley (1991, p. 59), premises in an argument support a conclusion *conjointly* – that is, the argument is linked. If taken separately, the premises provide little or no support for the conclusion, but taken together, they do provide support. According to Hurley (p. 58), the horizontal (convergent) pattern or structure consists of a single argument where two or more premises support the conclusion independently of each other.

A good example of a typical linked argument is used as an exercise by Copi and Cohen (1990, p. 23):

Case 3.2
Competent individuals are at liberty to make their own medical treatment decisions; incompetent individuals are not. Thus, competence and liberty are inextricably interwoven. (George J. Annas and Joan E. Densberger, 'Competence to Refuse Medical Treatment: Autonomy *vs.* Paternalism,' *Toledo Law Review* 15 [Winter 1984], 561)

Numbering the three propositions in their order of occurrence in case 3.2, the argument can be represented by the characteristic diagram (figure 3.2), for the linked argument with two premises.[3]

Both the first proposition, 'Competent individuals are at liberty to make their own medical treatment decisions,' and the second proposition, 'Incompetent individuals are not [at liberty to make their own medical treatment decisions],' go together to support the conclusion, 'competence and liberty are inextricably interwoven.' Each premise helps the other to support the conclusion. The two reasons are combined, and work cooperatively to support the conclusion, marked by the indicator-word 'thus.'[4]

Many of the familiar kinds of deductively valid arguments commonly found in logic textbooks are clearly linked arguments. Consider arguments of the familiar form *modus ponens*.

Case 3.3
If Sally has agreed to run, Jane will not be elected.
Sally has agreed to run.
Therefore, Jane will not be elected.

In this case, the two premises go together to support the conclusion. Each premise needs the other. Without the first premise, the second premise would not support the conclusion. And the first premise, by itself, is merely hypothetical. It needs the addition of the second premise in order to be brought to bear as a reason to lead us to conclude that the third proposition is established as true. In this case, each premise helps the other to support the conclusion. The two premises are combined, and each is used to prove the conclusion through the mediation of the other. They work cooperatively rather than independently.

Instances of practical reasoning[5] are another clear type of linked argumentation where the two premises function together to support the conclusion.

Case 3.4
My goal is to get to Leiden.
Taking the Maaldrift is the way to get to Leiden.
Therefore, I should take the Maaldrift.

In this argument, both premises function together to support the conclusion. If the one premise is absent, or does not obtain, then the other one, by itself, does not bind the arguer to the conclusion as a practical (prudential) course of action.

A convergent argument has more than one premise, where each premise gives an independent reason for accepting the conclusion.[6] Convergent arguments can have any number of premises, but the simplest type has two premises, and each premise stands on its own to support the conclusion, without having to depend on the other one.

According to Beardsley (1950, p. 19), 'in a *convergent* argument, several independent reasons support the same conclusion.' According to Copi and Cohen (1990, p. 19), in a convergent argument, each of the two premises supports the conclusion independently: 'Each supplies some warrant for accepting the conclusion and would do so even in the absence of the other premise.' Copi

88 Argument Structure

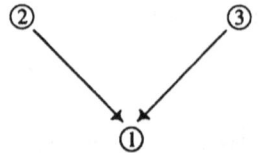

Figure 3.3 Convergent Argument

and Cohen add (pp. 19–20) that we could even speak of it as being one argument with two (independent) premises.

A good example of a convergent argument is the following case, from an exercise in Copi and Cohen, 1990 (p. 22).

Case 3.5
I've opposed the death penalty all of my life. I don't see any evidence that it's a deterrent and I think there are better and more effective ways to deal with violent crime. (Governor Michael Dukakis, in the Bush–Dukakis presidential debate, Los Angeles, 15 October 1988)

Numbering the propositions, the argument begins with the proponent's putting forward the conclusion, ①: 'I've opposed the death penalty all my life.' The following two premises give reasons for this opposition. First, 'I don't see any evidence that it's a deterrent,' and second, 'I think there are better and more effective ways to deal with violent crime.' Let's number these premises ② and ③, respectively.

A minor point of analysis is that the conclusion is probably better reconstructed as the proposition 'The death penalty is a bad thing,' or perhaps as 'The death penalty should be abolished,' or 'My stand against the death penalty is reasonable.' But let's not worry too much about these finer details for our purposes here.

If we use the numbers ①, ②, and ③ to represent the component propositions, the argument can be represented by figure 3.3, a characteristic diagram for convergent arguments with two premises. The diagram represents the idea that the two premises, ② and ③, each support the conclusion independently of the other. Each supplies a reason on its own.

Note that the text of discourse in case 3.5 could possibly be interpreted as an explanation rather than an argument. Perhaps Mr Dukakis could be interpreted as explaining why he has opposed the death penalty, rather than giving reasons to support his stand against the death penalty in the form of an argument. But let's assume that case 3.5 is an argument. If so, it is a good example of a conver-

The Art of Diagramming   89

Figure 3.4 Serial Argument

gent argument, where two independent reasons for the conclusion are given. Here is another reminder of the additional problem of how to distinguish between explanations and arguments, treated in chapter 2, above.

4. Serial and Divergent Arguments

A *serial argument* is composed of two or more stages (subarguments) where the conclusion of the first argument also functions as a premise in the second argument.[7] A good example is the following argument from Beardsley, 1950 (p. 18):

Case 3.6
The room was sealed, and empty when we entered.
Therefore, no one could have left it. And therefore, the murderer was never in the room.

Numbering the three propositions that occur in the argument, in their order of appearance, we get the structure shown in figure 3.4. This structure is characteristic of the serial argument, or 'horizontal pattern,' as it is called by Hurley (1991, p. 58). The first proposition, 'The room was sealed, and empty when we entered,' is a premise leading to the second proposition 'Therefore, no one could have left [the room].' This second proposition is a conclusion, as indicated by the word 'therefore.' But it also functions as a premise in the next subargument, which has the conclusion 'the murderer was never in the room' (the third proposition).

In case 3.6, the conclusion came last in order of appearance in the passage, and the indicator word 'therefore' clearly marked both conclusions. In the following case, there are no indicator-words at all. Yet it is not difficult to see that a serial argument is being put forward.

90 Argument Structure

Figure 3.5 The Argument in Case 3.7

Case 3.7
Philosophy and classics, the historic focus of university education beset by fears of extinction in the 1980s, is turning into the boom area of the 1990s.
  Applications in both subject areas have reached record levels again this year. The Universities Central Council on Admissions received 5,190 applications for philosophy courses, up 16.7 per cent, and 4,239 for classical studies – an increase of 10.8 per cent. (Huw Richards, 'Record Applications for Philosophy and Classics,' *The Times Higher Education Supplement*, 6 September 1991, p. 1)

The argument in this passage starts out with a general claim, that philosophy and classics are turning into a boom area. Then, a more specific claim is made that gives evidence in support of the first claim. The evidence given is that applications have reached record levels again this year. Then, this statement is backed up, in turn, by an even more specific citing of figures – philosophy courses are up 16.7 per cent, and classics courses are up 10.8 per cent. In this serial argument, the conclusion is stated first (call it ①). Then, the other two propositions are premises of a serial argument leading into that conclusion.

Thus, the argument in case 3.7 can be diagrammed as in figure 3.5 (numbering the propositions in order of appearance in the discourse). Despite the lack of indicator-words in case 3.7, it is quite clear that the structure of the argument is that represented in figure 3.5. What makes this clear is that each proposition is a more specific instance of the prior one. Each one serves to give specific evidence that backs up the previous claim.

The level of abstraction of a sequence of propositions is often a good internal indicator of how the propositions are structurally related to each other in an argument diagram. Specific indicator-words, like 'thus' or 'therefore' for a conclusion, or 'because of this' or 'for this reason' for a premise, can be used in

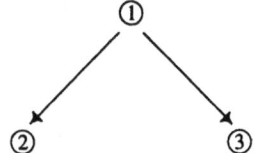

Figure 3.6 The Argument in Case 3.8

conjunction with internal evidence like abstraction. *Abstraction* refers to the level of generality or specificity of a proposition.[8]

A *divergent argument* is one in which two separate conclusions are each supported by the same reason. Case 3.8 provides a simple example.

Case 3.8
Holmes turned to Watson and said: 'So you see, Watson, Smith is not the murderer. Therefore, Robinson had nothing to do with the crime. Therefore also, incidentally, Lady Gregg's display of grief was merely a tactic to cover up the finding of the revolver.'

To see the structure of this argument, we number the three propositions as follows.

① Smith is not the murderer.
② Robinson had nothing to do with the crime.
③ Lady Gregg's display of grief was merely a tactic to cover up the finding of the revolver.

The structure of the argument is represented by figure 3.6. In this case, there are two independent conclusions, both being inferred from the same, single premise.

It is also possible to have cases in which two independent conclusions are inferred from more than one premise. This kind of structure can occur where a linked argument is combined with a divergent argument.

Case 3.9
To achieve equality is the goal of the movement. The only way of achieving this goal is to have a social revolution. Therefore, an empowering group must be unified. And therefore also, anger at any oppression that stands in the way of the goal of equality must be expressed in demonstrations.

When we number the propositions in order of their occurrence, the argument in

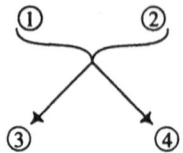

Figure 3.7 The Argument in Case 3.9

this case has the structure depicted in figure 3.7. The first two propositions are linked together as premises in a practical inference. But, instead of a single conclusion, two separate conclusions are drawn.

In the past, formal logic appeared to be preoccupied exclusively with arguments that have a single conclusion. In fact, an argument is typically, and even predominantly, defined in logic textbooks as a set of propositions, *one* of which is the conclusion.

This proclivity for single-conclusion arguments has, however, been challenged from time to time. Shoesmith and Smiley (1980) have even developed a formal logic for arguments with multiple conclusions. This kind of logic adapts very well to diagrammatic representations of sequences of argumentation. Indeed, Shoesmith and Smiley even use a method of representing arguments by graphs (directed graphs, in which propositions are points, and inferences are arrows or 'arcs' that join the points).

Once you put a whole network of propositions together in an argument diagram – joined by linked, convergent, serial, and divergent subarguments – you can model the 'flow' or sequential structure of an extended chain of reasoning. Using this method, you could even map out the overall structure of an argument in a piece of discourse as long as a book.

Graphs, structure diagrams, and flow charts are widely used in all kinds of scientific fields, including chemistry, economics, and sociology, for modelling sequential processes in an orderly way that gives you a broad picture or model of the structure of the events or phenomena you are studying. It is quite natural, therefore, to apply directed graphs to modelling the structure of a sequence of extended argumentation in logic or discourse analysis, prior to evaluating the argument.

5. Combined Structures in Diagrams

It is easy to appreciate how argument structures can be combined to diagram longer sequences of argumentation. Case 3.10 is an extended argument that combines two types of structures.

The Art of Diagramming 93

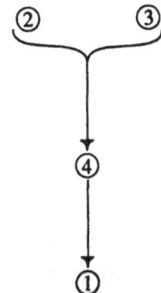

Figure 3.8 The Argument in Case 3.10

Case 3.10
I think that active euthanasia, in the form of helping someone else to die, is something that will come to be accepted in the future. For when people become old or debilitated by illness, they may lack the means or strength to end their own lives. Such individuals may try many times, unsuccessfully to end their own lives, causing themselves and others great suffering. Therefore, the need to have assistance in ending terminal pain is becoming more evident.

Here, the first proposition stated, ①, prefaced by the words 'I think,' indicating it is the main conclusion of the argument that follows. The next two propositions (② and ③) are linked together as premises to support a subconclusion, ④, prefaced by the indicator-word 'therefore.' The middle two propositions go together to support ④, which in turn provides support for the final conclusion, ①.

The argument diagram in figure 3.8 makes it clear that the structure of this sequence of argumentation combines a linked argument with a serial argument. From this example, it is easy to see how serial argument structures can be used, in combination with linked and other structures, to model extended sequences of argumentation. In some cases, an argument diagram could be quite large.

Even from a simple case like this, we can see the promise and the potential usefulness of argument diagramming as a technique. The argument diagram can give us a map of the extended and connected sequence of reasoning in a long argument. Looking over the many examples of lengthy and complex arguments modelled in logic textbooks like Beardsley's (1950), Scriven's (1976), Thomas's (1981), Acock's (1985), Copi and Cohen's (1990), Freeman's (1988), and Hurley's (1991), we can see how the technique of argument diagramming has caught on as a mainstream tool for informal logic. Its advocacy and use in works on discourse analysis such as van Eemeren and Grootendorst's

94   Argument Structure

(1984) also makes clear the centrality of this technique for the study of argumentation structure in speech communication and such allied fields as rhetoric and cognitive science.

It is also not difficult to see that an argument diagram (broadly speaking) appears to have a familiar mathematical structure – that of a directed graph. The propositions (the circled numbers) are the points (vertices, nodes) of the graph, and the arrows are the arcs of the graph. Since the arrows go one way, it is a digraph, or directed graph. Specific techniques to model argument diagrams as directed graphs have already been proposed by Shoesmith and Smiley (1980), Walton (1980), Walton and Batten (1984), and Walton (1991). So the technique of argument diagramming shows promise, not only of being practically useful, but of being amenable to mathematical modelling, as having a formal structure or 'logic.'

Moreover, the pedagogical promise of argument diagramming as a technique to teach critical thinking is extremely promising. In introductory critical thinking courses, one of the most basic skills needed is that of argument recognition and identification. Students need to be able to locate the premises and conclusion of an argument, prior to attempting to analyse or evaluate that argument. Yet it seems (from discussions with Gerald Nosich and other experts in critical thinking, and teachers of informal logic) that this is precisely the kind of skill that most students (who are new to critical thinking) lack. They tend to confuse arguments with descriptions, explanations, and other speech acts that are not really arguments (see chapter 2). And they have trouble identifying the premises and conclusion in a text of argumentative discourse. These important and necessary skills of argument identification are the first steps needed prior to any adequate evaluation of an argument, for example, one that may claim that a fallacy or error of reasoning has been committed.

Given all this promise and potential use of the technique of argument diagramming, why hasn't it caught on even more than it has? Many informal-logic textbooks now use the technique (more and more, lately), but probably just over half of the textbooks do not use or refer to it at all. Copi and Cohen, 1990, the most widely used logic textbook – in North America, and probably in the world, although it may now be giving way to the popularity of Hurley, 1994 – employs the method of argument diagramming right at the very beginning of the book. Why isn't there more analysis of the technique as an organized 'logical' method that can be studied and refined theoretically?

The answer may reduce to the difficulties posed by the three fundamental problems inherent in the application of the method to real-life cases of texts of discourse that we have cited. The one problem is the difficulty, in practice, of telling whether a given argument is linked or convergent. The second problem is

The Art of Diagramming 95

the difficulty of clearly being able to tell whether a given passage of discourse contains an argument, as opposed to an explanation or some other kind of speech that is not an argument, for example, a description or narration. The third problem is that of identifying 'missing' premises, that is, premises that are part of an argument, but are not explicitly stated. In the author's experience of teaching, students have great difficulty with all three of these tasks, and the problem of providing some decisive method for proving that your interpretation can be justified by objective evidence has no universally accepted solution.

The examples given in the textbooks may at first seem clear enough. But, when we try to apply diagramming to everyday texts of discourse from magazines, books, and so on, we find an impressive variety of cases in which it just seems very hard or impossible to say – or to prove definitely – whether the passage is an argument, and, if so, whether it is linked or convergent. Some typical examples are given in section 6, below.

But then, as is shown in even more detail in chapter 4, once we review the examples given in the leading textbooks, it even becomes unclear whether many of them are arguments, or whether they are linked as opposed to convergent. Surprisingly, as we will see, the textbooks even conflict with each other on what are (supposedly) the most elementary examples.

6. Some Problem Cases Introduced

The following case consists of a sequence of three propositions that appeared at the very beginning of an article on ethics in a work environment.

> Case 3.11
> Today's public managers face increasingly complex ethical dilemmas, often having to weigh personal and professional values against current public opinion and the law. In a climate of expanded concern over ethical conduct in government institutions – heightened by a decade of well-publicized cases of both willful and negligent abuses of public trust – administrators confront new challenges in the practice of public service. There is a growing realization among local governments of the cost of unethical behavior and, conversely, of the benefits of ethical behavior. (Stephen J. Bonczek, 'Creating an Ethical Work Environment,' *Public Management*, October 1991, p. 19)

Is the first proposition the conclusion of an argument, and the other two propositions premises that back up this conclusion? Or are the three propositions simply being listed – three items of information meant to fill the reader in on what is happening in government today?

Or perhaps the discourse does not represent either an argument or a simple presenting of information. Perhaps it is an explanation of how today's public managers face increasingly complex ethical dilemmas. On this interpretation, the first proposition is a given fact, to be explained (an *explanandum*). And the other two propositions are parts of an explanation (an *explanans*). In this case, there are no indicator-words given, and it seems hard to rule out any of these three possible interpretations decisively.

It is just this kind of case that proves to be a major, and very widespread problem in applying the technique of argument diagramming. Once students get accustomed to using the method, they tend to apply it indiscriminately to passages of discourse, even ones that do not contain an argument. This is a kind of error, because, as already shown (chapter 1, section 9), it can make a difference in some cases, when determining if a passage of discourse contains a fallacy or logical error, whether that passage is in fact an argument or not.

Moreover, it is particularly easy to confuse arguments and explanations. As Scriven (1976) and Hoaglund (1987) have pointed out, reinforcing our contention of chapter 2, both arguments and explanations often use the same indicator-words, such as 'because' and 'for this reason.' Compounding the problem are cases like 3.11, which are very common, where there are no indicator-words at all, and where it seems impossible, or at any rate very difficult, to tell decisively whether something is an argument or an explanation.

Thomas (1981) concedes that there are a lot of cases like this, where we can't tell the difference, but concludes that it does not matter because, whether we are justifying (arguing) or explaining, we are putting forth a claim supported by reasons, that is, reasoning. However, as already observed to some extent in chapter 2, most authorities are against Thomas on this matter. In particular, Kasachkoff (1988, p. 26) says flatly that Thomas is 'wrong in this,' because arguments and explanations need to be reacted to in conversation (and, in particular, criticized) in different ways. We will support Kasachkoff's point of view by showing, in this chapter, how evaluations of whether something should be criticized as a fallacy or not depend very much on whether it is an argument or an explanation.

The clue to attempting to deal with case 3.11 lies in looking at the context of conversation or dialogue in which it occurs. We see that the passage occurred in a journal article. We need to ask, then, what was the purpose of this article, and where did this particular passage occur as part of whatever it was the author was trying to do (to explain, to argue, to educate, to inform, and so on)? It appears, then, that our judgment in this case should be that we do not have enough information to decide definitely, one way or the other, what it is we have – an argument, an explanation, or something else.

In other kinds of problem cases, we can be fairly sure that what we have is an argument, but, for various reasons, we may not be able clearly or definitely to fit it into one of the structures required for argument diagramming.

In some cases, a discourse contains a sequence of propositions that do seem to be putting forward an argument, or to be part of an argument, but they do not appear to be related to each other as premises and conclusion.

The following case is part of an article on recent discoveries of new structures in carbon molecules. One type of molecular structure, called a 'bucky ball,' is made up of hexagons that have a soccer-ball architecture, providing a rigidity like the hexagon-shaped cages studied by Buckminster Fuller in 1954.

Case 3.12
If bucky balls populate interstellar space in large numbers, as I suspect they do, they may be the oldest of all molecules. Almost certainly they would have been created in the first generation of stars, when they went through their red giant phase some ten to twenty billion years ago. And many of the rugged little molecules created then could have survived. (Richard E. Smalley, 'Great Balls of Carbon,' *The Sciences*, March/April 1991, p. 26)

It seems that the first proposition makes a statement that is put forward as a claim or conjecture. It does seem like a good candidate to be the conclusion of an argument.

But the following two propositions do not seem like premises put forward to support the first one as conclusion. Instead, they seem more like additional conjectures or consequences drawn out from the first one. (More cases of this type are considered under the section on hypothetical arguments, section 9, in this chapter.)

In another kind of problem case, it is not immediately clear whether the argument is linked or convergent.

Case 3.13
Carbon, one of the commonest substances on earth, is also one of the best-understood. For in spite of the almost unfathomable complexity of the organic compounds it forms in living systems, carbon in its pure form has been studied for thousands of years. Until recently all the evidence suggested it forms only two basic structures, diamond and graphite. Thus to the modern chemist a continuing study of pure carbon would seem to offer little hope for excitement. (Richard E. Smalley, 'Great Balls of Carbon,' *The Sciences*, March/April 1991, p. 22)

It seems that, in order to judge whether the argument in this case is linked or

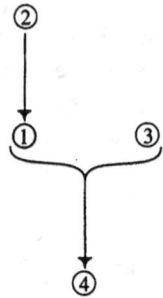

Figure 3.9 The Argument in Case 3.13

convergent, we have to reflect on the content of the propositions contained in the argument.

①: Carbon, one of the commonest substances on earth, is also one of the best-understood.
②: In spite of the almost unfathomable complexity ... for thousands of years.
③: Until recently ... diamond and graphite
④: To the modern chemist a continuing study of pure carbon would seem to offer little hope for excitement.

The indicator-word 'for' suggests that ② backs up ①. The conclusion-indicator 'thus' shows that ④ is the final conclusion.

But how are ① and ③ related, as premises that go together to support ④? On the assumption that ① and ③ are linked together in support of ④, the diagram for the argument has the structure shown in figure 3.9. But how do ① and ③ really function to support ④? That is the puzzling question. To answer it, the evidence of context does not appear useful. Instead, it seems we have to reflect on what the component propositions really mean.

That carbon has been studied for thousands of years does give some reason for concluding that carbon offers little hope for excitement to the modern chemist. Anything studied that long has probably yielded all the easier discoveries already. But this reason is not, in itself, very conclusive. Even though carbon has been studied for a long time, it could still yield new discoveries when studied further, perhaps from a new angle.

In a case like this, then, the problem is that it seems hard to say decisively whether the argument is linked or convergent. In chapter 2, many cases of this kind were studied. This kind of case is very discouraging to students who are just starting to learn the technique of argument diagramming. To construct the diagram, one has to decide whether the argument is linked or convergent. But,

The Art of Diagramming   99

in a case like this, one could go either way. There doesn't seem to be any way to get a clear answer, and in fact, in a classroom, opinions will differ. Who is right? Or can both opinions be justified? These questions are highly problematic, and it seems hard to know where to look for answers. It seems that the linked–convergent distinction is clear enough in principle. But, once we start to look at actual real-life discourse in natural language, there are many cases where it is unclear whether the given argument is linked or convergent.

These problem cases are classified into several types in chapter 4. One of the major, and most common, types of problem cases is the kind of argument in which there is a series of premises, and each premise gives only a little bit of evidence to support the conclusion, but this support grows as one proceeds from one premise to the next. In chapter 4, these arguments are called 'evidence-accumulating arguments' (section 6). The classic case of this type is that of the detective finding clues to the mystery of who committed a crime, illustrated by the 'Study in Scarlet' case.

7. The 'Study in Scarlet' Case

The following case will be familiar to readers of the Sherlock Holmes stories. It occurs in chapter 1, part 2, of 'A Study in Scarlet' (the section entitled 'The Science of Deduction').[9] Watson, returning from Afghanistan after being wounded on a military campaign, is looking for rooms in London. After he is introduced to Holmes, the two of them eventually decide to share a flat at 221B Baker Street.

A few days later, Holmes is describing to Watson the technique of deduction, based on observation, that he uses in his detective work. Watson, sceptical, asks how Holmes knew, on their first meeting, that he had come from Afghanistan. Holmes replies that a 'train of thoughts' had run 'swiftly' through his mind and, as a result of this 'train of reasoning,' he arrived at the conclusion that Watson had come from Afghanistan.[10] According to Holmes's account, this train of reasoning ran as follows:

Case 3.14
Here is a gentleman of a medical type, but with the air of a military man. Clearly an army doctor, then. He has just come from the tropics, for his face is dark, and that is not the natural tint of his skin, for his wrists are fair. He has undergone hardship and sickness, as his haggard face says clearly. His left arm has been injured. He holds it in a stiff and unnatural manner. Where in the tropics could an English army doctor have seen much hardship and got his arm wounded? Clearly in Afghanistan.[11]

This sequence of argumentation is made of several stages or subarguments. The

100   Argument Structure

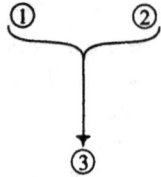

Figure 3.10 The First Subargument in Case 3.14

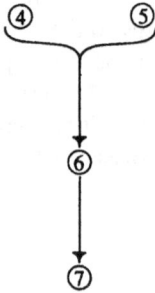

Figure 3.11 The Second Subargument in Case 3.14

first one is a linked argument, composed of three propositions (as numbered in figure 3.10, where 'he' refers to Watson).

①: He is a gentleman of a medical type.
②: He has the air of a military man.
③: He is an army doctor.

The next subargument is made up of four propositions:

④: His face is dark.
⑤: His wrists are fair.
⑥: That is not the natural tint of his skin.
⑦: He has just come from the tropics.

This argument could be diagrammed as in figure 3.11. As shown in figure 3.11, this argument is a linked argument combined with a single argument.

The next subargument in the train of reasoning is a single argument, shown in figure 3.12, made up of two propositions:

Figure 3.12 The Third Subargument in Case 3.14

Figure 3.13 The Last Subargument in Case 3.14

⑧: He has a haggard face.
⑨: He has undergone hardship and sickness.

Similarly, the last subargument is a single argument composed of two propositions (shown in figure 3.13).

⑩: He holds his left arm in a stiff and unnatural manner.
⑪: His left arm has been injured.

Finally, Holmes shows how this sequence of arguments are combined, leading to his conclusion, when he asks the question 'Where in the tropics could an English army doctor have seen much hardship and got his arm wounded?' The answer yields the final conclusion of the sequence:

⑫: He came from Afghanistan.

Along the way, Holmes has also inserted one further proposition into his train of reasoning:

⑬: He is English.

This completes our account of all the component propositions and subarguments in Holmes's reasoning. Now the question is: how is it all put together?

The way Holmes put all the subconclusions of each of the component arguments together in his final question suggests that all these subconclusions are linked together, in order to enable the final conclusion to be derived. This inter-

102   Argument Structure

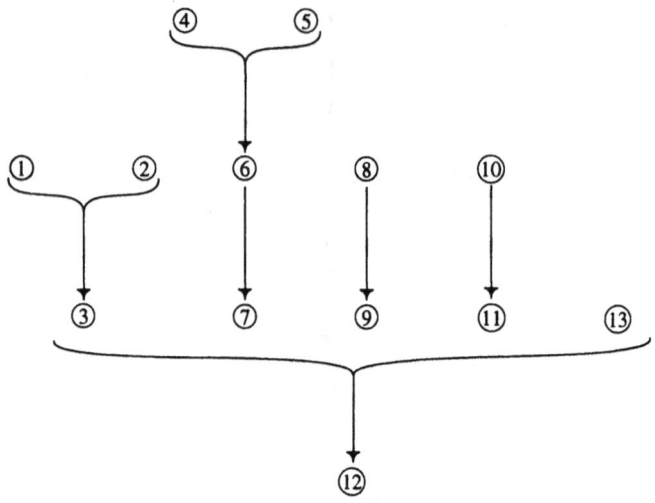

Figure 3.14 The Argument in Case 3.14

pretation would suggest the structural diagram of the whole sequence of argumentation shown in figure 3.14. According to the reconstruction in figure 3.14, all of the subconclusions 'He is an army doctor,' 'He has just come from the tropics,' 'He has undergone hardship and sickness,' 'His left arm has been injured,' and the added premise 'He is English,' are linked together to produce the final conclusion, 'He came from Afghanistan.'

But is the argument structure definitely linked in this case? There seem to be no indicator-words, such as 'These facts together enable us to conclude ...' that would definitely show the inference from ③, ⑦, ⑨, ⑪, and ⑬ to ⑫ is definitely linked, as opposed to convergent. And there appears to be no known argument structure, or warrant of inference, like *modus ponens*, for example, that would link all these propositions together as premises for the conclusion, ⑫. How can we be sure, then, that the overall structure of this train of reasoning is linked, rather than convergent?

To try to answer this question, let us look more closely to see what kind of argument it is. Despite Holmes's own analysis of his argument as deductive, it does not seem to be a deductive argument. Nor does it seem to be inductive or probabilistic in nature, in any obvious or straightforward way. It is not based on statistics, sampling, probabilities, and so on. Instead, it seems to be guesswork – a kind of presumptive (defeasible) reasoning based on drawing out likely interpretations or plausible conjectures from observations, used as premises.

How the overall sequence of reasoning works is that, once all the subconclusions are drawn out, it seems to complete the 'big picture,' and the conclusion falls into place. With each successive subinference, we work gradually towards the ultimate conclusion, but once the whole sequence of the four subconclusions, plus ⑬, are in place, the plausibility of the final conclusion appears to escalate. This is perhaps why the argument seems linked.

This type of argumentation is a very serious problem. In chapter 4, we will see that some textbooks classify it generally as linked, others as convergent. Evidence-accumulating arguments of this type almost seem to defy classification as linked or convergent, and this poses a fundamental problem of argument structure. Our main basis for solving this problem is presented in chapter 6.

8. Arguments and Explanations

A second basic problem with argument diagramming is that, once students get used to using the technique, they tend to apply it even to texts of discourse that do not contain an argument at all. As we saw in chapters 1 and 2, this can be a serious error. If one criticizes a text of discourse for containing logical weaknesses or committing fallacies, one's criticisms could be highly inappropriate and misleading if the discourse was really meant to be merely an explanation, description, or some other form of discourse, and not really an argument at all.

The problem here arises from the fact that arguments and explanations both use sequences of propositions, and also often use the same words to connect them, such as 'because' or 'for this reason.' In some instances, it is quite clear that a given case is meant to be an argument, and not an explanation. But, in others, it is very difficult, or even impossible, to tell the two apart, as we saw in chapter 2. To indicate how widespread this problem is, however, it serves to reflect on some examples of very common and familiar cases of everyday reasoning.

Consider the following case:

Case 3.15
He went south because the northern route is closed to traffic, and he knew that.

Is it an argument or an explanation? If it is an argument, then presumably the conclusion, that he went south, is being drawn on the basis of the two indicators given in the premises. If it is an explanation, then presumably his having gone south is being explained by the person's knowledge of the other route's being closed. But which one is it? We can't really say. It could be either.

Only if we put the discourse in case 3.15 in some more extensive context of dialogue does it come out clearly as an argument or an explanation.

For example, consider the following profile of dialogue:

Case 3.15a
Q: Which way did he go, north or south?
A: He went south because the northern route is closed to traffic, and he knew that.

Here, the proposition under *A* is clearly an argument. It is a question of which way he went, north or south. And the answer is an argument for the one side: 'He went south because ...' The context indicates the purpose of the statement.

But consider another profile of dialogue.

Case 3.15b
Q: Why did he go south?
A: He went south because the northern route is closed to traffic, and he knew that.

In this case, the proposition under *A* is clearly an explanation of why he went south. The respondent is not arguing that he went south, as opposed to going north. Instead, the respondent is trying to explain why the person in question acted as he did.

The pedagogical problem is posed by the need to be sure that, when one begins an argument diagram, it is really an argument one is dealing with, and not, say, an explanation. But the examples used by the textbooks to teach this skill are typically short cases, with very little context indicated. This often leaves room for more than one interpretation, and once students perceive ambiguities, they become uneasy.

For example, even after most of the class has been convinced that some given case is really an explanation as opposed to an argument, one student will raise her hand and say, 'Well, couldn't it really be an argument if the context were the following situation?' And, in many cases, being reasonable people, the rest of us will have to concede that such an interpretation is possible, and that, in such a case, the passage could be viewed as containing an argument.

These problems appear devastating to students just beginning a course called 'logic.' In logic, they (justifiably) have an expectation of precision and some rigour. To admit, right at the beginning, that we don't really know whether such-and-such is an argument or not, or that it could be interpreted either this way or that, seems to have a psychologically devastating impact on students. They need lots of reassurance that there is some sort of clear or definite basis for giving an objective, verifiable answer to this sort of question. Otherwise, it seems their confidence is shaken right at the beginning of the course, where it needs to be strongest.

9. Enthymemes Introduced

A third basic problem soon encountered in identifying arguments is that not all premises (or conclusions) used in an argument are explicitly stated. Traditionally, an enthymeme is described in the logic textbooks as an argument in which one or more premises (or a conclusion) is missing, and needs to be filled in, because it has not been explicitly expressed.

A straightforward example of an enthymeme is the following case, similar to one used as an exercise in Hurley, 1991 (p. 273).

Case 3.16
All nonprofit organizations are exempt from paying taxes, so churches must be exempt from paying taxes.

In this case, there is a non-explicit premise: churches are non-profit organizations. Once we fill in this premise, we get the following linked argument.

All nonprofit organizations are exempt from paying taxes.
Churches are nonprofit organizations.
Therefore, churches must be exempt from paying taxes.

This linked argument can be reconstructed, with a little paraphrasing, as a valid syllogism. At any rate, it is a straightforward matter to see what the missing premise is, and how it is needed to make the argument valid.

Other cases can be less straightforward, however. As soon as we get into enthymemes, we are in a problematic area of argument identification, because, if a premise has not been explicitly asserted as part of a speaker's argument, there may be doubts and uncertainties about whether or not she really meant to assert that premise.

An example may help to indicate the nature of the problem. According to Hurley (1985, p. 231), the following argument is an enthymeme, because it has a missing premise, identified as follows:

Case 3.17
Ms. Jackson must be a businesswoman because she subscribes to the *Wall Street Journal.*

Missing premise: Any woman who subscribes to the *Wall Street Journal* is a businesswoman.[12]

Using the missing premise cited above, Hurley (ibid.) 'translates' the enthymeme into the following complete argument:

All women who subscribe to the *Wall Street Journal* are businesswomen.
Ms. Jackson subscribes to the *Wall Street Journal*.
Therefore, Ms. Jackson is a businesswoman.

Hurley notes (ibid.) that this argument is valid, but not sound. That is, the conclusion follows from the premises deductively, but, according to Hurley, at least one of the premises is not true.

But, here, a problem arises. Is the argument above really the argument expressed in the enthymeme in case 3.17 made explicit? The word 'must' suggests that it could be. Or would it be more accurate to say that the major premise non-explicitly used in the enthymeme is something more like this proposition: Generally women who subscribe to the *Wall Street Journal* can be expected to be businesswomen (subject to exceptions). This way of interpreting the missing premise is not as an absolute (all) proposition, but as a presumption, a kind of stereotype statement that is held to be normally true, but can also be expected to be false in some cases.[13]

Surely interpreting the missing premise in this case as an absolutistic all-proposition that makes the argument deductively valid (meaning that it is logically impossible for the premises to be true and the conclusion false) is just the kind of overly rigid thinking that logic should counsel us to avoid, and even warn us against. Or, if the argument is really meant in this absolutistic way, it is an instance of overly rigid thinking. This kind of error could even be a fallacy – the fallacy of *secundum quid* or 'in a certain respect,' referring to the neglect of qualifications in overly rigid stereotypical thinking.

Thus, one can see a kind of dilemma posed by the problem of enthymemes. People use arguments with non-explicit premises quite often. And logic cannot be brought to bear on these arguments without some sort of method for filling out enthymemes, or making presumptions about what the argument is in such a case. Yet, the questionable nature of even an introductory example of this process, given in one of the most widely used logic textbooks, indicates how problematic the process is. This clearly indicates the danger of venturing into the area of enthymemes. Once we start filling in people's premises for them, there is grave danger of falsely attributing premises or conclusions to them that they do not accept, and might repudiate if confronted with the interpretation.

10. The Pedagogical Problem Revisited

The pedagogical problem with the technique of argument diagramming is that it is usually taught right at the beginning of the course, perhaps because it seems logical in writing a textbook to identify arguments before starting to evaluate them. But, if any very realistic cases are used as exercises, where it is not absolutely and non-arguably clear, for example, that the argument is definitely linked or convergent, the students ask questions: 'I know that this argument is supposed to be linked/convergent, but couldn't we interpret it another way so it would be classified the other way around?' The instructor, then, to be perceived as being reasonable, has to admit that, yes, it might be possible to interpret the argument that way. And then the seeds of doubt are sown. This is supposed to be a logic course, but it is not clear what the right answer is.

This is a pedagogical problem, because of the order of subjects in the course. If the evaluation part is taught first, then, the impact of borderline cases of argument identification encountered later would not be so great. Part of the problem is that many students have difficulty interpreting even straightforward texts of discourse in natural language, because of poor reading skills.

Another way out of the problem is to stick to only clear cases, where it is very definite that the argument is linked or convergent, according to the stated criteria. Hurley (1991), for example, has done this with some success, but as we saw in chapter 2, section 5, even these supposedly straightforward cases can lead students to impressively wrong outcomes. So, it is much harder to have pedagogical success using a very broad range of examples. The more realistic are the cases used, the more likely that they will admit of differing interpretations and student discomfort.

The other thing that compounds the problem is that the cases, as given, are typically very short, and are thus very remote from their context of use. Often, the main indicator of context is the title and source of the example argument cited by the textbook. This lack of contextual information makes it very likely that different interpretations of how the argument is being used are possible.

The problem is precipitated by the students' quite natural expectation that, if they are taking a logic course, there will be quite exact, definite, and unambiguous judgments made on whether an argument is correct or not. This expectation may or may not be reasonable, in an informal logic course. But, once it is in place, there is likely to be an intolerance for too much ambiguity too soon.

One solution would be to teach only the hard, calculative methods of argument evaluation first, such as the syllogism and propositional logic, reserving the teaching of practical techniques of argument identification and structure analysis for later. This way, the students can be led later into the idea that arguments need to be identified; that this is a non-trivial job in many cases, though not in all; and that skills of interpretation need to be built on one's already-existing intuitions in understanding what is meant by a given text of discourse. At this stage, it may not seem so much like the whole course is going to founder on subtle and difficult ambiguities of textual interpretation.

The existing problem is compounded, as already mentioned, by the use of short, non-contextual examples as arguments, conjoined with the use of a test that appears to be precise, decisive, and non-contextual. It seems here that the use of a decisive-appearing test is an attempt to keep in tune with the rest of logic, where exact, mechanical procedures and tests predominate. Unfortunately, however, this attempt at precision is pretty well doomed to failure in all but the most calculated examples. Both students and instructors consequently find this part of the course frustrating and difficult – somewhat needlessly, it would seem.

It has been encouraging in recent years to see so many leading logic textbooks introduce sections on argument identification, because it is a laudable attempt to try to make logic more applicable to the realities of everyday argumentation. Unfortunately, however, this part of the text too often turns out to be more of a liability than an asset.

What can be done about this? Well, of course, one thing that is needed is more research on techniques of argument identification – beyond that, in effect, being carried out in the textbooks themselves – so that at least some uniformity and consistency could be worked towards in the tests used, and some of the bugs gotten out of them. But the other thing is that, if this research tends to the conclusion that argument identification is more of a question of enhancing existing skills of interpreting a text of discourse, and less of a mechanical question that can be resolved exclusively by a mechanical test that does not need to take context of use in a conversation much into account, then the place of argument identification in the curriculum may need to be rethought.

One implication of the results of the research in the present book is that such a rethinking is badly needed. Prior to taking a course on symbolic logic, or emphasizing techniques of evaluating arguments by some normative or logical standards, the current generation of students may benefit from improving their skills of interpretation of a text of discourse in natural language to become familiar with arguments and their structures.

4

Linked and Convergent Arguments

The first problem with the linked–convergent distinction is the bewildering variety of tests in the literature used to determine whether an argument is linked or convergent. This chapter assists the reader in dealing with the problem by introducing a convenient system of classification and terminology for the various tests.

The second problem is that the tests conflict with each other in some instances on ruling whether an argument is linked or convergent. In other instances, the tests appear to conflict, or it is unclear how they would rule, in a given case. This chapter identifies the key cases at issue, and discusses possible reasons or explanations for the conflicts and apparent conflicts.

The third problem with the linked–convergent distinction is the various counter-examples – cases that intuitively appear to be linked arguments, but are ruled as convergent (or non-linked) by a particular test, or vice versa: cases that appear convergent but are ruled as linked (or non-convergent). This chapter poses the key counter-examples for the various tests, and discusses some possible solutions, or ways of dealing with the problems posed by the counter-examples.

The ultimate solutions recommended as the best ways to deal with these problems are reserved for chapter 9. The present chapter is primarily meant as a survey (but also partly an explanation and discussion) of the existing criteria and methods in use for determining whether an argument is linked or convergent in a given case.

1. Standard Tests Used in Logic Texts

The account of the linked–convergent distinction presented by Copi and Cohen (1990, p. 20) is given in terms of whether the premises 'work cooperatively' or

110   Argument Structure

'independently.' In the linked argument, both premises are 'needed,' and each premise supports the conclusion 'through the mediation of' the other premise.

The first example of a linked argument given by Copi and Cohen (1990, p. 20) illustrates their criterion well.

> *Case 4.1*
> If an action promotes the best interests of everyone concerned, and violates no one's rights, then that action is morally acceptable. In at least some cases, active euthanasia promotes the best interests of everyone concerned and violates no one's rights. Therefore, in at least some cases active euthanasia is morally acceptable.

This argument is supposed to be a linked type, according to Copi and Cohen (p. 20), because neither premise supports the conclusion 'independently':

> Here neither of the two premisses supports the conclusion independently. If the principle expressed in the first premiss were true, but there were no case in which active euthanasia promoted everyone's best interests, the conclusion would have been given no support at all. And if there were cases in which active euthanasia promotes everyone's best interests, but the principle expressed in the first premiss were not true, the conclusion – that active euthanasia is morally acceptable in some cases – would remain without support.

The test being applied in this case by Copi and Cohen is, in effect, the following. For purposes of simplicity of exposition, let us assume that the argument to be tested as linked or convergent has only two premises (we will frequently adopt this assumption in discussing the various tests in this chapter).

The Copi–Cohen Test: Assume the first premise is true and the second premise is false, and ask: 'Does the conclusion have any support at all?' Assume the second premise is true and the first premise is false and ask: 'Does the conclusion have any support at all?'

In order for the argument to qualify as a linked argument, the answer must be 'no' to both questions. That is, in both cases, the conclusion must be given no support by the single premise.

The second premise of the argument in case 4.1 appears to convincingly pass the Copi–Cohen test, because the first premise is a general principle or statement that says nothing about euthanasia. However, there is some question whether the first premise clearly passes the test. If active euthanasia promotes

Linked and Convergent Arguments   111

the best interests of everyone concerned and violates no one's rights, then that is surely at least a partial indication, a small but not complete sign, that active euthanasia is morally acceptable. It gives a little support to the conclusion, surely. We couldn't say that it gives no support at all to the conclusion.

But, even so, what if the first premise is false? Then, does the second premise still give any support to the conclusion? This depends on how we interpret the conditional expressed by the first premise. If it is a strict conditional, meant to express an absolutely sufficient set of conditions for an action to be morally acceptable, then the other premise would give the conclusion no support if the first premise were false. But, if it is taken, not as a strict conditional, but only as saying that the two conditions stated are among those that make an action morally acceptable, then there still could be room for the other premise to provide some small support for the conclusion, even if the first premise were false. These two types of conditionals are discussed at length in chapter 5, below.

The Copi–Cohen test seems fairly tough because it requires that each premise give no support at all to the conclusion, in the absence (or assumed falsity) of the other premise. It tests more than just whether the premises 'work cooperatively' together. It tests whether each is absolutely needed for the other to provide any support at all to the conclusion.

The contrasting example of the convergent type of argument presented by Copi and Cohen (1990, p. 19) is the following case. The first statement is the conclusion, and the other two are premises.

Case 4.2
The time for a national high-speed passenger railroad system has come. Airlines cannot keep up, and in their frenzied attempt to do so have subjected passengers to poor service and, what is worse, life-threatening conditions. The upkeep costs of the heavily traveled interstate highways, never intended or constructed to take such pounding, are soaring. (Leo D. Marks, 'Time to Start on High-Speed National Rail,' *New York Times*, 15 October 1988)

In this case, it is said that the two premises support the conclusion *independently*, meaning 'each supplies some warrant for accepting the conclusion and would do so even in the absence of the other premiss' (p. 19). This contrasts with the linked argument in case 4.1, where both premises are needed.

If we reflect on case 4.2, we can see that each premise gives some support to the conclusion, even in the absence or assumed falsity of the other premise. The two premises do 'work together' in the sense that, when put together, they both give more support to the conclusion collectively than each one would individually. But, even so, it is not a linked type of argument, because each premise still gives some support by itself.

There is a sense, however, in which the premises in case 4.2 do 'work cooperatively' together. Each premise rules out an alternative type of transport to high-speed rail. Thus, they are in a way 'linked,' because, when we put the two together, they give more support to the conclusion than either one does separately. Still, the argument is not 'linked,' in the sense Copi and Cohen intend, as indicated by the Copi–Cohen test: when we pull one premise away, the other premise still gives 'some warrant' or support for the conclusion. Even if we assume one premise is false, the other still appears to give at least some warrant for the conclusion.

Note, finally, that the Copi–Cohen type of test for linked arguments could be modified by posing the requirements in stronger or weaker ways. Instead of adopting the stronger requirement of making the premise in question false, the test could have adopted a weaker requirement of simply taking the premise away, that is, assuming it is not known or presumed to be true. This weaker version would call only for a suspension or removal from consideration of the premise, as opposed to its falsification. The sense of 'linked,' meaning that the premises are necessary or 'needed' for the argument, could possibly be interpreted in either of these ways, as far as its operational rendering in a test is concerned.

The test to distinguish between linked and convergent arguments proposed by Freeman (1988, p. 178) is quite different from the type of test used by Copi and Cohen. In Freeman's test, we begin by asking what would happen if the other premise was not known to be true. As Freeman puts it, we should ask what would happen if we 'blocked the other premise completely out of our mind.' By contrast, Copi and Cohen's test begins by asking what would happen if the other premise was false.

According to Freeman (p. 178), we should ask the following question in order to determine whether two premises are linked, or whether they are convergent on a conclusion.

> If we knew that just one of the premises were true, and had no knowledge of the other, would we see why that premise was relevant to the conclusion? If we blocked the other premise completely out of our mind, would we see why the first still gave a reason for the conclusion?

If the answer is 'yes,' the premises are convergent. If the answer is 'no,' they are linked.

Linked and Convergent Arguments   113

What does Freeman mean by 'relevant'? For Freeman, a premise is *relevant* to a conclusion if it gives '*some* justification' for that conclusion (1988, p. 164; Freeman's italics). According to Freeman (1991, p. 97), to say that one statement is relevant to another is to say that the one statement gives a reason for the other: 'it must give some evidence, even if that evidence is very slight.' Freeman (ibid.) cites with approval the definition of relevance given in Johnson and Blair (1977, pp. 15–16), where R (a reason) and Q (a conclusion) are propositions:

> If R is relevant to Q, ... then R's being true would increase the likelihood that Q is true, while R's being false would increase the likelihood that Q is false ... If there is no effect one way or the other, then you have ample grounds for your claim that R is irrelevant to the acceptability of Q.

The concept of relevance appealed to here is what is called in Walton (1989, p. 79) 'probative relevance,' meaning that one proposition is relevant to another if it gives some reason, justification, or basis for proving the other. This is contrasted with 'topical relevance,' whereby one proposition shares some subject-matter with another. For example, 'Bananas are yellow' and 'Bob likes bananas' are topically relevant to each other. The shared subject-matter is bananas. But they are not probatively relevant to each other – in the absence of further information that might link them, at any rate. For the one's being true does not give us any reason or justification for concluding that the other one is true.

What Freeman's test basically comes down to, then, is this: if we suspend the one premise, does the other give any reason at all to support the conclusion? If the answer is 'no,' the argument is linked. In short, this could be called a 'suspension/no support' test. A linked argument tests out as one where, if the one premise is 'blocked out of our mind' (suspended), the conclusion is not given any support at all by the remaining premise. Doubts remain concerning exactly what Freeman means by 'relevance.' But without inquiring further into the meaning of relevance, Freeman's version of the linked–conversion distinction can be interpreted as basically coming down to the above test.

Govier (1985) gives a type of test for linked arguments that is essentially the same as the Copi–Cohen test. In a 'Quick Summary' (p. 131), she gives the following statement of this test:

> The linked support pattern. Several premises support the conclusion, and they do this interdependently. That is, they require each other in order to support the con-

clusion. If premises are linked, and one is false, then the others do not support the conclusion at all.

However, in earlier statements of the criterion, Govier appears to be stating something more like Freeman's version of the test. At the very beginning of the section on 'Linked Support,' Govier (p. 126) phrases her definition as follows:

> Most often conclusions are drawn from more than one premise. In many cases the premises work *interdependently* to support the conclusion. This means that in their support for the conclusion the premises depend on each other. One premise could not lend the conclusion any support without the others. In these arguments, premises *link* to support the conclusion.

This suggestion of suspension as opposed to falsity is made even more explicit during the discussion of an example (p. 127): 'the premises work interdependently in the sense that if one were not there, the others would lend no support to the conclusion at all.' Here, the use of the phrase 'not there' suggests suspension or bracketing, as opposed to the stronger assumption of falsity.

In general, though, going by the 'Quick Summary' statement, which is the last, and presumably the most definitive of the three, it seems right to classify Govier's test as being of the 'falsity/no support' type.

Van Eemeren and Grootendorst give yet another type of test.

2. Tests Used in Speech Communication

The distinction between linked and convergent arguments is put by van Eemeren and Grootendorst (1984, p. 91) in explicitly dialectical terms. The distinction turns on the relationship between the protagonist or proponent of an argument – the other who has advanced the argument to prove a conclusion or claim made in a critical discussion – and the antagonist or respondent – the one whom the argument was put forward to convince. The point of putting forward an argument in a critical discussion is for the proponent to convince the respondent that the conclusion is true or acceptable. The function of the premises is to remove the respondent's critical doubt with respect to this conclusion. For van Eemeren and Grootendorst, the linked–convergent distinction turns on whether or not the premise in question is necessary or sufficient to accomplish this objective. If both premises are each individually sufficient for this purpose, the argument is convergent.

Van Eemeren and Grootendorst (1984, p. 91) define 'convergent,' or as they call it, 'multiple argumentation,' as the kind of case in which there is 'a series of separate and individual arguments' for a conclusion, and 'it is necessary that at least *one* of these argumentations actually be advanced, but in principle it does not matter *which* argumentation is chosen.' They offer the following example:

Case 4.3
Premise 1: He was on the wrong side of the road.
Premise 2: He had no lights.
Premise 3: He went through a red light.
Conclusion: He was breaking the law.

This case is a convergent argument, because each premise is by itself sufficient to prove the conclusion, that is, to remove the respondent's doubts about the conclusion.

By contrast, in a linked, or as they call it, 'co-ordinative compound argumentation,' each premise is individually necessary, but the premises are only sufficient when taken together (p. 91). The following case is used to illustrate a linked argument:

Case 4.4
Premise 1: The style is defective.
Premise 2: The dialogues sound artificial.
Premise 3: The plot contains no surprises.
Conclusion: This book has no literary qualities.

This type of argument is judged to be linked (or co-ordinative compound) by van Eemeren and Grootendorst on the grounds that, although each premise gives some support to the conclusion, we need them all together in order to get enough support to prove the conclusion. The proponent needs to support all three premises in order to make enough of a case to establish or prove the conclusion.

Van Eemeren and Grootendorst make it very clear that their view of the linked–convergent distinction is inherently dialectical in nature when they phrase it explicitly in terms of removing the antagonist's doubts (p. 91).

> A crucial point of difference between *multiple* argumentation and *co-ordinative compound* argumentation is that the antagonist's calling into question of statements adduced has different consequences. In the example of the traffic offense it is not necessary for the protagonist to be able to furnish evidence for all the argumentative statements he makes. If he succeeds in removing the antagonist's doubts about only *one* of his arguments, that will be enough to resolve the dispute. In the case of the book that has to manage without literary qualities this is not so. The antagonist will only be convinced, we may suppose, when the protagonist succeeds in provid-

116 Argument Structure

ing evidence to support *all* his argumentative statements to the antagonist's satisfaction; removing the doubts about only one of his statements will not be enough.

The test here is put in terms of what the protagonist needs, what will be sufficient, in order to succeed in proving the conclusion to the antagonist, by removing the latter's doubts. Is the one premise sufficient by itself? Or are the other premises necessary? If the answer to the first question is 'yes,' the argument is convergent (multiple). If, on the contrary, the answer to the second question is 'yes,' the argument is linked (co-ordinative compound).

There are some questions here, however, about what is meant by 'sufficient.' In case 4.4, for example, the conclusion is a universal proposition – a universal negative or 'no-proposition' – which is generally a difficult type of proposition to prove. Are the three premises given sufficient, when taken together? Well, perhaps not. Suppose that, even though the style is defective, the plot contains no surprises, and the dialogue sounds artificial; still, the book might have some literary virtues. Perhaps it might have characters that are interesting, easily recognizable, and portrayed with depth. Or perhaps, despite its crude style, the book could be very funny, and have a quirky humour that is very appealing. So it would seem, then, that the premises in case 4.4 are not (at least, in some sense) sufficient to prove the conclusion.

A lot depends on what is meant by 'sufficient' here. Does it mean sufficient to prove the conclusion beyond any further dispute? Or could it mean just sufficient to shift a burden of proof to the other side in a dialogue provisionally, even though room is left for further discussion or dispute? A dialectical approach could leave this question open, declaring it contextual, but that might make it of limited practical use as a criterion for judging individual cases as linked or convergent.

This dialectical approach of putting the distinction in terms of what would be sufficient for an arguer (protagonist) to prove a proposition to an audience (antagonist, respondent) was also clearly and compellingly put forward by Windes and Hastings (1965, pp. 215–18). The example of a typical linked argument they give (although they do not use the word 'linked' to describe it) is one in which an advocate has to prove the proposition 'Mr X is guilty of embezzlement.' To prove this claim, the advocate must prove (p. 215) that Mr X 'willfully misappropriated property without the consent of the owner for his personal use.' To prove this, the advocate must answer each of the following four questions or 'issues' (p. 216): How much money was it? Did he actually take it? Was it an accident or a deliberate theft? How was the money used? An example argument that would satisfy these requirements is given by Windes and Hastings (p. 217):

Linked and Convergent Arguments   117

Case 4.5

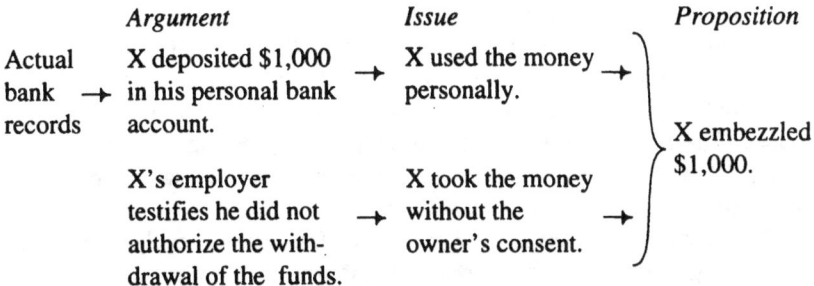

The two premises cited under 'Argument' each individually support the two premises cited under 'Issue.' And the two premises under 'Issue' make up a linked argument for the conclusion cited under 'Proposition.' Indeed, Windes and Hastings write that these latter two premises are linked in precisely the following sense: 'If any issue is not proved, then the proposition is not proved' (p. 216).

To contrast this linked type of case with a convergent type of case – again, they do not use the word 'convergent' – Windes and Hastings (p. 216) present the following example, where (1) is the conclusion:

Case 4.6
1. Dullnia is buying corn on the world market. (Reasoning from effect to cause)
2. The testimony of an agricultural expert who visited Dullnia. (Testimonial evidence)
3. The presence of drought and poor growing conditions this year. (Cause to effect)

In this case, there is not a clear or predetermined set of issues to be established in order to prove the conclusion. Instead, it is a question of the 'number and plausibility' (p. 217) of the premises: 'In such cases one strong one may be sufficient, but the more independent arguments which lead to the same conclusion, the more probable is the conclusion' (p. 218). In case 4.6, each premise gives only a small reason, by itself, to support the conclusion. But each is independent, in the sense that, if one of the others 'falls down' or fails to be proved, it does not follow that the conclusion 'falls down' or fails to be proved.

According to the conception of a linked argument given by Windes and Hastings, neither premise could be sufficient to prove the conclusion in just this sense – no matter how strongly the one premise was supported, it could never be sufficient to prove the conclusion by itself, because the failure to support the other one would always leave a gap. In case 4.5, for example, even if the prosecuting attorney proved beyond reasonable doubt that X took the money without the owner's consent, by all kinds of powerful, convincing arguments, that by itself could never be sufficient to prove the conclusion that X embezzled the money. The reason: because of the structure of argumentation required in the criminal law to prove embezzlement, the prosecution also has to prove that X (the accused) used the money personally.

Thus, in the account given by Windes and Hastings, the legal structure of the kind of argument needed in any proof of embezzlement defines a clear and predetermined prior set of issues to be established.

The criteria for the linked–convergent distinction given by Windes and Hastings is different from that given by van Eemeren and Grootendorst. For van Eemeren and Grootendorst, it is a question of whether or not each premise is individually sufficient to prove the conclusion. For Windes and Hastings, it is a question of whether such a premise might be sufficient by itself, if it were a strong one, even though more independent premises would be required, no matter how strongly the other one was supported, in order to prove the conclusion. Despite these differences of detail however, both accounts of the linked–convergent distinction are dialectical in nature – both define sufficiency in terms of reasonably satisfying a respondent's doubts where two parties reason together to resolve a conflict of opinions.

3. The Variety of Tests

In general, the distinction between the concepts of linked and convergent arguments is clear. In a linked argument, both premises are necessary, meaning that, if either falls down, the conclusion fails to be supported adequately by the other alone. In a convergent argument, the opposite is the case. The one premise is adequate to support the conclusion, without the other.

A physical analogy is to the distinction between parallel and series circuits. In a series circuit, both switches have to be 'on' for the output of the circuit, for example, a lightbulb, to be 'on.' If either switch is 'off,' the lightbulb fails to be lit. This is like a linked argument. But, by contrast, in a parallel circuit, if the one switch is 'on,' that is enough to light the bulb. This is like the convergent argument, where one premise is enough, by itself, to support the conclusion.

In principle, then, this distinction is clear enough, and simple physical examples of it can be given. It is even similar to the distinction between conjunction and (inclusive) disjunction in formal logic. But the problem is that, in practice,

Linked and Convergent Arguments 119

as applied to real arguments, various different tests are being used to determine whether the given text of discourse contains a linked or convergent argument.

As will be shown in more detail in chapter 5, in practice we have to ask: 'Sufficient for what?' 'Sufficient' here means 'sufficient to prove the conclusion,' but burden of proof would seem to vary in different contexts of dialogue.

Judging from the literature, there are various different ways of making specific tests to identify arguments as being linked, as opposed to convergent. These different operational varieties of tests have to do with different ways the premise-requirement and the conclusion-requirement are stated. In some versions, the premise is assumed to be false. By contrast, in other versions, the premise is assumed not to be proved (established, supported, or known to be true). In some versions, the conclusion is not given *any* support when the premise is removed. In other versions, the conclusion is not proved, that is, not given *enough* support to be proved or established.

Let us call the two premise-requirements the 'falsity requirement' and the 'suspension requirement.' According to the first, the premise is assumed to be false. According to the second, the premise is suspended (bracketed), meaning it is 'blocked out of mind'; that is, we assume that it is not known to be true, and, thus, it is assumed to have an undetermined truth-value.

The two conclusion-requirements can be called the 'no-support requirement' and the 'insufficient proof requirement.' The former means that the conclusion is not given any support at all when the premise is removed. The latter means that the conclusion is not given enough support to prove it, once the premise is removed. An equivalent, shorter way to put it is to say that the conclusion is 'not proved.' This finding is compatible with the finding that the conclusion is given some support. But it is the opposite of the finding that the conclusion is not given any support.

There are four ways of putting the test to determine a linked argument. For simplicity of statement, let us consider only the type of case in which two premises are involved.

Falsity/No Support (*Fals./No Supp.*) Test: *If one premise is false, the conclusion is not given any support.*

Suspension/Insufficient Proof (*Susp./Insuf. Prf.*) Test: *If one premise is suspended (not proved, not known to be true), the conclusion is not given enough support to prove it.*

Falsity/Insufficient Proof (*Fals./Insuf. Prf.*) Test: *If one premise is false, the conclusion is not given enough support to prove it.*

Suspension/No Support (*Susp./No Supp.*) Test: *If one premise is suspended (not proved, not known to be true), the conclusion is not given any support.*

The *Fals./No Supp.* test and the *Susp./Insuf. Prf.* test are by far the most common in the logic textbooks. But the *Fals./Insuf. Prf.* and *Susp./No Supp.* tests are occasionally found. In some textbooks, as we will see, there is ambiguity. That is, one type of test may be explicitly stated, while there is a tendency in practice to drift towards using one of the other tests. Copi and Cohen (1990) state and consistently use the *Fals./No Supp.* test. Windes and Hastings (1965) and van Eemeren and Grootendorst (1984) are leading exponents of the *Susp./Insuf. Prf.* test.

The *Susp./Insuf. Prf.* test appears to be based on the Windes and Hastings (1965, p. 216) conception of the chain of arguments that could be called the 'weakest-link principle': if any one premise falls down, the whole argument falls down, and the conclusion fails to be established.

This same conception would appear also to express the meaning of linked argument (or 'co-ordinative compound argumentation,' as they call it) found in van Eemeren and Grootendorst (1984, p. 91). According to this requirement, the protagonist has to support (remove doubt from) both premises, and only then will the antagonist be convinced of the conclusion. This conception fits in with and requires a *Susp./Insuf. Prf.* type of test. For, if doubt fails to be removed from either premise, the argument will be insufficient to prove its conclusion to the antagonist. This conception ties the test for linked arguments in with the concept of burden of proof.

The following case is an example where the outcome of the *Fals./No Supp.* test is different from that of the *Susp./Insuf. Prf.* test:

Case 4.7
This one marble is red.
This other marble is red.
Therefore, neither marble is black.[1]

This argument is not linked, according to the *Fals./No Supp.* test. If one premise is false, the other still gives some support. For example, if the first premise is false, the other premise (if true) still gives a support of 0.5 probability to the conclusion. But it is linked, according to the *Susp./Insuf. Prf.* test. If one premise is suspended, the other is not sufficient to prove the conclusion (assuming the burden of proof is greater than 0.5).

In many cases, however, there appears to be no difference in the outcome of the two tests. The following example will illustrate how the tests work:

Case 4.8
This crow is black.
This crow is representative of the general population of crows (with respect to colour).
Therefore, all crows are black.

This argument intuitively appears to be linked. And according to the *Fals./No Supp.* test, it is linked. If the first premise is false, the second premise gives no evidential weight to the conclusion. And, if the second premise is false, the first premise would give no evidential weight to the conclusion. Normally, the first premise would give some small reason to accept the conclusion, even if it only gives a very small evidential weight towards accepting the conclusion as true. But that is defeated if, in fact, this crow is not representative of the general population of crows, with respect to its colour.

The argument in case 4.8 also comes out as linked on the *Susp./Insuf. Prf.* test. If the second premise is suspended – if we do not know whether it is true or not – then the first premise does not give sufficient evidential weight to prove the conclusion. It gives a small weight of evidence, because it is an argument from example (argument from a single case). But it would not be enough evidence to prove the conclusion. And, if the first premise is suspended, the second premise, by itself, does not give sufficient evidence to prove the conclusion, even by inductive standards.

The same can be said for the types of deductively valid arguments commonly used as examples in the logic textbooks, for example, *modus ponens* and syllogisms. These arguments come out as linked on both the *Fals./No Supp.* test and the *Susp./Insuf. Prf.* test.

Although the *Fals./No Supp.* and *Susp./Insuf. Prf.* tests are the prevalent ones in logic textbooks and writings on argumentation generally, another type of test exists that does not fit into any of the four test categories described above. This test, described in section 5, below, rules an argument as linked if the conclusion is more weakly supported than it was before, if we take one premise away. Such a type of test could perhaps be called a 'suspension/diminishment of support' test.

All four tests discussed previously are based on the idea of whether the conclusion is given any support at all, or whether the conclusion is given enough support to prove it. These are absolutistic, 'all-or-nothing' kinds of tests. The new test, in contrast, makes the linked–convergent distinction a matter of degrees. It is a question of how well the conclusion was supported before the premise was removed versus how well it is supported once the premise is taken away.

122 Argument Structure

Let us discuss the first four tests a bit more, however, before going on to this fifth test.

4. Problems in Applying the Tests

The following argument is the leading example given by van Eemeren and Grootendorst (1992, p. 4) to illustrate a linked argument. It is said by them to be a co-ordinatively compound (linked) argument because 'all the single argumentations are, in principle, necessary for a conclusive defence of the standpoint [conclusion]':

Case 4.9
You can be sure that a letter will be delivered next day.
You can be sure that a letter will be delivered to the right address.
You can be sure that a letter will be delivered early in the morning.
Therefore, postal deliveries in Holland are perfect.

All three premises refer to a letter mailed before 5:00 P.M. in Holland. This is a typical linked argument, according to van Eemeren and Grootendorst (p. 4), because each premise is only a 'partial support' for the conclusion that represents a 'conclusive defence' of the conclusion only 'in combination with' the other premises.

According to the *Susp./Insuf. Prf.* test, this argument comes out as linked. Reason: if one premise is suspended, the others fail to give enough evidence to (conclusively) prove the conclusion. Note that the conclusion requires 'perfect' postal deliveries. This proposition requires a high burden of proof – for it is hard, indeed, to prove that anything is 'perfect.'

Their use of this case would suggest that van Eemeren and Grootendorst are advocating the *Susp./Insuf. Prf.* test. While this may be so, the wording of their evaluation at one point suggests that they may be using a falsity/insufficient proof (*Fals./Insuf. Prf.*) test – a kind of hybrid test that is fairly unusual. For, they write of the argument in case 4.9: 'If either of the single argumentations proves to be incorrect, the entire co-ordinatively compound argumentation falls apart.' If 'incorrect' here means 'fails to give enough evidence to prove the conclusion,' then it is a *Fals./Insuf. Prf.* test that is being used.

At any rate, it seems that van Eemeren and Grootendorst are not using or advocating the *Fals./No Supp.* test. And it also seems that the *Fals./No Supp.* and the *Susp./Insuf. Prf.* tests would differ sharply in how they classify the argument in case 4.9. If we apply the *Fals./No Supp.* test, the argument in case

4.9 comes out as not linked. If one premise is false, the others still each give some reason to support the conclusion. Suppose the first premise is false, for example. Even so, the second premise, that one can be sure a letter will be delivered to the right address, gives some small and partial reason in support of the conclusion that mail deliveries in Holland are perfect.

This application of the *Fals./No Supp.* test to case 4.9 could be disputed, however, along the following lines. Assume that the second premise, for example, is false. Assume, in other words, that sometimes letters are delivered to the wrong address in Holland. Then, given this single counter-example, the conclusion, that postal deliveries are perfect in Holland, has to be false. Hence, none of the other premises is of any use in proving that conclusion, or giving any reason to accept it. Following this interpretation, it seems that the argument in case 4.9 could be classified as linked, after all.

The principle at work in this interpretation is the following: if a universal generalization is false (because of one known counter-instance), then no new positive instance can ever give any support to it.[2] Using this principle, case 4.9 comes out as linked on the *Fals./No Supp.* test.

But is this interpretation right? For even if the second premise were false, still one of the other premises, such as the first, would give us some evidence to support the conclusion. It still gives positive evidence, or a reason to support the conclusion. Even if the conclusion is false, there could still be evidence that supports its being true. In other words, it appears wrong to suggest that this premise gives no support at all to the conclusion, even if the assumption is that the conclusion is false. We can have one proposition giving some support to another, even if that other proposition turns out to be false.

In short, whether or not case 4.9 comes out as linked on the *Fals./No Supp.* test depends on how we interpret the test. And two interpretations are possible. This reveals an important ambiguity in the *Fals./No Supp.* test.

What does the test mean? Does it mean that the other premise would support the conclusion if it (the other premise) were true? Or does it mean that the other premise does support the conclusion as true? The second finding could never obtain, of course, if the chosen premise proves that the conclusion is false.

It is hard to be sure, but probably the exponents of the *Fals./No Supp.* test mean to advocate the first interpretation. If so, then case 4.9 comes out as not linked on the *Fals./No Supp.* test.

Is this argument really linked or convergent? There seems to be room for two (opposed) points of view here. According to the point of view advocated by van Eemeren and Grootendorst, it is linked, because one needs all three premises to (conclusively) prove the conclusion.

But we could view it as a kind of convergent argument in the sense that each of the three premises represents a different line of argumentation that is based on a different line of evidence needed to support the conclusion. The first premise has to do with the speed of delivery, whereas the second premise has to do with the accuracy of delivery to the right address. These two things are independent, in the sense that giving evidence that one is true involves a different chain of reasoning, and different kinds of facts, from giving evidence that the other one is true. Even if the one premise turned out to be false, or could not be proven, still the other premise might turn out to be true or provable, and go forward by itself as a good reason to support the conclusion.

Thus, we can see that, even with a simple example like case 4.9, our intuitions appear to be sharply divided on how or why to classify it as linked or convergent. It was meant to be a clear and straightforward illustration of a common type of linked argumentation. And at first it did seem to come out as linked, on the *Susp./Insuf. Prf.* test.

But on the *Fals./No Supp.* test, it came out as convergent, that is, not linked. But then, after some rethinking, it even began to seem that it might come out as linked on the *Fals./No Supp.* test. These doubts concerning the classification of case 4.9 suggest that the tests are not as clear or unambiguous as they might seem. In particular, the *Fals./No Supp.* test has been shown to conceal an important ambiguity concerning how it is to be applied.

This is not the end of the problems raised by case 4.9, however. An even more basic problem is the meaning of the term 'sufficient' when it is claimed that, in case 4.9, the premises, taken together, are sufficient for the conclusion. Presumably, to say that a set of premises is sufficient for a conclusion is to say that, if all the premises are true, then the conclusion must be true; that is, the premises (if true) represent a conclusive defence of the conclusion, so that no further doubts or critical questioning of the truth of the conclusion is possible. But, in case 4.9, this does not apply. It could be, for example, that the postal service often delivers the letters in a damaged form that makes them unreadable, or that the costs of mailing a letter are prohibitively high. Such postal deliveries would hardly be called 'perfect.'

Perhaps, then, 'sufficient' means being conclusive enough to remove the doubts or objections that a critic would normally have concerning a conclusion. Or perhaps it could mean something even weaker, like being worthy enough to require an appropriate and convincing response from any respondent who would criticize it, or otherwise be presumed to be acceptable.

We return to these problems about the meaning of 'sufficient' in section 10, below.

5. Degrees of Support Tests

A test different from all the ones previously outlined was given by Thomas (1981, p. 52), who defined a 'linked argument' as one that 'involves several reasons, each of which is helped by the others to support the conclusion.' This is taken by Thomas to mean that the addition of the one premise to the other makes the argument stronger than it was before. The test for a linked argument is: if one premise is taken away, the conclusion is more weakly supported than it was when that premise was in the argument. This is the suspension diminishment of support type of test mentioned in section 4, above.

The same type of test would appear to be advocated by Acock (1985, p. 83), who defined an argument as linked 'when its two premises taken together give more support to its conclusion than the sum of supports that each premise individually gives to the conclusion.' The test for a linked argument is: 'the sum of the amount of support [the two premises] given independently is less than the amount of support they give to the conclusion when taken together' (ibid.).

This test contrasts with the previous ones. According to the *Fals./No Supp.* test, if the premise is made false, the conclusion gets no support at all. According to the *Susp./Insuf. Prf.* test, if the premise is bracketed or removed, the conclusion is not proved; that is, it now has insufficient support to prove it. But, according to the Thomas–Acock test, if the premise is bracketed or removed, the conclusion becomes less supported than it was before the removal.

According to the Thomas–Acock test, evidence-accumulating arguments are linked. Thomas (1981, p. 56) gives the following example to show that he explicitly agrees.

Case 4.10
His swimming suit is wet.
His hair is plastered down.
Therefore, he's been swimming.

When the Thomas–Acock test is applied, this argument comes out as linked. If one premise is taken away, the support for the conclusion is made weaker than it was before.

Note that this outcome is different from that given by the Copi–Cohen test, for example. Applying the latter test, even if one premise is false, the conclusion does not get 'no support at all.' It still gets some support from the other premise. Therefore, the argument is not linked.

By the Thomas–Acock test, inductive generalizations from single instances also come out as linked.

Case 4.11
Crow 1 is black.
Crow 2 is black.
Therefore, crows are black.

Interpreting this argument as an inductive generalization from specific instances (confirmatory instances), it qualifies as linked by the Thomas test. Reason: if one premise is taken away, the conclusion is more weakly supported than it was before.

The Thomas–Acock criterion appears to be a peculiar one. It would seem that the general tendency is to think of cases such as 4.10 and 4.11 as convergent rather than linked arguments. Indeed, curiously enough, the very paradigm example of a convergent argument given by Copi and Cohen (1990, p. 19), would come out as a linked argument on the Thomas–Acock test.

In this argument, case 4.2 above, two reasons are given for a conclusion: ③ is the reason that the costs of highways are soaring, and ② is the reason that the airlines cannot keep up. The conclusion is ①, the proposition that the time for a high-speed railway system has come. According to Copi and Cohen (p. 19), each premise gives some support for the conclusion, even in the absence of the other premise. Hence, they classify the argument as not being linked.

But, using the Thomas–Acock test, the very same argument definitely comes out as linked. The reason is that the two premises 'work together' in the sense that the two together give more support to the conclusion than either does separately. If one is taken away, the support for the conclusion is lessened.

Hence, there is radical disagreement between the textbook accounts on linked arguments. The very paradigm of the convergent (non-linked) argument used in the one leading textbook is judged as linked by the criterion of another prominent textbook.

Ironically, the example Thomas used to illustrate a linked argument, case 4.10, is remarkably similar to the example used by Beardsley (1950, p. 19) to illustrate a convergent argument.

Case 4.12
His rubbers are muddy.
His raincoat is wet.
Therefore, he has been walking in the rain.

Beardsley was the first person to use the technique of argument diagramming in a logic textbook, and case 4.12 was the first example of a convergent argument given by Beardsley (1950). As far as it is known, Thomas, in the first edition of

Linked and Convergent Arguments   127

his textbook (1973), was the first to use the expression 'linked argument.' Thus, it is worth noting that these two sources flatly disagree on the primary and most basic examples they give to teach students the technique of argument diagramming.

Perhaps the problem with the Thomas test is that it needs to specify exactly how weakened the support for the conclusion needs to become for the argument to qualify as linked. If the Thomas test required that support become much weaker when one premise is removed, in order for the argument to be linked, then the problems with cases such as 4.10 and 4.12, above, could be removed. On such a modified criterion, these arguments would not come out as linked, because the support for the conclusion would not be weakened enough. But how much is enough? Yanal (1988; 1991) provides a numerical answer.

According to the test advocated by Yanal (1988, p. 42), a linked (dependent) argument is identified as follows: 'Reasons are *dependent* when together they make the overall strength of the argument *much greater* than they would considered separately.' Reasons are *independent* (convergent) 'when together they *do not* make the overall strength of the argument much greater than they would if considered separately' (p. 43). Let's call this the degree of support, or *Degree Supp.*, test. Yanal (pp. 53–5) even presents a method of calculating what is meant by 'much greater' in applying the *Degree Supp.* test to a given case.

Using the following illustration (p. 54), Yanal presents an 'ordinary' method of summing probabilities that enables us to calculate how much greater is the weight of evidence introduced by a second premise.

Case 4.13
Suppose it is known that three out of every ten apples in Farmer Brown's orchard are Grade A. Suppose also that you have a device that detects the presence of Grade A apples. Unfortunately, this device is right only half the time. You are presented with an apple from Farmer Brown's orchard, and you test it with your detecting device. The device shows it to be Grade A ...

The probabilities sum in the ordinary way: 0.3 plus 0.35 (which is 0.5 times the 'unknown,' 0.7) equals 0.65. *When probabilities sum in the ordinary way, reasons are independent.*

The argument diagram in figure 4.1 exhibits Yanal's analysis of the structure of case 4.13: ① is the premise 'This apple is from Farmer Brown's orchard'; ② is the premise 'The detection device shows that this apple is Grade A'; and ③ is the conclusion 'This apple is Grade A.' Together, the two premises do not make the overall strength of the argument much greater than if they were considered separately. Hence, this argument is convergent.

128   Argument Structure

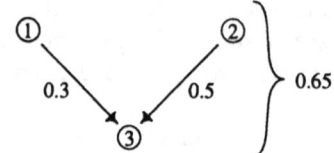

Figure 4.1 The Argument in Case 4.13

By contrast, Yanal gives an example where the probabilities do not sum in the ordinary way (p. 55). In this case, the probability of the conclusion given the first premise is one-half (0.5). And the probability of the conclusion given the second premise is very small (0.001).

Case 4.14

He's either in the kitchen or the bedroom.
He's not in the bedroom.   0.001   0.5
Therefore, he's in the kitchen.

In this case, summing the probabilities in the ordinary way, we get 0.5 + (0.001 × 0.5) = 0.5005. But this cannot be correct! The argument is deductively valid; hence, the two premises give a value of 1.0 to the conclusion. The disparity of results indicates a linked argument.

In the first case, the probabilities summed in the ordinary way – the argument did not become much greater in strength when the second premise was added to the first. But, in the second case, the probabilities 'jumped' – the strength of the argument became much greater when the two premises were put together than when each was considered separately. Hence, the second case is a linked argument, according to this species of *Degree Supp.* test. Yanal's specific numerical test could be called the 'summing test,' to use a short term for it.

One problem with the summing test is that it assumes that in a given argument, numerical values in the form of probabilities can be attached to the support of each premise individually for the conclusion. This practice becomes highly questionable, however, in dealing with presumptive reasoning of the kind that is very common in everyday argumentation, like many of the cases encountered above. In such cases, the margin of error in assigning probabilities in the form of numbers would be so high that it would make the assignment meaningless. In many cases, indeed, assigning numerical probabilities would be inherently misleading – a sort of fallacy of misleading precision, perhaps.

Linked and Convergent Arguments   129

A second problem with the summing test is that it does not enable us to identify linked arguments where the conditional probabilities are already high. Consider what would happen in case 4.14, where the conditional probability of the conclusion given each premise individually is very high, say 0.9. Then the probabilities summed in the ordinary way are $0.9 + (0.9 \times 0.1) = 0.9 + 0.09 = 0.99$. But the argument is deductively valid, so the probability of the conclusion given both premises is 1.0. Here, the probability of the conclusion does not increase very much (0.01). So, it appears that, by the summing test, the argument is not linked. However, case 4.14 has the form of a disjunctive syllogism, indicating presumably that it is a linked argument.

A third problem concerns the following argument (Conway, 1991, p. 153). The assumption expressed by the third premise is that antifreeze is a mildly effective cobra antivenom.

Case 4.15
Harvey handles cobras barehanded, and 80% of people who handle cobras barehanded die young.
Harvey drinks antifreeze for breakfast, and 90% of people who drink antifreeze for breakfast die young.
Harvey drinks antifreeze for breakfast and handles cobras barehanded, and 60% of those who drink antifreeze for breakfast and handle cobras barehanded die young.
Therefore, Harvey will die young.

As Conway points out (p. 153), the usual way of summing gives a probability value of 0.992 to this argument, but linking the premises together gives a total support of 0.6. Therefore, the argument must be diagrammed as convergent by the summing test. Conway concludes that this is the wrong outcome, because the argument in case 4.15 is linked.

A fourth problem is that the summing test does not appear to deal very well with presumptive argumentation, typically a weak and defeasible kind of argumentation in which any conditional probabilities we could assign would tend to be on the low side to begin with. And then, even when the argument is linked, the value of the conclusion, given the premises, would not increase by very much.

Consider the following instance of argumentation from sign:

Case 4.16
Someone's having red spots all over is a sign that this person has the measles.
Bob has red spots all over.
Therefore, Bob has the measles.

130   Argument Structure

In this case, let's say that the probability (or plausibility) of the conclusion, given the second premise, can be assigned a value of 0.5. But the probability of the conclusion, given the first premise (by itself, in the absence of the confirmation of the other premise), is very low, say, 0.01. According to Yanal's ordinary way of summing the probabilities, the overall strength of the argument can be calculated as $0.01 + (0.5 \times 0.99) = 0.505$. But it could quite possibly be that the probability of the conclusion, given both premises together, is only 0.505 or so. This could be because diagnosis of measles on the basis of these two indicators alone is a tentative (defeasible) judgment. Is this reasonable, or should a reasonable assessment require a radical 'jump' in this evaluation, indicating the argument is linked?

This is a tough question, because it is hard to know how to assign any numerical probabilities at all to this kind of argument. Perhaps the best we could say is that, if having red spots is roughly a fifty-fifty indication of having the measles (other things being equal, and in the absence of further diagnostic information), then perhaps our assessment of the overall strength of the argument could also be rated at around fifty-fifty. This outcome doesn't differ much from the usual way of summing the probabilities. If anything, it reduces the overall strength assigned to the argument a little. So, case 4.16 is not a linked argument, according to the *Degree Supp.* test. But, intuitively, it is a linked argument.

It seems, then, that the *Degree Supp.* test does not handle presumptive or plausible kinds of argumentation very well. These arguments tend to be weak and defeasible, so the 'jump' in probability is not large. Yet they are a very important and common kind of argumentation in natural language conversations.

6. Evidence-Accumulating Arguments

One common type of argument has a sequence of premises, each of which gives a sign or indication that a conclusion is true, and, as you go from each premise to the next, that likelihood increases. In this type of argument, which we might call an 'evidence-accumulating argument,' each premise provides a little bit of evidence, a slight indication that the conclusion is true, but, when you go from one premise to the next, the evidence accumulates so that, collectively, the premises give a stronger indication that the conclusion is true than does any proper subset of them. These arguments are typically plausible or presumptive in nature, rather than conclusive. They are often based on argument by sign. An example already encountered in chapter 3, section 7, is the 'Study in Scarlet' case.

Medical diagnosis often has arguments of the evidence-accumulating type, as

Linked and Convergent Arguments 131

is shown in more detail in chapter 6. The following example is taken from the artificial-intelligence system MYCIN for diagnosis of infectious diseases (see chapter 8, section 2):

Case 4.17
The gram stain of the organism is gramneg.
The morphology of the organism is rod.
The aerobicity of the organism is anaerobic.
Therefore, there is suggestive evidence that the identity of the organism is bacteroides.

Each premise gives a sign or indication that the conclusion is a plausible presumption or hypothesis to go on. But, once you get all three premises confirmed as true, the argument is a 'clincher' – it becomes a good indication of the identity of the organism – not a conclusive indication, but one at least worth taking seriously as a basis for action or further investigation along particular lines.

Now, in this type of case, we could say that the argument is 'linked,' in that all three premises 'work together' to clinch the diagnosis as plausible. But it would definitely not be a linked type of argument in another sense. For clearly, in case 4.17, each premise does, by itself, give some warrant, or grounds for support of the conclusion. Each premise, by itself, does provide a sign of the identity of the organism. Each premise does give some support to the conclusion, even if it is only a small support that is not very strong, by itself. It seems to be the linkage that gives such an argument its strength.

Another question remains to be asked in reference to this case, however. Does the failure of a positive finding for any one of the three premises rule out the identification of the organism as bacteroides? Or could the truth of one premise still be a good sign of the truth of the conclusion even if one or both of the other premises were found to be false? Presumably, in this case, all three characteristics must be present in an organism to get the identity of the organism specified by the conclusion.

On this second interpretation, case 4.17 turns out to be a linked argument according to the *Fals./No Supp.* test, because, if any premise is assumed to be false, then the remaining premises give no support at all to the conclusion.

This outcome may seem strange to some, because it does seem like each of the premises represents a separate and distinct line of evidence on which the conclusion could be based. The premises are not 'linked together' in the same way that the premises of a deductively valid argument, like one of the form *modus ponens*, are linked. Moreover, if one of the premises is true, then even if neither of the other premises is known to be true, or has any evidence behind it, the one premise that is known to be true does give some support or warrant for the conclusion. Thus, the argument is convergent according to the *Susp./Insuf. Prf.* test. But, at least on the second interpretation above, it is a linked argument according to the *Fals./No Supp.* test.

Perhaps the apparent strangeness of this outcome can be mitigated by another example of an evidence-accumulating argument. In this type of case, each premise by itself provides a plausible sign that the conclusion may be true, but, if the one sign is not present, the other premise still lends some weak support to the conclusion.

Case 4.18
Bob is sneezing a lot.
Bob has a sore throat.
Therefore, Bob has a cold.

In this case, suppose the one premise is true but the other is false. Still, the true one by itself provides some weak support or warrant for the truth of the conclusion. Hence, this specimen of an evidence-accumulating argument is not a linked argument according to the *Fals./No Supp.* test. According to this test, it comes out as a convergent argument. Whether it is linked or convergent on the *Susp./Insuf. Prf.* test depends on the burden of proof. But, if neither premise by itself is enough to 'prove' the conclusion, the argument is linked, on the *Susp./Insuf. Prf.* test.

How the summing type of *Degree Supp.* test deals with this kind of case is uncertain, because the conditional probability of the conclusion, given both premises, would appear to be variable. Let's say, for example, that the conditional probability assigned to the conclusion, given each premise individually, is 0.3. Then, summing the probabilities in the usual way, the support for the conclusion is $0.3 + (0.3 \times 0.7) = 0.3 + 0.21 = 0.51$. So, should the conditional probability of the conclusion, given both premises, be higher than 0.51 or not? There seems to be no general way to judge. So, on the summing test, it is uncertain whether the argument in case 4.18 is linked or not.

The conclusion to draw from our discussion of these cases is that evidence-accumulating arguments are neither linked nor convergent *per se* in every case. Sometimes they are linked, and sometimes they are convergent, depending on the case.

Still another kind of evidence-accumulating argument shows a difference between the *Fals./No Supp.* test and the *Susp./Insuf. Prf.* tests. Suppose that, in case 4.19, neither premise by itself is sufficient to prove the conclusion, but both premises together, if true, would provide sufficient evidence to prove the conclusion beyond reasonable doubt (thereby fulfilling the requirement of burden of proof).

Case 4.19
Bob was seen at the scene of the crime, holding a smoking gun.
Bob confessed to the crime.
Therefore, Bob committed the crime.

This argument would probably appear to be convergent to many commentators, but perhaps it could also be looked at as linked, from some perspectives.

On the *Susp./Insuf. Prf.* test, the argument is linked, because, if the one premise is suspended, the other by itself does not supply sufficient evidence to prove the conclusion. But, on the *Fals./No Supp.* test, this same argument comes out as not linked. The reason: even if the one premise is false, the other premise still gives some support to the conclusion.

When the *Fals./No Supp.* test is applied to evidence-accumulating arguments, it seems to arrive at an outcome, not on the basis of the form of the argument, but on a factor determined by context. Consider a simple but general kind of argumentation from sign:

Case 4.20
Sign S_1 of condition C is present.
Sign S_2 of condition C is present.
Therefore, condition C is present.

This type of argument could be classified as either linked or convergent in a given case by the *Fals./No Supp.* test, depending on whether the finding that a sign (say, S_1) is definitely not present means that condition C is also not present. The classification of the argument as linked or convergent depends on this additional factor. Curiously, the *Fals./No Supp.* test, in such cases, seems more contextual than purely semantic.

In discussions in informal-logic circles, it is sometimes presumed or stated that evidence-accumulating arguments are a distinct category of argumentation in their own right. This view has now been stated in print, in at least one place, according to Snoeck Henkemans (1992, pp. 26–8), who tells us that, in an unpublished manuscript, Robert Pinto and Anthony Blair have presented such a view. It is also mentioned in Pinto (1994, p. 315). Pinto and Blair distinguish three ways a set of premises may depend on each other (Snoeck Henkemans, p. 26): they may be linked, cumulative, or complementary. If the premises are *linked*, 'each premise is needed, and no single premise taken by itself supports the conclusion' (p. 26). If the premises are *cumulative*, 'each premise alone lends some support to the conclusion, but with each additional premise the sort of support in question gets stronger and stronger' (p. 26). Cumulative arguments, in this sense, appear to correspond to what we have been calling 'evidence-accumulating arguments.'

Finally, if the premises are *complementary*, some premises complete others. Snoeck Henkemans cites the following case (p. 27), attributed to Pinto and Blair:

Case 4.21
(P1) I promised my girlfriend I'd take her to see the latest Woody Allen movie tonight. (P2) She'll be really disappointed if I don't go to that movie with her, and (P3) I don't have any excuse for not doing so. So I guess (C) I should take her to see that movie tonight.

According to the account of Pinto and Blair, the argument in this case is neither linked nor cumulative. It is complementary, because (as quoted by Snoeck Henkemans, p. 27), 'a promise is more urgent if the person to whom it was made is anxious that it be kept, and sometimes the obligation to keep a promise is overridden by weightier considerations (as denied by [P3]).'

The kind of viewpoint represented by Pinto and Blair is very significant for our understanding of the linked–convergent distinction, because, if true, it implies that we can no longer simply define convergent argumentation as non-linked, and define linked argumentation as non-convergent. This simple process of definition of the one category as the negation or complement of the other may no longer be possible.

Moreover, we have the problem of deciding whether cumulative (evidence-accumulating) arguments are a special species of linked arguments, or are different from linked arguments altogether. Pinto and Blair evidently think of cumulative arguments as not linked, but as a subspecies of dependent arguments, alongside linked arguments (another subspecies of dependent arguments).

7. Key Counter-Examples

Both the *Fals./No Supp.* and *Susp./Insuf. Prf.* tests are open to refutation by clear counter-examples. Also, with respect to both counter-examples, the two tests come out with opposite results on how to classify the argument as linked or convergent. Thus both these types of counter-examples are fundamental.

The first one is the following case, which intuitively appears to be a linked argument:

Case 4.22
Bob is wearing a yellow shirt.
Bob is wearing a green tie.
Therefore, Bob is wearing two items of clothing that are not red.

To back up the intuition that this argument is linked, we could fill in a little background context of dialogue. Suppose Karen said to Albert: 'Bob likes red. How do you know that he is wearing two items of clothing that are not red?' Albert replies with the argument in case 4.22. Here, the way Albert is using the argument, the two premises go together to support the conclusion. If true, the premises provide conclusive support for the conclusion, in the sense that the argument is of a deductive type.

According to the *Fals./No Supp.* test, however, the argument in case 4.22 comes out as not linked. Reason: even if the one premise is false, the other premise still gives some support to the conclusion. For example, suppose that it is false that Bob is wearing a yellow shirt. Even so, if Bob is wearing a green tie, that gives some support to the conclusion that Bob is wearing two items of clothing that are not red.

By contrast, however, the same argument comes out as linked on the *Susp./Insuf. Prf.* test. For, if one premise is suspended, the conclusion is not given enough support to prove it (by the other premise alone).

In this case, then, the *Susp./Insuf. Prf.* test comes out with what appears to be the correct result, while the *Fals./No Supp.* test comes out with the opposite result. And this latter result appears to be intuitively incorrect.

The *Degree Supp.* test appears to make the argument in case 4.22 come out as linked, but not very decisively. Individually, the probability of the conclusion, given the premise, is, in both instances, 0.5. Summing these probabilities in the usual way, we get $0.5 + (0.5 \times 0.5) = 0.5 + 0.25 = 0.75$. However, the conditional probability of the conclusion, given both premises, is 1.0. Hence, the overall increase in strength is 0.25. Is this enough for us to certify the argument as linked? We do not know, for neither Yanal nor anyone else has given us an exact number to define the threshold required to make such an increase count as identifying a linked argument. However, it could arguably be the case that the 0.25 increase is enough in this case to classify the argument as linked, according to the summing test.

The other counter-example concerns the following case:

Case 4.23
Marcia and Ted are discussing what colour of tie Bob is wearing today. Neither has seen Bob yet, but Marcia says:'Well, Bob likes red a lot. And I

have another indication as well. Linda thought she saw Bob pulling into the parking lot, and she wasn't sure, but it looked like he was wearing a red tie.'

In this case, Marcia's argument has two premises, and they intuitively form a convergent pattern to support the conclusion.

> Bob likes red a lot.
> Linda thought she saw Bob, and it looked like he was wearing a red tie.
> Therefore, Bob is wearing a red tie.

Each premise provides a small amount of support for the conclusion, independently of the other premise. The argument is a presumptive type of reasoning which, as used in case 4.23, is convergent.

According to the *Susp./Insuf. Prf.* test, however, this argument comes out as linked. Reason: if one premise is suspended, the other premise does not, by itself, give enough support to prove the conclusion. Each premise, by itself, gives only a small weight of presumption in favour of the conclusion, and is insufficient to prove the conclusion. The *Susp./Insuf. Prf.* test, therefore, gives an intuitively incorrect result in this type of case.

By contrast, the *Fals./No Supp.* test yields the opposite result, classifying the argument as convergent. Reason: even if one premise is false, the conclusion is still given some small degree of support by the other premise. At least, this would be how most observers would likely apply the test, even though some might say that, if one premise is false, it tends to cancel out the weight of the other. This is dubious, however. For it seems that the other premise could still give some small support to the conclusion.

The *Degree Supp.* test would not appear to be applicable to this kind of case because (like case 4.15) the conditional probability of the conclusion, given both premises, would not appear to be defined.

All in all, then, these two cases appear to be fundamental. Case 4.22 contains an argument that is intuitively linked, but comes out as convergent on the *Fals./No Supp.* test. The reason seems to be that the argument is 'too tight' for the *Fals./No Supp.* test to work. If a premise-falsity type of test is wanted, we are forced to move to a *Fals./Insuf. Prf.* test, which makes the argument (correctly) come out as linked. Reason: if one premise is false, the conclusion is not given enough support to prove it.

The second case (4.23) is an argument that is intuitively convergent, but comes out as linked on the *Susp./Insuf. Prf.* test. The reason seems to be that neither premise by itself, nor even both premises taken together, give enough support to prove the conclusion. Both are weak reasons, and highly fallible, even though each carries a small presumptive weight of evidence in favour of the conclusion. But this is enough to make the argument come out as linked, on the *Susp./Insuf. Prf.* test, even though the premises do not really function together to support the conclusion.

These two cases are basic counter-examples indicating that the *Fals./No Supp.* and *Susp./Insuf. Prf.* tests are inadequate, at least by themselves, to determine whether an argument in a given case is linked or convergent. They are not the only problems, however. Even deductively valid arguments pose some fundamental problems for the contention that these tests are adequate to drawing the linked–convergent distinction.

8. Valid Arguments

There seems to be a general acceptance of the idea, in informal logic, that deductively valid arguments tend to be linked.[3] But it is easy to see that this is not so, absolutely (without exceptions). Consider the following deductively valid argument:

Case 4.24
Bob is wearing a red shirt.
Bob is wearing a red tie.
Therefore, Bob is wearing at least one item of clothing that is red.

Even where one premise is false, the other premise, whether it is true or false, by itself, makes the argument deductively valid, and, if true, proves the conclusion. So, by any of our five tests, the argument in case 4.24 comes out as not linked.

Intuitively, also, this argument does not seem to be linked. It would seem to be a convergent argument, because each premise gives a separate and independent reason for accepting the conclusion as true.

In this argument, each premise (if true) is individually sufficient to prove the conclusion. All that is needed is one premise – the other is superfluous, as far as proving the conclusion is concerned. Some would say, therefore, that there is something peculiar about this argument – it is not the kind of argument that would naturally occur in everyday conversation.

It is true that in teaching deductive logic as a method of evaluating arguments, we are used to dealing mainly with examples of two-premise, deductively valid arguments in which, in fact, both premises are needed to get the conclusion. These cases are linked arguments. Familiar examples are the categorical syllogisms in which, because of the way a syllogism is defined, both premises have to be used to get the conclusion.

In a syllogism, a middle term has to be used in both premises, there has to be exactly two premises, and both end terms have to occur once in each premise and once in the conclusion. The result is an argument having the following sort of structure:

Case 4.25
All Athenians are Greeks.
All Greeks are philosophers.
Therefore, all Athenians are philosophers.

With a syllogism, like the argument in case 4.25, both premises must be used in order to deduce the conclusion, because of the way a syllogism is defined as a type of argument. The end terms, 'Athenians' and 'philosophers,' occur once each in the conclusion, and once each in both premises. Hence, both premises are necessary in order to infer the conclusion.

The situation is similar for familiar types of valid inference forms used in propositional logic, such as *modus ponens* and hypothetical syllogism. These arguments are linked, because both premises are used to get the conclusion. Perhaps this is why one often hears it said in informal-logic circles that it can be presumed that deductively valid arguments are generally linked.

However, if we reflect on this presumption more analytically, we can begin to realize that it is simply not true in all cases. Case 4.24 shows this. And, in general, there are a lot of arguments like case 4.24, because of the monotonic property of deductively valid arguments – no matter how many premises are added to a deductively valid argument, it always remains valid if it was valid to begin with.

The presumption that all deductively valid arguments are linked is, therefore, not absolutely true. It only seems plausible as a general rule perhaps, because, in our pedagogical practices, we are generally used to dealing with cases of valid arguments in which both premises are used to get a conclusion through a warrant such as *modus ponens*.

But this doesn't mean that all deductively valid arguments are linked. Far from it. It means only that all deductively valid arguments, where both premises are needed to get the conclusion, are linked. This, however (as stated), is a vacuous claim, a tautology, or close enough to it to rob the principle of any real bite, as far as its usefulness to informal logic is concerned, as a definition or sole test of 'linked' argument.

All that said, nevertheless, we will come back to the idea, in chapter 5, that

Linked and Convergent Arguments   139

one source of evidence for judging an argument as linked in a given case is the use of a known argumentation structure or scheme to generate the conclusion from the pair (or set) of premises.

9. Bad Arguments

One serious kind of counter-example to the *Fals./No Supp.* type of test is the 'bad' convergent argument, that is, a convergent argument in which both premises are inadequate, incorrect, or even irrelevant reasons for accepting the conclusion.

> *Case 4.26*
> George appears nervous.
> Rodney says that George is guilty.
> Therefore, George is guilty.

Let's say that, in this case, we know that Rodney has a criminal record, is a habitual liar, and has been bribed to testify against George. Let's say that we also know that George is terrified that the charges against him will ruin his career and reputation. In short, let's say that neither premise gives any reason to accept the conclusion. Let's say that also, in this case, the conclusion is false.

The argument in case 4.26 is (intuitively) a convergent argument. But it comes out as linked on the *Fals./No Supp.* test because, if the one premise is false, the other gives no reason to accept the conclusion. This is true because neither premise, in itself, gives any reason to accept the conclusion.

On the summing species of *Degree Supp.* test, case 4.26 comes out as not linked (if probabilities could be given, in such a case).

Case 4.26 functions as a serious type of counter-example to the *Susp./Insuf. Prf.* test, however, for essentially the same reasons as it did for the *Fals./No Supp.* test. If one premise is suspended, the other gives insufficient support to prove the conclusion. Hence, on the *Susp./Insuf. Prf.* test, the argument is linked. But, in reality, it is not a linked argument; rather it is convergent.

It could be, however, that we are misinterpreting the *Susp./Insuf. Prf.* test here. According to the account of linked (co-ordinative compound) argumentation given by van Eemeren and Grootendorst (section 2, above), in a linked argument, not only is each premise insufficient (as shown by suspending the other premise), but both (or all) premises are sufficient when taken together. But, in case 4.26, it is not the case at all that both premises are sufficient, when taken together.

So construed, the *Susp./Insuf. Prf.* test should require two findings: (1) suspending the one premise, to see if the other is sufficient by itself, and hence whether the suspended premise is necessary; and (2) checking both premises together, to see if both together are sufficient for the conclusion.

This stronger interpretation makes the *Susp./Insuf. Prf.* test tougher to apply, because it requires the additional finding of whether the premises are collectively sufficient for the conclusion – a finding, as noted above, that may be difficult to determine in many cases. But this interpretation does help in dealing with some counter-examples.

Another serious kind of counter-example to both tests is the type of argument in which each premise is unrelated to the other, and neither premise gives any good reason for accepting the conclusion. Such an argument appears to be neither linked nor convergent; if anything, it is convergent. Intuitively, at any rate, it is not a linked argument.

Case 4.27
Crocodiles make safe, friendly pets for children.
Surfing is popular in Winnipeg in January.
Therefore, Aristotle was born in Rome.

According to the *Fals./No Supp.* test, this argument comes out as linked. Reason: if the one premise is false, the other premise gives no reason at all to accept the conclusion as true. It is also linked according to the weaker version of the *Susp./Insuf. Prf.* test. For, if the one premise is not known to be true, the other premise is insufficient to prove the conclusion.

What do these results show? They certainly show that the *Fals./No Supp.* and weaker *Susp./Insuf. Prf.* tests do not work on all arguments. They also show that these tests do not work on outrageously bad arguments – arguments in which the premises and the conclusion are clearly false, or unrelated to each other (or both).

Is this a serious limitation? We could perhaps argue that it is not, on the grounds that these tests are designed only to distinguish between linked and convergent arguments in the kinds of cases we would normally encounter in everyday argumentation. These are cases where the premises are relevant to the conclusion, or at least not outrageously irrelevant, and where the premises do give at least some support to the conclusion.

Commenting on this kind of case, Yanal (1992, p. 143) says that the probability of the conclusion, given the premises, is zero, no matter whether it is summed up 'ordinarily or nonordinarily.' Hence, Yanal concludes that, in such a case, the two premises cannot be said, by his criterion (the summing *Degree Supp.* test), to be dependent or independent (linked or convergent).

But this does not really pose a problem, according to Yanal (p. 143), because the sequence of propositions in case 4.27 does not really constitute an argument. Yanal argues that those who claim that the premises in such a case are either dependent or independent must defend the proposition that the sequence of propositions in the case 'is an argument at all' (p. 143). He adds that, presumably, this claim would be defended on the ground that the case contains the word 'therefore.' Still, Yanal doubts that this is enough evidence to say that the set of propositions in such a case really constitutes an argument. It seems, then, that Yanal is presuming some sort of additional requirements on a case that make it an argument.

Perhaps, then, some additional requirements could be added to the tests, so they apply only to cases of genuine arguments in which the premises have some initial plausibility and are relevant to the conclusion. Or with the *Susp./Insuf. Prf.* test, the requirement could be added that the premises be individually or collectively sufficient to prove the conclusion. This implies that the tests work only when applied to genuine or useful arguments, and that we can exclude artificial cases of the kind we have been considering. On the other hand, it seems that these kinds of counter-examples do give good reasons for concluding that the *Fals./No Supp.*, *Degree Supp.*, and *Susp./Insuf. Prf.* tests cannot be universally applied in the simple and straightforward way that the logic textbooks are suggesting. This remains somewhat worrisome because, although these tests should primarily apply to arguments encountered in everyday argumentation, it should also be possible to extend them to unusual arguments as well, if these unusual arguments pose a problem. Otherwise, we cannot be sure that the tests are based on a distinction between linked and convergent arguments that holds generally.

Another kind of unusual case where peculiar results appear to come out is an argument in which one premise is not used to get the conclusion, even if it could be used.

Case 4.28
All crocodiles love chocolate sauce.
All birds love any kind of sauce.
Therefore, all birds love chocolate sauce.[4]

First, try applying the *Fals./No Supp.* test. If the first premise is false, the second premise still gives some support to the conclusion – in fact, it deductively implies the conclusion. This makes the argument in case 4.28 convergent, according to the *Fals./No Supp.* test.

But applying the *Fals./No Supp.* test, starting with the second premise, seems to yield a different result. If the second premise is false, the first premise gives no support at all to the conclusion. This makes the argument linked, according to the *Fals./No Supp.* test.

The same asymmetry attaches to the *Susp./Insuf. Prf.* test. Even if the first premise is suspended, the second premise is still sufficient to prove the conclusion. But, if the second premise is suspended, the first premise is not sufficient to prove the conclusion.

We see here the presence of the asymmetry problem, where applying the test to one premise yields a different (opposite) result from that obtained when the test is applied to the other premise.

Some would say that, in case 4.28, the first premise is redundant. The first premise is not topically irrelevant to the conclusion, but it is irrelevant in the sense that it is of no use in proving the conclusion. Hence, we could say, it seems, that case 4.28 is really a single-premised argument – a single argument that is neither linked nor convergent.

This interpretation may not be wholly justified, however. The first premise in case 4.28 could possibly be used as a way of proving the conclusion. Suppose, for example, there could be a non-explicit premise in case 4.28 saying that birds love whatever crocodiles love, when it comes to sauce. Thus, although the first premise, by itself, is not used to prove the conclusion, it could, at least potentially, be a line of support for the conclusion. Hence, it is a real or legitimate premise, even though it provides no support for the conclusion as things stand in case 4.28.

On the summing test, case 4.28 poses no problem. It is convergent, not linked, because the summing of probabilities gives the same result (1.0) as that of the deductively valid argument. If this interpretation is feasible, then peculiar cases like 4.28 do pose a problem for both the *Fals./No Supp.* and *Susp./Insuf. Prf.* tests, but not for the summing species of *Degree Supp.* test.

Case 4.29 is an example of another peculiar case of a bad argument.

Case 4.29
All men are mortal.
Socrates is a man.
Therefore, bananas are yellow.

Is this case linked or convergent? It seems neither, perhaps, because neither premise (with or without the other) would be used to get the conclusion. Or perhaps it seems linked, if one has to make a choice, on the grounds that the two premises do appear to go together.

On the *Fals./No Supp.* and the weaker version of the *Susp./Insuf. Prf.* tests, case

4.29 is a linked argument. Neither premise gives any support at all to the conclusion, whether the other premise is false or suspended. This is a peculiar result.

Another simple case of a bad argument that is problematic is the following:

Case 4.30
Erik is in Amsterdam.
Erik is in Groningen.
Therefore, Erik is in France.

By the *Fals./No Supp.* test, it is linked, because, if one premise is false, the other gives no reason in support of the conclusion. By the *Susp./Insuf. Prf.* test, the argument is also linked. If one premise is suspended, the other is insufficient to prove the conclusion. But, intuitively, the argument does not seem linked, because the two premises do not 'go together' to support the conclusion. In fact, the two premises contradict, or 'go against,' each other.

By the stronger version of the *Susp./Insuf. Prf.* test, determining whether or not this argument is linked is problematic. It depends on whether the premises are collectively sufficient for the conclusion. Intuitively, they are not sufficient as a basis of argumentation that could be used to prove the conclusion. But, together, the two premises are at least implicitly inconsistent – they conflict with each other. If so, in at least one sense, the premises are 'sufficient' for the conclusion – the argument from the premises to the conclusion is deductively valid (on the assumption it is not possible for Erik to be in both Amsterdam and Groningen).

Moreover, on the summing *Degree Supp.* test, the argument in case 4.30 would come out as linked. The conditional probability of the conclusion based on each premise individually is 0, but the conditional probability of the conclusion based on both premises (an inconsistent set) is 1. Thus, by the summing test, the argument is linked.

These sorts of cases appear highly problematic in refuting all five types of tests, unless some restrictions on the tests can be devised to rule them out as exceptional counter-examples.

10. Initial Conditions of Use

Of the three leading tests, the *Fals./No Supp.*, *Susp./Insuf. Prf.*, and *Degree Supp.*, the one that seemed to survive our barrage of problematic cases and counter-examples the best was the *Degree Supp.* test. This does not necessarily mean that the *Degree Supp.* test is the best of the three, or of all those we considered. It may just be that we have not yet discovered the key counter-example that refutes the *Degree Supp.* test, or shows it to be problematic. Perhaps it also might be the case that the *Fals./No Supp.* and *Susp./Insuf. Prf.* tests need some kind of supplementary conditions that limit their area of application in a way that can exclude, or deal with, the various problems we encountered in applying them to realistic cases.

Also, we did find, in cases 4.14 and 4.16, that the *Degree Supp.* test does not appear to manage some kinds of argument very well. But how serious these problems are remains to be seen. They do seem like the kinds of problems that could possibly be resolved by further analysis of these two cases.

The *Fals./No Supp.* and *Susp./Insuf. Prf.* tests are meant to be practical by their exponents – tests that are applied to the kinds of arguments that students are likely to encounter in common argumentation in everyday reasoning. They are not designed to cope with, or function well in use against, the 'weird' or invented types of philosophers' cases cited in section 9, above.

Still, in order to see whether these tests can be generalized to cover all arguments, it has proved useful as an analytical exercise to see whether counter-examples can refute them, even if these counter-examples are unusual or contrived arguments. Where the tests have appeared to fail, it may just be shown that some additional conditions need to be built into them to restrict their range of applicability.

What, then, are these necessary additional conditions? In this section, an attempt is made to formulate such a set of conditions.

Clearly, the main thing is that the premises should actually be used – or be usable – to support the conclusion. That is, we need to rule out cases in which the premises (and/or the conclusion) are clearly false, or would be of no use in supporting the conclusion. We also need to rule out cases in which the premises are irrelevant to each other, or to the conclusion, and cases in which the premises are inconsistent with each other, or with the conclusion.

The basic idea behind the type of tests being considered here is that the premises do function, either together or separately, to prove or to give some evidence to support the conclusion. Then, the test is based on what happens if we take away (or falsify) one of these premises. The tests then tell us whether this premise is necessary to prove or provide any support for the conclusion. But this presumes that the premises (if true) do provide proof, or at least some support, for the conclusion in the first place. In the contrived cases in section 9, above, this presumption is not met.

The basic presumption is that the premises are being used, in some fashion, to support the conclusion. This basic presumption can be broken down into three specific conditions.

1. *Plausibility Condition.* The premises are somewhat plausible, or could be. At any rate, they are not known to be false.
2. *Consistency Condition.* The premises are consistent with each other. As well, together and/or separately, the premises are consistent with the conclusion.
3. *Relevance Condition.* The premises are relevant to the conclusion. We mean probatively relevant – one proposition is probatively relevant to another if it gives some reason, justification, or basis for proving the other.

This is probably not the final formulation of these initial conditions of use for the tests. No doubt there will be new counter-examples to challenge this set of conditions, leading to further refinements. But it is a good first pass, or place to start. Although the conditions are formulated only in a rough way, and depend on defining probative relevance and other ideas more precisely, they do appear at least to enable the contrived counter-examples of the previous section to be dealt with.

Case 4.26, with 'George is guilty' as conclusion, could be excluded from the test on the grounds that the premises are not relevant. The premises are weakly relevant (perhaps), but their probative strength is minimal, or perhaps even nonexistent. The next case (4.27), with the conclusion 'Aristotle was born in Rome,' is excluded because the premises are not plausible, and also because the premises are irrelevant to each other, and to the conclusion. Case 4.28, with the conclusion 'All birds love chocolate sauce,' is excluded because the first premise is redundant, that is, not used, or at any rate not useful or needed to prove the conclusion. Case 4.29, with the conclusion 'Bananas are yellow,' is excluded because the premises are irrelevant to the conclusion. The next case (4.30), with the conclusion 'Erik is in France,' is excluded because the premises are inconsistent with each other, and each of them is inconsistent with the conclusion.

Note that the set of three conditions is not circular, as an addition to one of the tests, because it does not, by itself, require that any argument be linked or that any argument be convergent. It may require that any argument being tested be either linked or convergent, meaning that the premises, either together or individually, give some support to the conclusion. But it is not evident that this makes the application of any test circular. For, once the test is applied, the outcome could go one way or the other, depending on the particulars of the given case.

Adding this set of conditions for use makes whichever of the tests you prefer inherently pragmatic. We can still say that the linked–convergent distinction is in the reasoning, that is, the set of premises and conclusion of the argument. But to determine whether an argument is linked or convergent in a given case, you have to look at how the argument is being used, or is meant to be used, to prove a point or support a conclusion.

Is it really fair to exclude all these counter-examples by building in conditions of use that simply bar them from the test? This is a question that is sure to be the subject of further debate in informal logic. However, it seems reasonable to think that the formulation of some explicit set of conditions for use like those expressed in the three statements above is needed. For it seems that, in practice, the tests are based on the tacit, but unarticulated presupposition that the premises are being used to prove, or at least give some support to, the conclusion. This presupposition does, in fact, match the theory of argument attributed to van Eemeren and Grootendorst in chapter 1. However, there, we opted for a different theory of what an argument is. We have argued against this general presumption. Once this presumption falls away, both the *Susp./Insuf. Prf.* and *Fals./No Supp.* tests seem to become arbitrary, and not useful any more.

One thing we might notice is that the *Susp./Insuf. Prf.* and *Degree Supp.* tests are very similar, in general outline. The *Susp./Insuf. Prf.* test says that, if we remove (suspend) the one premise, the other premise becomes insufficient to prove the conclusion. We are not told, in general, what level of support is required to 'prove' the conclusion in a given case, only that, if the one premise is removed, the remaining argument falls below this level. The *Degree Supp.* test is very similar in its general upshot. It says that there is a marked increase in support for the conclusion if we take both premises together, as opposed to taking each one separately. In other words, it too says there is a certain drop in the level of support for the conclusion, if we consider the premises one at a time. Like the *Susp./Insuf. Prf.* test, it does not quantify this drop of support by citing any specific number that can be applied to a given case.

There do appear to be some key differences between the two types of tests, however. The *Susp./Insuf. Prf.* test requires that we take the one premise alone, and suspend the other, to get a degree of support to compare with the degree of support given by both premises together. The *Degree Supp.* test is somewhat different. It requires that we take the one premise alone, and then the other alone, and then combine these two values of degrees of support (by summing, in the case of the summing test), as the basis of comparison. This is an essential difference. The summing type of *Degree Supp.* test sums the two premises together, while the *Susp./Insuf. Prf.* test uses the degree of support provided by each single premise as the basis for comparison. Perhaps this discrepancy in the tests can be reconciled somehow, but, as things stand, it does appear to be an essential difference in how the tests work.

The other difference is that the *Degree Supp.* test appears to be non-contextual; that is, it assigns numbers to each of the relationships in an argument (conditional probabilities), and calculates on the basis of these given or assigned values. In contrast, the *Susp./Insuf. Prf.* test appears to be highly contextual in that it presumes that, in the context of a given case, there is enough information to tell us whether a set of premises is, or should be, sufficient or insufficient to convince the respondent, putting an end to the dispute. The *Degree Supp.* test seems much more exact and calculative in nature, while the *Susp./Insuf. Prf.* test is much more contextual and interpretative in nature.

On the whole, the *Susp./Insuf. Prf.* test did better against the counter-examples than did the *Fals./No Supp.* test, and it seems that, if the right conditions were to be attached to the *Susp./Insuf. Prf.* test, it could survive the difficulties we posed for it.

It is a different story with the two key counter-examples, however – the 'Bob is wearing two items of clothing that are not red' case (4.22) and the Marcia and Ted case of the red tie (4.23). Both these cases meet all the requirements set by the conditions of use. The premises are at least somewhat plausible, or could be in the right circumstances. The premises are relevant to each other, and to the conclusion. The premises are consistent with each other, and with the conclusion. And the premises do give at least some support to the conclusion, or prove the conclusion. So, these cases are very deep and genuine counter-examples for the *Fals./No Supp.* and *Susp./Insuf. Prf.* tests, respectively. They cannot be removed by deploying the conditions of use for the applicability of the tests (at least, any conditions considered so far).

A fourth key presumption built into some of these tests is the assumption that, in the argument to be tested, the tester can judge whether or not the premises are sufficient for the conclusion. This presumption is especially marked in the analysis of the linked–convergent distinction given by van Eemeren and Grootendorst, as we noted in our presentation of cases 4.3 and 4.4, above. In their analysis (1984, p. 91), a convergent argument is one in which each premise is individually sufficient, and a linked argument is one in which the premises are sufficient only when taken together. In both types of arguments, on their analysis, it is possible to determine in a given case whether the premises are sufficient for the conclusion.

What happens, then, when we try to apply this test to weak, defeasible types of arguments, like case 4.21, ones in which the premises are insufficient to prove the conclusion? Such arguments could be presumptively of some value in a dialogue, even though the premises do not meet the burden of proof required to convince the respondent and settle the issue beyond further questioning. It seems that the test (so conceived) is simply not applicable to such cases. Small wonder, then, as we found, in section 9, above, that this type of test is open to counter-examples such as case 4.22, where the premises are not sufficient as evidence to prove the conclusion. This will turn out to be a major liability of the *Susp./Insuf. Prf.* test, when it is argued, in chapter 5, that these kinds of arguments not only are very common, but represent a distinctive kind of reasoning that is fundamental to argument.

Is it fair that such a test should be restricted only to relatively good or successful linked arguments? Or could it be that, for practical purposes of the kinds of methods appropriate for use in speech communication, restriction to cases where the premises are sufficient is appropriate and acceptable? Clearly much depends here on what is exactly meant by 'sufficient.' This question must be explored further before we can reach any final judgment about the worth of the *Susp./Insuf. Prf.* test.

The term 'sufficient' in the *Susp./Insuf. Prf.* test could mean one of at least two things, when it is said that the premises of an argument are sufficient for the conclusion: (1) that the premises, as they stand, are sufficient evidence to show that the conclusion is true; or (2) that the premises, *if true* (or if backed up by sufficient evidence), would show that the conclusion is true. These two things are quite different.[5] The first is a categorical or absolute claim, whereas the second is only a hypothetical or relative claim. The first states that, in fact, the burden of proof for the conclusion is met, while the second states only that the burden could be met by these premises, subject to the right sort of further argumentation.

If (1) is meant, then the *Susp./Insuf. Prf.* and *Degree Supp.* tests are quite distinct. But if (2) is meant by 'sufficient' in the *Susp./Insuf. Prf.* test, then the *Susp./Insuf. Prf.* and *Degree Supp.* tests, in practical terms, come closer towards being the same test. For the summing test compares two conditional relationships, the conditional probability of the conclusion, given the premises taken individually (calculated by summing them up in the usual way), *versus* the conditional probability of the conclusion, given the premises taken as a linked unit. When the weight of the former relationship falls significantly below that of the latter conditional relationship (expressed by Yanal as probability-values), the argument is linked. Otherwise, it is convergent. But this appears to be pretty much the same general kind of finding as that stipulated by the *Susp./Insuf. Prf.* test, as a basis for drawing the linked–convergent distinction (at least if we interpret [2] as the appropriate meaning of sufficiency). On the *Susp./Insuf. Prf.* test, so interpreted, to say that the premises are collectively sufficient for the conclusion means that, conditionally speaking, if these premises were true, taken all together, then they would be sufficient to prove the conclusion. But, if you take each of them individually, no single one of them is sufficient. That is, no single one is such that, if true, it would prove the conclusion to be true, or acceptable as true. The only difference is that, in the summing version of the *Degree Supp.* test, there is a 'summing up' (in what Yanal calls 'the usual way') of both, or all, the premises. By contrast, in the *Susp./Insuf. Prf.* test, the basis for comparison is the strength of the one premise taken individually, while the others are suspended. What the summing test introduces that is distinctive of it is the 'summing up' idea of adding the evidential value of the two (or more) premises together.

Even so, in basic upshot, the ideas behind the *Susp./Insuf. Prf.* and *Degree Supp.* criteria seem basically comparable. Both are based on a comparison between two calculations: (a) the value of the premises taken together, as a collective unit of support for the conclusion; and (b) the value of the premises taken individually, as though they were not interacting with each other but were both (or all) functioning as single units of support. And it is this type of basic comparison, broadly speaking, that does seem to reflect (in the author's experience) how we tend to differentiate, in practice, between linked and convergent arguments.

But the difference between the *Susp./Insuf. Prf.* test, and the summing species of the *Degree Supp.* test – the way they are advocated, in particular, by van Eemeren and Grootendorst and by Yanal, respectively – is the following. The *Susp./Insuf. Prf.* test is based on the underlying presumption that sufficiency of a set of premises for a conclusion, in a given case of an argument, can be determined in that case. On the most plausible version of the *Susp./Insuf. Prf.* test, the two premises are together sufficient, but, if you pull either one away, the remaining premise becomes insufficient to prove that conclusion. Everything depends then, if this test is to be useful, on the presumption that what is sufficient or insufficient can be defined or determined in an argument in a given case. With the summing test, everything depends on whether numerical probability- or plausibility-values can be defined on the conditional relation between the premises and the conclusion (both separately and collectively, for the set of premises) in a given case.

Neither of these presumptions, as we have shown, is very plausible in the cases of most everyday arguments we want to classify as linked or convergent. Perhaps, then, the best way to put the question is in the negative – which type of test is less applicable to the broad range of cases we need to classify? In chapter 5, after clarifying and rethinking these two tests, we will come to a conclusion on recommending which one is the better.

The final problem to be discussed is how to deal with evidence-accumulating arguments. They tend to be classified as linked or convergent by the *Susp./Insuf. Prf.* and *Degree Supp.* tests, depending on how complete they are in a given case. Each premise gives only a little weight of evidence, by itself, and, in some cases, you might have two or more of these premises, yet the argument is not complete enough to yield a big jump when the premises are all put together. But then, typically, when you get enough of these 'small' premises, you get a 'lock,' and the value of support for the conclusion jumps dramatically. So, the complete argument would qualify as linked, because of the significant increase, when all the premises are taken together as a unit. Yet, in an incomplete case, where some premises are present but others are lacking, so that there is no 'lock' yet, the argument would be classified by the *Susp./Insuf. Prf.* and *Degree Supp.* tests as not linked. The reason: there is not a big enough jump (to sufficiency), when all the given premises are considered together.

So, evidence-accumulating arguments pose an interesting problem. For the moment, at least, it is best to think of them as a special category in their own right – a category of some importance.

5
Rethinking the Linked–Convergent Distinction

In spite of all the difficulties we encountered with the linked–convergent distinction in chapter 4, the need for this distinction as part of the method of argument diagramming has been established. In chapter 1, section 9, it was shown how the distinction is important for fallacies such as begging the question. And, as chapter 7 will show, being able to identify an argument as linked is one of the key skills in identifying non-explicit premises. In this chapter, therefore, we put forward a recommended basis for determining, in a given case, whether the argument is linked or convergent.

However, in this chapter, we do not claim, nor have we tried, to close off the issues posed by the various tests beyond all doubt or further discussion. The central part of the chapter is addressed to the partly unresolved problem of whether the different tests represent different concepts of the linked–convergent distinction, or merely different tests for some common concept of the linked–convergent distinction.

What is especially important about this chapter is that it shows why the tests, all by themselves, do not provide a good-enough basis for determining whether a particular argument is linked or convergent in a lot of cases, and should realistically not be expected to. Here, it is shown how the tests work best as one limited piece of evidence within a framework where other pieces of evidence should function together with the use of the test.

Our conclusion will be that the *Susp./Insuf. Prf.* test does not function very well as a test – that is, a specific finding to be determined from the evidence of discourse in a particular case. Instead, it is better conceived of as being an analysis of the meaning of the linked–convergent distinction, generally, in an ideal argument in which the premises are collectively sufficient for the conclusion. As an analysis, its key element is the concept of a set of premises being sufficient for a conclusion, in a critical discussion where both parties are following the rules. But this concept should be seen as an ideal model of rational argument. Unfortunately, many of the cases we have to deal with do not meet the requirements of this model. To say that a set of premises is sufficient for a conclusion means that, *if* the premises are true, or acceptable as commitments, then the conclusion is true too, or should be acceptable too as a commitment to a degree of support appropriate for the type of argument and its use in the context of a critical discussion, but possibly (in some cases) subject to further critical questioning in the dialogue. But, in many cases of arguments used in everyday conversations, of the kind we have to analyse using the method of diagramming, the premises are not sufficient in this sense. In these cases, the *Susp./Insuf. Prf.* test turns out not to be helpful.

The general question confronted by this chapter is: how do we judge in a particular case when a set of premises is sufficient or not, in this sense, so we can judge on the basis of good evidence that the argument is linked or convergent? Our answer will be that there are four kinds of evidence which need to be put together: (1) structural evidence of the type of argument; (2) textual evidence – the indicator-words; (3) contextual evidence of the purpose of the discourse; and (4) the *Degree Supp.* test. In other words, our recommendation is that the *Degree Supp.* test be used when a test is needed as a supplement to the other kinds of evidence to judge whether argument is linked or convergent in a particular case.

However, we will conclude that some of the problems raised by the uncertainties and difficulties encountered in chapter 4 are attributable to the unrealistic expectations set in place by trying to use a simple mechanical type of test on examples of arguments in which little context of dialogue is given. The quest for exactness is generally appropriate in logic, but trying to force a clear 'yes' or 'no' outcome by applying a mechanical test can lead to problems (even to fallacies) in some cases, if the best answer should be: 'We don't know.' Our advice here is to learn to live with cases where not enough context is given to diagram the argument unconditionally.

1. Problems with the *Susp./No Supp.* and *Fals./No Supp.* Tests

The *Susp./No Supp.* test does not work on case 4.1, the case of the argument about the acceptability of active euthanasia. This case was supposed by Copi and Cohen to be a linked argument. If we construe the major premises as referring to 'in all cases,' the argument in case 4.1 could be deemed to be deductively valid. (It can be construed as having the form of *modus ponens.*)

As we noted in chapter 4, section 1, Freeman's test asks the following question: if we blocked the one premise 'completely out of our mind, would we see

Rethinking the Linked–Convergent Distinction 153

why the first still gave a reason for the conclusion?' The problem is that, when we apply this test to the argument in case 4.1, it makes it come out as convergent rather than linked. And, intuitively, the argument is linked.

For example, try blocking the first premise out of your mind completely. Then, the other premise, 'in at least some cases, active euthanasia promotes the best interests of everyone concerned and violates no one's rights,' does still give a reason for the conclusion, 'In at least some cases, active euthanasia is morally acceptable.' If 'blocking completely out of your mind' means suspending the other premise (not knowing or assuming it is true or false), still it does seem that the second premise in this case gives some reason (though not a conclusive reason) for the conclusion. It still gives some support to the conclusion.

You could say the same for the other premise. It also seems to give a reason for the conclusion, even if the other premise is 'blocked out of your mind' or suspended.

Even on this first case, then, supposedly a perfectly straightforward and uncontroversial case of a linked argument (according to Copi and Cohen, and plausibly so), the *Susp./No Supp.* test gives a wrong result. Of course, it is possible we are somehow interpreting this test incorrectly. But, on the face of it, it appears that the test is not helpful, and is, at least arguably, liable to give wrong results.

It seems likely that, in fact, Copi and Cohen adopted the *Fals./No Supp.* test precisely because of this problem with the *Susp./No Supp.* test. If we make the premise in question false, instead of just suspending it, then the test seems to work (at least better, in a case like 4.1). Then, the conclusion is given no support.

We can see, as well, in case 4.1, why Copi and Cohen are using the *Fals./No Supp.* as opposed to a *Susp./No Supp.* or *Susp./Insuf. Prf.* type of test. By itself, the second premise would tend to give some support to the conclusion, even in the absence of the first premise. If, at least in some cases, active euthanasia promotes the interests of everyone concerned and violates no one's rights, then that in itself is a pretty good reason to support the conclusion that, at least in some cases, euthanasia is morally acceptable.

The problem evidently perceived by Copi and Cohen is that, if the student is using a *Susp./Insuf. Prf.* or *Susp./No Supp.* test, it seems unclear whether the argument in case 4.1 is really linked or convergent. It does intuitively seem like a linked argument, because clearly the two premises function together to support the conclusion. But, on the other hand, as noted above, the second premise, if taken by itself, would appear to give some support to the conclusion. What to do about such a borderline case, which could lead students to be very confused?

The solution adopted by Copi and Cohen, and clearly meant to deal with the

154   Argument Structure

problem of management posed by this type of case (4.1), is to go for the stronger *Fals./No Supp.* test. Using this test, the argument in case 4.1 definitely comes out as linked. If the first premise is assumed to be definitely false, then the support given by the second conclusion is taken away. The premise-falsity requirement makes such an argument clearly linked. Here, the test seems useful, but in other cases it did not do so well.

The *Fals./No Supp.* test had trouble with quite a few of the counter-examples posed in chapter 4, but the key counter-example seems to be case 4.22. There doesn't seem to be any way of revising or interpreting the *Fals./No Supp.* test in any acceptable way that would preserve its character in order to cope successfully with an argument such as that in case 4.22. For, in this case, even if the one premise is false, the other premise still gives some support to the conclusion.

In this case, the burden of proof requires both premises (or some other finding citing the colour of at least two items of clothing) to prove the conclusion (adequately or conclusively). But, proving just the one premise still gives some (relevant and important) support for the conclusion, even if the other premise is false. If there is some way of getting around this unacceptable outcome for the *Fals./No Supp.* test, it is not obvious what it is, other than admitting that the test is *limited*, in the sense that it is not meant to apply to all arguments.

However, there do appear to be some significant limitations on the *Susp./Insuf. Prf.* test as well. But do they mean that this test is also limited in the above sense?

2. Problems with the *Susp./Insuf. Prf.* Test

How serious a problem is case 4.23 for the *Susp./Insuf. Prf.* test? In chapter 4, section 7, we judged that case 4.23 comes out as linked, according to the *Susp./Insuf. Prf.* test. But the argument in case 4.23 seems, at least intuitively, more likely to be convergent. For each premise gives a small amount of support to the conclusion in a way that makes it seem independent of the other premise. Yet, by the *Susp./Insuf. Prf.* test, the argument comes out as linked, because each premise gives such a small amount of evidence for the conclusion that neither is sufficient, by itself, to prove the conclusion.

From this standpoint, the argument in case 4.23 would seem to be linked, because, if we suspend one premise, the other, by itself, is insufficient to prove the conclusion.

But before we can arrive at any firm results in judging the status of this case, an important question remains to be asked: Are the two premises together sufficient to prove the conclusion?

In effect, this question asks: what is the burden of proof in case 4.23? Are the two premises, together, supposed to be enough for acceptance of the conclusion? Or are both premises very weak evidence that, together, give some reason, but not a sufficient reason, to accept the conclusion? Either interpretation is possible. We are not given enough information in the context of case 4.23 to decide the question.

Now, let us go back to the van Eemeren and Grootendorst version of the *Susp./Insuf. Prf.* test, as outlined in chapter 4, section 2. They defined multiple or convergent argumentation as the kind of case in which there are separate arguments, and at least one of them is necessary, but it does not matter which is chosen. Case 4.23 could be an example. The arguments do seem separate, and we could choose one or the other. But, if we choose both, the argument is stronger.

According to the van Eemeren and Grootendorst account, a linked, or co-ordinative compound argument, is one in which each premise is necessary, but both are only sufficient when taken together.

According to one possible interpretation, case 4.23 is like this. Each premise gives only a little evidence, but both are sufficient when taken together. But, according to the other interpretation, each gives a little evidence, but not enough so that both are sufficient for the conclusion when taken together. According to the first interpretation, the argument in case 4.23 comes out as linked when the van Eemeren and Grootendorst test is applied. According to the second interpretation, the same case comes out as containing a convergent argument, using the same test.

The difference appears to reside in the question of whether the premises, taken together, are supposed to be sufficient for the conclusion. What exactly is meant by 'sufficient' here is a serious problem in its own right. Blair (1991, p. 335) claims that standards of sufficiency vary with the established practices of intellectual communities, and are subject to review and revision (see section 7, below).

One solution is to say that we don't really know whether the premises in the argument in case 4.23 are sufficient or not, so that's the end of the matter. But that doesn't really solve the problem, because we can simply postulate two new cases in which this information is given. In case 4.23a, the two premises are sufficient for the conclusion, given the burden of proof reasonable to prove the conclusion in that case. In case 4.23b, the two premises are not sufficient to meet the burden of proof required in that case. In case 4.23b, we need to be more sure that Bob is wearing a red tie, given the nature of the decision to be made in that context.

In case 4.23a, the argument is linked, according to the *Susp./Insuf. Prf.* test,

156   Argument Structure

in the van Eemeren and Grootendorst version, because the two premises are individually necessary and jointly sufficient. This is a problem because, as the context of case 4.23 given in chapter 4 showed, the indicator-words provide evidence that the argument is convergent.

In case 4.23b, the argument appears most likely to come out as convergent on the *Susp./Insuf. Prf.* test, although, as noted above, there is some uncertainty. At first, the argument seems linked, because if we suspend one premise, the other is insufficient to prove the conclusion. But, according to the van Eemeren and Grootendorst version of the test, an argument is linked where each premise is necessary but both together are sufficient. By default, then, case 4.23b has to come out as non-linked (convergent), because the premises together are not sufficient to prove the conclusion. Moreover, it does not seem to matter, in principle, which argument (premise) is chosen. We could construct a line of argument from the one or the other, each independently of the evidence provided by the other.

In short, then, case 4.23 and its variants provide a genuine problem, or set of problems, for the *Susp./Insuf. Prf.* test. The one major problem is that it seems that, for an argument to be linked (and perhaps also for an argument to be convergent), the premises collectively have to be sufficient for the conclusion. But what does 'sufficient' mean here? And, more pointedly, how do we deal with arguments, of a kind that are presumably plentiful, in which the premises are not sufficient to prove the conclusion? Case 4.23b is a case in point. In particular, since the van Eemeren and Grootendorst test seems to presume that the premises are, either individually or collectively, sufficient for the conclusion, how can it apply to the many arguments in which the premises are not sufficient for the conclusion? To say we simply cannot judge such cases is not very convincing as a reply, because it seems to leave too many common kinds of cases of everyday argumentation unclassifiable, which should not be so left.

Intuitions differ with respect to case 4.23. On the one hand, it seems like a convergent argument, because the two premises do seem to function as lines of evidence for the conclusion independently of each other. Moreover, these two premises do not seem to be structurally linked within a single warrant or argumentation scheme. The premise 'Bob likes red a lot' is based on Bob's general preferences, or dispositions to like something. The other premise, 'Linda thought she saw Bob, and it looked like he was wearing a red tie,' is based on a report of testimony. They are different types of argumentation. Each stands on its own, without (apparently) having to depend on the other.

On the other hand, case 4.23 does seem to be a sort of linked argument, in the sense that the two premises, taken together, give more support to the conclusion than either would independently. But this is perhaps a special sense of the concept 'linked,' one which seems to be characteristic of evidence-accumulating arguments. Each premise gives a little support, but we need a whole collection of them together to build up enough support to make the conclusion begin to appear plausible enough to be taken very seriously as a candidate for acceptance. It begins to seem, perhaps, that the evidence-accumulating type of argumentation is neither linked nor convergent (at least in many cases), and could be a separate type of argument structure in its own right. Or could it be a special type of linked argument? This whole area is an outstanding problem that resists any easy solution, as we saw in chapter 4, section 6. However, we have now achieved a better understanding of how argument from sign works.

The analysis of co-ordinative (linked) and multiple (convergent) argument structures given by Snoeck Henkemans (1992) uses the pragma-dialectical framework of van Eemeren and Grootendorst, but expresses the linked–convergent distinction in terms of how an argument is regarded by the speaker, as a response to the critical questioning of the hearer (as anticipated, in context). Snoeck Henkemans also, significantly, adds a category of cumulative arguments in her account of the criteria for structures (p. 174):

> The conceptual clarification of coordinative and multiple argumentation thus obtained makes it possible to distinguish multiple from coordinative argumentation in argumentative discourse. If it is clear that one of the arguments that are advanced cannot serve as a means to make the other argument(s) a more acceptable defence of the standpoint, the argumentation must be multiple. If one of the arguments is to be regarded as a means to answer criticism of the sufficiency of the other argument(s), the argumentation is coordinative. If the attempt to answer criticism consists of adding another argument that supports the standpoint directly, the coordinative argumentation is cumulative.

This analysis leaves more options open for dealing with case 4.23. One option would be to classify the argument in case 4.23 as cumulative, on the Snoeck Henkemans analysis. Another would be to pay most attention to the indicator-words, which, in case 4.23, clearly indicate how the structure of the argument in this case is 'regarded' by its proponent, and rule that the argument is multiple (convergent).

Snoeck Henkemans's account seems to rescue the *Susp./Insuf. Prf.* test, because it allows specifically for cumulative argumentation as a separate category, and because it defines 'sufficient' in terms of what the proponent (speaker) regards as a sufficient means to answer the criticisms of the respondent (hearer) in a given case. But this approach still leaves open the practical question of how to deal with cases in which there is insufficient information on what the proponent regards as a sufficient means to answer criticisms.

3. Argument from Sign

Evidence-accumulating arguments tend to be generally problematic to classify as linked or convergent. They seem intuitively to be more like linked arguments, but none of the tests studied in chapter 4 appeared to do an adequate job of clearly or decisively identifying them as linked. It begins to seem that they are a special category of linked arguments in their own right. Something like this was suggested by the Pinto and Blair designation of a special class of arguments called 'cumulative' – see chapter 4, section 6 – but Pinto and Blair did not appear to think of cumulative as being a subclass of linked arguments. Snoeck Henkemans (1992, p. 174) does, however, specifically define 'cumulative' argumentation as a subspecies of linked argumentation.

In an evidence-accumulating argument, each premise or component argumentation gives a small bit of support for the conclusion. Then, as we go from one sign, or small bit of evidence, to the next, support for the conclusion increases. In the end then, when we put all the premises or signs together, we get a more substantial (but not conclusive or indubitable) basis of support for the conclusion. There seems to be a kind of incremental build-up as we go from one premise or component argumentation to the next.

The classic case we return to once again is the case of Sherlock Holmes's train of reasoning in 'A Study in Scarlet,' concluding that Watson came from Afghanistan (case 3.14). Holmes argues from a number of signs that he infers from observations of Watson – he is an army doctor, he has a tan, he has undergone hardship and sickness, his left arm is injured, and he is English. Given Holmes's unstated common background knowledge of the then-recent English campaign in Afghanistan, he is able infer the presumptive but firm conclusion that Watson must have come from Afghanistan. As we go from one sign to the next, support for the conclusion gradually builds up.

Argument from sign has long been known to researchers in speech communication as a distinctive type of argumentation. As noted in chapter 8, Hastings (1962, pp. 55–64) analysed argument from sign as a species of causal reasoning. Presumptive, defeasible reasoning, including argumentation from sign, has also been the subject of intense research in artificial intelligence in recent times, as shown in chapter 6.

The problem for us is that arguments from sign, and evidence-accumulating arguments generally, are not, at least straightforwardly or clearly, categorized as linked arguments by the tests in chapter 4. Yet, they do seem (in at least some cases) to be linked arguments of a sort, as also recognized in the analysis of Snoeck Henkemans (1992).

As noted in chapter 4, section 5, the *Degree Supp.* test seems to work accept-

Rethinking the Linked–Convergent Distinction 159

ably well when dealing with simple, two-premise cases of argument from sign, such as case 4.12. Evidently, as Thomas interprets this case, each premise – 'His rubbers are muddy' and 'His raincoat is wet' – gives a small amount of evidence for the conclusion – 'Therefore, he has been walking in the rain.' But, if either premise is removed, the other (by itself) gives less support to the conclusion. This is a plausible interpretation of the context of case 4.12 (though not the only one, for, as we saw in chapter 4, section 5, Beardsley judged this case as convergent). Presumably, the Yanal formula could also be gotten to work in classifying this case as linked, if it would make sense to give numerical probability-values to the premises and the conclusion.

What is the argumentation scheme implicit in case 4.12, in virtue of which the premises are linked together to support the conclusion? According to our analysis in chapter 8, it is a scheme of the form 'S_1, S_2; therefore, C,' where S_1 and S_2 are the two signs (muddy rubbers and wet raincoat), and C is the conclusion that the wearer has been walking in the rain. In such a scheme, then, S_1 gives some support to C, but, then, when you add S_2, the level of support for C goes up. Presumably, this kind of argumentation is symmetrical, in the sense that, if S_2 were taken first, the addition of S_1 would also give increased support to C.

The 'Study in Scarlet' case seems to be similar, except that more component arguments are involved. It has the form, 'S_1, S_2, S_3, S_4, S_5; therefore, C.' But here the degree of support test is more variable. If the premise 'His left arm is injured' were removed or dropped out, it would reduce the support for C by only a small amount (presumably). But, if the premise 'He has a tan' were dropped, presumably it would reduce the support for the conclusion by quite a bit more. Another factor here is that normally it would be quite evident to Holmes whether Watson had a tan or not. So, if there was no observation that he did have a tan, there would be a presumption that he didn't have, which would lower the support for the conclusion (that he came from Afghanistan) dramatically.

Generally, however, in this case, each component argument gives only a small bit of evidence for the conclusion. But, once the whole set is in, if any one premise were dropped, it would lower the plausibility- or acceptability-value of the conclusion by a significant weight of support. Hence, we can see how this type of argumentation would be classified as linked by the *Degree Supp.* test. When we put all the premises together, the support for the conclusion does go up significantly, as would seem to be required by the Thomas–Acock and Yanal tests. Each premise, by itself, gives only a little support for the conclusion (with the possible exception for some, as noted above). But support builds up gradually and cumulatively in the evidence-accumulating argument of this type. As we go along, starting at S_1, and proceeding ultimately to S_5 (or whatever is the last premise S_n), the support for the conclusion gradually builds up to a greater, but not a conclusive or overwhelming level. Yet, if we drop any premise S_i out, support may be diminished significantly. The *Degree Supp.* summing test captures this idea, in classifying such an argument as linked.

This type of case seems to be a problem for the *Susp./Insuf. Prf.* test, because it raises the question of what is meant by 'sufficient.' If we drop out one premise, such as 'His left arm is injured,' this may take enough support away from the conclusion that we need to say that the argument is no longer sufficient for the conclusion, whereas it was sufficient before the suspension or deletion of that premise. But, even where a set of premises is sufficient for a conclusion in argumentation from sign, it does not mean that these premises conclusively establish the conclusion beyond further doubts. It means only that, once the right set of premises are 'in,' their collective support for the conclusion is boosted up significantly higher than is the case when some of them were still not 'in.' Presumably, the nature of this linkage is accounted for by the argumentation scheme for the argument from sign.

One problem with this field is that we have knowledge of familiar deductive forms of argument such as *modus ponens* and disjunctive syllogism to give us some structures to apply to cases, and help us to determine whether a given argument is linked, but our knowledge of non-deductive structures is much less well established. Our knowledge of argumentation schemes for presumptive reasoning is growing, but so far it is based on recent research that is not widely known outside the argumentation community, and not even very well established within it. As we get more systematic knowledge of these argumentation schemes, our basis for judging both enthymemes and the linked–convergent distinction in many common types of argumentation often used in everyday conversation will become more exact and useful.

In particular, many common cases of argumentation can be revealed as linked only when we see them as instances of connected sequences of practical reasoning.

The main clue to judging whether an argument is linked or convergent is the argument's structure. But another main clue is the use of indicator-words. However, these two determinants may possibly even conflict with each other, as will be seen graphically in case 8.1. This is so because the argument structure is an indicator of need – of what is rationally needed to complete an argument of a certain type of structure – whereas the indicator-words are indicators of use – they give evidence as to what the arguer herself thinks about the nature of the sequence of reasoning she has put forth. We can have the same kind of problem here we had with enthymemes, because we are identifying arguments partly on the basis of need and partly on the basis of use.

Rethinking the Linked–Convergent Distinction   161

However, as case 3.2 has shown, some arguments can be indicated as linked or convergent, but there is no identifiable structure in virtue of which this determination can be made (as far as anyone knows). And, in chapter 4, we saw abundantly that the given indicator-words are often insufficient to tell us whether an argument is linked or convergent.

Here, then, is where we seem so often to be cast back upon the expedient of trying to determine whether a given argument is linked or convergent by means of one of the tests. And it is exactly in these cases where the *Susp./Insuf. Prf.* test is less useful than the summing test.

4. Cases Lacking Known Structure

One problem type of case worth noting is that in which the argument plausibly appears to be linked, but the premises are not linked together by any known structure. Case 3.2 was such a case, but there it was quite evident that the argument is linked because the conclusion stated that the two factors stated in the premises are 'inextricably interwoven.' Also, in other cases, the argument is linked simply because we need both premises in order to support the conclusion adequately, but the premises are not linked together by any known structure. In case 4.5, for example, we need to prove both premises, 'X used the money personally' and 'X took the money without the owner's consent,' in order to prove the conclusion, 'X embezzled $1,000.' But there is no (known) argumentation structure or form of argument linking the two premises together in this case. It is a general principle that proving embezzlement requires that one proves both that the money was taken without consent and that the money was used personally. But this principle does not seem to express, or to be based on any argumentation scheme or formal structure of argument, such as *modus ponens*. It is perhaps based on common or legal knowledge about what one needs to prove to make a case in an alleged embezzlement.

Case 4.5 fits the *Susp./Insuf. Prf.* test well. We need both premises, in the sense that neither is sufficient to prove the conclusion without the other. And both are sufficient, when taken together. But, let us examine another case of a type that is somewhat more difficult to classify unproblematically, using the tests.

The following case is given as an exercise for students by Copi and Cohen (1990, p. 25):

Case 5.1
Proponents of the bill ... argue that legalizing heroin for medicinal purposes would not contribute to the nation's drug abuse problem because the amounts

involved – about 400 pounds a year – would be small, and because the heroin would be manufactured, stored and administered under strict security. (Jean Cobb, 'Heroin in Hospitals,' *Common Cause* 10/6 [November-December 1984], p. 35)

The solution given by Copi and Cohen (1990, p. 11) classifies the argument in this case as convergent. This seems to be the right classification according to the Copi–Cohen *Fals./No Supp.* test. Each premise would still give some support to the conclusion even if the other one were false. For example, even if the amounts of heroin involved were not small, their storage and administration under strict security would still give *some* reason to think that legalization would not contribute to the nation's drug problem. And, even if security was not strict, the small amounts would give at least *some* support to the negative conclusion that the medicinal heroin would not contribute to the drug problem.

In sharp contrast, however, the argument in case 5.1 would appear most plausibly classified as linked according to the van Eemeren and Grootendorst *Susp./Insuf. Prf.* test. Reason: if either premise is questionable, the conclusion becomes open to doubt. For example, suppose it is dubious whether the amount of heroin involved is small or large. Then, even if storage and administration of that heroin are under strict security, if large quantities are involved, there could be risks of its contributing to the nation's drug problem. Or, conversely, if it were in doubt whether security was strict, even if only a small amount of heroin was involved, it could contribute to the nation's drug-abuse problem.

In this case, if the one premise is questionable, then the other, by itself, is not sufficient to prove the conclusion. Therefore, according to the criteria of van Eemeren and Grootendorst, the argument cannot be convergent. It would most plausibly be classified by them as linked, because, if either premise is questionable, the conclusion is open to doubt.

So the Copi–Cohen test and the van Eemeren and Grootendorst test flatly conflict on how to classify the argument in case 5.1. On the Copi–Cohen test, it is convergent. On the van Eemeren and Grootendorst test, it does not appear to be convergent, and would seem most likely to be classified by them as linked (possibly depending on whether the two premises are meant to be jointly sufficient to prove the conclusion).

At a guess, it probably seems most plausible to most readers to classify the argument in case 5.1 as linked, because the two premises do seem somehow to function together in generating the conclusion. But all these classifications seem a little dubious. A further study of the case can reveal why.

On the *Susp./Insuf. Prf.* test, the question is whether each premise is, by

Rethinking the Linked–Convergent Distinction 163

itself, sufficient to resolve doubts about the conclusion being true or not. But can we really make this judgment without jumping to conclusions that might not be fully supported by the evidence? A closer examination of this case raises questions about what sort of evidence we need to say justifiably that a premise is sufficient for a conclusion.

In this case, there is no structure, no form of argument or argumentation scheme that clearly links the two premises together to support the conclusion. Thus, we are cast back upon the tests to seek some basis for judging whether the argument is linked or convergent. But the tests just raise further questions – in particular, questions of whether each of the following pair of conditionals represents a sufficient-condition relationship:

1. If the amounts of heroin – about 400 pounds a year – would be small, then legalizing heroin for medicinal purposes would not contribute to the nation's drug-abuse problem.
2. If the heroin would be manufactured, stored, and administered under strict security, then legalizing heroin for medicinal purposes would not contribute to the nation's drug-abuse problem.

In each of these cases, we need to ask: would the antecedent, taken together with the conditional, produce a *modus ponens* argument that would be sufficient to prove the conclusion? For example, in the case of (1), we need to examine the following argument, with its two premises:

If the amounts of heroin – about 400 pounds a year – would be small, then legitimizing heroin for medicinal purposes would not contribute to the nation's drug problem.

The amounts of heroin – about 400 pounds a year – would be small.

Legitimizing heroin for medicinal purposes would not contribute to the nation's drug-abuse problem.

This argument appears to have the form of *modus ponens*, a deductively valid form of argument. But it has this form (in reality) only if the first premise is a strict conditional, according to the analysis of conditions by Walton (1992b, pp. 75–80). According to this analysis, strict conditionals are absolute in nature, as contrasted with presumptive conditionals. The latter are defeasible in nature, meaning that the conditional 'If A then B' can still be held, even in some cases where A is true and B is false. A strict conditional fails where, even in one single case, A is true and B is false.

Now, let us go back to considering the conditional in the first premise of the argument just above. Is it a strict conditional? Is the truth of the antecedent strictly sufficient for the truth of the consequent? That is the question. If the answer is 'yes,' then the argument in case 5.1 is convergent. If the answer is 'no,' then the argument in case 5.1 is linked, at least according to the *Susp./Insuf. Prf.* test, and assuming that both premises in the argument in case 5.1 are together sufficient for the conclusion.

But the problem here is that we can't say absolutely, one way or the other. If the amount of heroin is small, then, yes, we can say that legitimizing heroin would not contribute significantly, or to any great extent, to the nation's drug-abuse problem. But how much is 'significantly' or 'to any great extent'? It doesn't seem that we, as argument evaluators and interpreters, could fairly or non-arbitrarily assign an exact number to this degree of support. On the other hand, we can't deny that even a small amount of heroin in the amount of 400 pounds a year could contribute, to some extent, to the nation's drug problem.

What we need to do, in case 5.1, is cast about for more information from the context. But, as soon as we look carefully back to the information given in case 5.1, we see that the discourse is actually a report of someone else's argument – it is a report on what 'proponents of the bill' argue. Not having any more information on who these proponents are, or what case they have made for legalizing heroin, it seems presumptuous for us to categorically say whether their two contentions are meant to be linked together or are supposed to be two separate arguments that stand on their own to support the legalization of heroin. Trying to determine the question on behalf of these proponents even begins to seem like it could be a kind of 'straw man' argument of imposing a distinction where (as far as we can say) none may exist.

Wouldn't it really be better to say, in cases where the evidence is insufficient for us to judge, that we simply don't know whether the given argument is linked or convergent? The usual approach is to invoke the principle of charity, or some comparable principle, to force a decision one way or the other. Perhaps we should reconsider this way of proceeding (see chapter 6, section 9).

A recurring problem we had with many of the cases studied in chapter 4 was that we simply didn't know, intuitively, whether a given argument is linked or convergent, even apart from the tests. This was an especially acute problem with the *Susp./Insuf. Prf.* test, in those cases where it seemed like we simply could not tell where the premises are (in the appropriate sense) sufficient for the conclusion.

Could it be, however, that the real problem is our expectation that the test should work in every case? For some reason, the textbook treatment seems to imply that the test should apply to every argument, and produce a decisive result one way or the other. But we need to rethink this expectation. Isn't it more reasonable to expect that, in everyday conversation, we will encounter many arguments in which it is simply unclear, from the given information, whether the premises (or any subset of them) are sufficient to prove or support the conclusion? And haven't many of our cases in fact borne out this expectation?

If this is right, we need to rethink the use of the tests, and take this element of incompleteness more prominently into account. The upshot of this rethinking of the nature of the decision to be made is the modified version of the method of argument diagramming put forward in chapter 6. According to this new approach, the principle of charity and other principles of interpretation will be used. But, even so, room will be made for cases where we simply don't know whether an argument is linked or convergent. The existence of undetermined cases is something that very much needs to be acknowledged, it will be argued, and is not something that, in itself, should be taken as a reason for judging any particular test as a failure.

5. Precision of the Tests

A problem with all the tests is that they seem more precise and quantitative than they really are when implemented in practice, in many real cases. The van Eemeren and Grootendorst test depends for its applicability on what we mean by 'sufficient' in a given case. This word looks precise, but the appearance of precision fades away as we realize that the burden of proof not only is highly variable from case to case, but is, in many cases, simply not indicated in any precise way.

The summing test requires numerical assignments of probabilities for degrees of support given by an argument. But, in the majority of cases dealt with in informal logic (where we have to evaluate alleged fallacies and the like), exact numerical assignments are not feasible. Here, the margin of error attached to such a numerically exact probability would be so high that it would cancel out the usefulness or appropriateness of the original numerical assignment. Then, we revert to the Thomas–Acock version of the *Degree Supp.* test, which is explicitly vague. The problem is: how much support do we need, in a given case, to make the argument linked, as opposed to convergent?

There is a kind of dilemma here. If we make the tests very precise, by using numbers, applying them to well-behaved deductive and probabilistic cases, and so forth, they work decisively in some cases. But it is this very precision that makes them fail in many other cases, or appear to flounder. Here, van Eemeren and Grootendorst seem to be taking a less ambitious kind of approach by admitting that the test is bound to be uncertain in its outcome in many cases, requiring a 'benefit of the doubt' strategy in its application to real discourse.

Once we realize that both the *Susp./Insuf. Prf.* test and the *Degree Supp.* test represent a trade-off between two different kinds of vaguenesses of application, and are imprecise indicators as opposed to clear litmus tests in some cases, the differences between them appear to be less conceptual and more practical in nature.

Indeed, at a conceptual level, the two types of tests could be really saying the same thing, or something that works out to be very closely equivalent, in practice. The *Susp./Insuf. Prf.* test says that, in a linked argument, the premises were, to begin with, sufficient, but then, later, when one was dropped, the remainder became insufficient. 'Sufficient' here means 'meeting the burden of proof required to make the conclusion acceptable.'[1] The *Degree Supp.* test says that, in a linked argument, if we pull one premise out, the degree of support for the conclusion provided by the remainder goes down a whole lot. But how much is 'a whole lot'? Well, we could define it as meaning that the level of support goes down so much that the argument is no longer strong enough to meet the level of burden of proof (or a reasonable level of such) that would be required to make the conclusion acceptable. So construed, the *Degree Supp.* test amounts to the same finding as the *Susp./Insuf. Prf.* test.

But we don't have to interpret the *Degree Supp.* test this way. All it literally says is that, when we remove the premise (or component argument) in question, the level of support for the conclusion drops considerably. But the problem remains of defining 'considerably' in a way that would be both precise and applicable to the various cases and contexts of dialogue we have considered.

Another way to interpret the *Susp./Insuf. Prf.* and *Degree Supp.* tests reveals that, in terms of how they work generally, they are closely related to each other. When we apply this type of test to an argument, there will be an initial level of support given to the conclusion. When we pull one premise (or subargument) away, there will be a final (or secondary) level of support for that same conclusion. It is a question of how to measure or identify the difference between the two levels of support.

According to the *Susp./Insuf. Prf.* test, the difference has to be enough to make the burden of proof insufficient. According to the *Degree Supp.* test, it has to be enough to meet some kind of measure or mark of being a 'considerable' or 'significant' drop. But 'significance' need not be defined here in terms of burden of proof, or failure of burden of proof (although, as noted above, it could be in practice, making the two tests equivalent).

Whether we call it 'burden of proof' or 'level of support,' then, both tests essentially turn on a diminishment of level of support. And the problem for both

Rethinking the Linked–Convergent Distinction 167

tests, as practically useful indicators, is how to measure or identify that drop in level of support of a kind appropriate to identify the given argument as linked or convergent.

The advantage of the *Susp./Insuf. Prf.* test in this regard is that, by making the test turn on burden of proof, the application of the test is made relative to the context of dialogue and the given information appropriate for the text of discourse in a given case. Burden of proof varies from case to case, from context to context, and often may not be set or determined exactly. The summing version of the *Degree Supp.* test suggests, in contrast (and unfortunately, it would seem, judging by the cases studied above), that the drop in level of support can be quantified or somehow measured by assigning it a precise evidential value, in every case.

Hence, to the extent that there is any real difference between the two tests, the *Susp./Insuf. Prf.* test seems preferable, judging from the point of view of its usefulness and worth in evaluating the cases in chapter 4. However, this asset of the *Susp./Insuf. Prf.* test is counterbalanced by our finding that it fails to give any result on many cases where it should give a result. Even worse, we have seen that, in some cases, it clearly gives counter-intuitive results that are difficult to explain.

Perhaps, then, the clue to the effective use of these tests is to realize that they are best seen as ancillary diagnostic indicators only, as opposed to sufficient determinants, to be used only in conjunction with other factors in judging whether an argument in a given case is linked or convergent. Perhaps the precision suggested by these tests is misleading.

This is a good place to remember Aristotle's advice that 'precision is not to be sought for alike in all discussions' (*Nicomachean Ethics*, 1094 b 13), and that, therefore, we should not expect more precision than the discussion in a case admits of. This expectation of more precision than the case is appropriate for is a kind of mistake that Aristotle equates with a lack of education (1094 b 23–7): 'it is the mark of an educated man to look for precision in each class of things just so far as the nature of the subject admits; it is evidently equally foolish to accept probable reasoning from a mathematician and to demand from a rhetorician demonstrative proofs.'[2] Aristotle's advice, although it comes from his ethical rather than his logical writings, seems strikingly appropriate to the problem posed by the various tests for the linked–convergent distinction.

One point to take from this advice is that we should expect that our methods of testing for the linked–convergent distinction to vary in different contexts of dialogue. In mathematical reasoning, the specific test used might be different (particularly with regard to the precision expected) from that used where the discourse is a political debate in a parliament or congress.

The other point to take from Aristotle's advice is that it would be a serious error or fallacy to infer that, because it is difficult to test precisely or quantitatively for the linked–convergent distinction in many cases, the concept of the linked–convergent distinction is inherently unclear, useless, or incoherent. A parallel fallacy is the inference that, because some cases can be judged more precisely or quantitatively than others, this variation itself demonstrates the worthlessness or incoherence of the linked–convergent distinction.

Perhaps, then, what might be suggested here is that the expectations of precision that appear to be presumed by the treatments of the current logic textbooks are inappropriate, and too high, in general, for the nature of the work that the linked–convergent distinction should properly be expected to do. This suggestion should lead us to focus less on the differences between the tests, and more on the concepts behind them.

6. Concepts behind the Test

To use any test for the linked–convergent distinction on cases of real arguments, it is vital to be clear about certain aspects of burden of proof, in relation to some aspects of the practical test being performed. In using such a test, the test is normally applied to a relatively short (and incomplete) text of discourse containing an argument that is, in reality, a subargument of a larger sequence of argumentation. What is the purpose of this relatively short subargument chosen for testing? Its purpose generally is to 'make a point,' which is a localized move in a broader context of dialogue in which some ultimate thesis or conclusion provides the underlying direction and goal of the subargument. What 'sufficient' means is 'sufficient to make a point' at the local level appropriate for the chosen case. In a linked argument, if one premise (or component argument) drops out, the point is no longer made (or is lessened, if you like, according to the *Degree Supp.* test). Thus, whether an argument is linked or convergent depends on how we view the given argument as making a particular point, in the context of a conversation (dialogue).

To take a typical example, consider a global context of dialogue in which two participants are having a critical discussion on the subject of tipping. Helen thinks that tipping is not a good thing, in the sense that it should not be continued as a general practice in paying for services. Bob thinks that tipping is a good thing, meaning that he thinks it ought to be continued as a general practice in paying for services. This conflict of opinions represents the disagreement between the ultimate theses of both parties, and gives the dialogue its underlying, global purpose – to resolve this conflict of opinions.

However, at the local level, during the argumentation stage, various subarguments will be brought forward by both sides, as they take turns 'making a point.' Suppose, for example, Helen puts forward the following argument, during the course of the dialogue on tipping:

Case 5.2
Tipping makes people feel inferior.
When a person feels inferior, it makes her feel undignified.
Therefore, tipping makes people feel undignified.

In this case, it is fairly clear that the two premises are meant to go together to support the conclusion, so that the argument in case 5.2 is linked. But what does 'sufficient' mean in relation to this argument, in the sense that, if either premise is dropped, the argument remaining is no longer sufficient to prove the conclusion?

First, notice that the two premises are probably not meant to be sufficient for the conclusion in the sense of proving it beyond all possible exceptions, or in all possible instances. Perhaps there are some people who do not feel inferior when they receive a tip. Perhaps there are some people who do not feel undignified when (or whenever) they feel inferior. But such exceptions do not invalidate or refute the argument in case 5.2. They only refute it, or subject it to enough doubt to make it fail to prove the conclusion, if such exceptions are widespread enough to bring the generality of the premises into doubt.

Second, the argument in case 5.2 is not, by itself, sufficient to prove Helen's ultimate thesis, that tipping is a bad practice generally. But we can see the point made in the argument in case 5.2 by noting that it does, or could, contribute to Helen's ultimate goal in the dialogue.[3] It could be 'sufficient' in the sense put forward by Snoeck Henkemans (1992, p. 96), that the opponent has called its insufficiency into question. But how do we know that? In this case, we do not have any information, one way or the other. And this is a strange sense of 'sufficient.' If I merely call into question the insufficiency of A, how can this make A sufficient?

The argument in case 5.2 is sufficient in another sense. Unless Bob challenges one or the other of the premises, then he has to concede that Helen's use of the argument in case 5.2 has made a point against his side of the disputed question. And, in general, this is exactly what the linked–convergent distinction should come down to, in a particular case. If Bob would have to attack both premises to make Helen's argument lose its power to make a point in the discussion, then the argument is convergent. If questioning or refuting the one premise is enough, then the argument is linked.

If we look more closely at the way van Eemeren and Grootendorst (1984,

p. 91) draw the distinction between linked and convergent arguments, it appears evident that they mean the distinction to apply only to cases in which the premises (or some subsets of them) are sufficient for the conclusion. They define convergent (multiple) argumentation as the kind in which each of the several premises (or groups of them) advanced is individually sufficient for the conclusion (p. 91). They define 'linked' (co-ordinative compound) argumentation as the kind in which each premise is individually necessary, but the premises are sufficient only when taken together. In both kinds of cases addressed here, it is generally presumed that the given premises, or some subsets of them, are in fact sufficient to prove the conclusion.

What happens when this presumption is not met in a given case of argumentation? It seems that the answer is that the van Eemeren and Grootendorst test for making the distinction is simply not applicable to that case. It seems that the van Eemeren and Grootendorst criterion works only when applied to successful arguments, that is, arguments in which the premises are sufficient for the conclusion.

What happens, then, when we try to apply it to non-successful arguments? This is an important question because, in everyday conversation, plausible arguments in which the premises are not sufficient to prove the conclusion are very common.

Consider the 'George is guilty' case (case 4.26). We presume that this is an unsuccessful or 'bad' argument. Neither premise provides good evidence. Nor do the two premises, separately or together, give any evidence that would prove, or even give a good argument for, the conclusion.

Yet, because of the indicator-words 'one reason for' and 'my other reason for believing,' there is good linguistic evidence from the discourse text for saying that the argument is convergent.

But because neither premise is sufficient to prove the conclusion, nor are both sufficient when taken together, the van Eemeren and Grootendorst test would simply not seem to be applicable to this case. Neither premise is individually sufficient, as a line of argumentation to prove the conclusion, that is, to convince a respondent in a critical discussion that the conclusion is true or acceptable. Hence, the argument in case 4.26 can surely not be classified as convergent by van Eemeren and Grootendorst's test.

The same point could be made concerning all the cases studied under the heading 'Bad Arguments' (chapter 4, section 9). In such arguments, where the premises (or subsets of them) are not sufficient for the conclusion, the van Eemeren and Grootendorst criterion would simply seem to be inapplicable.

Is this a problem or not? And, if so, could it be fixed somehow?

It may not be a problem, or too serious a practical problem for some pur-

Rethinking the Linked–Convergent Distinction   171

poses, on the grounds that it could be argued that the van Eemeren and Grootendorst type of criterion stems from a background of working discourse analysis. It is generally presumed that the kinds of cases encountered in such a background are relatively successful arguments – or, at least, not obviously or spectacularly bad ones – in which the premises, either jointly or separately, do give some good or relatively plausible reasons to accept the conclusion. On the other hand, the cases studied under 'Bad Arguments' are philosophers' counter-examples, that is, made-up cases that are meant to be unpersuasive and spectacularly bad. These are not the kinds of arguments likely to be encountered in the normal texts of discourse dealt with by working case-studies of persuasive argumentation.

But the assumption that the premises are sufficient for the conclusion in the arguments generally encountered in everyday speech does not seem to be a very plausible one, even for practical purposes. It seems more likely that there are about as many bad arguments as good ones in everyday argumentation practices – 'bad' or 'good' here referring to the sufficiency of the premises for the conclusion.

Hence, we regard the *Susp./Insuf. Prf.* test as having been shown to be seriously deficient by its evident inability to deal with the various counter-examples discussed above. In too many cases of arguments, either the premises (together) are clearly not sufficient for the conclusion, or it is unknown whether they are or not.

Also, however, a lot depends on what is meant by 'sufficient' in the test. Does a sufficient argument have to be deductively valid or inductively strong, or could 'sufficient' refer to meeting the kind of burden of proof appropriate to weaker kinds of plausible, but inconclusive arguments? This is a key question, and our consideration of the important role of abductive arguments in everyday reasoning suggests this whole area needs to be rethought.

7. Defining Necessity and Sufficiency

The crux of the *Susp./Insuf. Prf.* test for the linked–convergent distinction is based on the necessary–sufficient condition distinction. A linked argument (in the simplest two-premise case) is one in which both premises are individually necessary in order (sufficiently) to support the conclusion. A convergent argument is one in which each premise is by itself sufficient to support the conclusion, without the other being necessary.

At least in the abstract, we have a pretty good idea of what the terms 'necessary' and 'sufficient' condition mean. And, indeed, one can be defined in terms of the other. Given the expression 'proposition A is sufficient for proposition B'

as primitive, the concept of necessary condition can be defined as its converse: proposition B is necessary for proposition A. For example, saying 'My graduating from State University is a sufficient condition of my having taken two basic arts courses' is equivalent to saying, 'My taking two basic arts courses is a necessary condition for my graduating from State University.'[4]

At least as far as the subject of logic is concerned, it is easy initially to accept the idea that we have a pretty good idea of what 'sufficient condition' means. One proposition (or a set of propositions, like premises) is sufficient for another if we can prove the one from the other(s). But this basic idea, as clear or straightforward as it initially seems, begins to appear to be something of an illusion once we try to put much practical weight on it. For 'sufficient to prove' in this context clearly amounts to, or is equivalent to, the concept of burden of proof. But burden of proof varies, depending on the type of dialogue in which an argument occurs. It could be higher in a scientific inquiry than in a practical deliberation. And it could be higher in a practical deliberation, particularly, for example, where human safety is concerned, than in a critical discussion concerning a controversial conflict of opinions. An argument that is sufficient to prove in one context might not be sufficient in another context.

One way to solve this problem could be to restrict the concept of sufficiency to a particular type of dialogue. For example, Walton (1984) posits the goal of both participants in a persuasion dialogue as for the one party to persuade the other that a particular proposition (the first party's thesis to be proven) is true. In such a context, it is exactly clear what constitutes a successful fulfilment of the goal. The proponent (the one who has the goal of proving her thesis) has to construct an argument that meets two criteria: (1) the premises all have to be commitments of the respondent (the other party); and (2) the warrant, or structure of inference linking the premises to the conclusion, has to be of a type acceptable to both parties in the dialogue, meaning that, for both parties, if the premises of such an argument are commitments, then the conclusion will be a commitment too.

For example, suppose the premises are two propositions of the form 'A' and 'If A then B.' And suppose that the respondent has previously committed himself to the acceptance of both 'A' and 'If A then B.' Even further, suppose both parties accept *modus ponens* as a warrant, or structure of inference that is valid. Then, if the proponent puts forward the argument 'A; if A then B; therefore B,' her argument is (or should be, in the context of a critical discussion) sufficient to prove B. 'Sufficient' can be equated with 'sufficient to prove' in this context, because the basic purpose of putting forward arguments in a critical discussion is to prove something (ultimately, your thesis, or proposition designated to be proved by you at the beginning stage of the dialogue).

Rethinking the Linked–Convergent Distinction 173

This answer to the question of what is meant by 'sufficient' is useful, up to a point. But it is open to two key objections. One is that it is relative to a context of dialogue, presuming that the type of dialogue can be identified in a given case in which argumentation occurs.

The other objection is that this criterion of sufficiency works well enough for deductively valid arguments, but appears more problematic when confronted with non-deductive inference structures.

Blair (1991, p. 332) gives a very nice summary of how van Eemeren and Grootendorst define the concept of sufficiency in argumentation.

> Van Eemeren and Grootendorst (1984) hold that someone asserting a thesis – the protagonist of a point of view – has sufficiently defended it just when that person has *successfully* defended (a) the inference from the grounds or premises to the point of view and (b) the premises (see Rules 11 and 12, 169–71). Such successful defences consist of successfully meeting the challenges of any critical interlocutor – the antagonist; and meeting such challenges amounts to securing the agreement of the antagonist (164–5). Successful defense of (a), the inference, occurs when either (i) the antagonist accepts appropriately formulated missing premise(s) (see Ch. 6) that render(s) the argument deductively valid (145), or (ii) the antagonist agrees that the inference satisfies the rules of inference validity (of whatever sort) that the two parties had agreed in advance would govern their arguments (169). Successful defense of (b), a premise, occurs when either (i) the antagonist grants that the premise is equivalent to one of the propositions both parties accepted as their initial shared commitment store (165–6), or (ii) the antagonist accepts the premise as validated by one of the proposition-testing methods both parties agreed at the outset to regard as authoritative (167–8), or (iii) the premise is itself sufficiently defended by a further argument (170, see Rule 11).

Blair objects to this analysis on the grounds that: (a) disputants might 'agree too readily to rules of inference, propositional commitments or authorities'; and (b) there might be 'stupid or dogmatic holdouts who simply fail to appreciate the genuine force of the argument' (p. 333). Blair's basic problem with this definition of sufficiency is that it doesn't deal with the concept of rational commitment to a proposition in a way that does not depend on agreement.

> By making the sufficiency of the argumentation dependent in the end on the relatively unconstrained agreement of the participants, the pragma-dialectical model as it stands tolerates resolution of disagreements by the use of arguments that are demonstrably insufficient, and it tolerates the failure to resolve disagreements when the argumentation of one side is demonstrably sufficient. For these reasons,

the criterion of interlocutor agreement cannot serve, without qualification, as a general answer to our question: 'When is the support provided for taking a propositional attitude sufficient to justify it?'

We can see, from Blair's remarks, that the concept of what is sufficient to defend a conclusion in a critical discussion is a lot more complex than it initially seemed. What seems to be presupposed is the concept of a participant's commitment to a proposition in a context of dialogue where two parties are reasoning together.

It is our contention that, in the literature on argument structure, the use of the term 'sufficient condition' should be rethought, and redefined more precisely as meaning 'sufficient to give the amount of support for the conclusion, given the premises appropriate for that type of argument.' The problem is that we tend to think of 'sufficient' in absolute terms; for example, in a deductively valid argument, the premises are sufficient (absolutely) for the conclusion, meaning that it is impossible for the premises to be true and the conclusion false. But, where we are dealing with presumptive arguments of the abductive kind, based on argumentation schemes, the degree of support for the conclusion tends to be much weaker, and more provisional in nature.

Freeman (1991) has presented a dialectical theory of argument structure that is specifically based on an attempt to avoid the unclarity of the problems posed by having to try to decide, in particular cases, whether each of a set of premises is insufficient to support a conclusion. Instead of using the concept of sufficiency, Freeman bases his criterion of linked and convergent arguments on the concept of relevance. According to Freeman (1991, p. 94), 'premises are linked when we need to take them together or they are intended to be taken together to see why we have a relevant reason for the conclusion.' However, as Pinto (1994, p. 320) points out, this approach has the problem that some arguments are classified as both linked and convergent at the same time. Generally, the problem with this approach seems to be that the concept of relevance is as much a source of conceptual confusion as the concept of sufficiency.

8. The Purpose of the Distinction

To solve our problem of which of the various tests is best to identify linked and convergent arguments, we have to go back to the question: what is the purpose of attempting to identify an argument? All along, the purpose was to serve as a basis for evaluating arguments as valid, strong, weak, fallacious, and so on. So, we need to ask: what do we need to know, for this purpose?

The answer to this second question is: we need to know, once we have

Rethinking the Linked–Convergent Distinction

established what the premises are and what the conclusion is in a given case, which subsets of premises need to be grouped together, that is, as linked premises. And why do we need to know this, in order to evaluate the argument? The reason is that we need to know whether a group of premises are supposed to be sufficient, by themselves, as an argument for the conclusion, or whether the remaining premises are also needed for that purpose. And why do we need to know that? The answer is that many of the ways of evaluating the argument (corresponding to types of criticisms represented by the major informal fallacies, and other types of criticisms and refutations of arguments) depend on it.

A good example is the case of the *petitio principii* fallacy, as outlined in chapter 1, section 9. Suppose we find a particular premise in an argument that is on a circle; that is, the argument diagram shows a line of reasoning going from the conclusion to that premise. But suppose the argument also has another premise, not on the circle (according to the argument diagram). In order to judge whether the circular reasoning exhibited by the argument diagram is a case of the fallacy of begging the question, we need to know whether the two premises are linked together, or whether each of them represents an independent (convergent) line of argument for the conclusion. For, if the premises are linked, then we can't avoid the circle, and we couldn't therefore use the premises (as a linked set) to fulfil the probative function. Reason: if the conclusion is non-evident, it can't be used as a required basis for proving a premise that is supposed to be pre-evident. This would be a hopeless conflict in how the argument is supposed to be used to prove something. (For detailed analysis of several extended cases of this sort, see Walton, 1991.)

The key, then, to understanding the purpose of determining whether an argument is linked or convergent resides in looking at the argument from a critic's point of view. The critic needs to know whether it is necessary to refute both these premises, or if is it enough to find fault with just the one, in order for the whole argument to fall down. The key need resides in what a rational critic needs to know about the argument in order to subject it to the kinds of criticisms appropriate for informal logic – criticisms that determine whether the argument was used appropriately or not in its given context of dialogue.

From this point of view, the pragma-dialectical viewpoint represented by the van Eemeren and Grootendorst conception of the linked–convergent distinction is basically the right one, because it is centrally concerned with the question of whether a set of premises is sufficient for a conclusion, where 'sufficient' means adequate to resolve the other party's doubts in a context of a critical discussion. This same pragma-dialectical concept of sufficiency is represented by Snoeck Henkemans (1992). Presumably, such a set of premises is 'adequate to resolve the other party's doubts' only if they are such that the other party ought (as a participant in a critical discussion) to reasonably cease doubting.

This general philosophy behind the linked–convergent distinction could be called 'the respondent's doubt conception': In order to refute (or successfully cast doubt upon) the argument, does the respondent have to refute (cast doubt upon) both premises, or will attacking one only suffice? This question is what we should generally have in mind as what we are testing for in applying any test of the linked–convergent distinction to a given case. Because it does appear to us to express this general philosophy, the analysis of linked, convergent, and cumulative argumentation given by Snoeck Henkemans (1992) is a considerable advance on the approach to testing given by van Eemeren and Grootendorst. However, in our opinion, the use of the *Degree Supp.* test would better support Snoeck Henkemans's approach.

The best way to think of the respondent's doubt conception of the linked–convergent distinction is to see it as concerning the obligation of the proponent of an argument to make a point in the context of a dialogue, and the obligation of the respondent to concede that point. What 'sufficient' means is 'sufficient to shift that obligation from the one side to the other, in the context of a global dialogue between a proponent and a respondent.' Hence, this view of the linked–convergent distinction is explicitly dialectical in nature, as expressed by Snoeck Henkemans.

However, the respondent's doubt conception, as intended here, is meant to be broader than that of van Eemeren and Grootendorst and that of Snoeck Henkemans, in two respects. First, it can, in principle, be applied to types of dialogue other than a critical discussion. And, second, it can be applied to abductive arguments (like argument from sign) where 'sufficient' is defined more variably, weakly, and broadly than the way indicated by the Amsterdam School.

9. The Functional Perspective

According to the pragmatic theory of argument developed in chapters 1 and 6, 'argument' is defined as 'reasoning used in a context of dialogue.' 'Reasoning' is defined as 'a chain of inferences modelled by an argument diagram.' An 'inference' is 'a set of premises connected to a conclusion by a warrant, or bridging proposition, often a conditional (called a 'rule' in computer science).' Inferences are of three kinds: deductive, inductive, and abductive (presumptive). Argument is conceived of, in this theory, as a species of organized verbal exchanges in which two parties reason together for a common purpose. Argument is seen, in this framework, as a kind of goal-directed social activity conforming to maxims of politeness (cooperative rules of exchange).

In chapter 1, three distinctive uses of reasoning in argument were identified.

Rethinking the Linked–Convergent Distinction   177

In the *probative use*, the proponent's goal is to prove a particular proposition (conclusion) to her respondent in dialogue. In a critical discussion, the proponent is obliged to do this by securing the respondent's commitment to the premises, and to the line of reasoning leading from the premises to the conclusion. By contrast, in the *hypothetical use*, the proponent needs to fulfil only the second obligation. The *provisional use* is a mixed function, where the aim is to move forward in the dialogue by securing only partial (provisional) commitment to the premises on the part of the respondent.

In the hypothetical use of argument, there is no burden of proof. We are free to assume any proposition we like, for the sake of argument, even if it is known to be false (and can be proved false). The probative use carries with it a positive burden of proof. The provisional use has a 'negative' or oblique burden of proof – the respondent is entitled to base the argument on presumptions that are accepted without being proved. However, if the respondent can disprove them (refute them by good evidence), the proponent must give up the argument.

This dialectical definition of the concept of an argument is partly semantic and partly pragmatic. An argument is defined in part as a set of propositions – an inference, or a sequence of reasoning made up of propositions held together by deductive, inductive, or presumptive argumentation schemes. But an argument is also defined, *qua* argument, as reasoning used for a purpose in a context of dialogue. From this point of view, argument is a dialectical concept, a reasoned interaction between two parties who are engaged in some kind of organized, conventional, verbal activity with each other.

When argument is viewed in this way, it is not surprising that the linked–convergent distinction should be viewed in terms of how the premises of an argument function together as reasoning used for a purpose in a context of dialogue.

What the counter-examples of chapter 4 can now be revealed as showing is that the linked–convergent distinction is *functional*, meaning that it relates to how the premises of an argument function together in supporting the conclusion in a context of dialogue. An argument is linked if the two premises function together, so that the one is structurally interlocked with the other to support the conclusion. To the extent that there is evidence of this functional interlocking in a given case, we can say that the argument, as used in that case, is linked rather than convergent.

On this view of linkage, no simple, purely propositional test on the truth-values or probabilities of the premises and conclusion will (always) be sufficient to determine whether an argument is linked or convergent in a given case. While such tests may be useful in some cases, the known argument structures and the indicator-words will be necessary evidence in other cases. And, in many cases, the context of dialogue is an important indicator.

Having adopted a functional interpretation of linkage, it becomes apparent that there will be many cases where we have an argument (a set of premises and conclusion) but it is not known, nor can it be determined from the given information, whether the argument is linked or convergent. It becomes possible to see that there are lots of cases of arguments in everyday discourse like this, and that it is not an indication that the linked–convergent distinction is vague or incoherent. This situation seems problematic only (or mainly) because of our expectations that some simple semantic test can be used to decide all cases. Once we give up this idea, and move to a functional view, it is possible to see why, in many cases, it is difficult or even impossible to determine categorically whether the argument is linked or convergent. The reason: there just isn't enough evidence given to enable us to determine how the argument is being used in the given context.

There are three basic kinds of evidence for judging, in a given case, whether an argument is linked or convergent.

1 Structural Evidence. What is important here is the type of reasoning used, and if it has a recognizable inference warrant or argumentation scheme. (See the typology of argumentation schemes in Kienpointner, 1987.) For example, if the argument is deductive, and if two premises fit together in a *modus ponens* form to generate the conclusion, this is good evidence that it is linked. Or, to take another kind of example, suppose the premises and conclusion have the argumentation scheme for practical reasoning as their structure.

Case 7.3
My goal is to pass this course.
The way for me to do it is to study tonight.
Therefore, I must study tonight.

In this case, it is clear that the two premises are structurally linked together, because the whole argument conforms to the argumentation scheme for practical reasoning.

2 Textual Evidence. Indicator-words can be very important in showing how an argument was meant to be used by its proponent. For example, in a convergent argument, the text of discourse might read: 'My one reason for believing it is this, and my other reason is that.' Or, in a linked argument, we might find the words, 'This reason, taken along with my other reason (such-and-such) shows that my conclusion is true.' Such indicator-words are not, by themselves, completely decisive in determining whether an argument is linked or convergent. They only give a clue, by indicating how the arguer evidently means his argument to be taken. But such a clue is normally a very important kind of evidence.

3 Contextual Evidence. The first thing that is important here is the type of dialogue. For the standard of burden of proof in an inquiry, for example, may be very different from that in a critical discussion. It is also important what stage of the dialogue the argument is supposed to be in. Generally, what is important here is the global thesis to be proved in the dialogue – for example, if it is supposed to be a critical discussion. If we are given a short (localized) argument with a few premises and a conclusion, it may be crucial to our assessment to know where the argument came from. Was it part of a book or a magazine article, for example? And if so, what is the title of the book or the article, and what kind of magazine did it appear in (in the case of an article)? To judge the argument as linked or convergent, it may be important to know what the ultimate purpose of the argument was supposed to be, in proving some thesis or making some general point.

Another crucial kind of evidence in this category is, of course, the burden of proof in the given case, which will (presumably) be given as part of the contextual evidence.

According to the approach recommended here, then, the first task of argument recognition (identification) in a given case will be to determine the reasoning in the case, that is, the propositions that make up the ostensible premises and conclusion, and the warrants, or argumentation schemes that bind these premises to the conclusion. This step comprises the gathering of the structural evidence.

The second task is the collection and interpretation of the textual evidence including the indicator-words and other relevant textual evidence relating to interpreting the argument as linked or convergent.

The third task is the identification of the purpose of the reasoning as it is presumably being used in a context of dialogue (of which there are various conventionalized types that can be recognized by a reader). Finally, once all this evidence is in, the test can be applied, as a fourth resource that may help in the identification of the argument.

10. Recommendation on the Best Test

Our evaluation of the usefulness of the various tests studied in chapter 4 is the following. The *Susp./Insuf. Prf.* test is congenial to our pragmatic theory of argument because of its frankly dialectical conception of an argument as a dialectical exchange. But the problem with it, as a useful test, is that the concepts of necessary and sufficient condition employed by it are too vague, inapplicable to real arguments, and potentially ambiguous to be of much help in many cases. It works least well in cases where the premises are insufficient to prove the conclusion, but still give some presumptive weight (although perhaps not very much) to support the conclusion. And it works not at all in cases of 'bad arguments' where the premises, or some subset of them, have no weight as evidence.

If we want a test based on numerical values of degree of support, the *Degree Supp.* summing test is the best one. It works best where conditional probabilities can be assigned in an argument. But it, too, is somewhat vague, because it does not give exact numerical limits on how much the degree of support must go up for an argument to be judged as linked as opposed to convergent. Moreover, it cannot be applied to cases where we cannot assign numerical values to degree of support, without committing a fallacy of inappropriate precision. Also, the summing test works least well on cases of presumptive argumentation where the premises together give only a small degree of support to the conclusion (as in evidence-accumulating arguments, arguments from analogy, and other kinds of arguments based more on weight of presumption than on conditional probability of the more familiar sort). But, as noted in chapter 4, these are common cases.

All the other tests, including the *Fals./No Supp.* test and the *Susp./No Supp.* test, are rejected, on both theoretical and pragmatic grounds. These tests do not grasp the right theoretical conception of the linked–convergent distinction needed to support argument evaluation from a normative and critical point of view. And, perhaps for that reason, they did not perform well in giving intuitively acceptable results in ruling on the various cases studied in chapter 4.

Our conclusion, then, is that the *Susp./Insuf. Prf.* test is basically not the best test to be used as part of the set of criteria for distinguishing between linked and convergent arguments. Our recommendation is that, if a working test based on numerical values of degrees of support to be assigned to arguments is wanted, then the summing test is the appropriate test to be used. However, as shown in our analysis of abductive arguments in chapter 8, the assigning of such numerical values, while it can be useful in some cases, has its limitations.

A key difference between the *Susp./Insuf. Prf.* test, as presented by the Amsterdam School, and the summing test, as presented by Yanal, is that the *Susp./Insuf. Prf.* test is highly contextual, whereas the summing test is based on numbers assigned to the propositions in an argument (apparently independently of the context of dialogue). The *Degree Supp.* (summing) test appeals to logic textbooks precisely because it does appear to free us of the need to worry about the broader context of dialogue in which the argument was used. The *Susp./*

Insuf. Prf. test, in contrast, at least as deployed by van Eemeren and Grootendorst, is very much dependent on viewing the argument as being used in the context of a critical discussion.

We find the *Susp./Insuf. Prf.* test as providing a right-minded contextual framework, and a sensible pragmatic viewpoint on what is meant by the linked–convergent distinction generally. But we find the *Degree Supp.* test works best as an indicator, that is, as a specialized aid that can be used in conjunction with contextual indicators to determine whether an argument has a linked or convergent structure in a given case.

The version of the *Susp./Insuf. Prf.* criterion provided by Snoeck Henkemans works best when there is enough context of dialogue given in a particular case so that indications are present to tell us what the respondent is trying to doubt, and how the proponent is trying to answer these doubts in her argument structure. Unfortunately, however, the kinds of argument examples cited by the logic textbooks generally are cases in which this contextual background is simply not given, and has to be presumed, or simply conceded as not known. And it is just this type of case where the test – especially the *Degree Supp.* test – is most useful to give some basis for judging the argument as linked or convergent.

It should be added here that, in our opinion, the value of the tests has been blown somewhat out of proportion by the logic textbooks. What is most important in judging an individual case is the structure of the argument, the indicator-words, and the evaluator's interpretation of how the argument is being used, in the context of dialogue, to make a point. In most cases, these three indicators are the main basis for making a judgment, and we may have no need at all to apply the *Degree Supp.* test. The test should be seen as more of an adjunct indicator that can be applied if these other indicators are not very decisive.

This point of view, however, makes the judgment a highly contextual one, based on the evaluator's interpretation of how the argument is being used in a context of dialogue. In traditional logic, allowing this much of a role for contextual interpretation appears hazardous (or so it seems, judging from the textbook accounts surveyed in chapter 4). This contextual insensitivity, we argue, needs to be corrected. Hence, in chapter 6, as throughout the rest of this book, we emphasize the use of other kinds of contextual evidence, along with the test.

The best test is the following version of the *Degree Supp.* test. First, block one premise out of your mind, and then ask what degree of support the other premise (if true) gives (by itself) to the conclusion. Then, reverse the process, and block the other premise out of your mind, asking what degree of support the first premise (if true) gives (by itself) to the conclusion. Then, you add these two weights of support together, and ask what degree of support both premises together give to the conclusion. If there is a significant jump from the first joint

182   Argument Structure

degree of support to the second, the argument is linked. Otherwise, it is convergent.

For simplicity, the test as outlined above is for two premises, but the same principle applies to any number of premises in an argument. You need to consider all non-empty subsets of all the premises, grouping those subsets together as linked where the degree of support goes up significantly when the test is applied.

How significant is a question that cannot be given a general answer with any numerical precision, for it depends on context and burden of proof, matters that are very often not definable by an appropriate number. However, Yanal (1988) is right to claim that, in those cases where probability-values can be justifiably assigned, then a mathematical calculation of the basis for comparison can be made. In very many cases of arguments in everyday conversation, however, the *Degree Supp.* test is best regarded as only a rough and ready indicator, used to supplement other criteria. In many cases, it is not an exact method of determination, and by itself may give no meaningful or useful result. It is best seen as just one kind of evidence, useful to help fill in a larger picture.

In many instances, this thought experiment can determine whether there is a significant jump, in a particular case, without assigning exact numerical values to the degree of support of the individual and collective premises for the conclusion. However, in those cases where it is useful and appropriate to assign specific numerical values to these relationships, then the summing (Yanal) test is recommended.

We caution the user, however, that the use of numerical values should not suggest that the test alone is sufficient to determine whether an argument is linked or convergent, in many cases. The test should be seen as one indicator or sign, to be used along with others, as shown in chapter 6.

6

The New Method of Diagramming

To this point, the method of argument diagramming has been developed well enough so that many serious objections to it have been answered (provisionally but adequately). However, the various cases we have studied have included many outstanding difficulties that were resistant to completely effective and convincing solutions. These problems give those who might be sceptical about the method of argument diagramming a basis for having serious worries about its reliability. The most outstanding problems concerned the cases of arguments that were difficult to classify as linked or convergent, and the cases where it was difficult to tell whether a sequence of reasoning was an argument or an explanation.

Clearly, we have found some significant problems to object to. The state of the art of diagramming leaves room for improvements of a practical, as well as of a theoretical kind. In this chapter, we present a new version of the method that is adaptable to automation (in a computer program), and has a very clear and exact mathematical structure. By separating the exact (calculative) part of the method from the inexact (interpretative) part, we present the method in a positive light, as one with inherently limited precision as applied to particular cases, but that is nevertheless a theoretically valid and practically useful tool, subject to care being taken in how it should be used. We will also see that some of the objections to the method are made into worse problems by the particular way the diagrams are drawn. Consequently, we will introduce and recommend an improved method of diagramming that uses a different notation from the one currently in use.

In order to provide the needed basis in theory to solve these problems, section 2, below, sets out our basic framework of analysis, that of a reasoning structure. A reasoning structure is a kind of directed graph (digraph) where the points of the graph are thought of as propositions and the arcs of the graph are

184   Argument Structure

thought of as inference steps. Section 2 formulates how the notion of a sequence of reasoning can be represented in a reasoning structure. The reasoning structure below will be the basis of the new method of diagramming, modelling how a sequence of reasoning has been used in different contexts of argument and explanation. The reasoning structure provides a new method of diagramming that deals with the problems revealed in the standard method, and overcomes these difficulties much more easily.

Also, in this chapter, some of the leading objections to the method of argument diagramming (based, in part, in our own negative findings of problems in the previous chapters) are presented. Then, some key refinements and clarifications of the new method are made, based on the difficulties dealt with in the previous chapters, to reply to the objections as adequately as possible.

The use of digraphs to diagram arguments is not entirely new. So we begin by looking at previous attempts to use this kind of technique.

1. Use of Digraphs to Model Argumentation

Digraphs were used to model logical implications among a given set of propositions by Harary, Norman, and Cartwright (1965, pp. 13–14). The example they give (p. 13) uses four propositions in Euclidean geometry.

Case 6.1
$p1$: ABC is an equilateral triangle.
$p2$: ABC is an equiangular triangle.
$p3$: ABC is a triangle in which at least two sides are equal (an isosceles triangle).
$p4$: ABC is a triangle in which at least two angles are equal.

According to Harary, Norman, and Cartwright (p. 13), the following information about the implications among these four propositions is known.

1. It is known from Euclidean geometry that propositions $p3$ and $p4$ are logically equivalent; that is, each implies the other.
2. It is also known that every equilateral triangle is equiangular, and conversely.
3. It is immediately obvious that, in addition, $p1$ implies $p3$, and $p2$ implies $p4$.
4. But it is known from propositional logic that the relation of implication among propositions is transitive. This applies to the digraph (see figure 6.1), in which the lines $p1p3$ and $p3p4$ occur. Thus, it follows that $p1$

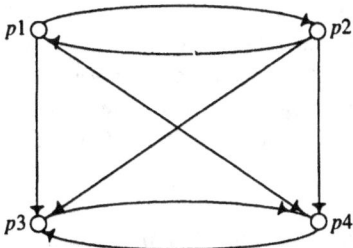

Figure 6.1 The Implication Relations for Case 6.1

implies p4. Similarly, from the presence of lines p2p4 and p4p3, we conclude that p2 implies p3.

All of the implications that hold for the four propositions p1, p2, p3, and p4 are shown in figure 6.1. There are eight implications, shown by the eight lines connecting the four points.

Generally, in an *implication digraph* the points are interpreted as propositions and the lines are interpreted as implications among these propositions. A *total implication digraph* 'displays all possible implications between the propositions which constitute its points' (Harary, Norman, and Cartwright, 1965, p. 14). This concept is very important for analysis of enthymemes, and for argument diagramming generally. It means that a given diagram can be expanded to reveal all possible ways a given conclusion could be inferred from a set of premises.

This is the first use (as far as the author is aware) of digraphs to model argumentation – or, at least, to model something (logical implications among a set of propositions) that could be considered to represent a kind of argumentation, or an aspect of it. However, it is predated by the use of arrows by Beardsley (1950) to identify premises and conclusions in arguments. Beardsley was not advocating what is technically defined as a digraph (see below). But he was using a technique of argument diagramming that, if we are right, is better seen as a digraph structure.

As part of a project to analyse circular arguments, the proposal of considering an argument diagram (of the kind commonly used in the logic textbooks) as a digraph was made by Walton (1980, pp. 47–51). A digraph was defined, following Harary (1969), as a non-empty set of points, V, and a set, X, of ordered pairs of points, called lines. The idea of considering an argument diagram as a graph was presented (p. 50) as follows:

A *walk* of a graph G is an alternating sequence of points $v_i \in V$ and lines $x_i \in X$, v_0,

$x_1, \ldots, x_{n-1}, x_n, v_n$, beginning and ending with points, and where each line is incident with the two points immediately preceding and following it (Harary, 1969). In terms of the theory of relations, the notion of a walk permits a kind of transitive closure – if there is a line from v_i to v_j and a line from v_j to v_k, it does not follow that there is a line (arc) from v_i to v_k, but it does follow that there is a walk from v_i to v_k.

In terms of argument analysis, what this means is that, if there is an argument from one premise-set to a conclusion, and then from that conclusion (as premise) to a second conclusion, and so forth from that point to some end statement, then we can say, after Hamblin (1970), that there is a 'thread' or 'development' of arguments, as we put it earlier a 'chain' of argument, from the initial premises to the end conclusion.

With a somewhat different purpose in mind, Shoesmith and Smiley (1980) proposed looking at deductive logical reasoning in arguments with more than one conclusion using graph structures. Their motivating idea was that deductive, formal logic had traditionally considered only arguments with a single proposition designated as the conclusion. They extended logic to arguments with multiple conclusions, that is, to what are called 'serial' and 'divergent' arguments in informal logic (see chapter 3, section 2, above).

The concept of a digraph is very simple, and not much different from that of a traditional argument diagram. A graph is simply a set of points (representing propositions, in this application), and a set of arrows (arcs) joining these points. The arrows or directed lines represent steps of inference, from premises to a conclusion. When all the lines and points are put together in a particular case, the resulting digraph diagram gives an overall picture of all the steps of reasoning in an argument, and how they connect together. We can see how the argument represents a chain of reasoning or development of inference steps from a set of initial premises to a final conclusion.

A further development (Walton and Batten, 1984) was the mapping of a digraph onto a sequence of argumentation in a dialogue in order to model and evaluate cases of circular argumentation. The motivating idea behind this use of digraphs was to begin with a set of propositions called 'initial premises' and a set of rules of inference (*modus ponens* and so forth) that could be applied to the initial premises to generate arguments in the form of new premises and conclusions. The resulting sequence of argumentation was modelled as a digraph. This structure was then used to model different kinds of circular argumentation, and to provide various ways of evaluating such arguments as fallacious or non-fallacious. The goal, in other words, was to provide a basis for evaluating the traditional fallacy of *petitio principii*, or begging the question.

The New Method of Diagramming 187

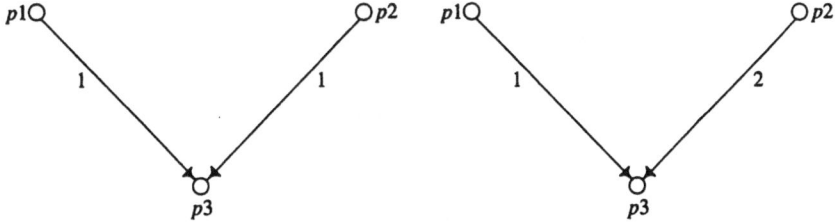

Figure 6.2 Linked and Convergent Diagrams

The method used by Walton and Batten (1984) was to number the rules of inference used in a given case, and to represent the application of a rule in an argument by writing the corresponding number on the line of the digraph. Thus, in a linked argument, the lines would all have the same number (to indicate the same rule used), while a convergent argument would have different numbers on the lines. For example, in figure 6.2, the argument on the left would be linked, while the argument on the right would be convergent. This method of diagramming was used by Walton (1991) to evaluate many cases of circular arguments of varying degrees of complexity.

What is most important, for present purposes, is not so much the technical question of what type of graph or graph-like structure is used. The most important thing is to see that, by changing from the old notation to the graph method, we are freed from always being forced to model an argument as either linked or convergent. It is for this reason that the recommendation is made here that we should move from the existing method of argument diagramming to the new method of reasoning graphs, based on reasoning structure.

2. Reasoning Structure

First, we define the concept of a reasoning structure, generally. Within this structure, the concept of a line of reasoning is defined. In a line of reasoning, the reasoning progresses from a single starting-point, where all the premises are collected together as that single point, to the end-point, or conclusion of the reasoning, which is also a single point.

Then, we define the concept of a sequence of reasoning. In a sequence of reasoning, reasoning can start from several premises, each of which is a separate starting-point. Also, a sequence of reasoning can go from a premise to more than one distinct conclusion.

A *reasoning structure* $\bar{\mathbf{R}} = (\mathbf{P}, \mathbf{I}, \mathbf{F})$ consists of: (1) a finite non-empty set $\mathbf{P}$ of *propositions (points)*, $p_1, p_2, \ldots, p_n$, (2) a finite set $\mathbf{I}$ of *steps (arcs)*, $i_1, i_2, \ldots,$

188 Argument Structure

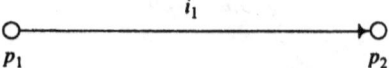

Figure 6.3 An Inference Step

Figure 6.4 An Inference-Step Loop

Figure 6.5 Not a Reasoning Structure

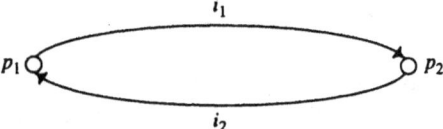

Figure 6.6 Back-and-Forth Steps of Inference

i_m, called *inference steps*; and (3) a function $\mathbf{F}: \mathbf{I} \rightarrow \mathbf{P} \times \mathbf{P}$ which maps each step into an ordered pair (p_i, p_j) of propositions. An inference step is drawn as a directed line from one proposition to another. In figure 6.3, p_1 represents the premise or starting-point, and p_2 represents the end-point, or conclusion of the inference step.

It follows from the definition that *inference-step loops* are permitted, that is, that an inference can go from a proposition p_1 as premise back to that same proposition p_1 as conclusion (see figure 6.4). The reasoning pictured in figure 6.4 is allowed because the p_i need not be distinct points, according to the definition. We will say that the step (p_i, p_j) goes from p_i to p_j and that p_i is *incident with* p_j. There can be, at most, one inference between an ordered pair of points in a reasoning structure. Thus, figure 6.5 does not represent a reasoning structure. But figure 6.6 *does* represent a reasoning structure because i_1 and i_2 are distinct steps, but (p_1, p_2) and (p_2, p_1) are distinct ordered pairs.

However, there can be at most two steps incident with a pair $\{p_i, p_j\}$, and clearly each must be directed the other way from its mate. Where two such

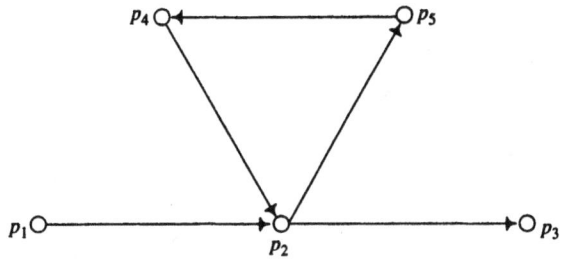

Figure 6.7 A Line of Reasoning

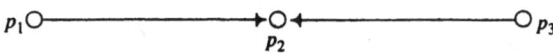

Figure 6.8 A Sequence of Reasoning

inference steps join the same pair of points, we call the reasoning 'back-and-forth steps of inference.' Below, when circular reasoning is defined, it will be apparent that a case of back-and-forth steps is the simplest type of circular reasoning (apart from a loop). Thus, we repeat that, for each pair of propositions $\{p_i, p_j\}$, there can be at most one inference going (directly) from p_i to p_j. There does not have to be at least one inference step per pair of propositions however, and thus a set of points (propositions) with no arcs (inferences) also constitutes a reasoning structure. Such a diagram represents a case of reasoning structure where no inference steps have been made. It is a kind of absence or lack of reasoning case. It also follows that there can be, at most, one inference-step loop at any given point, and that there need not be an inference-step loop at every given point in a reasoning structure.

A *line of reasoning* is an alternating sequence of propositions and steps, p_0, $i_1, p_1, \ldots, i_m, p_n$, where each step i_i goes from p_{i-1} to p_i. The line of reasoning is *circular* if $p_0 = p_n$ and otherwise is *non-circular*. A *pathway of reasoning* is a line of reasoning in which all the propositions are distinct. If $n \geq 3$, a circular line of reasoning is called an 'extended line of circular reasoning.' A circular line of reasoning is called a 'circle,' for short.

In figure 6.7, $p_1 p_2 p_5 p_4 p_2 p_3$ is a line of reasoning but not a pathway of reasoning; $p_1 p_2 p_5 p_4$ and $p_1 p_2 p_3$ are pathways of reasoning; $p_2 p_5 p_4$ is an extended line of circular reasoning. It follows that a pathway of reasoning can never contain circular reasoning. A *sequence of reasoning* is an alternating sequence $p_0, i_1, p_1, \ldots, i_n, p_n$ of propositions and steps, but an inference is allowed to be $p_{i-1} p_i$ or $p_i p_{i-1}$. Figure 6.8 shows a sequence of reasoning but not a line of reasoning.

190 Argument Structure

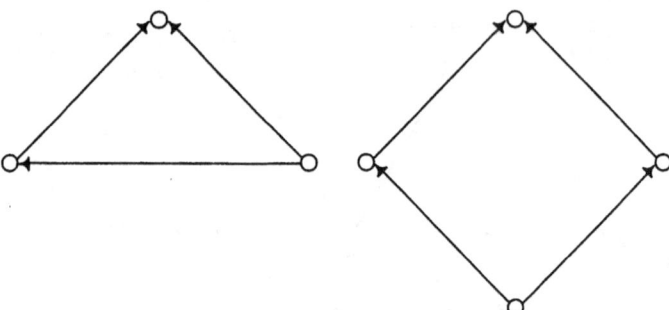

Figure 6.9 Cyclical But Not Circular Reasoning

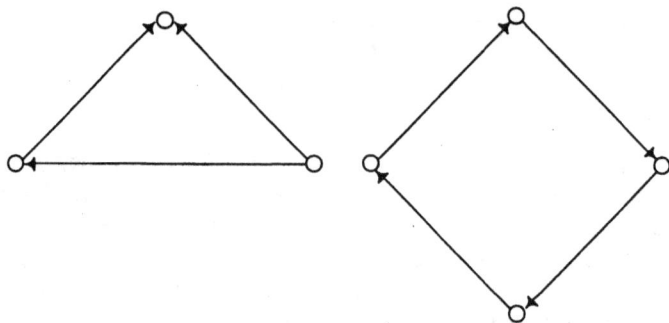

Figure 6.10 Examples of Circular Reasoning

However, every line of reasoning is also a sequence of reasoning. Similarly to a line of reasoning, a sequence of reasoning is *semicircular* if $p_0 = p_n$ and otherwise non-semicircular, and a *semipath* is a pathway in which all points are distinct. Again, in parallel fashion, a non-trivial ($n \geq 3$) semicircular sequence of reasoning is called an 'extended sequence of semicircular reasoning.' Figure 6.9 represents extended sequences of cyclical reasoning that are not circular. But the reasoning represented in figure 6.10 is circular, and consequently also semicircular.

A sequence of reasoning is *loop-free* or *free of back-and-forth steps* if it, respectively, has no loops or back-and-forth steps at any points or pairs of points. Any line of reasoning with n points is said to be *circular* if it is a loop ($n = 1$), a back-and-forth step ($n = 2$), or an extended line of circular reasoning ($n > 2$). A line of reasoning with no loops, multiple steps, or extended circles is said to be *circle-free*.

If there is a sequence-of-reasoning path from p_i to p_j then, p_j is said to be *accessible from* p_i. The set of all points from which a given point p_i is accessi-

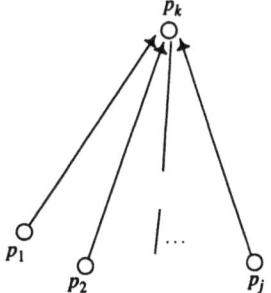

Figure 6.11 Choice of Interpretations

ble is called the 'inspread (predecessors)' of p_i. The set of all points that are accessible from a point p_i is called the 'outspread' of p_i.

A *converse reasoning structure* $\overleftarrow{R}$ has the same points (propositions) as a reasoning structure $\overrightarrow{R}$, but a step $p_i p_j$ is in $\overrightarrow{R}$ if, and only if, the step $p_j p_i$ is in $\overleftarrow{R}$. Thus, the converse reasoning structure is obtained by reversing the direction of every step. When it comes to the question of interpreting reasoning structures in studying argumentation at a practical level of informal logic, we think of a reasoning structure $\overrightarrow{R}$ as modelling a forward-chaining line of reasoning by which a proposition is proved from a set of prior premises. Each step represents a probative advance from the previous stage of reasoning. Then the converse structure $\overleftarrow{R}$ becomes a backward-chaining use of reasoning – by 'reasoning backwards' we are trying to determine the justification or explanation of each given proposition by seeking out the premises or starting-points that it was based on. Thus, informally, depending on whether we take a forward-looking or backward-looking perspective, we can view a reasoning structure as exemplifying a series of inferences in reasoning in two different ways. This feature will come to be extremely important in analysing the notion of abductive reasoning in chapter 8.

3. Circular Reasoning

Reasoning can go forwards, or it can go backwards. Reasoning can even be aimless. It can proceed in a particular direction without any real purpose to guide it, other than seeing where the line of reasoning goes. Moreover, as we have modelled it so far, reasoning does not take into account the linked–convergent distinction. But we now need to consider how that might be done.

A choice is possible in practically interpreting reasoning structures for the analysis of arguments that use reasoning. We can construe the situation pictured

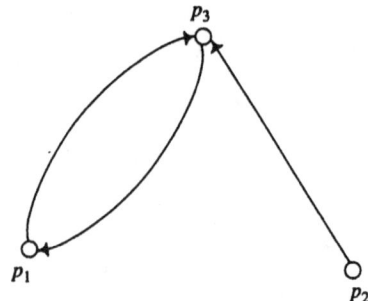

Figure 6.12 Alternative Line of Justification

in figure 6.11 in two ways. *First reading*: $p_1, p_2, \ldots, p_j$ are alternative possible steps of reasoning used in justification of p_k, any one of which is an adequate justification by itself for p_k. *Second reading*: all of $p_1, p_2, \ldots, p_j$ are required for adequate justification of p_k. According to the first reading, the p_is are like a *disjunction*, or a *convergent* set of lines of reasoning to p_k; that is, p_k is thought to be based on either p_1 or p_2 or ... or p_j. According to the second reading, the p_is are like a *conjunction* of propositions, or a *linked* set of lines of reasoning to p_k; that is, p_k is thought to be based on p_1 and p_2 and ... and p_j.

Initially, it might seem that the best way to confront this choice is to avoid it. That is, given all the problems with the linked–convergent distinction encountered in chapter 4, it may now seem best to leave reasoning structures neutral in this regard, so that, in individual cases, we are not forced to make a choice between linked and convergent reasoning. In a way – as shown in section 4, below – that does turn out to be the best approach to diagramming arguments. But the problem – as shown in chapter 1, section 9 – of determining whether a sequence of reasoning involves a linked or convergent premise structure is extremely important when trying to analyse cases where the fallacy of begging the question is a problem.

As shown in the kind of case illustrated in figure 1.2, the linked–convergent distinction is crucial in the analysis of circular reasoning. The kind of problem case confronted in chapter 1, section 9, can be appreciated if we consider the type of situation exemplified in figure 6.12.

According to the second reading, both p_1 and p_2 are required to adequately justify p_3. Therefore, the argument represented, from the premise-set $\{p_1, p_2\}$ to the conclusion p_3, *must* be circular. Whereas, according to the first reading, only one of the premises $\{p_1, p_2\}$ is needed. Thus, even though the argument

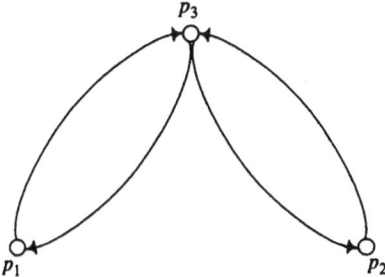

Figure 6.13 Inevitable Circle

from p_1 to p_3 would be circular by reason of the multiple steps between p_1 and p_3, an alternative possible line of justification for p_3 remains open – namely p_2. And, therefore, the argument represented by figure 6.12 can evade the charge of circularity.

Both alternatives are open to us, but let's say we opt for the first reading. Let's say we interpret figure 6.12 as representing a situation in which the argument from p_1 to p_3 would be circular, but not every possible line of reasoning for p_3 would be circular. This contrasts with a situation like that in figure 6.13, in which any argument for p_3 *must* be circular.

The reasoning displayed in figure 6.13 represents an *inevitable circle* because, no matter which alternative possible line of justification for p_3 is chosen, p_1 or p_2, the only possible sequence of reasoning that could be used to support p_1 or p_2 comes from p_3. A case where circle-free justification of a conclusion is available would be one like the reasoning represented in figure 6.14. In this reasoning, p_4 can be grounded on p_2 without circularity because p_2 can, in turn, be grounded on p_1, and p_1 is not on any closed walk that p_4 is also on.

Generally, an *inevitable pathway* from p_i to p_j is a set of pathways starting at p_i such that every pathway passes through p_j, as figure 6.15 illustrates. It is clear that an inevitable circle is simply a special case of an inevitable pathway, and this follows from the next two definitions. First, a *circular reasoning pathway* between p_i and p_j is a circular pathway such that both p_i and p_j are on it. This means that a circular pathway may be a loop ($i = j$), a back-and-forth step ($n = 2$), or an extended sequence of circular reasoning ($n > 2$), for points n. An *inevitably circular pathway* from p_i to p_j occurs where every pathway from p_i to p_j is a circular pathway.

Different ways of using reasoning graphs to display circular reasoning in

194   Argument Structure

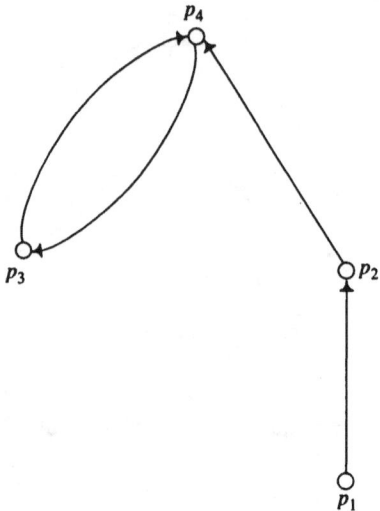

Figure 6.14 Case of Circle-Free Justification Available

arguments are evaluated by Walton (1991). Generally, the approach taken is that circular reasoning is not, in itself, inherently fallacious, but only becomes fallacious when used in an argument in a particular context of dialogue. In other words, certain reasoning structures can be appropriate (non-fallacious) in some uses in arguments in a context of dialogue, yet the same reasoning structure could be inappropriate (fallacious) when used in an argument in a different type of dialogue.

The kind of reasoning characteristic of the inquiry is a cumulative increment of verified and established propositions. The kind of structure appropriate for this type of dialogue is one in which the reasoning always moves forwards, and never loops back to a previous point. As shown by Walton (1991), a tree-like structure is characteristic of argumentation in the inquiry.

A *reasoning tree* is a reasoning structure that is free of semicircles and where $p_n = k_n + 1$. Every line of reasoning in a reasoning tree is a pathway. If there is a pathway from p_i to p_j, we will say, as before, that p_j is *accessible from* p_i. A *source* in a reasoning structure is a unique proposition from which all other propositions in the structure are accessible. If a reasoning tree has a source, it will be called an 'out-tree,' pictured in figure 6.16. The source is p_s. Not only is a reasoning tree free of semicircles, and consequently free of circles, but it follows from the definitions above that reasoning trees cannot contain loops or multiple steps.

The New Method of Diagramming 195

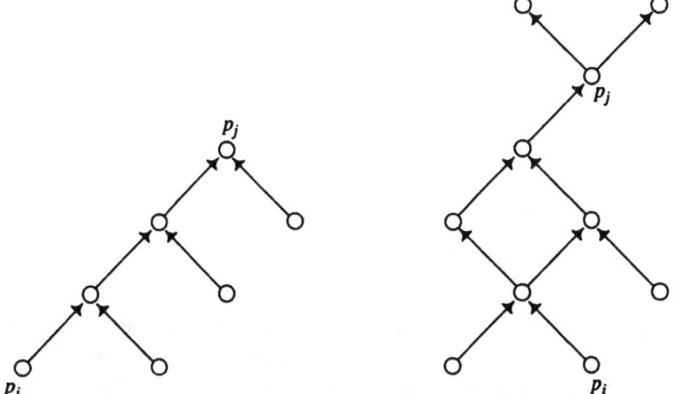

Figure 6.15 Cases of an Inevitable Pathway from p_i to p_j

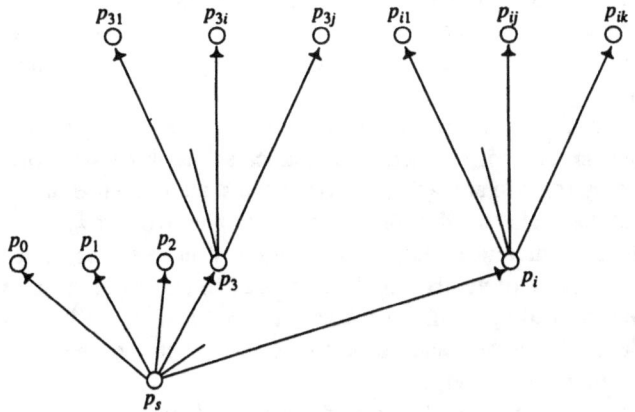

Figure 6.16 A Reasoning Out-Tree

Not all reasoning takes the form of a reasoning tree. However, if we want to restrict our attention to the kind of reasoning in an inquiry, then circular reasoning is excluded as fallacious in this context. It does not count as reasoning of the type allowed in the inquiry.

Thus, reasoning structures enable us not only to diagram circular argumentation, but also to formulate conditions under which circular reasoning is not allowed at all. Hence, reasoning structures are a highly useful tool for analysing cases of the fallacy of begging the question.

196   Argument Structure

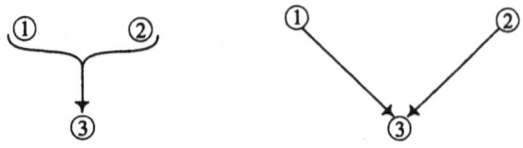

Figure 6.17 Linked and Convergent Arguments

4. Diagramming Incompleteness

A serious problem with the conventional method of argument diagramming is that it forced us to diagram an argument as linked or convergent. The diagramming technique leaves no third option, in a case where it is best to say that we don't know whether the argument is linked or convergent. This is essentially because we have to diagram every argument, as in figure 6.17, one way or the other. The use of digraphs offers a way out of this dilemma, in cases where the evidence is incomplete to judge an argument as either linked or convergent. The way out arises from the technique, illustrated in figure 6.2, of putting numbers on the arrows.

As shown in figure 6.2 on the left, in a case where the argument is linked, having the same number on each arrow indicates that both steps of inference (represented by the two arrows) are parts of the same inference. In contrast, in the figure on the right, the different numbers on the two arrows indicates two separate steps of inference, marking the argument in this case as convergent. Using this technique of numbering the arrows in an argument diagram, we can devise a way of dealing with cases where it is not known, on the basis of the given evidence of the text and context of discourse in the case, whether the argument is linked or convergent.

In such cases, we can simply fail to put any numbers on the lines of the diagram at all. Then the diagram would still be useful to indicate what the premises and conclusions are, at each stage of an argument. It simply would not tell which subarguments are linked and which are convergent.

This solution will not be adequate for all cases, however. Suppose, in a given case, we know that some subarguments are definitely linked, and some are definitely convergent, but, in still other subarguments, there isn't enough evidence to say definitely whether the argument is linked or convergent. What do we do here? If we want to consistently use the same method, we can't assign numbers to the lines in a diagram in some, but not all instances.

But there is a solution available for this kind of situation. We can let the special number 0 stand for the kind of case in which we don't know whether the

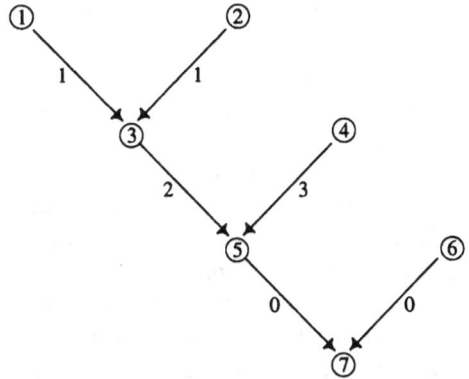

Figure 6.18 Case Involving a Subargument Not Known to Be Linked or Convergent

argument is linked or convergent. Thus, we could have argument diagrams like the one shown in figure 6.18. In this figure, the top subargument is linked, the second subargument is convergent, and the third subargument is one in which there is not enough evidence to say, one way or the other, whether it is linked or convergent.

The use of this new method is no better or worse than the old method, in many respects. The change to the use of the new notations is not significant in many cases. But, in addition to the practical improvement in diagramming linked and convergent argumentation cited above, the new method has the strong theoretical asset that it is mathematically generalizable. An argument diagram using the new method can be expanded, for example, so that it could show all possible ways of proving a conclusion from a given set of premises.

Using the method of graphs, many aspects of the diagramming method can now be calculated on a mathematical basis. As is shown in chapter 8, for example, a computerized method of managing abductive reasoning in enthymemes is possible.

Many more technical details need to be worked out to see how the method of graphs is best used for argument diagramming. But it is easy to see that the method of using graphs offers important advantages over the existing, conventional techniques of argument diagramming found in the textbooks. From the point of view that has arisen from our analysis of the key problems of argument diagramming above, however, one consideration stands out as being of vital importance. It would seem to be much better, judging from what we have found, to have a method of diagramming that allows us to acknowledge incompleteness in some cases, and to mark explicitly on the diagram that there is not enough evidence to say clearly that a given argument is linked or convergent.

It is this advantage of the use of graphs that leads us to suggest that the change to this new method of argument diagramming is the best way to reply effectively to one of the most damaging of a number of objections to the method of argument diagramming that we now turn to considering. For, according to this objection, it could rightly be said that, if we are classifying arguments as linked (or convergent) where the evidence is insufficient for such a classification, we are in fact distorting what a speaker may be saying.

Many commentators are extremely sceptical of any method that is supposed to be used to 'deconstruct' a text of discourse prior to making criticisms of the arguments in it. Many social scientists and philosophers feel that any interpretation is inescapably a subjective process which incorporates the critic's bias, and that therefore no 'logic' or method of objective argument representation could ever be possible.[1] Clearly, these doubts and worries are significant, and reflect some genuinely important questions about the place and limits of interpretation of discourse in logic.

5. Abstraction Distorts Diagramming

Objection 1: *Every case is different, and the flow of argumentation in a given case is dynamic and changing. A diagram is a fixed entity that inevitably is an abstraction from the real argument. Hence, argument diagramming is inevitably an oversimplified representation of what the argument really is.*

This objection applies, not just to the particular tests or criteria used in argument diagramming, but to the whole method itself. It is an old kind of objection that can be used against any mathematical technique of analysis that abstracts from reality but is meant to be applied to real cases.

This objection can be applied to any abstraction, but it seems especially serious when applied to diagramming, because that method gives a very simple and sketchy model of an argument, leaving out a lot of details.

One thing this objection forces us to reflect on is the use of the diagram in argument evaluation. Clearly, the diagram itself is not the whole account of an argument. It is best seen as merely an initial sketch that identifies (often provisionally, and subject to conditions and interpretation) what the overall general structure of the reasoning is, as a series of steps or inferences from one proposition to another. As such, the diagram is a preliminary step, prior to analysis and evaluation of the argument. Hence, it should not be meant to represent the argument completely, or in all respects. Even so, this objection still has sting.

One of the most serious criticisms of the method of argument diagramming is that no formalistic tool of abstraction like a diagram can ever adequately capture an arguer's intentions, or what that arguer is really thinking. For an argument is an actual verbal transaction between people in a particular situation, and depends on non-verbal cues and unexpressed knowledge shared by the speaker and her audience. Any attempt, therefore, to 'deconstruct' a speaker's argument by modelling it with a diagram must inevitably leave so much out that it can never completely or adequately represent the argument that the speaker really advocates.

Willard (1976) raised the objection that argument diagrams do not actually describe the way people think when they put forward an argument. According to Willard (ibid., p. 314), argument diagramming is not a useful technique because it does not solve 'the central descriptive problem for the student of argument,' which 'must be how the people who use arguments in social situations account for the relationship among propositions.' An argument diagram is always something fixed and definite, according to Willard – some lines on a sheet of paper. However, persuasive arguments in real cases of human argumentation are 'too complex and dynamic to be adequately depicted diagramming' (ibid., p. 309). Hence, according to Willard, an argument diagram is worthless as a tool for identifying arguments in the 'real world.'[2]

This objection is based on a true premise. An argument diagram does abstract from the psychological reality of a particular case. However, we should not conclude that all abstraction is worthless. We need to remember a few points about normative evaluation of arguments.

In evaluating how useful the method of argument diagramming is as a tool for the identification of arguments, we need to ask what job this tool is supposed to perform. The job should be seen, not as descriptive or psychologistic – as a test to determine what an arguer's motives are, what that particular arguer really meant (in his own mind), or what his audience took him to conclude or advocate. Instead, the job should be seen as normative – as a test or set of criteria to determine what it is reasonable to take the argument to be, given the text of discourse and the context of dialogue the argument was supposed to be part of (as far as we can tell). Thus, the argument diagram that reconstructs (what may presumably be taken to be) the line of reasoning in an argument in a discourse should be seen as a kind of provisional construct. But it should also be seen as based on certain kinds of characteristic evidence that can be reproducibly verified as being present (or absent) in a given case.

An argument diagram is an interpretation, one which, in many cases, can be expected to be partial, incomplete, and conditional in some respects. It is a point of view or judgment that anyone, especially the proponent of the argument, is free to accept or reject. But there is, or should be, requirements citing certain definite kinds of evidence, or indicators, by which the interpretation expressed by the diagram must stand or fall. Thus, it is not a purely subjective interpretation, but one based on public evidence, of the kind cited by the relevant criteria and tests.[3]

It seems to really help in understanding the method of argument diagramming if you stress that the purpose of informal (applied, practical) logic is to apply objective tests for validity, invalidity, and so on, to argumentation in everyday conversations. The objective is pragmatic – it is to apply logic to the real world of natural language exchanges in discourse. But, in order to do this, we have to take the first step of identifying arguments. We have to have some set of criteria or method for telling us, in a given case, whether what we have is really an argument, as opposed to, say, an explanation or some other type of speech act.

One problem we have encountered is that explanations and arguments often look alike, and even use the same indicator-words. Indeed, in some cases, the same discourse could function both as an explanation and as an argument.

But the problem is, then, that if we go ahead and presume that something is an argument, and then determine by our objective methods that it is an invalid argument, this criticism could be unfair. For it could be that the discourse in question is really an explanation, not an argument. So, to say it is a bad or faulty argument of some sort is a kind of error of misapplying logic.

A comparable kind of error is condemning an argument that was clearly meant to be taken as inductive by a speaker on the grounds that it is an invalid deductive argument. It may be quite true that the argument in question is deductively invalid. But so to criticize it could be a misleading and fallacious misapplication of logic, if in fact the argument was presented by its proponent as being inductively strong, and in fact it is inductively strong (as judged by the appropriate standards of inductive strength).

In understanding the method of argument identification, then, it is helpful to emphasize that, while it is not as exact and decisive as the methods we have for testing deductive validity (which are by their nature, binary or 'black and white'), it is nevertheless useful to apply it as a first step in the process of logical evaluation of arguments, in order to prevent the error of misapplying logic to things that are not really arguments at all, or of misapplying logic to an argument of the wrong type.

So introduced, the method of diagramming can be seen as a pragmatic method of discourse analysis or interpretation that is useful preparatory to the later stage of argument evaluation. Because the method of argument identification is applied to argumentation in everyday conversation – where people are often unclear about whether they are arguing or not, or what their argument is, and so on, judgments may in some, but not, all cases have to be dependent on conditional assessments or presumptions on how an argument should be taken, given the textual evidence. In some cases, two interpretations may even be legitimate, and can be conceded, given the reasons citing evidence on both sides. Hence, if the method is properly understood and applied, no distortion of the original argument needs to be involved.

The method is not meant to describe the way people actually think, but is meant to base argument evaluation on a prior hypothesis that a given text of discourse contains an argument that can be identified, based on textual evidence supporting that hypothesis.

6. Vague Concepts Are a Problem

Objection 2: *The tests and criteria look precise, but they use words like 'sufficient condition' that turn out to be too vague and mushy when you try to apply them to real cases. Hence, they lack the precision necessary for logic.*

We have seen that this objection has real force, and is basically legitimate (given the present state of the art of diagramming). Even the word 'argument,' as we have seen, is inherently vague, and is subject to various philosophical or theoretical interpretations. So, if we don't know exactly what we are testing to find, naturally it will be unclear whether we have found it, or even how to test for it.

However, we have argued that this objection can be overcome, at least to a considerable extent. A precise but provisional analysis of the concept of an argument was presented in chapter 1. To the extent that this analysis is acceptable (even though it is subject to debate and criticism), the entity called an argument can be identified with a reasonable degree of accuracy in enough cases to make the method of diagramming accurate and useful.

Our way of making the tests useful was to preconceive them in a pragmatic way, making the vagueness of the test commensurate with the vagueness of the cases to be tested. Thus, it is to be expected, for example, that it cannot be said absolutely that a given argument is linked or convergent. But, in many cases, it can be said that we can provisionally interpret it one way or the other, given the evidence of indicator-words, text, and context that is cited.

All that said, this objection does have particular force when applied to the *Susp./Insuf. Prf.* test. One of the most serious problems in making the *Susp./Insuf. Prf.* test both clear and useful is that of defining what is meant by the term 'sufficient' (as shown in chapter 5, section 7). What does it mean (exactly) to say that two premises are sufficient for a conclusion, but neither, by itself, is sufficient? As Blair (1991) pointed out, the definition of sufficiency offered by van Eemeren and Grootendorst (1984) – see the details in chapter 5, section 7 – ties sufficiency to the agreement of the interlocutor (respondent in the dialogue) to the premises. There is a problem here. How can such a conception of argument deal with hypothetical arguments like case 1.1 and abductive arguments like those studied in chapter 8?

Our general solution to this problem, advocated in chapter 1, is to tie the concept of sufficiency to the concept of burden of proof in a context of dialogue. In the sense we advocate, to say that two premises are sufficient for a conclusion means that the two premises, taken together, would make a point that would shift the burden of proof (the obligation to provide critical questioning) to the other side, *if* the premises were proven (or accepted by the respondent). This is a kind of hypothetical meaning of sufficiency, meaning 'these premises would be sufficient as a basis of argument (justification) for the conclusion if the respondent were to accept them as justified (good evidence).' On this account, it is the structure or the function of the argument, not the content of the premises, that makes the argument linked or convergent. Similarly, it is the function of the argument, not the content of the premises, that makes it an argument as opposed to an explanation (or anything other than an argument).

Even though we think that sufficiency can be generally defined, we have also argued that the *Susp./Insuf. Prf.* test does not work well enough, mainly because, in so many cases of arguments in everyday conversational use, the premises are not in fact sufficient for the conclusion. Hence, to some extent at least, we agree with that objection.

All this said, however, it remains important, as stressed in chapter 1, to distinguish between the probative and hypothetical use of an argument. Copi and Cohen, along with van Eemeren and Grootendorst, have laid stress on the probative use of argument in their tests for linked versus convergent and argument versus explanation. This can be justified, because the probative use is the paradigm of how arguments are most commonly and straightforwardly used in everyday discourse. However, as argued in chapter 1, despite the conceptual subtleties and complications required, it is necessary to include hypothetical and provisional uses of argument as well, if justice is to be done to some of the more subtle and problematic cases we have studied. Within this framework, we have argued, the concept of sufficiency of a set of premises for a conclusion, can generally be defined in a way that is neither 'mushy' nor unduly vague. No doubt further studies will give this concept greater precision but, as Aristotle reminded us,[4] it could be an error to expect (inappropriate) precision where none exists.

Any test that is applied to interpretation of a text of discourse in real, everyday cases of argumentation will have to be based on a recognition that, in some cases, the participants are going to be confused about things like whether they are really putting forward an argument, or what their premises and conclusion are supposed to be. It would be a conceptual error to expect the method to give a precise result, or designation of the argument structure in such cases.

However, the method we have advocated is, at least to some extent, quite precise. To get a better grasp of what is precise and what is vague in the method, consider our proposed solution to the problem of enthymemes in chapter 7. Part of this method is quite 'objective' and calculative in nature. This part we called the 'need,' as opposed to the 'use,' part of the process of analysing an enthymeme to seek out the non-explicit premise(s).

The objective part of the process can be carried out by an automated search method of abductive reasoning in an expert system. The computer program is told what the conclusion of the argument is, and what one given premise is, and then it searches through the knowledge base (the set of 'facts' and 'rules,' so called in the knowledge base), to find what other premise(s) is/are in that knowledge base that could go along with the designated premise(s) to complete the inference, by the given standards and forms of inference. This part of the process is perfectly mechanical, and calculative in nature. It would not be appropriate to describe it as 'vague' or 'mushy.'

It is the second part of the process – corresponding to the 'use' aspect – that is more subject to objection 2. In a knowledge-based system, the knowledge base, that is, the set of possible premises, is a clearly demarcated set, stored in the memory of the computer. So, when you conduct an abductive search for premises, the computer either will find a particular proposition in the set or will find that it is not there. However, in evaluating an argument in a text of discourse, for example, in a logic-course section on enthymemes, we have to ask whether or not the needed premise really is a commitment of the arguer, as determined from the given text of discourse. This aspect is the problem, as far as objection 2 is concerned, because such a determination can be uncertain and conjectural, in some cases. This is really the problem of dark-side commitments posed by Walton (1984; 1991; 1992b; 1993). For example, although George may have gone on record as advocating communist principles, declaring he is a communist, and so on, can we presume that, in an argument on whether the post office should be run by the state or free enterprise, George is committed to a non-explicit premise in his argument to the effect that the post office should be run by the state? In such a case, we have to draw an inference to a presumption that George *probably* is committed to this premise, yet leave open the possibility that he could (if asked) deny or repudiate such an assumption.

This kind of case admittedly is a difficult problem about commitment and enthymemes, and the best we can say here, for the present, is that current work on the concept of commitment (Walton and Krabbe, 1995) is developing precise methods for the determination of commitment in such cases.

7. Interpretation of Discourse Is Subjective

Objection 3: *The tests and criteria for linked–convergent, enthymemes, and arguments may work well enough in some clear cases of argumentation, where one side is clearly trying to prove some clearly identified disputed conclusion to the other side. But, as we saw abundantly, not all cases are like this. There are too many difficult and undecidable cases where the various tests don't work very well, or even at all, and hence the criteria used are not too subjective.*

This objection is based on some good evidence, as we have abundantly seen in previous chapters. In some cases, for example, it is clear that a discourse is an argument as opposed to an explanation, because the conclusion at issue is clearly in dispute, rather than being taken for granted. But, in other cases, this distinction is much less clear, and the tests don't seem to work.

The linked–convergent criteria and the test for argument versus explanation are not foolproof. They work best when applied to pro- or contra-argumentation in a critical discussion. They work less decisively in cases of hypothetical argumentation, or where the argument is in a context other than a critical discussion, for example, a pedagogical dialogue or a negotiation. Although not without exceptions, they work effectively, if somewhat roughly and conditionally, in many cases. And, not surprisingly, the more information we have on the context of dialogue in a given case, the better the test works.

It is not surprising that van Eemeren and Grootendorst concentrate on pro- and contra-argumentation in a critical discussion as their model of what an argument is. For that is the very kind of case most often encountered, and that we need to deal with, in evaluating arguments as fallacious, open to critical questioning, and so on.

However, we have seen that, in order to deal effectively with the problems posed by a broader range of cases in which there really does exist an argument (though the context is not that of a critical discussion specifically), the adequacy of the method of diagramming can be improved by extending it to see how it should be dealt with in these kinds of cases too. Recently, Fisher (1988) and Snoeck Henkemans (1992) have stressed the importance of hypothetical arguments as well.

Unfortunately, the impression tends to be given, the way the tests are presented in many logic texts, that the test itself (the *Fals./No Supp.*, *Susp./Insuf. Prf.* tests and so on) bears the decisive brunt of the load in determining whether an argument is linked, convergent, or whatever. This impression of decisiveness and precision is reinforced by words like 'sufficient condition' and so forth, and in some cases even mathematical formulas, included in the test. However, as we saw, with this kind of pressure put on such a test, it tends to collapse when applied

The New Method of Diagramming 205

to all kinds of problematic cases from everyday argumentation. This kind of expectation put on the test, by itself, is not very realistic or practical.

Far better to think of the test as just one more indicator or diagnostic criterion that supplements all the other criteria, such as the indicator-words, the structural evidence, and the contextual evidence. None of these criteria can be summed up, very usefully, in a one-line 'quick test.' And that is the reason, perhaps, why the logic textbooks prefer the test, which looks brief, decisive, and quantitative, over a more lengthy consideration of these other factors. But this misleading impression of precision and simplistic applicability can be offset or corrected by reinterpreting the tests pragmatically.

One thing about the tests is that there appears to be a high level of expectation, as the tests are presented and used in logic textbooks, that they will definitely and clearly give a positive or negative result when applied to discourse containing argumentation. But, when you start to think of what function the test is performing, this expectation reveals itself as a little naïve. For, in many cases of argumentative discourse, a speaker can be vague, confused, rambling, even incoherent. For example, in a novel using techniques of free association, there may be some sort of argumentation involved, but the actual reasoning may be vague and virtually incoherent (perhaps even purposely so). To expect that one of the tests is a failure because it fails to work decisively in such a case seems somewhat ridiculous. No test could ever bear this kind of load, and we should not expect it to.

Since we are dealing with real cases of everyday discourse in natural language, it is much better to lower our expectations of any set of tests or criteria we might devise. A good test should work well and straightforwardly to give a positive or negative result in some cases, whereas, in many other cases, we should expect the outcome to be conditional upon certain interpretations of the discourse. In many cases, it is perfectly reasonable to reach the decision that there is not enough information given concerning items of the text or context of the argument to say definitely, yes, it is linked versus convergent, or an argument versus an explanation. This incompleteness of information in a given case is perfectly normal, and we should learn to expect it. It does not mean that the test is useless, incorrect, and so on.

In many cases, a conditional judgment on how to identify an argument is extremely useful in making criticisms and evaluations. As long as we are clear that the evaluation is conditional on what was meant, there is nothing wrong with making such a conditional evaluation.

It should be perfectly acceptable that there are going to be a lot of cases of discourse where the test won't tell us whether the argument is linked or convergent, or whether it is really an argument as opposed to an explanation. In many such cases (too often, the ones in the logic textbooks are of this type), simply not enough information is given for a real basis of differentiation. This, in itself, is not necessarily a failure of the test.

Also, it is clear that the tests will work better in some contexts of dialogue than others. For example, in the 'risks for managers' and the 'foundations of philosophy' cases cited by Thomas (see chapter 2, sections 8 and 9), the context was that of a pedagogical dialogue – a type of dialogue that tends to be mixed: it is partly critical discussion, partly explanation, and partly information-presenting, and generally involves an expert talking with a novice. In this type of dialogue, it is much harder to sort out than, say, in a critical discussion, what is an argument and what is an explanation. The two speech acts tend, inherently, to be mixed in together. What you have to do, in such a case, is look more carefully at the context, and find out what the purpose of the dialogue was supposed to be. Both these cases were taken from university textbooks.

What is to be stressed is that some contexts of dialogue are more difficult to apply the test to than others. Van Eemeren and Grootendorst (1984) rightly stress the critical discussion as a central context of dialogue for argumentation, and one where the tests tend to work better, perhaps, than they do in some other contexts. This leads to another objection.

Objection 4: The linked–convergent distinction, the argument–explanation distinction, and the analysis of enthymemes have now all been portrayed (in the previous chapters) as requiring a context of a text of discourse. That is, they depend on the purpose of a discourse. This makes argument diagramming too relative and subjective for logic.

By making the tests and other criteria relative to different contexts of dialogue, for example, the critical discussion, the pedagogical dialogue, and the scientific inquiry, we have introduced a certain amount of relativity into the concept of an argument diagram. We see the diagram as representing reasoning, but also reasoning used in argument (or explanation) in a given context of dialogue the speaker and hearer are supposed to be engaged in.

Some will see this as too much relativism, as too much of a pragmatic orientation. From the point of view of traditional logic, it seems to make the concept of an argument too context-dependent. From the point of view of van Eemeren and Grootendorst, it may seem too kaleidoscopic, too fragmented, in considering types of dialogue other than the critical discussion. Others will say that any process of interpretation of a text of discourse is a kind of 'deconstruction' that is inherently subjective, and simply reflects the advocacy and interests of the analyst.

But we think that the method of argument diagramming can live with some degree of relativism, and indeed flourish within it as a useful method for informal logic. The diagram represents an interpretation of how to look at a text of discourse in a given case. But, given the nature of discourse in natural language, a particular case can often be susceptible to many interpretations. 'What makes this particular (or any particular) interpretation using a diagram the right one?' a critic can always ask. The answer is that nothing makes it absolutely the right one, or the only permissible one. It is only the conventions of certain types of dialogue that are understood by both speaker and audience which make it possible to put forward a particular interpretation (as represented by a diagram) as expressing what the speaker presumably meant to say, according to the text of what he or she actually said, taken together with the cooperative (Gricean) principles for the type of dialogue the speaker was supposed to be engaged in.

Such an interpretation, by its nature, tends to be conditional and presumptive. It can be challenged, quite often, and in many cases other interpretations may be possible. Even so, an argument diagram can be justified as a legitimate interpretation because evidence, both textual and contextual, can be given to support it as a hypothesis, to the extent such evidence is available in a given case.

The bottom line, then, is that the argument diagram never stands by itself, as the exclusive interpretation of what a speaker really meant to say. It stands only side by side with the account of the evidence that supports it, as a provisional interpretation of what we can take the speaker's argument to be, subject to revisions or corrections should new evidence come in. Even so, it is a necessary tool, because no evaluation of an argument in a given case can go ahead (on a sound basis) without having as a foundation some provisional interpretation of what the argument is, as expressed by that case.

An argument diagram needs to be viewed, not as a final, exact, and exclusive representation of the line of argumentation implicit in a given text of discourse, but rather as merely a heuristic device or tool that is part of the analysis of a given text of discourse. Such an analysis typically involves a good deal of 'cleaning up' a given text of discourse – deleting matter judged to be unimportant, and inserting new matter that needs to be made explicit. In some cases, where there is ambiguity, for example, it may be necessary to formulate two different argument diagrams, each of which represents an interpretation that is consistent with the data. The diagram itself, then, is only one part of this larger task of argument reconstruction. But the diagram is important, because we cannot evaluate an argument unless we have reached some prior agreement on what its premises and conclusions are taken to be.

Of course, such agreement can be provisional and hypothetical – based on evidence, and subject to refutation – but, even so, it is a necessary first step before any evaluation of the argument as correct or incorrect can begin.

Consideration of these issues takes us to an extension of objection 4 that is even stronger, and more worrisome, in certain respects.

8. Distortion and Commitment

Objection 5: *An argument diagram is only a subjective interpretation of what some critic thinks an arguer means. By using an argument diagram, you are imposing your own version of the argument on the arguer. Because of human bias, this viewpoint is inevitably a distortion, and commits the 'straw man' fallacy.*

This objection is based on a true premise – namely, the proposition that, when we identify a non-explicit premise, or judge something to be an argument as opposed to an explanation, we are not basing the attribution on the arguer's explicit say-so (assertion). Instead, our attributions of these things should be seen as assumptions or hypotheses. This observation is quite important and is correct. But what is also important is that, in using the method of diagramming, we mark clearly (by means of some notation), which propositions in an argument are explicit assertions, as opposed to non-explicit (presumed attributed) premises or conclusions. Only if we separate these two things clearly is the method of diagramming acceptable.

But the conclusion drawn in objection 5 does not follow. It is true that the argument identification represented by an argument diagram is only a 'viewpoint' or hypothesis, but it is one that can be supported by reproducible evidence, of the various kinds cited in the previous chapters. So, it is a hypothesis that can be challenged, questioned, or put against competing hypotheses, even by the original arguer himself, if he is present to dispute the case.

In many cases, as we have seen, however, this evidence is not conclusive. In some cases, as well, it could be perfectly reasonable to have two alternative argument diagrams representing two different possible interpretations of the line of an argument in a given case. Ambiguity is quite possible in these cases, and there could be legitimate evidence for two different (incompatible) interpretations of the text of discourse in a case.

This should not be worrisome, however. For, when dealing with real arguments in natural language, we are going to find, in some cases, that people's arguments are ambiguous, or they themselves are unclear about what their argument really is. Alternative diagrams can model such cases. Also, use of such principles as that of charity helps to prevent unsympathetic interpretations, in cases where stronger or weaker interpretations are possible – see sections 9 and 10, below.

In using the technique of argument diagramming, it is necessary to ask: 'What are we really doing here?' In particular, it is useful to begin by distinguishing two questions, taking the linked–convergent distinction as the case in point: (1) Is this argument really linked or convergent, according to its internal structure? and (2) Was this argument meant to be linked or convergent by the person who put it forward? The second question is subjective and is related to the intentions of the speaker. The first question is objective and concerns the structure of the argument, for example, whether one proposition is necessary or sufficient, as a proof or justification of another.

Now it appears from the treatment of the logic textbooks, judging from how they use the method of argument identification, that it is (at least primarily) the first task that they are engaged in. For they use criteria, such as indicator-words, that are presumably evidence of how an argument was put forward, or was meant to be put forward, by a speaker. The objective evidence, in answer to question 2, above, seems to be relevant as well. But its function seems to be to support (or refute) the finding that is supposed to be the answer to question 1.

Let's take a somewhat artificial example to pose the issue in a concrete way.

Case 6.2
Bob puts forward an argument that has the form of *modus ponens* and is clearly a linked argument in its structure. But he makes it clear to the respondent that he is putting it forward as a convergent argument by saying: 'Here is my one premise, and here is my other premise, which can be used as a quite distinct and separate basis for proving my conclusion.'

Here, Bob is making clear, by the language he uses, that each premise is meant to be a separate line of argument for his conclusion. That is, he is clearly telling us that, as he sees it, his argument is convergent. Yet, since the argument has the form *modus ponens*, and both premises are needed to adequately prove the conclusion, the argument (in itself, apart from the way Bob is presenting it) is linked.

The question is: according to method of argument identification, do we judge the argument to be linked or convergent? Judging from the way the method of argument identification is used by the textbooks, as we have seen, they would probably be inclined to judge the argument as convergent. But the question poses a key problem that should be thought about, and specifically addressed by the textbooks. No doubt this problem will provoke different answers, because it seems that the case puts forward an argument in which the evidence is inherently contradictory. By one kind of evidence (the indicator-words), the argument is convergent. But by another kind of evidence (the internal structure of the reasoning in the argument itself), the argument is linked.

The solution to the problem that we propose here is to view the question as being about the commitment of the speaker who put forward the argument. Commitment, viewed in the way advocated by Hamblin (1970), Walton (1984), van Eemeren and Grootendorst (1984), and Walton and Krabbe (1995), is not a psychological matter of the arguer's intentions or beliefs. It is a normative question to be judged by the evidence given in the text of discourse in a given case, for example, the indicator-words, and by contextual evidence concerning the type of dialogue (conversation) in which the speaker is supposedly engaged with some respondent or audience. An arguer's commitments are determined by the type of move she makes in a conversation, for example, an assertion or the asking of a question, in a type of dialogue where commitment rules determine which propositions are inserted into, or retracted from, that participant's commitment set. (For the definition of a commitment set, see Hamblin [1970, pp. 257–8], and see Walton and Krabbe [1995] on how such sets are regulated in different types of dialogue exchanges of argumentation.)

When we ask whether an argument in a given case is linked or convergent, it is somewhat misleading to see the answer as a choice between the oppositions posed by questions (1) and (2), above. For commitment is a kind of blend of the objective and subjective factors posed by questions (1) and (2), but it is misleading to see it as falling into either category. Commitment is determined partly by objective matters of the internal structure of an argument – for example, whether it is a deductive argument of a particular form, like *modus ponens*. But it is also a function of how that argument was used, or put forward, by its proponent in a context of conversation. That is not a psychological or purely subjective question of what the speaker meant to say 'in his own mind,' for example, Bob, in a particular case. Rather, it is a question of what we ought to judge that arguer of being committed to claiming in that particular case, given the evidence furnished by the text and context of discourse.

It is important, then, to ask what we are doing when we make an argument diagram. The answer is that we are trying to identify an argument, prior to evaluating or criticizing it. In short, we are asking the question 'What is the argument?' But the problem is that, in many cases, people are not clear themselves on what their premises and conclusions are supposed to be, or on how those items are related, or even on whether they are advancing an argument or not. Thus, we have to expect that, in many cases, our reconstruction of an argument using the diagram method will be, at least to some degree, conjectural in nature. But that in itself is not inherently bad or logically wrong, provided it is clear that conjectures (hypotheses) are being made, and provided that they can be supported by evidence that is open to inspection.

What we are doing when we diagram an argument is trying to give some sort of account of what the argument is, or what we may take it to be, prior to entering into the task of attempting to evaluate it. This task of argument identification can be seen as a type of dialogue relationship between the arguer, who originally put forward the argument in question (in some written text, normally), and the would-be evaluator, who has taken on the task of making some critical remarks about the strengths or weaknesses of the argument.

In a typical case, however, the dialogue relationship is a special type, because the arguer is no longer present to dispute how his argument should be taken. Even so, the evaluator does have a text at her disposal, and the verbal or written evidence provided by this text can serve as a basis for advancing or refuting conjectures about what sort of claims are made by the arguments in the text. It is this kind of objective evidence that should rightly be used in determining whether an argument in a given case commits the 'straw man' fallacy or not.

9. The Principle of Charity

The principle of charity, according to Johnson and Blair (1992, p. 1) has its origins in debates in philosophy of language on the indeterminacy of translation. However, Johnson and Blair attribute the first formulation and naming of the principle, 'as applied specifically to argument reconstruction,' to Nicholas Rescher. Rescher (1964, p. 162) stated the principle as a rule for use in deciding between candidates to be missing premises in enthymemes: 'The governing rule in the reconstruction of enthymematic arguments is the principle of charity – one should, insofar as possible, try to *make the argument valid and its premisses true*.' Although Rescher's version of the principle of charity was restricted to deductive arguments, subsequent formulations extended it to other uses.

For example, Little, Groarke, and Tindale (1989, p. 15) used the principle of charity to distinguish between arguments and passages of discourse that do not contain an argument, for example, passages that should be treated as an explanation, as opposed to an argument: 'If there are no logical indicators, look at the *context* of the discourse. If it is clear that the author is trying to convince you of some claim, treat it as an argument. If it is unclear, ask yourself whether it is *charitable* to treat it as an argument. If your answer is "yes," treat the discourse as an argument; if "no," do not treat it as an argument.'

In other textbooks, the principle of charity is generally applied to argument reconstruction. For example, according to Soccio and Barry (1992, p. 235), the principle can be applied either to determining missing premises or to judging whether an argument is linked or convergent: 'The principle of charity in rational reconstruction is the rule that whenever two possible interpretations of an argument are equally likely, choose the one that most strengthens the argument.' In this version, the principle is no longer restricted to a deductive framework, and could be applied to any kinds of arguments, whether deductive or not.

Van Eemeren and Grootendorst (1992, p. 81) use a different principle, in order to judge whether an argument is linked (co-ordinative) or convergent (multiple), in borderline cases:

> In borderline cases ... , it is a good strategy to start by analysing the argumentation as multiple if no good reason can be found to opt for coordinative. That way, at least there is a guarantee that the strength of each single argumentation will be duly examined. Because, in following this course of action, we attribute a maximum of argumentative force to each individual single argumentation, this recommended option is called the strategy of *maximally argumentative analysis*.

Van Eemeren and Grootendorst (pp. 81–2) see the principle of maximally argumentative analysis as different from the principle of charity:

> Analysing the structure of argumentation as multiple can, at the same time, be called more and less 'charitable' than analysing it as coordinative. It is more charitable, because in multiple argumentation each individual argument is supposed to have its own independent argumentative force and, in addition, dropping one unacceptable argument does not automatically undermine the whole argumentation. It is less charitable, because in multiple argumentation, in principle, all the individual arguments must be separately conclusive. More important than charity, however, is from a dialectical perspective that the quality of each and every individual argument should be examined critically. In cases that cannot be decided on pragmatic grounds, opting for a maximally argumentative analysis is the best way of ensuring that this will indeed happen.

The conflict between the two principles seems to stem from a difference of purpose in argument reconstruction. Presumably, the principle of charity gives the arguer the benefit of the doubt in order to prevent the committing of fallacies like the tactic of making an argument seem weaker than it really is, and then attacking the weak version. The purpose here is to prevent unjustified, illicit criticisms. In contrast, the purpose of the principle of maximally argumentative analysis is to ensure that no potentially legitimate criticisms are left out.

The problem here is that there seem to be several kinds of principles at work in guiding how we should interpret arguments. Berg (1987, p. 15) lists five such principles. Berg's account of the principle of charity is different from the previous ones. But the main thing to note, for the moment, is the possibility of a multiple set of principles for argument identification.

(a) *The Principle of Loyalty*: Be loyal to the text (written or spoken) – in formulating claims prefer the wording of the text, and in general prefer interpretations supported by the strongest, most direct textual evidence (including what is known of the circumstances under which the text was produced).
(b) *The Principle of Clarity*: Present the argument as clearly as possible – be literal, precise, and terse.
(c) *The Principle of Neutrality*: Formulate the claims in neutral terms.
(d) *The Principle of Charity*: Assume the arguer is not grossly deficient in either general knowledge or logical competence, i.e., that he would not make wildly absurd claims or inferences.
(e) *The Principle of Principled Preference*: The preferability of the favored interpretation over rejected competing interpretations must be justifiable in terms of the principles above; hence, alternative interpretations that cannot be dismissed must not be neglected.

The 'principle of neutrality' is illustrated (p. 15) by the following two phrasings of a claim: (a) 'The murderer who executes a poor defenseless fetus must bear full responsibility for his wicked crime'; and (b) 'An individual who performs an abortion must bear full responsibility for his action.' The 'principle of principled preference' is a way of dealing with conflicts which arise when various of the first four principles support incompatible interpretations of the text. This principle emphasizes that, in general, there may be more than one legitimate interpretation of a text of discourse. Hence, it is important that any interpretation must be treated as a claim that should be backed up by citing evidence from the wording of the text, or from the context of dialogue in the case, in both Berg's view and our own.

Added to the 'principle of loyalty' could be another, called the 'principle of breadth of view,' following the statement of it given by John Veitch, professor of logic and rhetoric in the University of Glasgow (1901, p. 32): 'There is an intellectual fairness and breadth of view characteristic of the trustworthy critic. This weighs a writer's statements, tries to find the meanings of his words, to compare and truthfully conciliate apparently conflicting expressions of them, with a view to elicit the real meaning.' Veitch criticized the bases of John Stuart Mill's attacks on the philosophical views of Sir William Hamilton, calling Mill's methods of attack unfair to the real meanings intended by Hamilton.

What is significant with respect to applying these principles is that we can see the potential for several different principles of argument reconstruction coming into play. And, most significantly, one principle could conflict with another, in a given case. So, the principle of charity should not be seen as an absolute or exclusive rule of argument interpretation. It represents only one factor to be judged against other factors that should also influence how we identify what the argument is, or whether something is an argument, in a given case.

So far, there has been no structured or automated way to apply these principles to a text of discourse in which argumentation exists. But current research is working towards this very objective. Walton and Krabbe (1995) have developed a method of reading off an arguer's commitments, as expressed in a text of discourse in a given case. This work studies the conditions in different types of dialogue exchange of argumentation, under which participants are committed to propositions in virtue of having made certain sorts of moves (like making assertions and asking questions) in a dialogue. Requirements are formulated under which commitments should be held to stand, or may be retracted, in different types of dialogue.

By formulating sets of commitment rules for the insertion and deletion of propositions in an arguer's commitment sets in a dialogue, this research provides a calculative method for implementing the principle of loyalty. This analysis of commitment gives us a way of calculating, relative to the context of dialogue in a given case, whether a given proposition should be judged to be a participant's commitment or not.

Hence, loyalty, as well as these other principles cited by Berg, are not just abstractions to be applied directly to a case. Current research in the pragmatics of argumentation is providing calculative methods that can be applied to profiles of dialogue (shorter sequences of exchanges of a particular type) to determine commitments.

One of the main problems with the principle of charity is that it requires a balanced judgment. The principle is needed to counterbalance the obvious tendency to interpret an opponent's argument as being weaker than it really is, by leaving out needed premises, and so forth. But, on the other hand, it could be an equally bad failure in interpreting an argument to take it as being stronger than it really is, in order to make it an easy target to demolish ('straw man' fallacy). It seems, then, that the principle of charity must aim for a middle way – an argument should be interpreted as being strong enough, but not too strong, to do the job it is evidently supposed to do, as far as we can judge from the evidence given in the text of discourse.

Govier (1987, pp. 151–2) has warned of this need for judgment, arguing that what we need is a moderate, rather than a strong, principle of charity. Using a moderate principle means that we should not accuse someone of committing a fallacy or having made a faulty inference unless there is good evidence from the text of discourse that she has done so. But, on the other hand, it should not require that, if someone leaps to a hasty or faulty conclusion, we should fill in the gaps needed to make the argument correct, thereby overlooking the fault altogether.

But how can we achieve this middle way? What is needed is an evaluation, in a given case, of what burden of proof, what level of support, is required for the given argument. Then the evidence of the text of discourse should be considered in judging whether this level has been successfully met or not. As we saw, such a judgment is crucial in analysing enthymemes, and in determining whether an argument is linked or convergent.

The first question to ask is: 'What kind of reasoning is it supposed to be?' It could be deductive reasoning, inductive reasoning, or presumptive reasoning. An example of presumptive reasoning would occur in an appeal to expertise. Presumptive arguments tend to be weaker than deductive or inductive arguments, and there is something inherently dialectical about them. Nevertheless, in some instances, they can be quite reasonable arguments to shift a burden of proof. In the case of an argument that is based on appeal to expert opinion, for example, we need to examine each case on its own merits, and determine whether the argument on the basis of expert testimony is weak or has been backed up on a plausible, presumptive basis.

As we saw in chapter 5, the key question in judging such a case is what meaning we attach to the idea that the premises must be sufficient to prove the conclusion. We need to judge what level of proof is needed to support the proposition, which in turn depends on the context of dialogue and the type of argument meant to be advanced by the proponent. For example, a plausible argument may require a different type of support, or perhaps less strong support, than an argument that is claimed to be deductively valid.

Every argument in reasonable dialogue has a certain burden of proof. Sometimes the burden of proof is determined by how strong a claim is made by the arguer. If an arguer claims to prove his conclusion beyond doubt, then his burden of proof is heavy. If he merely claims to question, or throw reasonable doubt on, a proposition, his burden of proof is reasonably judged to be lighter to prove his point. However, in some cases, the burden of proof is established by the procedural rules of the game of dialogue. For example, in a criminal trial, the burden of proof is laid upon the prosecutor to prove 'beyond reasonable doubt,' whereas the defender has only to find a weak point in the prosecutor's argument to win his side of the case.

Often, as we have seen, we simply don't know what the burden of proof should be, in a given case. The best we can do, in such instances, is to go by the indicator-words, and by the evidence from the context of dialogue. The best we can do here is to strive for a middle way of not making the argument too strong or weak, in accord with what is known. Here, Berg's principle of principled preference comes into play – we should always make such judgments relative to the known evidence. Furthermore, another principle should be brought into play, what could be called the 'principle of agnosticism': if you don't know, on the given evidence, that an argument is supposed to be of a certain type, or you don't know whether it is linked or convergent, then say so. This is a principle of admitting your ignorance. This principle will be made easier to implement by the new method of diagramming proposed below.

Given these qualifications, the 'principle of charity' can now be re-expressed as follows: whenever two possible interpretations of an argument are equally well supported by the other available evidence from the given text of discourse, choose the one closest to the burden of proof appropriate for the context of dialogue. According to this version of the principle of charity, it is not always the stronger interpretation that is chosen over the weaker. It could be that the weaker interpretation fits the context better.

In cases where the burden of proof is not known, or cannot be judged from the given evidence, even roughly or provisionally, it is best to choose neither possible interpretation, if both are equally well supported by the available evidence. In cases like this, we think it is best to admit it is not known which interpretation is right.

This new version of the principle of charity eliminates the problem of always (perhaps inappropriately) choosing the stronger interpretation of an argument, which could, in some cases, be committing a 'straw man' fallacy.

The principle of charity does have a place in the use of the method of diagramming, because techniques of diagramming, and enthymemes in particular, are based on Gricean presumptions to the effect that the participants are engaging in collaborative dialogue, and may be presumed to know, or take for granted, shared presumptions. But where there is a conflict, the principle of loyalty should take precedence over the principle of charity.

However, exactly how such conflicts should be resolved depends on the type of dialogue the argument is part of. As shown by Walton and Krabbe (1995), what is most important is the use of a commitment-store to build up a repository of an arguer's set of commitments, as known in a given case. It is against this set of propositions that the principle of loyalty should be implemented and tested.

10. Outline of the New Method

The new method of argument diagramming we have recommended can meet the five objections presented above because: (a) it frankly concedes that the

The New Method of Diagramming 217

argument diagram, as applied to a particular case of an argument in a natural language text of discourse, is a conjectural construction; but (b) it builds safeguards into the construction to prevent 'straw man' misrepresentations, and (c) the hypothesis represented by the identification is based on reproducible evidence. Thinking of the argument diagram as a kind of complete model or picture of all that is going on in an argument (admittedly, a dynamic interaction, on our view) is unacceptable. But, in the method recommended, the argument diagram is seen as normative reconstruction, based on explicit assertions and presumptions about non-explicit parts of a given argument, based on an interpretation of the given text of discourse. The method is based in part on hard evidence and calculations but also in part on an attribution of commitment as known or judged in a particular case. Despite this interpretative aspect, the method of argument identification of premises and conclusion is a necessary first step in the analysis and evaluation of any argument.

In preparing to evaluate any argument, your first step should be to try to identify the conclusion being argued for. Once the conclusion is identified, the second step is to identify the premises being advanced in support of the conclusion. In some cases, the premises and conclusion of an argument are clearly stated by indicator-words and can easily be identified. But, in other cases, the question 'What is the argument?' cannot be answered adequately without evaluating evidence from the *corpus* which indicates the context of dialogue.

The method has two basic steps – an abductive step and a commitment step. The abductive step begins with all the explicitly given propositions in the argument (premises and conclusions), and the warrants (inference forms or argumentation schemes) that are appropriate for this type of argument (deductive, inductive, or abductive). Then the second stage of the first step is the use of the method of graphs to fill in the non-explicit premises and conclusions needed to complete the graph. This step identifies the missing premises on a need basis, and is purely mechanical.

The second step is the checking of these needed premises against the commitments of the proponent that can be identified or inferred from what is known of the context of dialogue in the given case. If a needed premise can be justified as one of the arguer's commitments, then it is inserted into the diagram as a non-explicit premise.

The context of dialogue should ideally indicate what the issue of the dialogue is supposed to be. The issue is the pair of propositions set as the conclusion (thesis) of each participant, the proponent and the respondent. But the problem of identifying the conclusion is by no means trivial in many cases, or even of determining that what we are dealing with is really an argument, as opposed to an explanation, and so on. Ideally, the participants in the argument should be clear on what the purpose of their conversation is, and what their dispute (if that is what it is) is supposed to be about. But, of course, in a real case, they may not be, or at any rate the purpose of the argumentation may not be evident to the critic who is supposed to identify a specific argument in that case. In such cases, conditional argument-structure identification may have to be made, and it may be a good idea to have alternative argument diagrams to represent two or more possible interpretations.

Another tool to be applied are argument structures, such as argumentation schemes and deductive argument forms. These determine what the argument needs as missing premises, and determines instances of linked arguments versus convergent ones. In making these determinations of need, the principle of charity comes into play, helping us to judge what type of argument is appropriate for the context. But we have to evaluate on the basis of use, as well as need.

The arguer's position or commitment set is one crucial factor in evaluating which propositions may reasonably be taken to be enthymematic in an argument. Unfairly attributing premises or conclusions to an arguer that do not represent a reasonable interpretation of his or her position in the dialogue can be a case of the 'straw man' fallacy. The error is a very serious one, for it is a necessary goal for any skilled critic to be able to attain enough objectivity to understand a position she is not committed to and does not agree with. Without this ability to identify an arguer's set of commitments, no reasonable basis for evaluating arguments in particular cases would be practically applicable to argumentation in everyday discourse exchanges.

The argument diagram is simply a sketch of the key stages in the argument that is useful to present a visual summary of the flow and direction of the argument. The critics of diagramming are right to say that the diagram itself does not model everything that goes on during an argument.

Throughout this book, we have found that each individual argument we have encountered is to some extent unique, and must be evaluated on its own merits. In each case, it is necessary to examine carefully the text of discourse of the argument, and then to study the evidence to identify the argument in that particular case as a particular sequence of propositions. Although we set forth general guidelines for identification, each argument must be identified as an individual case. This orientation towards a case-study method of evaluation is inevitable in practical argument analysis, precisely because the objective of such analysis is the evaluation of real arguments, as they occur in daily transactions in natural language.

Applying the method of diagramming is, therefore, in some (but not all) respects, different from traditional logical theory of the formal sort. The goal of argument diagramming is the applied task of identifying the premises and conclusions in each case of argument as it occurs and in the required detail specific to each case. Argument diagramming is best seen as not purely descriptive in nature, but as partly normative. It applies a normative model of reasoned dialogue to the specific case.

Identifying an argument as a possible object of criticism should always begin by identifying the reasoning in it, and in particular, by identifying three items.

1 Conclusion
2 Premises
3 Burden of Proof

But, in approaching any particular argument, much depends on how much given discourse is presented as the *corpus* for analysis or the focus of the criticism. The argument may be only a sentence or two, and the context of dialogue may be implicit. Or the argument could be a lengthy paragraph or more, which may contain many premises and more than one conclusion. Where to start depends on how much information is given and in what form. Thus, an argument diagram is best seen as a reconstruction of a sequence of reasoning based on a given *corpus*. To the extent that the *corpus* is incomplete, ambiguous, obscure, or even incoherent, the diagram will reflect the same uncertainties and incompleteness. The verbal account of how the diagram relates to the evidence from the *corpus* should play an important role in cases of this sort.

7

Enthymemes

Perhaps the biggest single problem of argument diagramming is that so many arguments in natural discourse are incomplete, in the sense that they have premises or conclusions that are not explicitly stated. This is the so-called problem of enthymemes. In logic textbooks, enthymemes are variously called arguments with 'missing premises,' 'unstated premises,' 'suppressed premises,' 'unexpressed premises,' and 'implicit premises.' Each of these terms appears to mean something different. The more neutral term 'non-explicit premises' (enthymemes, as we will see, are taken to include arguments with non-explicit conclusions as well) is generally used here.

It is generally known that enthymemes pose a difficult problem, for various reasons explored in this chapter. But it is a problem that cannot be avoided if we wish to apply logic to evaluate argumentation as it occurs in natural language settings. For, in order to evaluate an argument using some logical standard or structure, you first have to identify what the premises and conclusion are. If you arbitrarily 'designate' these propositions when evaluating a given argument, then of course there is no guarantee you are really evaluating that given argument, and not some other one.

There might be all kinds of reasons for filling out an argument, by filling in non-explicit premises or conclusions. How one should properly go about such a task depends very much on the purpose that one has in engaging in it. It might sometimes be the case that the proponent of the argument is present to answer questions to resolve the problem of how the premises should be made explicit. In such a case, for example, the proponent and respondent could be engaging in a critical discussion, and the purpose of making the missing premises more explicit could be to resolve the conflict of opinions posed in the discussion.

Gilbert (1991) has proposed a mechanism for filling in non-explicit premises in a situation of precisely this type. Basically the mechanism of the 'enthymeme buster' is for the respondent to question the proponent by posing a series of potential counter-examples, in order to secure the proponent's agreement on exactly what she meant to say with respect to the unstated premise.

Gilbert's method is indeed a good one. In fact, it could be said that it represents the optimal method of filling in non-explicit premises. If the proponent of the argument in question is present, and one can engage in continued dialogue with that person, then the best method of completing enthymemes is to actually ask that person, 'Is this what you meant to say as your premise?' This is the ideal or optimal method of completing enthymemes.

However, in practical terms, the ideal method is very often not (at least, directly) applicable. This is really the crux of the problem. Generally, when one is engaged in attempting to provide an evaluation of an argument in a given, specific case, it is from the basis of a written text of some sort, and the proponent of the argument is not present to verify or rebut any assumptions one might make in interpreting what the argument is. In judging what the premises and conclusion should be taken to be, typically in the kinds of cases we routinely deal with in informal-logic argument diagramming, we do not have the luxury of actually consulting with the proponent. Instead, we must operate on the basis of making conjectures or hypotheses, based on the text of what was said. Such an evidential basis will generally be incomplete, making any interpretation or evaluation of an argument on this basis conditional in nature.

This process of interpretation of a text of natural language discourse in a given case makes any logician nervous, because it is not purely a calculative process. Even worse, misinterpretation, in the form of the 'straw man' fallacy, becomes a very real possibility. But the alternative to attempting an interpretation is that evaluation of the argument may not be possible. For, in many cases, before we can make any useful evaluation of an argument, we have to have some account of what the premises and conclusion are, even if it is only provisional. In practice, this means we have to go beyond Gilbert's method, and extend the process of completing enthymemes to less than ideal situations.

1. The Tradition of the Textbooks

In the logic textbooks, enthymemes have traditionally, at least very often, been treated under the heading 'syllogistic logic.' The use of enthymemes functions as a way of extending the application of syllogistic logic to cases of arguments that can be treated as a syllogism, once an unstated (non-explicit) premise is filled in.

222   Argument Structure

This tradition was already well established in the Middle Ages. For example, in Peter of Spain's *Tractatus* (*circa* 1270), we find the statement 'It is important to know that every enthymeme must be reduced to a syllogism' (Peter of Spain, 1988, p. 227). The definition of an enthymeme given by Peter is: an incomplete syllogism in which some proposition is not asserted in advance, but is tacitly understood (p. 227):

> An enthymeme is an incomplete syllogism, that is, discourse in which the hurried conclusion is inferred from propositions that are not all asserted in advance. For example, 'Every animal is running; therefore, every man is running.' For in that argumentation, the proposition 'Every man is an animal' is tacitly understood; and it is not added to the argumentation (for if it were added [the argumentation] would be a complete syllogism).

Curiously, however, Peter also held that syllogistic logic is not by itself everything that makes up an enthymeme. According to Kretzmann and Stump (1988, p. 216), Peter's doctrine of the enthymeme attempted to combine syllogistic logic with Aristotelian topics. Peter held that a topical argument is an enthymeme, and that the function of the topic is to confirm the (syllogistic) validity of the enthymeme. Perhaps we could say, in Toulmin's (1958) terms, that the topic functions as a kind of warrant or backing yielding a premise upon which the syllogism is based (in Peter's theory).

A version of this doctrine of the enthymeme as an incomplete syllogism appears in the *Port-Royal Logic*. In Arnauld's *The Art of Thinking* (1662), we find an enthymeme defined as an argument in which only one premise is expressed. And such an argument, we are told, may be considered a kind of incomplete syllogism (1964, p. 177): 'The two premisses of a syllogism are not always expressed, for often the expression of but one premiss leads the mind to the other. An argument in which only one premiss is expressed is called an enthymeme. An enthymeme might be considered as an imperfectly expressed syllogism, since the conclusion is reached by the mind's entertaining a complete syllogism.' It seems, then, that the doctrine of the enthymeme as an incomplete syllogism was fairly well established in logic, long before the modern textbooks took it up.

Many of the modern textbooks have followed this tradition of treating enthymemes under the topic of syllogisms, and many of these in fact define an enthymeme as a syllogism with an omitted premise. Carney and Scheer (1964, p. 270) define an enthymeme as 'a syllogism with a premise or the conclusion left out of the explicit statement of the argument.' However, they add (p. 271) that there are 'many forms of argument, other than the syllogism, which are also relatively simple and which are often abbreviated in speech.' Presumably, however, according to their definition, these other abbreviated forms of argument are not classified as enthymemes.

Hyslop (1899, p. 133) also defined an enthymeme as 'an incomplete syllogism in which one of the premises, or the conclusion, may be omitted.' Adams (1954, p. 266) defines an enthymeme as 'an elliptical syllogism, one with a premise or conclusion suppressed but understood.' Castell (1935, p. 145) also defines an enthymeme as a syllogism 'in which one or more propositions have been omitted.' Cohen and Nagel (1934, p. 78) also define an enthymeme as an 'incompletely stated' syllogism. Hurley (1991, p. 270) defines an enthymeme as 'an argument that is expressible as a categorical syllogism but that is missing a premise or a conclusion.' Even Whately (1859, p. 125) defined an enthymeme as 'a syllogism with one premise suppressed,' but he mentioned in a footnote (p. 125) that this employment of the word is different from that of Aristotle.

According to the traditional treatment of enthymemes as incomplete syllogisms, there were said to be three orders of enthymemes (see, for example, Boyce-Gibson, 1908, p. 231). In an enthymeme of the *first order*, the major premise is omitted. In an enthymeme of the *second order*, the minor premise is omitted. In an enthymeme of the *third order*, the conclusion is omitted. The first account found by the author of this threefold classification is that in Sir William Hamilton's *Lectures on Logic* (1874, p. 392), quoted directly below, with case numbers added.

THE EXPLICIT SYLLOGISM

[*Case 7.1*]
Every liar is a coward;
Caius is a liar;
Therefore, Caius is a coward.

I. ENTHYMEME OF THE FIRST ORDER – (the Sumption understood).
[*Case 7.2*]
Caius is a liar;
Therefore, Caius is a coward.

II. ENTHYMEME OF THE SECOND ORDER – (the Subsumption understood).
[*Case 7.3*]
Every liar is a coward;
Therefore, Caius is a coward.

III. ENTHYMEME OF THE THIRD ORDER – (the Conclusion understood).
[*Case 7.4*]
Every liar is a coward;
And Caius is a liar.

This threefold classification found its way into many subsequent logic textbooks, and is still widely used in current texts.

Another extension of syllogistic theory was to link two syllogisms together, so the conclusion of one could also function as a premise of another one. A chain of syllogisms called a 'sorites' argument could be formed by this means. Where some of the component syllogisms in such a chain are enthymemes, the argument is called an 'epicheirema.'

A succinct explanation of the concept of an epicheirema is given by Joseph (1916, p. 352):

> A syllogism, whether expressed in full or as an enthymeme, is a single act of inference; it may be analyzed into premisses and conclusion, but not into parts which are themselves acts of inference. The premisses may, however, be themselves in turn conclusions reached by other acts of inference; and the conclusion may itself serve as premiss to a further act of inference. A syllogism proving one of the premisses of another syllogism is called, in relation to that, a *prosyllogism*: and a syllogism using as a premiss the conclusion of another is called, in relation to it an *episyllogism*; where the prosyllogism is expressed in the form of an enthymeme, the whole argument is sometimes called an *epicheirema*.

A good example, given by Joseph (p. 353), contains both a prosyllogism and an episyllogism, and the prosyllogism is also an epicheirema.

Case 7.5
Those who have no occupation have nothing to interest themselves in, and therefore are unhappy; for men with nothing in which to interest themselves are always unhappy, since happiness depends on the success with which we advance the objects in which we are interested; and so wealth is no guarantee of happiness.

Joseph (p. 353) provides the following analysis:

Here the central syllogism is:
All who have nothing in which to interest themselves are unhappy.
Those who have no occupation have nothing in which to interest themselves.
∴ Those who have no occupation are unhappy.

The major premiss is proved by a prosyllogism to this effect:
Happy men are those who succeed in advancing objects in which they are interested.
Men who have nothing in which to interest themselves do not succeed in advancing any object in which they are interested.
∴Men who have nothing in which to interest themselves are not happy.

And an episyllogism is added thus:
Those who have no occupation are unhappy.
Rich men may have no occupation.
∴Rich men may be unhappy.

From Joseph's treatment of this case, one can get a good idea of how the traditional logic textbooks effectively used the simple machinery of syllogistic logic to analyse longer, extended sequences of arguments. They reconstructed argumentation as chains of syllogism (*sorites* arguments), putting in non-explicit premises and conclusions to fill the gaps required to make an explicit syllogism at each stage.

It is not hard to see how this technique was an attractive way for the textbook authors to apply their basic syllogistic logic to extended sequences of argumentation characteristic of reasoning in a natural setting. The categorical syllogism itself, as a structure of argument with only two premises and a single conclusion, is highly artificial.[1] Not all arguments, for example, contain exactly two premises. Therefore, the devices of enthymeme and sorites made it possible for syllogistic logic to be used as a much more widely applicable normative structure for evaluating argumentation in natural language.

As deductive logics other than syllogistic logic began to be included in textbooks, the concept of the enthymeme was often broadened. Quine (1972, p. 169) commented on this evolution by saying logic has 'so far outstripped the syllogism' that an enthymeme can be taken to refer to any logical inference with a tacit premise.

Some of the textbooks have, accordingly, adopted a more liberal definition of enthymeme that applies to deductive arguments generally, and not just to syllogisms. Barker (1965, p. 276) sees this wider definition as a more modern development:

In ordinary discourse a person often presents a deductive argument without bothering to make explicit what all his premises are. Sometimes he has a premise fairly definitely in mind but does not bother to state it because it is common knowledge, too obvious to be worth mentioning. An argument is called an *enthymeme* if one or more of its premises are unstated. Originally the term 'enthymeme' was restricted to syllogism. Nowadays the term is extended to deductive arguments of any type having unstated premises.

Schwartz (1980, p. 146), for example, follows this use of deductive validity as a criterion for the enthymeme. Schwartz (pp. 146–7) recommends analysing arguments in natural language by determining invalidity, and then filling in the missing premises that are plausible and attributable to the author, and make the argument valid.

Rescher (1964) seems inclined to have it both ways. In the part on syllogisms, he defines an enthymeme as 'an argument that can become a categorical syllogism with the addition of one or more statements (as premise or conclusion).' But earlier (p. 65) he had defined an enthymeme as 'a deductive argument that is incomplete as it stands but is capable of being corrected.' This seems to combine both the traditional syllogistic and the more liberal deductive conceptions.[2]

Some textbooks have now taken an even more liberal approach of not restricting enthymemes to deductive arguments at all. Copi and Cohen (1990, p. 231) give the following definition: 'An argument that is stated incompletely, part being "understood" or only "in the mind" is called an enthymeme.' Soccio and Barry (1992, p. 228) also define an enthymeme broadly as 'an argument in which a premise or conclusion is suppressed or missing.' Yanal (1988, p. 237) defines an enthymeme as 'an argument with an unexpressed premise,' making no restriction that the argument must be deductive.

All these accounts are quite broad in that, not only do they not restrict enthymemes to syllogistic arguments, they do not even restrict them to being arguments that (when filled out) are deductively valid. Below, we will argue that restricting enthymemes to deductively valid arguments is not, on balance, a good thing. Yet it is not hard to see how this development occurred, historically, given the dominance of deductive logic (and Aristotelian syllogistic, especially, before the advent of modern symbolic logic) in the logic curriculum. The founder of logic, who first gave us the concept of enthymeme, would probably, however, not have anticipated this development of his idea along the lines it subsequently took in the history of his subject.

2. The Aristotelian Enthymeme

It may come as quite a surprise to see that Aristotle did not use the term 'enthymeme' (*enthymema*) to mean an argument (or, in particular, a syllogism) with a non-explicit premise. Instead, he defined an enthymeme (*Prior Analy-*

tics, 70 a 12) as 'a syllogism from probabilities or signs.' A reconstruction of one example he gives (70 a 15) is the following argument.:

Case 7.6
Women who have milk are pregnant.
This woman has milk.
Therefore, this woman is pregnant.

Aristotle classified this type of argument as an argument from sign. The major premise can be expressed as based on the sign relation; that is, it can be expressed as the proposition 'A woman's having milk is a sign of her being pregnant.'

The puzzling question here is whether or not the major premise in an enthymeme such as the argument in case 7.6 is a universal proposition. Does the major premise express the first or the second proposition below?

1. All women who have milk (without exception) are pregnant.
2. Generally women who have milk (subject to exception, in some cases) are pregnant.

It seems that Aristotle took the major premise in case 7.6 the first way,[3] but he clearly allowed for the major premise of enthymemes to be taken in the second way, in other cases.

Another example of an enthymeme given by Aristotle (*Prior Analytics*, 70 a 27) bears this out.

Case 7.7
Those who love honour are high-minded.
Pittacus loves honour.
Therefore, Pittacus is high-minded.

In such a case, Aristotle makes it clear (70 a 32) that the major premise is not (strictly) universal, and that, therefore, the syllogism can be refuted by the existence of contrary cases. In other words, the major premise expresses the proposition that a person's loving honour is a sign (but not a necessary sign) of his being high-minded; that is, there do exist (contrary to the general rule) cases of persons who love honour but are not high-minded.

Curiously enough, then, it appears that Aristotle is, to a great extent (but not wholly), taking a non-deductivist view. But there remain many perplexing questions on how to interpret Aristotle's conception of enthymeme. Bitzer

(1959) has stressed that, although some commentators have characterized Aristotelian enthymemes as being deductively invalid arguments based on probabilities, it is nevertheless clear that some enthymemes were thought by Aristotle to have necessary (as opposed to probable) premises. Thus, Bitzer concludes that probability, or, at any rate, non-necessity, is not an essential characteristic of the Aristotelian enthymeme. He does, however, concede that 'it is no doubt true that most enthymemes are probable, formally deficient and concrete' (p. 404). And even this is enough to differentiate Aristotle's concept of the enthymeme from the deductivist interpretation taken up and held in place for so many centuries by the commentators and textbooks.

One problem is that the concept of a 'necessary sign,' as supposedly exemplified by case 7.6, is somewhat puzzling. But without going into the historical question of what Aristotle might have really meant in any detailed examination, we can see that the notion of a non-deductive, probabilistic (or better presumptive and plausible) type of argumentation was an important feature of the enthymeme in the Aristotelian conception.

The doctrine of enthymemes was especially important to Aristotle's *Rhetoric*, because he saw enthymematic argument as powerful and common means of persuasion in deliberation (*Rhetoric*, I.II.11). In the *Rhetoric* (I.II.13), Aristotle saw the enthymeme as sometimes being a strict, deductively valid type of argument from sign, based on a universal major premise, but in other cases as being 'concerned with things which may, generally speaking, be other than they are ...' This doctrine is expressed very clearly in a passage in the *Rhetoric* (I.II.14) that is worth quoting in full:

> But since few of the propositions of the rhetorical syllogism are necessary, for most of the things which we judge and examine can be other than they are, human actions, which are the subject of our deliberation and examination, being all of such a character and, generally speaking, none of them necessary; since, further, facts which only generally happen or are merely possible can only be demonstrated by other facts of the same kind, and necessary facts by necessary propositions (and that this is so is clear from the *Analytics*), it is evident that the materials from which enthymemes are derived will be sometimes necessary, but for the most part only generally true; and these materials being probabilities and signs, it follows that these two elements must correspond to these two kinds of propositions, each to each. For that which is probable is that which generally happens, not however unreservedly, as some define it, but that which is concerned with things that may be other than they are, being so related to that in regard to which it is probable as the universal to the particular.[4]

Aristotle's real conception of the enthymeme as a kind of argument is not widely known, and is quite surprising, with quite radical implications for informal logic, in two respects particularly.

One is that Aristotle clearly meant to say that not all syllogistic argumentation is deductive in nature. He also allowed for non-strict syllogistic reasoning based on 'signs and probabilities.' What he meant by 'probability' was not the same thing that we (most likely) take the word to mean, after the advent of statistics as a science. According to Grimaldi (1953, p. 90), *eikos* is not, for Aristotle, what generally happens in the sense of probability or chance. *Eikos* has to do with real and true opinions, for Aristotle, but not with scientific knowledge, writes Grimaldi (p. 91). *Eikos* is 'concerned with what is,' and what has 'a certain stability' (p. 91). Grimaldi quotes Aristotle's definition of *eikos* (p. 89), given in the *Rhetoric* (1357 a 34), as 'that which generally happens, not simply and unreservedly; rather it is that which usually prevails in the case of things which can be otherwise.' According to this interpretation, Grimaldi (p. 92) thinks that what makes reasoning from *eikota* distinctive is that it is always open to objection. (See also McBurney [1936b, p. 492], who quotes the *Rhetoric* (1402b) in support of the view that enthymemes based on *eikota* are 'always open to refutation.')

It seems fair to conclude from this that Aristotle very much appeared to have default reasoning in mind, that is, arguments based on a major premise that is not strictly universal, not based on numerical calculation of probabilities in the modern sense, but on generally accepted presumptions subject to qualifications and exceptions, as will be shown further in section 3, below.

Another surprising aspect of Aristotle's doctrine of the enthymeme is that it is quite different from the meaning of this term now standard in logic textbooks, where it is taken to refer to arguments (particularly syllogisms taken to be deductively valid) with non-explicit premises.

One can see how this misinterpretation of Aristotle easily took place, however. Just before the passage in the *Rhetoric* quoted above, Aristotle wrote that the enthymeme is a kind of syllogism often deduced from fewer premises than the regular syllogism (I.II.13), and used the following example to illustrate his point:

Case 7.8
For instance, to prove that Dorieus was the victor in a contest at which the prize was a crown, it is enough to say that he won a victory at the Olympic games; there is no need to add that the prize at the Olympic games is a crown, for everybody knows it.[5]

230   Argument Structure

This example has often been used to support the non-Aristotelian meaning of enthymeme as an argument with a missing premise, and indeed it is a good example of it, using a non-explicit premise based on general knowledge of the arguer and respondents.

Sir William Hamilton (1861, p. 153) noted: 'Aristotle's meaning has been almost universally mistaken' in the 'vulgar doctrine' that the enthymeme is a species of syllogism with one of its premises 'not expressed, but understood.' Contrary to this vulgar misinterpretation, Hamilton (p. 153) claimed, correctly, that Aristotle defined the enthymeme as a species of syllogistic reasoning based on 'signs and likelihoods.'

Apparently, this corruption of Aristotle's doctrine of the enthymeme started from the earliest commentators. Hamilton (pp. 154–7) writes that the word *enthymeme* in its modern meaning of a 'syllogism with one expressed premise' was used by 'the oldest commentators on Aristotle' (p. 155). According to Hamilton (pp. 155–6), this 'appears clearly' from Sextus Empiricus, all the later Greek logicians, and Boethius. (See also the remarks in McBurney [1936a, pp. 68–71] on the history of the enthymeme after Aristotle.)

Hamilton added that, during his time, 'there seems not to be present a logic author ... who is even aware of [this] controversy' about the meaning of the enthymeme. This could still be truly said, even today, apart from a few notable exceptions.

3. The Question of Terminology

Finding out that the usual meaning of the word *enthymeme* found in the logic textbooks is based on a misinterpretation of Aristotle's original use of this term poses a terminological problem. Should we go back to the original Aristotelian meaning, or stick with the corrupted one, given that it is now so well established?

One of the few textbooks to be clearly aware of this problem (Joseph, 1916) went along with the established meaning, but put in a long footnote (pp. 351–2) explaining the Aristotelian meaning of 'enthymeme.' Joseph (p. 351) explains very clearly that Aristotle took 'enthymeme' to refer to a generalization that is open to exceptions, and, therefore, is not universally true (like the A-proposition in syllogistic). This can take the form of argument from sign, or of what Aristotle called *eikos,* meaning 'likely, probable, or reasonable' (1968, p. 484). Joseph (p. 351) explains this concept clearly: 'Roughly speaking, *eikos* is a general proposition true only for the most part, such as that *Raw foods are unwholesome*; in applying this to prove the unwholesomeness of some particular article of diet, we are open to the objection that the article in question may form an exception to the rule; but in practice we are often compelled to argue from such probable premisses.' Joseph goes on to add that argument from sign (*semeion*) is a kind of argumentation where one particular fact is taken as a sign or indicator of the existence of another. A typical example (*Rhetoric* 1357 b 19) would be to infer from the existence of a symptom in a particular patient the conclusion that the patient has a particular disease or condition.

Nowadays, the general type of reasoning Aristotle called the 'enthymeme' would be called 'default', 'defeasible', or 'plausible' reasoning (Rescher, 1976; Reiter, 1987), or plausible argument (Walton, 1992b). Since this type of argumentation is now well recognized (especially in computer science) as a distinctive type of reasoning in its own right, it would be inappropriate to suggest it now be called 'enthymematic' reasoning. Better, we think, to follow Joseph's suggested course of giving in to the established (if somewhat confused) traditional terminology, while correcting the historical corruption along the way.

Several traditional textbooks support the 'missing proposition' account of the enthymeme by claiming that the term is derived from the two Greek words *en* (in) and *thymos* (mind). Castell (1935, p. 145) makes the comment that 'the word *enthymeme* is derived from two Greek words meaning *in the mind*. The missing proposition, deliberately suppressed or merely unformulated, is thus *in the mind* as contrasted with the rest which is expressed.' Jevons (1878, p. 153) wrote that the term 'enthymeme' is 'often supposed to be derived from two Greek words (*en* and *thymos*) so as to signify that some knowledge is held by the mind and is supplied in the form of a *tacit*, that is a silent or understood premise.' This derivation of the word is taken to support the traditional conception of an enthymeme as an argument with a non-explicit premise.

Some modern textbooks (Kilgore, 1968, see p. 85; Copi and Cohen, 1990, see p. 231) simply assert that 'enthymeme' means 'in the mind' without making mention of any Greek words or derivations specifically. This is potentially confusing, none the less, and is a very misleading account of the Greek origins of the concept.

What does *enthymema* really mean, as used by Aristotle? As noted above, the *Prior Analytics* definition (70 a 11) is a 'syllogism from probabilities or signs' (*syllogismos ex eikoton e semeion*). But according to the *Greek-English Lexicon* (Glare, 1968, p. 567), *enthymema* generally means 'thought, piece of reasoning, or argument,' and can also mean 'consideration or reflection.' Latta and Mac-Beath (1956, p. 215) interpret Aristotle to use the word in this sense.

> The word *enthymema* literally means 'a consideration,' as distinct from a logical demonstration. This is the sense in which Aristotle used it. He recognized that there are many arguments which we constantly employ and which are good

enough for practical purposes, good enough within certain ill-defined limits, but which at once appear as invalid if we express them in strict syllogistic form. Syllogism he regarded as rather an ideal to which a perfect argument ought to conform than a statement of the form which every argument that has any worth must take. Arguments that are good enough so far as they go without being absolutely or unconditionally valid he calls rhetorical. Such arguments are sufficient in an ordinary case to convince us, although they are not ideally perfect demonstrations. Those of the rhetorical arguments that take the syllogistic form Aristotle called enthymemes. He distinguished two main kinds: (a) Arguments based on probable statements, i.e. statements true on the whole but not universally true [and] ... (b) Arguments based on a sign or symptom, i.e. a fact which indicates the existence of some other fact.

According to this interpretation, there are two contrasting types of reasoning. One is the deductively valid type, called the 'syllogism', in which the major premise can take the form 'All F are G' for terms F and G, where 'all' means 'absolutely all,' that is, admitting of no exceptions. The other is the enthymeme, which is (at least in many instances, and even typically) not a deductively valid type of argument. The major premise in enthymematic reasoning takes the form 'Generally F are G,' subject to exceptions. Enthymematic generalizations are *defeasible*, or subject to exceptions, and are *nonmonotonic* in the kind of reasoning they support, meaning that the reasoning can cease to be valid (or presumptively correct) if new information comes to be known. This defeasible type of conditional has been the subject of recent investigations by Rescher (1977, p. 30), Reiter (1987), and Walton (1992b, pp. 69–72).

The confusion or misidentification of these two distinctive types of reasoning has also been related to the *secundum quid* fallacy (the fallacy of neglect of qualifications, sometimes also called 'hasty generalization.' [Walton, 1992b, pp. 72–80].[6] The key to the analysis of this fallacy is the distinction between a strict generalization, admitting of no exceptions, and a defeasible, presumptive type of generalization that is inherently non-strict in that it admits of exceptions in some instances.

Curiously, this notion of defeasible, presumptive reasoning based on 'probabilities and signs' (in Aristotle's terms, *eikos* and *semeion*) turns out to be the key idea in the analysis of enthymemes put forward below. But before proceeding to this analysis, we need to look at a range of examples of the typical kinds of enthymematic arguments encountered in conversational argumentation. This will give us a basis of casework to build on, before going on to theorize on what 'enthymeme' should really mean.

Further discussions of the relationship of the present-day meaning of 'enthymeme' to the original Aristotelian idea can be found in works by Madden (1952) and Lanigan (1974).

4. Types of Basis for the Enthymeme

One basis for the enthymeme is a premise that does not need to be stated explicitly because it is general knowledge shared by the speaker and hearer. A classic case illustrates this point:

Case 7.9
All men are mortal.
Therefore, Socrates is mortal.

The missing premise 'Socrates is a man' is an item of general (historical) knowledge which one would generally expect an educated, Western audience to know. When supplied, it makes the argument deductively valid. In this case, the premise could easily have been put in. But since, presumably, everybody knows it or accepts it as true, and nobody would likely dispute it, the argument does not suffer by its omission.

Quine (1972, p. 169) defines an enthymeme as 'a logical inference in which one or more of the premises are omitted from mention on the ground that their truth is common knowledge and goes without saying.' However, in some cases, a non-explicit premise is not a proposition that is known to be true. Instead, it is a controversial proposition that presumably is a commitment of the proponent, even though it may not be acceptable to many other people, including the respondent. Consider the following argument, part of a dispute on the ethics of abortion:

Case 7.10
Anything that is not a person has no rights.
Therefore, if a woman chooses to have an abortion, she violates nobody's rights.

Presumably, the non-explicit, additional premise appealed to by this argument is the proposition 'A foetus is not a person.' What suggests this proposition as a non-explicit premise is the explicit premise given, presumably used in order to rebut potential counter-argumentation based on the idea that the foetus may have some rights that could be claimed to be violated by an abortion.

The proposition 'The foetus is not a person' is very controversial, and could not be said to be something known to be true. But, presumably, it does represent a commitment of the proponent of the argument in this particular case.

234   Argument Structure

Another basis for the enthymeme is custom, habit, or a normal way of doing something known to the speaker and hearer, but which can be inferred to be such by the wider audience:

Case 7.11
Wayne's jeep is not in the driveway.
Therefore, Wayne is not home.

Here, presumably both the speaker and the hearer know that Wayne's jeep is his normal mode of transport, so that, if it is not parked (as it usually is, when Wayne is at home) in the driveway, we may presume that Wayne is not home. But when some person who has no knowledge of Wayne and his habits sees the argument in case 7.11, she quickly presumes that it is implied that the jeep is Wayne's normal method of transport, and that therefore its not being in the driveway is being taken as a sign that Wayne is not home.

In some cases, a non-explicit premise supplies a conceptual link that holds a chain of argumentation together. Often, the non-explicit premise implies that the speaker is defining a key term in her argument in a certain way.

The following argument is cited as an enthymeme by Gough and Tindale (1985, p. 101):

Case 7.12
Abortion is not murder. The soul does not enter the body until the first breath is taken. Up to this point, the foetus is a biological entity only.[7]

According to Gough and Tindale (p. 101), the argument in this case can be analysed as follows, revealing a conclusion (*C*), two explicit premises (*P1* and *P2*), and one hidden premise (*HP*).

- *C*:   Abortion is not murder.
- *P1*: The soul enters the body with the first breath.
- *P2*: Until such time the foetus is a biological entity.
- *HP*: Only ensouled entities can be murdered.

It seems that, in this case, the non-explicit or 'hidden' premise is a universal claim based on what we take to be the way that the arguer presumably would choose to define the term 'murder.' Presumably, the arguer would take this term to apply only to entities that have souls.

In some cases, enthymemes occur in practical reasoning used in an advice-giving dialogue. The following argument was used by a mother to try to get her young son to eat his vegetables:

Case 7.13
You wanna grow up to be big and strong? Eat your vegetables!

This argumentation could be paraphrased as a sequence of practical reasoning, revealing the use of a non-explicit premise, as follows:

If you don't eat your vegetables, you won't grow up to be big and strong.
You want to grow up to be big and strong.
Therefore, you should eat your vegetables.

The conclusion is a practical (prudential) should-statement associated with the imperative 'Eat your vegetables!' The second premise states a goal, attributed to the respondent, and explicitly stated in case 7.13. The first premise, a non-explicit premise, links the goal to a necessary means of achieving it.

5. Innuendo and Implicature

Another basis for the enthymeme is innuendo, where the conclusion of an argument is not explicitly asserted, but only suggested by means of implicature. Rescher (1964, p. 161) indicated this basis for the enthymeme when he contrasted two kinds of situations where enthymemes commonly occur:

1. when one of the premisses of a syllogism is omitted because it is regarded by the writer (or speaker) as so obvious that it need not be stated
2. when the conclusion of a syllogism is omitted either because it is regarded as obvious by the writer (or speaker), or because he is aiming at a rhetorical effect by letting his audience 'draw its own conclusions'

This use of rhetorical effect by letting the audience or reader draw the conclusion could be illustrated by the following advertisement:

Case 7.14
The bigger the burger, the better the burger.
The burgers are bigger at Burger King.

The non-explicit conclusion is that the burgers are better at Burger King.

236 Argument Structure

Another use of the non-explicit-conclusion type of enthymeme is the kind of case where the speaker wants to achieve plausible deniability of commitment by not actually stating the conclusion of her argument. For example, suppose that the leadership issue is being debated in a political caucus. One party member says, 'What about Smith? She is a good candidate for leader of the party.' The respondent replies as follows:

Case 7.15
Smith has been low in the polls lately.

Here, presumably, the conclusion to be drawn is that Smith would not be a good candidate for leader. Perhaps also the enthymematic basis for this conclusion is the generalization that anyone who is low in the polls is unpopular, and therefore would not be likely to do well in election campaigning for the party.

At any rate, the main point of putting the argument in the abbreviated way of case 7.15 is that the speaker has not actually said, 'Smith is not a good candidate for leader' in so many words. Later, if challenged by Smith or anyone else, the speaker can say, 'I never actually said you would not be a good leader for the party.' This plausible deniability could obviously have some value in future political negotiations.

Innuendo is the basis of fallacies, in many cases. For example, *ad hominem* attacks are often so powerful, even when based on little or no real evidence, because they are put forward on the basis of innuendo. And the power of innuendo to create doubts and misgivings in a balance of considerations situation can be considerable. However, innuendo is not itself a fallacy, or an inherently fallacious type of argumentation.

Innuendo is a contextual feature of argumentation, driven by the context of conversation in which an argument is put forward. It arises, not by deductive logical implication of one proposition by another, but by what Grice (1975) called 'implicature.' In implicature, one proposition is suggested as a presumption by the occurrence of another proposition in a context of conversation.[8]

In some cases, the basis of an enthymeme is the contribution of an utterance to a conversation, so that what is unstated explicitly arises from the context of a dialogue. A case of this sort is given by Grice (1975, p. 70):

Case 7.16
A: Smith doesn't seem to have a girl friend these days.
B: He has been paying a lot of visits to New York lately.

According to Grice (p. 70), in this case, *B* implicates that Smith has, or may have, a girlfriend in New York. This implicature arises from Grice's 'maxim of relation' (p. 68), which requires a speaker's 'contribution to be appropriate to immediate needs' at a given stage of a conversation. Here we can see that B is drawing the non-explicit conclusion that Smith has or may have a girlfriend in New York, in opposition to the claim made by A at the previous move in the dialogue. We know that what B explicitly says, 'Smith has been paying a lot of visits to New York lately,' is put forward to be used in the conversation as evidence, as a premise, from which one can draw or support the conclusion that Smith may have a girlfriend in New York.

Thus, in this case, we are able to extract the non-explicit conclusion by seeing that it stands in a relation of opposition or conflict with the assertion by another speaker in the dialogue. To determine the enthymeme, we have to look to the previous utterances made *by the other party* in a dialogue of which the speaker's assertion is a part. It is not the speaker's commitments, at least alone, that furnish the basis of the enthymeme in this kind of case. This is a contextual type of enthymeme which has its basis in the conversation exchange with two parties collaboratively taking part. Perhaps we could call this kind of enthymeme the 'conversational context' type. It is argued below that all enthymemes are of this type, fundamentally, as opposed to being deductively invalid arguments that need to be completed as deductively valid, by filling in the missing propositions sufficient for validity.

6. The Dangers of Deductivism

Thomas (1981, p. 171) concedes that, often, arguments are not deductively valid, even when all the implicit additional assumptions have been inserted in to the argument diagram. Even so, Thomas (pp. 171-3) recommends that his students learn the technique of inserting whatever assumptions are sufficient to make an argument deductively valid, for any given argument.

Thus, Thomas teaches his students two separate techniques for enthymemes. The first, carried out in his earlier sections (before p. 171), is to confine the diagram to premises and conclusions that were believed or intended by the arguer. The second, carried out after the student has learned the first technique, is to '*not* concern ourselves with accurate interpretations of the author,' and instead put in whatever missing assumptions are needed to make the argument deductively valid. Thomas (p. 171) calls this second technique 'supplying an argument's *formal* suppressed assumptions.'

It is interesting to see that Thomas clearly sees the second technique as a kind of formal exercise, and that he recognizes, in using the first technique, that, in some cases, an enthymeme does not turn out to be a deductively valid argument once all the missing premises or conclusions are filled in. But, even so, one wonders about the dangers inherent in teaching students the second technique. For any argument, no matter how inadequately supported the conclusion, or even if it is fallacious, can be made valid by the addition of some premises or other. Any invalid argument can automatically be made valid by, for example, adding a conditional premise that has as its antecedent the argument's explicit premise, or, if there is more than one, the conjunction of its explicit premises, and has, as its consequent the argument's conclusion, or, if there is more than one, the conjunction of its conclusions. This has sometimes been called 'the enthymematic ploy,' meaning that it is an automatic and purely formal move that you can make to defend, or to refute, any argument at all. One wonders, then, whether Thomas is teaching a technique of handling enthymemes that could encourage dubious practices, if not used with more care and circumspection than one might reasonably expect of a majority of logic students, at a beginning level especially.

Govier (1987) is sensitive to this danger, and sees the temptation to give in to it as widespread in philosophy. She defines 'deductivism' as 'the view that all good arguments are deductively valid.' She thinks this is a view that is very natural and familiar to many philosophers. Certainly, it is true that, in analytical philosophy, it is a common technique to evaluate argumentation by, first of all, specifying what sort of missing premises are needed to make the argument come out as deductively valid.

Govier has a number of objections to deductivism, but one of the central ones lies in her contention that many commonplace arguments are of a kind that can be correct, yet are not of a kind that are deductively valid. Arguments from analogy are a case in point. A good case, illustrating use of argument from analogy, is given by Gough and Tindale (1985, p. 103):

Case 7.17
A man who drives his car into the rear of another car is not guilty of careless driving if his brakes failed. Similarly, if a man kills another man he is not found guilty of murder if his mind failed to perceive reality due to mental illness.

Mental instability is not sufficient to establish insanity, as Mr. C. contends. Our judicial system justly requires that a person must have rationally formed the intention to kill another person to be considered a murderer. Insanity is, therefore, an appropriate defence for murder.

According to Gough and Tindale (p. 103), the non-explicit premise is an assertion of comparison which says: 'the two situations are comparable, so if you accept the principle in the case of the driver/brakes, you should also accept it in the case of the murder/mental illness.' This assertion of comparison supplies a warrant or argumentation scheme that functions to back up the conclusion by basing it on a case held to be analogous.

Such arguments are based on a comparison that shifts a burden of proof, yet is inherently open to counterclaims or rebuttals. This kind of argument is, by its nature, inherently inconclusive, because it is used in a context of balance of considerations where it does not need strictly to prove its conclusion by a deductively valid argument in order to meet a burden of proof appropriate to make it successful. In such a case, treating an argument from analogy as if it had to be deductively valid in order to be correct or successful is a distortion of this type of argument.

According to Govier, there are two opposed views of the nature of argument. According to the deductivist view, among whose proponents she classifies Thomas, premises needed to make an argument deductively valid must be a part of the original argument. The non-deductivist view denies that a correct or successful argument must be deductively valid and, hence, that adding to an elliptical argument sufficient premises to make the argument correct or successful is necessarily a matter of adding to it sufficient premises to make the argument deductively valid. Govier (1987, p. 84), for example, expresses the non-deductivist point of view on arguments from analogy as follows:

> If we add to an argument by analogy sufficient premises to make that argument deductively valid, someone who takes analogy to be a distinct nondeductive type of argument will see those added premises as going beyond the original. If those premises turn out to be false or unacceptable, from this position that will not indicate that the original argument was at fault. On this view, the original argument was nondeductive. The fact that a premise needed to make it deductively valid turns out to be a false premise shows nothing.

According to Govier (p. 84), Thomas is committed to disagreeing with this non-deductivist position, because he thinks that, if any premises needed to make an argument deductively valid turn out to be false, then we must conclude that the argument is unsound.

On this question, we certainly agree with Govier that there are many arguments commonly used in everyday language conversations that are not deductively valid, and yet are structurally correct according to appropriate standards of correctness for their use. Such arguments are of various kinds, and the structure of each type, and its conditions for correct use, are indicated by its argumentation scheme. Before the advent of these argumentation schemes, unfortunately, there was a lack of an account of the structures of these kinds of argumentation that could be used to evaluate instances of them. Naturally, this led to a tendency to try to apply the forms of deductive logic, in order to try to get some kind of formal structure to interpret and analyse these arguments.

Philosophers commonly do use deductive logic to see what premises need to be filled in to make an argument deductively valid, in the way that Thomas recommends as his second technique. This, in itself, is not incorrect or erroneous, as long as it is clear what is being done. Unfortunately, however, as Govier warns, there is a strong tendency to get carried away with this kind of analysis, and to take it for something it is not. It is too easy to slip into the assumption that, if the argument in question can be shown to have a premise that would make it deductively valid when filled in, the lack of this particular premise somehow makes the argument deficient, or any attempts to support or refute the argument must centre on this premise.

It is, therefore, appropriate to conclude this section by warning that it is a much more complex and subtle task than could ever be accomplished by simply filling in the deductive gaps in an argument. Before taking any such step, the prior question of what type of argument it is supposed to be needs to be asked. If the argument is of a presumptive, balance-of-considerations type, as opposed to a deductive type, then it would be a grave error automatically to go ahead treating it as if it had to be deductively valid to be any good.

What is shown here, generally, is the danger of taking any single structure and applying that structure to enthymemes as though it was the only one that could be applied. What this overlooks is that there can be different kinds of arguments, depending on the burden of proof and context of dialogue appropriate for a given case.

It is necessary to distinguish three different kinds of arguments – deductive, inductive, and presumptive. In a deductive argument, it is logically impossible for the premises to be true and the conclusion false. This is a strict conception of argument-structural correctness, admitting of no exceptions. Typically, deductive arguments are based on universal generalizations, which state that all F are G, for predicates F and G. Inductive arguments are not strict, but are based on probability. An inductive generalization takes the form: most (or a certain percentage) of Fs are Gs. Many philosophers think that there are only two types of arguments, but others have identified a third type, which may be called 'presumptive' or 'abductive' arguments, used for guessing intelligently that a conclusion is plausibly true.

Parenthetically, it might be noted that how deductive argument should be defined is a controversial matter. According to Vorobej (1992, p. 105), an argument should be defined as deductive if, and only if, the author of the argument believes that the truth of the premises necessitates (guarantees) the truth of the conclusion.

Presumptive arguments are inherently different from the other two types of arguments, because they are not put forward as assertions (see chapter 1) that are supposed to be based directly on evidence, the way the other two are. They are, instead, put forward as hypothetical arguments, presumed to be acceptable, based on practical considerations (a need to act), in the face of insufficient evidence to fulfil a burden of proof. When a speaker puts forward a presumptive argument in a dialogue, it is a tentative type of argument, subject to correction or rebuttal if further evidence comes in (Walton, 1992b, ch. 2). Here, the argument goes ahead, unless the hearer can present evidence to rebut it. Presumptive arguments are always arguments from ignorance, in the sense that they postulate that, since we don't know a certain proposition is true (false), we can provisionally assume that it is false (true). These arguments do not carry the same positive burden of proof as deductive and inductive ones, when put forward as pro- or contra-argumentation.

As far as enthymemes are concerned, the problem is that it would be a great error to go ahead and presume that all arguments can be reconstructed structurally as being deductively valid. Or, for that matter, it would be a great error to take any one of the three structures of argument as being the exclusively correct one, and forget about the other two. Such a policy would systematically misrepresent and distort argumentation. We could even say that it would be fallacious.

Reconstructing an enthymeme structurally to find the logical gaps is not as simple a job as tradition has so often suggested in the textbook accounts. One of the most important steps is the judgment of whether the argument in question is supposed to be deductive, inductive, or presumptive. Typically, the question comes down to whether the generalization premise in the argument is strict (universal), inductive, or presumptive (defeasible) in nature.

Thus, when our theory of the enthymeme is presented in section 9, below, it is crucial that a first step in the determination of any non-explicit premise or conclusion should be the identification of the type of argument in a given case. In fact then, the Aristotelian emphasis on presumptive, non-deductive arguments has turned out to be extremely important to our analysis of enthymemes.

7. The 'Straw Man' Fallacy

Gilbert (1991, p. 162) discusses the following case, which he calls a 'paradigmatic enthymeme':

242   Argument Structure

Case 7.18
Smoking should be banned because it's bad for you.

According to Gilbert, the usual approach to this type of case is to see it as an enthymeme that lacks a premise stating a general rule or principle of a universal form: All things bad for you should be banned. But is this a correct interpretation? Perhaps the proponent of the argument in case 7.18 might not be committed to such a universal rule at all. If questioned, he may even deny it.

Gilbert's solution, called the 'enthymeme buster' method,[9] is to ask the proponent a further question: 'So then you would ban alcohol as well?' (p. 162), and judge what the missing premise should be on the basis of the proponent's response. This is an excellent solution, if the proponent is present to engage in dialogue.

However, in a typical case of argument diagramming, the problem is that the proponent is not present to answer such questions. For such a case, then, we have to seek a different solution.

The general problem posed by this case is that attributing such a universal rule to the proponent's argument as an additional premise could be an instance of the 'straw man' fallacy. For, in reality, it could well be that the proponent is committed only to a much weaker rule – namely: If something is bad for you, then that is a reason (on balance of considerations, but not by itself a sufficient reason) for banning it. This principle is quite a bit weaker than the universal one first considered. In contrast to the universal rule, it is defeasible rather than absolute.

Trying to pin the universal rule on an arguer in case 7.18 could be highly unfair and prejudicial. It would be an instance of the 'straw man' fallacy, and would also be related to the *secundum quid* fallacy of ignoring exceptions to a rule.

The '*straw man fallacy*' is committed where the proponent (respondent) in a dispute misrepresents the position of the respondent (proponent), imputing to him a position that is implausible and easy to refute, and then goes on to argue against that position as though it really were his.

Case 7.19
Bob and Arlene are arguing about environmental laws that regulate industrial pollution, and Bob has taken a moderately 'green' position, Arlene argues, 'People like you want to make the planet into the pristine place it was hundreds of years ago. Therefore, what you are committed to is the elimination of all industrial manufacturing. Imagine the unemployment.'

Here, Arlene has committed the 'straw man' fallacy by exaggerating Bob's position to make it appear much more radical than (let's presume) it really was, as Bob presented it.

In a case like this, it is not too difficult for the respondent to correct the fallacy by insisting that his position is not what the proponent has pictured it as. If the proponent continues to press the argument, the two can resolve the problem by going back over what the respondent actually said in the previous dialogue, and discuss exactly what his commitments on the issue should be taken to be, given his record of explicit commitments.

Analysing and evaluating an allegation of 'straw man' fallacy in a given case is a problem of determining what the commitments of an arguer are. This is defined by the context of dialogue – namely, the type of dialogue the speaker is supposedly engaged in, and, if it is a critical discussion, the thesis the speaker is supposed to be arguing for. A third factor in determining a speaker's commitments is the record of what the speaker has actually said so far in the dialogue. Commitment, so conceived, is not a psychological notion. It can be defined normatively in relation to a model of dialogue (see Hamblin, 1970; van Eemeren and Grootendorst, 1984; and Walton, 1984). The concept of commitment is precisely defined for several different types of dialogue in which argumentation takes place by Walton and Krabbe (1995).

The problem of judging a case of the 'straw man' fallacy is more difficult when the respondent of the argument is not actually present or available to clarify his position, or specify exactly what his commitments are. But this is just the kind of case we are generally confronted with when attempting to analyse an argument with the method of argument diagramming. Indeed, in the typical type of case so often presented in the examples given in the logic textbooks, there is little contextual information to go on. In these cases, all we get are a few lines of text, and the context is pretty well left up to one's imagination to fill in. Therefore, we have to be especially on guard against the danger of committing the 'straw man' fallacy in using the method of argument diagramming.

The 'straw man' fallacy in diagramming is made even more dangerous by another factor. In dealing with enthymemes, it is generally very tempting to exaggerate an opponent's position by filling in a missing premise of the form 'Generally things that have property F also have property G, subject to exceptions' with an absolute, or strict generalization, of the form 'All things that have property F also have property G, without exception.' This move is actually a form of the *secundum quid* (meaning 'in a certain respect') fallacy, because qualifications have been ignored. However, it also relates to the 'straw man' fallacy, because the problem is one of misrepresenting an opponent's position by making it seem stronger, or stricter than it really is.

Indeed, this sort of fallacy is a systematic kind of danger to which the method of argument diagramming is inherently prone, given the tendency in the textbooks to fill in enthymemes by making arguments deductively valid. The deductivism that Govier warns about is indeed the heart of the problem here.

For example, if an arguer is putting forth an argument based on an appeal to an analogy, then she is generally best interpreted as claiming only that two situations tend to be similar in certain respects. And, if so, her argument is best seen as inherently presumptive and defeasible in nature, open to exceptions and qualifications. But, if we go on the assumption that the missing premise has to make her argument deductively valid, we are likely to take her argument as claiming that the two situations in question are exactly equal, in every respect. But this, as Govier has warned us, is a misinterpretation, and is taking the argument in a much stricter way than the arguer intended.

If the premise and the conclusion are both singular propositions, referring to a single instance, it may seem that the enthymeme can be filled in by linking the two instances by citing a universal generalization, or a general rule. Although this method often appears to work, in some cases it backfires badly. Scriven (1976, p. 166) cites such a case:

Case 7.20
The argument ['She's red-haired, so she's probably bad-tempered.'] consists of a single premise and a single conclusion – it could hardly be simpler. What is the missing premise? ... The usual first reply from a class is, 'red-haired people are bad-tempered' or 'all red-haired people are bad-tempered,' which are intended to mean the same. That's quite incorrect, quite unfair to the argument; it sets up a 'straw man.' If the argument had the conclusion, 'she *must* be bad-tempered,' it would require something more like this premise. But the argument is much more cautious, and to draw the conclusion in which 'must' is replaced by 'probably,' one only needs a premise referring to *most* red-haired people. Yet it is still incorrect to say that this argument assumes that most red-haired people are bad-tempered (or that a red-haired person is probably bad-tempered). The conclusion contains a further piece of information which narrows down the required assumptions; it is the reference to 'she.' The arguer may well believe that most red-haired *people* are not bad-tempered, only that most red-haired *women* are bad-tempered. [But] it might be argued that it's a little more plausible to suppose that the arguer believes that red-haired *people* are bad-tempered than that he or she believes that red-haired *women* are bad-tempered; roughly, because there seems to be no evidence about sex differentiation on this matter, and it might be thought there must be a gene combination that produces both a tendency to bad temper and redness of hair.

In this case, as Scriven points out, it would certainly be unfair to attribute the non-explicit premise 'All red-haired people are bad-tempered' to the arguer. The word 'probably' is a contraindicator to putting in this universal generalization, and to do so would be a form of 'straw man' fallacy. But if the missing premise is a probabilistic generalization, is it one about women specifically, or about people generally? It's hard to say, in the absence of any further context. Perhaps, as Scriven suggests, it is a little more plausible to take it to be about people generally, on the basis of generally known information of the kind Scriven cites.

But really it's hard to say what the missing premise is, in a case like this, in the absence of further contextual clues. It could be that the arguer is making an unthinking 'stereotype' judgment, or it could be that he or she has some sort of genetic information or conjecture in mind. It could be that he or she is generalizing about women, or about people. We do not know. The implications of this incompleteness are taken up in section 10 below.

8. Argumentation Schemes

A most important new tool for the analysis of enthymemes in the sense defined above is the argumentation scheme. Argumentation schemes, of the kind identified by Walton (1996), are the forms of argument (structures of inference) that enable one to identify and evaluate common types of presumptive argumentation in everyday discourse. Recent concerns with the evaluation of argumentation in informal logic and speech communication have more and more begun to centre around non-demonstrative arguments that lead to tentative (defeasible) conclusions, based on a balance of considerations. Such arguments do not appear to have structures of the kind traditionally identified with deductive and inductive reasoning. However, they are extremely common, and are often called 'plausible' or 'presumptive,' meaning that they are only tentatively or provisionally acceptable, even when they are correct (Walton, 1992b). In chapter 8, they are shown to be connected to the abductive type of reasoning identified by C.S. Peirce.

Walton (1996) provides argumentation schemes for the following types of arguments: (1) argument from sign; (2) argument from example; (3) argument from verbal classification; (4) argument from commitment; (5) circumstantial argument against the person; (6) argument from position to know; (7) argument from expert opinion; (8) argument from evidence to a hypothesis; (9) argument from correlation to cause; (10) argument from cause to effect; (11) argument from consequences; (12) argument from analogy; (13) argument from waste; (14) argument from popularity; (15) ethotic argument; (16) argument

246   Argument Structure

from bias; (17) argument from an established rule; (18) argument from precedent; (19) argument from gradualism; (20) the causal slippery slope argument; (21) the precedent slippery slope argument; (22) argument from vagueness of a verbal classification; (23) the verbal slippery slope argument; (24) the fully slippery slope argument. A summary of these schemes, with examples of each type of argument, is given by Walton elsewhere (1995).

Matching each argumentation scheme, a set of critical questions is given. The two things together, the argumentation scheme and the matching critical questions, are used to evaluate a given argument in a particular case, in relation to a context of dialogue in which the argument occurred.

According to the analysis given by Walton (1996) presumptive reasoning uses argumentation schemes based on limited generalizations that are subject to qualifications and exceptions, making it a species of so-called default or non-monotonic reasoning. Hence, the analysis of presumptive reasoning – and the analysis of the argumentation schemes themselves – is pragmatic and dialectical in nature, meaning that the argument in question is evaluated, not just in terms of its (semantic) logical form, but in relation to how it is, or should be, used in a given context of dialogue.

The species of presumptive argumentation based on argumentation schemes is strikingly similar to the kind of argument Aristotle (section 2, above) called the 'enthymeme.' Aristotle was the real founder of this field. But, perhaps owing to misinterpretation of his theory of the enthymeme, the study of plausible reasoning was virtually ignored by logicians after the Greeks. Carneades did develop a theory of plausible reasoning in response to scepticism, but his writings did not survive.[10] And the subsequent development of logic, right up to the twentieth century – with the notable exception of C.S. Peirce – stressed deductive logic almost exclusively, making little or no room for the study of plausible reasoning as a part of the logic curriculum.

Very little, in fact, was done with this field before Perelman and Olbrechts-Tyteca (1969; first published in French in 1958) identified many distinctive kinds of arguments used to convince a respondent on a provisional basis. Arthur Hastings's PhD thesis (1963) made an even more systematic taxonomy by listing some of these schemes, along with useful examples of them. In the recent literature on argumentation theory, argumentation schemes are often mentioned (van Eemeren and Grootendorst, 1984; 1992), and their place of importance is recognized.

An illustrative example is the use of argumentation from analogy in a deliberation. One situation can be said to be similar to another in certain respects, and this can be used as the basis of an argument from analogy. But, of course, the two situations will also be dissimilar in certain respects, as we can see from the example in case 7.17. Thus, any argument from analogy is, by its nature, defeasible and presumptive.

It is possible for some arguments from analogy to be inductive, rather than presumptive, in nature. But Govier (1989) supports our contention that many, common arguments from analogy are based on an unstated premise that is neither a deductive (universal) nor an inductive (based on probability) type of generalization. As she sees it (1989, p. 148), arguments from analogy are based on a comparison of key features in which two individual cases resemble each other, and where, generally, it is not possible to spell out a universal (absolute) claim that unites both cases in *every* respect. Typically, we cannot 'spell out' the important resemblances between cases 'exhaustively in just so many words' (p. 148).

Govier (p. 143) gives the following sample case of an argument from analogy:

Case 7.21
Smokers should be allowed to smoke only in private where it does not offend anyone else. Would any smoker walk into a restaurant and start eating half-chewed food on someone's plate, or drink a glass of water that previously held someone's teeth? Probably not, yet they expect non-smokers to inhale smoke from the recesses of their lungs. My privilege and right is to choose a clean and healthy life without interference. (P.T.B., *Cape Town Argus*, quoted in *World Press Review*, January 1988, p. 12)

Govier (pp. 149–50) gives the following reconstruction of the sequence of argumentation in this case:

1 Eating food which had been half-chewed by someone else or drinking water that had had someone else's teeth in it would be repugnant.
2 Breathing smoke which has been in someone else's lungs would be repugnant.
3 Smokers would not be willing to eat half-chewed food or drink water that had held someone else's teeth.
4* No one should expect anybody else to take into his body substances which have been partly used and contaminated by someone else.
5 So, smokers should not expect others to breathe air which has been in the lungs of smokers.
6 So, it is a person's privilege and right to choose a clean and healthy life without interference.
7 And, smokers should be allowed to smoke only in private where it does not offend anyone else.

248 Argument Structure

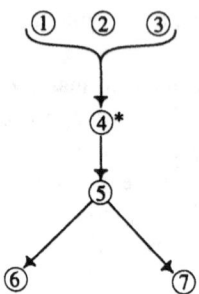

Figure 7.1 Argument in Case 7.21

And then she gives (p. 150) an argument diagram for the reconstructed argumentation, as shown in figure 7.1. Now the key question at issue is how to interpret proposition 4*. Is it a (strict) universal generalization, or an inductive generalization based on probabilities, or merely a presumptive (defeasible) generalization, distinct from the first two categories?

It appears to be a strict, universal generalization, and many would take it that way in reconstructing the argument. But Govier disagrees, seeing it as a defeasible, and not a universal generalization (what she calls a 'U-claim'). We agree, on the basis that there are important cases of exceptions to 4* as a generalization, for example, blood transfusions, or cases where a fireman or paramedic must give mouth-to-mouth resuscitation to a victim.

For detailed accounts of the argumentation scheme for argument from analogy, the reader can consult Govier (1987; 1989a) or Walton (1989). At least, it has been made clear, in principle, how one can apply an argumentation scheme with a non-universal, defeasible generalization as its major premise to a particular case, in order to extract non-explicit premises or conclusions indicated by the structure of the scheme.

It is generally true of argumentation schemes that they are based on presumptive generalizations that are non-universal, or non-strictly universal. Hence, we fully agree with Govier that it would be a very serious error to treat these kinds of arguments as though they were complete only if they were deductively valid. To deal with very common kinds of cases such as 7.21, the concept of enthymeme needs to be rethought and redesigned.

9. The Two Levels: Need and Use

The problem of enthymemes should be thought of in relation to the question of what it is we think we are trying to do when we pose the question of non-explicit premises. Basically, we are trying to analyse an argument. But to do this, we have to ask: 'What are the premises and the conclusion?' In practical terms, in order to apply logic to natural language argumentation, we have to ask this question. And to answer it, we have to fill in some propositions that were not explicitly asserted by the arguer. In order to do this, we have to make assumptions or hypotheses. But this, in itself, is not illegitimate, provided we recognize that what we are doing is making assumptions, and provided we base these hypotheses on evidence from the text or context of dialogue, evidence that can be produced and evaluated by anyone.

So, how do we undertake this task, once we have embarked on it? The answer comes in two stages. First, we impose some sort of structure on a given argument, to see what is required for that type of argument to meet its burden of proof, and to see what is missing to meet these requirements. To do this, we can use argumentation schemes, or we can use deductive forms of argument, such as syllogisms or forms of propositional reasoning. This step represents an analysis of what the argument needs in order to meet requirements for completion or correctness.

Over and above the recognition that an argument has an identifiable form, however, our main method for identifying non-explicit premises will be the method of diagramming itself. For example, if a stated premise is part of a linked structure that clearly requires some other unstated but presumed premise to support its conclusion, then that unstated premise can be identified by the method of diagramming. Hence, a large part of the best method for filling in enthymemes is, in fact, the identification of linked structures, as part of the method of diagramming. Hence, part of the route to solving the problem of enthymemes is to return to the problem of the linked–convergent distinction.

But this does not complete the task, for, in general, there may be many different candidates for missing premises that could be filled in, to make the argument meet these structural requirements. We need to go beyond this to ask which proposition the arguer was most likely to have used in getting the conclusion, given what we know from the text and context about the arguer's commitments and what seems most plausible.

In taking this two-levelled approach to the problem of enthymemes, we are following the important distinction of Ennis (1982, pp. 64–6) between *need* and *use*. According to Ennis (p. 64), used assumptions are unstated reasons that we look for 'when we are engaged in understanding someone.' A needed assumption is something an argument needs in order to be as good an argument as it can be (p. 65). This distinction is important because it represents, broadly speaking, two quite different things that one might be seeking in attempting to identify non-explicit premises or conclusions in an argument. In some cases, the two conceptions of enthymeme might actually conflict with each other. A premise an arguer actually used, implicitly but clearly, might not be the one she needs to complete her argument successfully, according to the appropriate criterion of argument success.

Judging what an arguer needs to offer an argument that is complete or structurally correct according to some criterion is the less complex and more potentially completable of the two tasks. What one needs for this purpose is a set of identifiable structures or forms of argument that indicate how to link sets of premises together to support a conclusion in some recognizable type of argument. We can use traditional syllogism for this purpose, or modern propositional and quantifier logic, or we can use argumentation schemes. Or, to get the best approach, one that can deal with the problems posed by the 'straw man' fallacy, we can use all of them, provided we have some means of knowing which structure is the appropriate one to apply in a given case. Once we have identified a particular form or structure of argument as appropriate, we can then apply it to a text of discourse, saying, 'Here is one premise, and here is the conclusion, so now with this type of argument, all one needs is this other particular premise (unstated) to fill the gap and give us a valid (or otherwise structurally correct) instance of this type of argument. So let's add the premise in question to the argument as a non-explicit premise.' Since we already have resources of this kind available in logic, we have a good many of the tools for this kind of job. More needs to be done, especially on the argumentation schemes, but at least there is promise with the project of supplying needed premises.

With respect to the task of identifying used premises, however, the resources are less readily available, at least according to the author's search of the state of the literature on enthymemes. The problem is that, while there has been a body of literature theorizing about enthymemes, there is an insufficient body of casework, that is, collection of illustrative examples of common types of enthymemes found in everyday argumentation. There is not enough of a body of this kind of casework to enable us yet to give any kind of relatively complete classification of the different kinds of enthymemes and the different bases they rely on in argumentation.

Moreover, there are different bases for determining implicitly used premises or conclusions in argumentation. Sometimes, for example, a premise can be seen to be used in an argument because it clearly represents the arguer's point of view or position, as made clear by the previous text and by the context of the dialogue. In other cases, a premise can be seen to be used because it is very plausible, and neither party in the dialogue would dispute it. But commitment and plausibility are two different things, and could even conflict in some cases.

Enthymemes 251

Thus, when it comes to determining what premise an arguer may be presumed to have used in her argument, there could be quite a few different ways of arriving at this finding.

The casework studies above have revealed six different bases for determining non-explicitly used premises in argumentation:

1 The general knowledge shared by the speaker, hearer, and audience (as indicated by the context of the conversation).
2 The position (as known) of the proponent. That is, the non-explicit proposition is not known to be true, but is presumably a commitment of the proponent, as far as we can judge by the dialogue.
3 Custom, habit, or normal ways of doing something.
4 Conceptual links holding an argument together.
5 Non-explicit premises (or conclusions) of practical reasoning.
6 Innuendo – conclusion not stated explicitly, but suggested by context of conversation.

This list is not likely to be complete, and will presumably be expanded somewhat by future research. But it does give a good idea of the variety of different criteria that can be appealed to when in argument identification we hypothesize that such-and-such proposition is a missing premise or conclusion.

It is to be emphasized that the two-levelled method of completing enthymemes advocated above is very much a contextual determination. Much depends on the type of dialogue the speakers are engaged in, relative to a given case. And much also depends on the commitments of the speaker who advanced the argument in the given case. In the analysis of commitment presented by Walton and Krabbe (1995), a key distinction is made between rigorous persuasion dialogue (*RPD*), where all commitments are explicitly stated, and permissive persuasion dialogue (*PPD*), where the so-called dark-side commitments, non-explicitly asserted commitments attributed to an arguer by presumption, are an important factor. Such dark-side commitments are revealed by viewing a case as an instance of a normative model of dialogue, for example, a critical discussion, where certain moves can be expected (or may be required) even if they are not explicitly articulated in the discourse by a speaker's actual assertions.[12]

The method for enthymemes is not wholly contextual, however. It is also partly structural, or 'logical' in the traditional sense of using structures of valid inference (argument forms of deductive and inductive logic, as well as argumentation schemes of presumptive reasoning). The method is a combination of these two levels.

We have seen, however, that there can be a conflict between these two levels

252   Argument Structure

of analysis. For example, filling in a premise needed to make an argument valid may in some cases not fairly represent an arguer's commitment, and may even commit a 'straw man' fallacy.

For this reason, we cannot yet say that the method is an algorithm that can be automatically applied without clashes or contradictions arising in it. Instead, each case needs to be looked into on its merits, and inserted non-explicit premises and conclusions must always be marked as such, separate from explicit assertions. The two levels must be balanced off against each other, on the weight of evidence.

10. Incompleteness

In some cases, an argument is clearly incomplete, in the sense that some non-explicitly stated premise appears to be presumed, yet we do not have any way of knowing what that missing premise is. The following argumentation was used as a supplement to case 7.13:

Case 7.22
Your brother eats his vegetables.

In this case, the conclusion is 'You should eat your vegetables,' just as it was in case 7.13. But what is the missing premise? It could be, 'You always do what your brother does' or 'You want to be like your brother, don't you?' or 'Your brother is big and strong.' It's very hard to say what the proponent might have had in mind to use in this case, and we can't seem to narrow it down further than a range of choices. Perhaps the mother knows that the argument in case 7.22 will convince her son to eat his vegetables, even though she might not be able to specify exactly why, if asked.

The problem is made more difficult in a case like this because we are deciding on a basis of use, rather than strictly a basis of need. Hence, we need to determine what the speaker is committed to, and to find out about this, more evidence from the context of dialogue about the speaker's argumentation on the subject of the brother eating his vegetables is needed.

But, if we were to decide on the basis of need, we could just plug in the missing premise 'If your brother eats his vegetables, then you should eat your vegetables.' This conditional, with the explicit premise stated in case 7.22, yields the conclusion cited, by *modus ponens*. But there is an additional problem of how to interpret this conditional premise.

We encountered essentially the same problem in Scriven's case 7.20, where it seemed impossible to say exactly how we should interpret the non-explicit premise 'All red-haired people are bad-tempered.' This case represented a different aspect of the problem, because the uncertainty was related to the structural question of what type of generalization and what type of argument were supposed to be involved. But this is all part of the same problem of incompleteness. What should we do if there is insufficient data given to determine exactly what the missing premise really is?

One commonly proposed type of solution is to apply the principle of charity (or some other comparable principle of interpretation), which suggests reconstructing the argument in a way that makes it as strong as possible. While we agree that something like this approach is needed, we have also seen that, at least on some versions, it can get us into a lot of trouble. The problem we encountered above was that taking the argument to be as strong as possible would most likely mean taking it to be deductively valid, and this could (in many cases) amount to committing the 'straw man' fallacy.

Better, we think, as a policy for analysis of arguments, to admit that you don't really know what the non-explicit premise (or conclusion) is, in those cases where the textual evidence is incomplete. Even better, in cases where two argument diagrams are both possible, based on two different interpretations of the text of discourse, the evidence for both reconstructions should be laid out. It could be, in some cases, that one interpretation is more plausible than the other, based on the given evidence. But this too, could be a part of the procedure used to identify the argument.

What is to be recommended, then, is that the diagram not be regarded as standing by itself. Part of the exercise of identifying the argument should be a presenting of the textual and contextual evidence in favour of a particular identification of the premises and conclusion (especially where some of these propositions are non-explicit).

This is not to rule out conditional evaluations of arguments, where an evaluation is made in the following form: if such-and-such proposition is a premise of this argument, then we can say that the argument is correct, valid, fallacious, and so on, based on this assumption. Sometimes conditional evaluations are revealing, because they can show (and here we agree, to some extent, with Thomas) what would be needed to make an argument complete or correct, according to some given standard (like deductive validity).

In the experience of teaching argument diagramming and identification, one finds there are three types of cases: (a) where it is clear to the whole class that some particular proposition is definitely the non-explicit premise; (b) where there is definite disagreement, that is, where one proposition is designated as the non-explicit premise on one interpretation of the argument, while another proposition is so designated on a different interpretation; and (c) where there is

254   Argument Structure

not enough evidence to say with any definite confidence exactly what proposition is supposed to represent the non-explicit premise. One's experience is that clear agreement can normally be reached on which category a given case falls into.

Even so, the experience of dealing with type (b) and (c) cases can be disquieting to beginning logic students, who expect logic to be an exact science, and who expect a clear, definite outcome that can be calculated by means of some algorithm. Some students do not expect to have to exercise skills of judicious interpretation of a text of discourse, and much, in this regard, depends on the objectives, expectations, and level of the course.

Despite these very real problems, it is generally fairly clear (subject to exceptions, of course) what the 'missing' premises or conclusions should be taken to be. And it is the conclusion of this chapter that these existing skills can be enhanced, and made into more objective judgments, by making explicit and carefully distinguishing between: (a) the need (structural) basis of the enthymeme; and (b) the use basis. The approach recommended in this chapter is to break judgment (a) into three categories representing three types or standards of argument – the deductive, the inductive, and the presumptive – and to break judgment (b) down into the different bases of the enthymeme outlined in the chapter.

Research is far from complete on this subject. The recommendations of the chapter may be regarded as an outline of a proposed research program for developing a useful method of dealing with enthymemes, in conjunction with the significant efforts already made in this direction by van Eemeren and Grootendorst (1984; 1992), Govier (1987), Snoeck Henkemans (1992), and Freeman (1991).

If we just stick to the more tractable problem of determining enthymemes on a need basis, there is a method already available, and widely in use in computer science. In what is called 'abductive' reasoning, the computer reasons 'backwards' from the conclusion, in order to determine which premises in a given database that conclusion could be generated from. For example, suppose the conclusion is B, and the conditional 'If A then B' is in the database. Then the computer will search through the database, looking for an additional premise, that, taken along with 'If A then B,' will generate B, by a recognized rule of inference. Suppose *modus ponens* is a recognized rule of inference. Then the computer, if it finds A in the database, will cite 'A' and 'If A then B' as the required premises.

Even more interestingly, from our point of view, is that, if the computer does not find A, or any other suitable premise in the database to complete the inference, it can cite A as the proposition that is needed for this purpose. Hence, the kind of computer programs widely in use today in expert systems technology can perform the function of completing enthymemes (at least, on a need basis). More about this notion of abductive inference in computer science is explained in chapter 8.

The method of digraphs presented in chapter 6 represents the purely calculative core of the method of diagramming. The method begins with the input of two pieces of data in a given case: (a) the explicitly given set of propositions that are the conclusion and premises; and (b) the set of rules of inference (such as *modus ponens*, or whatever) appropriate for the type of argument in the given case. Using this base, the method will then calculate a digraph showing potential non-explicit (missing) premises needed to generate the conclusion from the explicitly given premises (if any are needed), and the structure of the sequence of argumentation needed for this purpose. The structure of reasoning exhibited by the graph can be used to pinpoint the places in the argument where non-explicit premises (or conclusions) need to be filled in. Then an examination of the context of dialogue can be used to determine what the best candidates for these non-explicit premises (or conclusions) are.

8

Abductive Inference

Many times, now, the importance of separating deductive and inductive arguments, and a third type of argument called 'presumptive' or 'plausibilistic,' has been emphasized.[1] This task is important, both in the evaluation of arguments as fallacious or non-fallacious, and for diagramming the structure of an argument.

One particular type of presumptive reasoning, in fact, characteristically has a form of argument long recognized to be deductively invalid – namely, *affirming the consequent*: If A then B; B; therefore, A. However, it has occasionally also been recognized that, when interpreted as a species of plausible inference, as is appropriate in some cases, this form of argument can be reasonable. In a recent international meeting of a research group on practical reasoning in computer science,[2] it was commented by several participants independently to the author in discussions that the form of reasoning known to logicians as 'affirming the consequent' is not always an unreasonable inference (despite its traditional categorization in logic as a formal fallacy).[3]

A species of this type of inference that takes the form of affirming the consequent is called 'abduction' in computer science. It was first described as a distinctive form of inference having certain formal characteristics by C.S. Peirce, and it is now frequently called 'inference to the best explanation.' Because it combines the function of an argument with that of an explanation, it is especially interesting to explore for our purposes, in this book. In this chapter, we will link abduction to a type of presumptive reasoning we have frequently encountered already – argument from sign.

1. Peirce on Abduction

According to Misak (1991, pp. 91–2), Peirce, especially in his early work, distinguished among three kinds of inference, on the basis of their forms.[4]

Deduction proceeds from rule and case to result:

Rule: All the beans in this bag are white
Case: These beans are from this bag
Result: Therefore these beans are white

Induction proceeds from case and result to rule:

Case: These beans are from this bag
Result: These beans are white
Rule: Therefore all the beans in this bag are white

Abduction or hypothesis proceeds from rule and result to case:

Rule: All beans from this bag are white
Result: These beans are white
Case: Therefore these beans are from this bag

In the 1883 'A Theory of Probable Inference' (*CP* 2. 704), Peirce characterizes abduction as follows:

Rule: All *M*'s have the characters $P_1, P_2 ... P_n$
Result: S has the characters $P_1, P_2 ... P_n$
Case: S is an *M*

One can see from this account that abduction is a kind of reversal of one premise and the conclusion, as compared with the deductive type of inference.

If the rule premise in the example of abduction above is expressed as a universal conditional, it can be seen that the inference in this example also has a backwards-moving structure similar to that of *modus tollens*.

For all x, if x is a bean from this bag, then x is white.
a is white.
Therefore a is from this bag.

The inference involved in this kind of reasoning appears to be a presumptive one. The result that these beans are white suggests (rather than logically implies, or makes probable) that they are from this bag. For they could have come from somewhere else, and it seems that there is no basis in probability for calculating the chances of whether they came from somewhere else. All we know is that here we have a white bean, or some white beans, and here we also have a bag of beans, and all of the beans in the bag are white. Therefore, it is a reasonable presumption to infer that these beans are from the bag (barring contrary knowledge of where they came from).

The reasoning in the bean argument above is a kind of lack-of-knowledge inference of the type associated with the argument from ignorance. It is reasonable to assume that the beans came from the bag, assuming that there is no knowledge (in the case) that they came from somewhere else. Abduction was characterized generally by Peirce (Eisele, 1985, p. 898) as a kind of 'guessing' in which a statement is 'suggested' by some data that it is not contained in.

Fann (1970, p. 8) quotes Peirce (5.188), and commentators have remarked on this structural comparison, or found it deeply significant.

Peirce thought that abduction was especially characteristic of scientific inquiry at the discovery stage. In a work called 'The Proper Treatment of Hypotheses' (Eisele, 1985, pp. 890–904), Peirce describes abduction as a kind of 'interrogation' or questioning that saves money at the later testing stage by narrowing the inquiry down to the hypotheses that seem to be the more plausible candidates.

> By its very definition abduction leads to a hypothesis which is entirely foreign to the data. To assert the truth of its conclusion ever so dubiously would be too much. There is no warrant for doing more than putting it as an interrogation. To do that would seem to be innocent; yet if the interrogation means anything, it means that the hypothesis is to be tested. Now testing by experiment is a very expensive business, involving great outlay of money, time, and energy; so that comparatively few hypotheses can be tested. Thus, even the admission of an abductive conclusion to the rank of an active interrogation is a concession not to be too lightly accorded.

Clearly, Peirce saw abductive reasoning as leading only to tentative and plausible conclusions that do not commit us to a proposition – only to conjecturing that it is true as an explanatory hypothesis. Misak (1991, p. 94) quotes Peirce as writing that we must 'hold ourselves ready to throw them overboard at a moment's notice' (*CP* 1. 634, 1898), because they are merely conjectures. Peirce writes: 'Abduction commits us to nothing' (*CP* 1. 634, 1898; quoted in Misak, 1991, p. 94). Such conjectures can be verified or falsified at the later stages of the inquiry, when they are tested using inductive and deductive reasoning.

It seems fairly clear that Peirce thought that abduction involves explanation, and that, in the inference structure of abduction, one reasons 'backwards' from the 'surprising fact C' to the hypothesis A, because A functions as an explanation of C. Fann (1970, p. 10) describes Peircean abduction as 'an inference from a body of data to an explaining hypothesis.' And Misak (1991, p. 95) writes that, in abduction, we can 'infer a hypothesis to explain why we observed what we did.' Peirce, in describing abduction, frequently writes about abduction as a process of 'explaining' assumptions in the discovery stage that leads to a hypothesis (see 'The Proper Treatment of a Hypothesis,' Eisele, 1985, p. 899). Whether Peirce would have thought abduction the same as what is now called 'inference to the best explanation' is conjectural, but certainly he did think that abduction did involve a movement from an observed fact to a hypothesis that functions as an explanation of that fact. Fann (1970, p. 10) quotes Peirce (5.171) as writing: 'Abduction is the process of forming an explanatory hypothesis.' So abduction is a kind of backwards-directed inference to an explanation.

Harman (1965), who introduced the expression 'inference to the best explanation,' gave many examples to illustrate this type of reasoning. One example of Harman's is that, when we infer something about a person's mental state from some fact about her behaviour that was observed, we are inferring that this observed fact explains her behaviour better than any competing explanation. Another example Harman gives is that of a detective who puts the evidence together in a case, and concludes that the butler must have been the culprit. Harman describes this inference by commenting that the detective is reasoning that no other explanation that accounts for all these facts is as plausible.

Josephson and Tanner (1994, p. 5) define abduction, which they see as essentially equivalent to inference to the best explanation, as having the following form (where H is a hypothesis):

D is a collection of data (facts, observations, givens).
H explains D (would, if true, explain D).
No other hypothesis can explain D as well as H does.

Therefore, H is probably true.

Josephson and Tanner (1994, p. 5) see this type of reasoning as involving a choice between several explanatory alternatives, where one of these alternatives is selected out as 'the best,' or the most plausible, of the set. According to their account (p. 5), the 'core idea' is that 'a body of data provides evidence for a hypothesis that satisfactorily explains or accounts for that data (or at least it provides evidence if the hypothesis is better than explanatory alternatives.)' This account does suggest a sequence of reasoning that does have a form or structure.

But Peirce gave no indication of the logical form of abductive inference, aside from depicting its structure as having the form of affirming the consequent. The white bean example, above, illustrates an inference of this form, but leaves many questions unanswered. How and why is abductive inference useful, and what other defining characteristics does it have that can give us some clues to its structure as a distinctive type of argument? The form of affirming the consequent is deductively invalid, so why or how could this form be abductively valid?

2. Abduction in Computer Science

The term 'abduction' has now become a familiar technical term in computer science.[5] One type of reasoning used in computer searches of a database is *forward-chaining*, where, for example, a number of *modus ponens* steps of inference are linked together in a sequence of reasoning. First, the machine draws conclusion B from premises A and 'If A then B.' Then, in a next step, for example, B is used as a premise, along with a conditional, 'If B then C,' to derive a new conclusion, C. Abduction is identified with the reverse process of *backward-chaining*, where the purpose is to trace some information back to its source, to 'explain' to a user how this information was derived, or where it came from. For example, we might ask where a conclusion C came from, and the answer might be: 'From premises B, and "if B then C".' But then, if queried on where B came from, the computer might reply: 'from A, and "if A then B" is the source.' This sequence would be called 'abduction' or 'abductive inference,' in the sense that it tells you where a conclusion came from. What hypotheses or premises was it based on? It is an abduction in Peirce's sense, because the conclusion is a given fact, or outcome, and finding its premises yields an 'explanation' of where that conclusion 'came from,' that is, how it was, or could be, derived from premises. Such information could be useful for several purposes. But one of these purposes is that it could serve as an explanation of why the proposition is taken as data or knowledge by a knowledge base.

However, abductive reasoning is more than just 'backwards' reasoning in a database, in computer science. It is also thought to have other special characteristics that distinguish it as being inherently different from deductive reasoning. An example given by Spencer-Smith (1991) is helpful in indicating what computer scientists have in mind. Spencer-Smith (p. 40) cites a case where a person returns from a holiday, and is worried that there might have been a power cut. He reasons:

Case 8.1
(1) If there has been a power cut, everything in the fridge will be mouldy.

(2) There has been a power cut.
(3) Therefore, everything in the fridge is mouldy.

This inference is deductively valid. But the person might have also reasoned (p. 40) by inferring (2) from (1) and (3), that is, reasoning from the 'effect' (the mould) to 'its most probable cause' (the power cut). The abductive inference now has the following form:

Case 8.1a
If there has been a power cut, everything in the fridge will be mouldy.
Everything in the fridge is mouldy.
Therefore, there has been a power cut.

This inference is a classic case of abductive reasoning, in Peirce's sense. From the observed fact that everything in the fridge is mouldy, a hypothesis is surmised – there has been a power cut – that explains the observed fact. This abductive inference, according to Spencer-Smith, could be reasonable, even though it is not deductively valid (p. 41). Hence, one thing that is characteristic of abductive reasoning is that its correctness or reasonableness is inherently weaker than, and different from, that of deductive reasoning.

It can be seen from its use in expert systems technology that abductive inference is distinctively different, because it is based on a different kind of conditional warrant that is not 'definite' but is of an 'imprecise nature' (Bramer, 1982, p. 5), as expressed in the following form:

(R) *if* symptoms A, B and C are present *then* it is probable/it is possible/there is some reason to suppose that the cause is X.

Using rule (R) to explicate the inference in case 8.1 yields the following reconstruction:

Case 8.1b
If everything in the fridge is mouldy, there has been a power cut.
Everything in the fridge is mouldy.
Therefore, there has been a power cut.

In case 8.1b, the form of inference is that of *modus ponens*. But according to the theory in Walton (1992b), mentioned in chapter 4, section 4, the inference in case 8.1b would not be deductively valid. It is a plausible inference, because the first premise is a presumptive conditional. In this premise, there is an abductive transition from a sign to a hypothesis that functions as an explanation of that sign (in context). In abductive inference, this defeasible type of conditional is called a 'plausibilistic' rule.

Inferences based on plausibilistic rules[6] of this sort have proved to be useful in expert systems for medical diagnosis, based on signs or indicators of the presence of a disease. Clancey (1992, p. 16) offers the following rule of MYCIN (a knowledge-based expert system that provides consultations about diagnosis and treatment for infectious diseases), as an illustrative example:

Case 8.2
If: (1) The site of the culture is one of:
  those sites that are normally sterile, and
  (2) the gram stain of the organism is gram negative.

Then: There is strongly suggestive evidence (.8) that there is significant disease associated with this occurrence of the organism.

PREMISE: ($AND (SAME CNTXT SITE (LIST OF STERILESITES))
  (SAME CNTXT GRAM GRAMNEG))
ACTION: (CONCLUDE CNTXT SIGNIFICANCE YES TALLY 800)

The number 800 is a 'certainty factor' that indicates on a scale of −1,000 to +1,000 how certain the conclusion is, given that the premise is known with certainty.[7] Such a rule yields a strong indicator of disease, but the inference is defeasible (subject to cancellation in light of new information and testing of the hypothesis), and needs to be judged contextually in the sequence of what stage the program is in. Inferences of this sort in a system like MYCIN are generally not conclusive in nature (Jackson, 1986, p. 116), because it is possible for a single patient to be suffering from more than one disease at the same time. Abductive inferences, unlike deductive ones, but like inductive ones, are not 'guaranteed to be sound' (Jackson, 1986, p. 116), and can vary with the 'circumstances.' It is also interesting to note that Jackson (p. 116) cites the form of argument called 'affirming the consequent' as his account of the structure of abductive inference as a type of reasoning.

How then can we explain why the abductive inference in case 8.1a is different from the *modus ponens* type of inference in case 8.1b? *Modus ponens* is a deductively valid form of inference, whereas the 'affirming the consequent' type of inference used in case 8.1b has traditionally been classified as a fallacy in textbooks on deductive logic.

The explanation is that affirming the consequent must be rethought as a fallacy. It must no longer be taken for granted that inferences having the form of affirming the consequent are inherently fallacious, as case 8.1a clearly shows. We must now overcome our deductivist preconceptions about affirming the consequent. As an abductive inference, it can be presumptively reasonable in many cases.

The real explanation of the fallacy of consequent (see section 4, below) is the mistake of reversing the conditional premise – confusing inferences like 8.1a and 8.1b, where the two conditionals have different strengths as warrants. As usual with fallacies, the fallacy is based on a deception. For, in cases of abductive inference, typically a switching around of the conditional premise is a normal part of how this type of inference works, when it is used correctly. In the fallacious cases, this presumption of normal correctness is exploited.

For example, in case 8.1a, the conditional 'If there has been a power cut, everything in the fridge will be mouldy,' is a fairly strongly plausible conditional, because of the causal connections that would normally be expected to hold between the cutting of power, the stopping of the fridge, the lowering of the temperature of the contents of the fridge, and the subsequent proliferation of moulds in the food in the fridge. Because this sequence would be the normal chain of events in such a situation, the conditional also has some weight of plausibility going the same way, as in the inference in case 8.1b. Suppose that one arrives home and, whether or not the fridge is then running, sees mould on the food. The normal conjecture to be inferred (abductively) from this observed fact would be that the fridge had stopped running, for some significant period, while one was away.

Thus, in such a case, the *modus ponens* inference sets up and warrants the subsequent abductive inference. Characteristically, there is a switching around (transposition) of the conditional. This transposition is perfectly normal and is, indeed, characteristic of how abductive reasoning works. As we will see in section 4, below, it is only where the transposition is unwarranted that the fallacy of affirming the consequent really arises.

So far, then, we have come a little closer to getting a glimpse of how abductive reasoning works, and what its form is like. We can see that it is a kind of conjectural or plausible guessing by visible signs or indications that point towards an explanatory hypothesis. One of the best kinds of examples of its use – one that in fact indicates its usefulness graphically – is the abductive argument from MYCIN represented in case 8.2. The clue to the form of this argument lies in the distinctive, plausibilistic type of conditional cited by Bramer. This is clearly not a universally quantified, necessary, or material conditional of the type familiar in traditional deductive logic. The question is: how (more precisely) does it fit in with the form called 'affirming the consequent,' traditionally classified as a fallacy?

264   Argument Structure

3. Affirming the Consequent

The concept of a formal fallacy originated in the Middle Ages, at a time when Aristotle's theory of syllogisms was the accepted theory of inference in logic. According to Hamblin (1970, p. 194), the earliest account of formal fallacies occurs in the writings of Cassiodorus, a sixth-century contemporary of Boethius. The medieval treatises on logic tended to keep their discussions of formal and informal types of fallacies separate, apart from some exceptions noted by Hamblin (p. 194).

In the modern logic texts, many of the formal fallacies cited are closely related to inference forms of propositional logic. For example, one of the most commonly cited types of formal fallacies is the fallacy of affirming the consequent. The fallacy takes the form on the left (AC), an invalid form of inference, as contrasted to the valid form on the right, *modus ponens* (MP).

(AC) If A then B (MP) If A then B
         B A
         Therefore, A Therefore, B

For example, consider the argument 'If Bob is a pirate, he sails the sea for plunder; Bob sails the sea for plunder; therefore Bob is a pirate.' This argument is said to be an instance of the fallacy of affirming the consequent, because it is an instance of the invalid form on the left. Perhaps the argument above about Bob is a fallacy, not only because it is an instance of the invalid form AC, but also because it resembles the valid form MP.

It seems then that formal fallacies are differentiated on the grounds that they are each instances of a particular form of argument that is recognized in formal logic as invalid, and also perhaps because they resemble some form recognized as valid.

But perhaps this lesson is not so clear as it seems, however, as we can indicate by an observation made by Stebbing (1939). For it is easy to see a significant resemblance between the fallacy of affirming the consequent and the fallacy of undistributed middle in the following two cases cited by Stebbing (1939, p. 158).

($C1$) All weak people are sometimes tempted to lie.
        He is sometimes tempted to lie.
        Therefore, he is weak.

($C2$) If a man is weak, he is sometimes tempted to lie.

This man is sometimes tempted to lie.
Therefore, he is weak.

Both these arguments are fallacious. But they both seem fallacious for essentially the same reason. Whatever this reason is, if it is the same reason in both cases, then calling the fallacies by two different names may not be the best way to label, recognize, or analyse the fallacy. Sidgwick (1884, p. 221) confirms our conclusion when he wrote: 'The fallacy of "affirming the consequent" in hypothetical argument is essentially the same as that of employing an "undistributed middle" in a categorical one.' It's not the violation of any particular rule of formal logic that – uniquely, or characteristically, anyway – pinpoints the nature of the fallacy.

What is really the main problem in this kind of case generally is that the proponent of the argument has got the major premise switched around, as Aristotle pointed out. It seems like a mix-up between necessary and sufficient conditions, or perhaps a mix-up between 'If A then B' and 'If B then A.' This is not so much a formal fallacy at bottom as a kind of linguistic or conceptual confusion about conditional statements, in certain types of cases.

Consider a simple example given by Aristotle – see the quotation from *On Sophistical Refutations* in section 4, below. Being yellow is, in some typical and recognizable situations, a sign of something being honey. It is however, a defeasible sign. For the yellow something might be gall. On the other hand, being honey is an even more reliable sign that the substance in question is yellow. Here, too, the argument from sign is defeasible. But it is stronger. True, buckwheat honey is brown. But generally you can expect, in a typical case, that honey is going to be yellow. So the argument from sign is much weaker when the conditional goes one way than when it goes the other way. Surely this turning around of such a conditional, as Aristotle suggests, is the real root of the kind of fallacy at issue in the cases above.

The real problem in these cases is that there is a perfectly understandable propensity to get the major premise backwards, or to confuse the backwards and forwards interpretations of it. Hence, it may seem that the 'invalid' version, which is really a very weak argument, is much stronger than it is, due to the confusion with the 'valid' or stronger version. Clearly, *MP* and *AC* are involved in the explanation of this kind of error. But the really important thing about the fallacy is the confusion of the conditionals. It could best be called the 'fallacy of reversing the conditional' or, to use Aristotle's term for it, the 'fallacy of consequent' (see section 4, below).

What we see here then is that the very paradigms, the classical cases of formal fallacies, really have an informal element of interpretation of language that is the key element in the analysis of the fallacy. They have a formal aspect or element, but that is not the whole story, or perhaps even the most important part of them.

This aspect of interpretation in fallacy attribution has been analysed carefully by Adler (1994). Adler supports our contention that traditional formal fallacies are highly dependent on interpretation of a text of discourse in a given case. Adler (p. 271) cites an example offered by George (1983, p. 323) as 'clearly illustrating a formal fallacy.'

Case 8.3
He that is of God heareth God's words; ye therefore hear them not because ye are not of God. (John 8: 47).

George (ibid.) categorizes this argument as a fallacy on the grounds that it has the form called 'denying the antecedent': If A then B; *not-A*; therefore, *not-B*. Adler comments (p. 271): 'Perhaps the initial statement is not to be read as a conditional, but as a biconditional implying that "He that heareth God's words is of God." If so, the argument is valid.' Adler then proposes that, if there is a plausible alternative to the non-fallacious interpretation, the evaluation of the argument should turn, at least partly, on which interpretation is favoured by the evidence in the given case. These observations raise a number of questions about formal fallacies such as denying the antecedent and affirming the consequent, showing us how dependent the whole concept of a fallacy in such arguments is upon interpretation.

What is really characteristic of such cases of the fallacy of affirming the consequent is that the argument has a certain weight or degree of reasonableness when the conditional premise is interpreted one way. But it has less weight or degree of reasonableness when that premise is turned around, and interpreted the other way. As noted above, this solution is fairly close to Aristotle's own explanation of the fallacy. But to look into the matter further, let us examine what Aristotle wrote on this fallacy, or sophistical refutation.

4. Aristotle on the Fallacy of Consequent

Aristotle recognized the fallacy of affirming the consequent, including it as a specific fallacy, called 'consequent,' in his list of fallacies or sophistical refutations in *On Sophistical Refutations*. Aristotle's account of this fallacy provides a theory of how it works, and offers several interesting examples (*On Sophistical Refutations*, 167 b 1–20):

The refutation connected with the consequent is due to the idea that consequence is convertible. For whenever, if A is, B necessarily is, men also fancy that, if B is, A necessarily is. It is from this source that deceptions connected with opinion based on sense-perception arise. For men often take gall for honey because a yellow color accompanies honey; and since it happens that the earth becomes drenched when it has rained, if it is drenched, we think that it has rained, though this is not necessarily true. In rhetorical arguments proofs from signs are founded on consequences; for, when men wish to prove that a man is an adulterer, they seize upon the consequence of that character, namely, that the man dresses himself elaborately or is seen wandering abroad at night – facts that are true of many people, while the accusation is not true.[8]

Aristotle's theory is that the fallacy works because people get the antecedent and the consequent of the conditional backwards. They make the following inference:

Necessarily (if A then B).
Therefore, necessarily (if B then A).

Applying this analysis to the honey case, it would seem to be based on the presumption that the conditional 'If x is honey then x is yellow' is a strong enough sort of conditional so that, in Aristotle's view, it would express a necessary connection. This assumption appears dubious to us, raising questions about what Aristotle might have meant by 'necessary,' but let's go along with the idea that the conditional expresses a strong sort of connection. Then the converse conditional 'If x is yellow then x is honey' is less strong or plausible, given the existence of gall, a yellow substance that is not honey, and plenty of other common yellow substances that are also not honey.

What we might say today is that the conditional 'If x is honey then x is yellow' is a defeasible or default conditional, meaning that it is normally true, but is subject to exceptions, for example, in the case of buckwheat honey, which is brown. The other conditional, 'If x is yellow then x is honey,' is not even of this defeasible type, which provides a heuristic guide, because generally, if something is yellow, and that's all we know about it, then it would not be wise to generally presume or expect that this substance is honey.

Aristotle's case of the adulterer is even more interesting, because it shows how the consequent fallacy works in everyday argumentation to provide a basis for innuendo – a common basis of many fallacies. This example, as well, relates the fallacy of consequent to what is now called 'argument to the best explanation.' This case begins with the true conditional 'If x is an adulterer, then generally x will dress himself elaborately and x will wander around at night.' Let's say, at any rate, that these sorts of signs are characteristic generally of adulterers. Then the conditional is true. However, the converse conditional 'If x dresses himself elaborately and x wanders around at night, then x is an adulterer' fails to hold generally. The reason is, presumably, that there are plenty of people who commonly wander around at night dressed elaborately who are not adulterers. There may be other explanations for this behaviour. For example, they may be people going to a party or some sort of political function that happens to take place in the evening.

However, as Aristotle points out, these indicators could be used as the basis of an accusation, to throw suspicion of being an adulterer on some person. To refute the accusation, presumably they would have to give some other plausible explanation of this nocturnal behaviour.

Aristotle's general explanation of the fallacy of the consequent is the following. In a given case, a conditional is true, and the antecedent obtains, as can be observed, so we have the form of inference (*MP*). But then we presume, mistakenly, that the conditional premise is convertible, and we draw the inference (*AC*). But this inference is invalid. And hence, we have committed the fallacy of the consequent. At least, this is the traditional account of the formal fallacy of affirming the consequent so often given in the textbooks.

But there is more to it than this for arguments in the form (*AC*), as the honey and adulterer cases (as well as the MYCIN cases from the previous section) show, are sometimes reasonable, or abductively correct. So just to point out that (*AC*) is *deductively* invalid is not enough to pin down the committing of a fallacy, in a given case. The analysis of the fallacy in such a case (where there is a fallacy) must be more complicated than this account. It must be that the argument only seems valid because we get the conditional premise backwards, confusing a necessary conditional with a plausibilistic one. At any rate, this more complex analysis is certainly suggested by Aristotle's account.

The deeper problem underlying this analysis, however, is that we are still no closer to understanding the structure of abductive inference – what makes it legitimate and reasonable as a distinctive form of argument in some cases. The MYCIN use of abductive reasoning for diagnosis of diseases based on signs or indications gives us a clue where to look.

5. Ancient Views of Argument from Sign

The ancients were well aware of argument from sign as a distinctive type of inference to a conclusion, as we have already seen from our analysis of Aristotle's concept of enthymeme in chapter 5. The remark of Quintilian in *Institutio Oratoria* (1935; V. IX. 8–11) is also particularly interesting (p. 199):

> There are other indications or εὡκότα, that is probabilities, as the Greeks call them, which do not involve a necessary conclusion. These may not be sufficient in themselves to remove doubt, but may yet be of the greatest value when taken in conjunction with other indications. The Latin equivalent of the Greek σημεῖον is *signum*, a sign, though some have called it *indicium*, an indication, or *vestigium*, a trace. Such signs or indications enable us to infer that something else has happened; blood for instance may lead us to infer that a murder has taken place. But blood stains on a garment may be the result of the slaying of a victim at a sacrifice or of bleeding at the nose. Everyone who has a bloodstain on his clothes is not necessarily a murderer. But although such an indication may not amount to proof in itself, yet it may be produced as evidence in conjunction with other indications, such for instance as the fact that the man with the bloodstain was the enemy of the murdered man, had threatened him previously or was in the same place with him.

This account of argument from sign given by Quintilian identifies a number of features that are characteristic of this type of argument generally.

One is that this type of reasoning is weaker than that of the kind of argument which provides a necessary or sufficient condition for a hypothesis, at least in its typical use. Thus, it is a species of a kind of reasoning Quintilian classifies as being based on *eikos*, sometimes translated as 'probability.' But this does not mean 'probability,' in the modern sense – it could be better described as guesswork or presumptive (default) inference, based on what seems to be true, or what is the case generally or normally (subject to exceptions, in particular cases).[9]

Another related characteristic of this type of reasoning is that it is most useful in a balance-of-considerations argument, where there are many small pieces of evidence, but none of them is, by itself, conclusive (sufficient). Here, the case presented by Quintilian of the bloodstain on the person's clothes is an excellent example. This sign, by itself, is not sufficient to prove that the person in question is (necessarily) a murderer. But, 'in conjunction with other indications,' it may be produced as a significant piece of evidence.

According to this view of argument from sign, a sign is one element, in a given case, of a larger body of evidence. If the sign is present, then normally it will give a small push, or weight of supporting evidence, for a hypothesis. But, as Quintilian writes, such an indication 'may not amount to a proof in itself.' Instead, it needs to be weighed as only one factor 'in conjunction with other indications' in the given case. Nowadays we would say that argument from sign is a nonmonotonic type of reasoning, subject to default as more evidence is collected in a particular case. The sign functions as giving a tentative weight of presumption in favour of a hypothesis that can go in one of two directions as more evidence comes in: (a) it can support a greater weight of presumption in favour of the hypothesis, by fitting in with further evidence that also supports the hypothesis; or (b) the argument from sign can default, when refuted or contraindicated by the subsequent weight of evidence.

Hence, the conditional that links the sign to the hypothesis in the argument-from-sign warrant is not governed by the operator 'necessarily,' or even 'probably.' It is governed by the operator 'normally, but subject to exceptions' – see Rescher (1976) and Walton (1992b) on presumptive conditionals and plausible reasoning.

Argument from sign was well recognized in the ancient world as a common type of argumentation in everyday conversational reasoning. It was, as we have seen, an important type of argument for Aristotle's study of reasoning.[10] But somehow it became neglected or overlooked, as deductive logic (starting with syllogistic) became the dominant model of reasoning in the Western world. Perhaps argument from sign was felt to be too unreliable, because of its weak and defeasible nature as a type of evidence, to be appropriate for scientific reasoning.

However, signs have come to be studied by logicians, the most notable instance being Peirce's theory of signs. Peirce divided signs into icons indices and symbols, which indicate (respectively) by resemblance, causality, and conventional (or habitual) rule.[11] The problem is to see whether we can get a clear-enough grasp of what a sign is, so that argument from sign can be identified as a distinctive type of argument.

6. What Is a Sign?

A sign is an observable mark or trace of the presence of some object or event, in a case where the event or object cannot itself be directly observed, or directly verified as being present. Nevertheless, the presence of the object may leave some traces, or may have some associated features, that can be observed. These traces or patterns that are indicators of an event or object of a certain kind will have certain observable features that can be identified, and can perhaps even be measured and described quantitatively in some cases. When this characteristic pattern is identified, in a given case, then, in context, it can be used to suggest a conclusion by implicature. The sign points to a certain conclusion, but the conclusion is drawn, not by necessity, but only by pushing a (typically small) weight of evidence towards a hypothesis, presumptively.

What is a sign? A very good general definition is given in Sextus Empiricus (*Against the Logicians*, II, 143): a *sign* is that which seems to make something evident. What is presupposed by this definition falls into three components: (a) an object or event that is not evident to an observer; (2) another object or event that is evident to the observer; and (3) the second object or event is related to the first in such a way that it makes the first one evident to the observer. What is this relation of 'making evident'? It could mean 'explain.' But this interpretation by Sextus would be a precursor to the idea of the inference to the best explanation. But there is another possible interpretation. It could mean that the appearance of one object or event can serve to reveal (or make evident) another object or event, because the two are normally associated or connected to each other in common experience. Hence, when one is observed as present in a particular set of circumstances, the presence of the other can be inferred.

Sextus gives the example (II, 152) of a scar. It is a sign of a previous wound. However, we can no longer see the wound, because it is in the past. But, when we see the scar, we infer the prior existence of the wound.

Sextus also cites the case of smoke and fire (II, 153).[12] We may not be able to see the fire, but we can see the smoke – it is evident. Hence, we infer the (presumptive) existence of fire, even though the fire is not evident. Of course, we could be wrong. It may be that there is smoke but no fire, in some cases. But the smoke (in context) may shift enough of a weight of presumption towards the supposition of fire that, on a basis of burden of proof, we may be justified in calling the fire department. Here the smoke functions as a kind of evidence, or reason for drawing a conclusion that is defeasible. It is not like a deductively valid argument, or what might be called a 'necessary inference.' Yet it can be a good reason for drawing a conclusion pre-emptively that is strong enough in the right kind of situation to serve as a reasoned basis for taking action. Later on, it can be verified, one way or the other, whether there was actually a fire or not, as suggested by the smoke.

Argument from sign is highly contextual as a type of inference to be evaluated as reasonable or not, in a given case. In scientific inquiry, as Peirce pointed out, this presumptive or guessing type of inference is characteristic of the discovery stage, where questions are asked and plausible candidate hypotheses are selected out for later testing. At the closing or presentation stage of a scientific inquiry, the use of abductive-sign reasoning would be generally inappropriate. At this stage, the evidence furnished from testing the hypothesis or hypotheses is arrayed, and conclusions are drawn from reproducible evidence. Conjectures based on sign reasoning tend to be characteristic of the discovery stage, where plausible and testable hypotheses that show promise are selected out from the set of available alternatives. According to Peirce (as noted above), the function of this guessing or abductive reasoning is to reduce costs by cutting down the large number of possible hypotheses for testing to the ones that seem most promising.

This function of revealing the non-evident that is characteristic of sign for Sextus is not necessarily an indicator that Sextus had explanation in mind, as opposed to argument. For Sextus (*Outlines of Pyrrhonism,* II, 140) defined a *probative* argument as one that deduces something non-evident by means of evident premises, as we saw in chapter 1, section 5. Thus, to think that Sextus was defining the concept of sign by seeing it as a kind of explanation (or inference to the best explanation) would not be warranted. He could have been seeing it as a kind of probative argument, or as an argument that has some sort of probative function of enabling an observer to infer a non-evident conclusion from evident premises.

According to Sextus's account then, a sign is something that is evident, and seems to make something else – something that is not itself directly evident – indirectly evident, in virtue of some relationship the two things have. This relationship could be of a variable sort – it could be causation that connects the two things, but it might be other kinds of relations as well, depending on the type of sign involved.

7. Form of Argument from Sign

Argument from sign has the following general form, where A is a proposition describing a purported finding or observation, and B is another proposition that could be called a 'hypothesis,' or 'event signified.'

A is true in this situation.
B is generally indicated as true when its sign A is true, in this kind of situation.
Therefore, B is true in this situation.

Hastings (1962, pp. 55–64) identified argument from sign as a distinctive type of argumentation, or 'mode of reasoning,' and set out a form or argumentation scheme for it, comparable to the one above.

Hastings (p. 63) postulated two critical questions to be used when evaluating argument from sign in a given case.

Q1: What is the strength of the correlation of the sign with the event signified?
Q2: Are there other events which would more readily account for the sign?

Hastings argued, with respect to *Q1*, that the stronger the causal relation or association between *A* and *B*, the stronger is the argument from sign. With respect to *Q2*, Hastings argued (p. 64) that, for argument from sign to be strong or acceptable, other causes for the sign must be unlikely.

Argument from sign is very commonly used in criminal investigations, and is an important aspect of legal evidence of the kind commonly used in criminal cases. Some very illustrative, simplified cases are given in the Sherlock Holmes stories. Although fictional, these cases can be used to illustrate the function of argument from sign very effectively.

One example is also a good case of how arguments from sign are frequently used to cumulate evidence in a complex type of argumentation called an 'evidence-accumulating argument.' In an *evidence-accumulating argument*, the argument is an ordered sequence of arguments from sign, where each individual argument gives only a small weight of evidence for the ultimate conclusion, but, taken together, the whole sequence builds up a significantly greater weight of evidence for that conclusion.

The classic illustration is the 'Study in Scarlet' case from chapter 3, section 7. How did Holmes draw this startling conclusion, for we presume he knew nothing of Watson's background at this point? His reasoning took the form of a cumulative build-up of steps of inference, each based on a sign; for example, 'His face is dark.' Once the whole sequence is put together, Holmes draws a hypothesis and concludes that Watson is a physician who has recently done military service in Afghanistan.

In a given case, each individual instance of argument from sign generally gives only a small or inconclusive weight of support for its conclusion. Argument from sign is generally a presumptive and defeasible type of reasoning of the kind called presumptive reasoning by Walton (1992b, ch. 2). This is generally true, even though some signs can be relatively conclusive indicators of something in a given situation.

The presumptive nature of argument from sign as a type of reasoning is best seen in how individual instances of this type of argument should be evaluated. When the two premises of the argument from sign are justified by appropriate evidence in a given case, a burden of proof, or weight of presumption, is shifted from the proponent's side to the respondent (questioner's) side in a dialogue exchange. However, when one of the appropriate critical questions is asked, at the next move in the dialogue exchange, the weight of presumption shifts back to the other side. The argument from sign ceases to have a weight of presumption in favour of it until this critical question is answered appropriately.

The presumptive nature of argument from sign is also reflected in the transposition of the second premise of the argument scheme from a conditional of the following form: if *B* then generally (but subject to possible exceptional cases) *A*. The second premise of the argument scheme for argument from sign says that *B* is generally indicated as true when its sign *A* is true. This premise asserts a presumptive conditional of the form 'If sign *A*, then generally (but subject to exceptions) *B* is indicated.' But this conditional is based on the prior conditional 'If *B* then generally *A*.' There is a kind of circularity involved in the sequence of reasoning implicit in argument from sign. The reasoning goes from *A* to *B*, but it also presupposes a prior inference from *B* to *A*. But this circularity is not an instance of the fallacy of begging the question in the abductive reasoning process. Also characteristic of argument from sign is the kind of backwards or abductive form of inference identical to the so-called formal fallacy (see section 3, above) of affirming the consequent.

However, now this abductive type of inference can be seen, in some cases, as being a presumptively reasonable kind of argument from sign when it does shift a weight of presumption that can only be dislodged by the asking of appropriate critical questions. The argument, when reasonable, moves a dialogue forward by the posing of a defeasible hypothesis in a sequence of reasoned questions and replies – a hypothesis that is defeasible, and subject to possible future refutation should new evidence come in – but that nevertheless can have a provisional status as an inferred conclusion.

8. How Argument from Sign Works

Argument from sign works by picking out a promising or plausible hypothesis in a given case of a relatively familiar or recognizable type where certain normal patterns or regular features are present. For example, if bear tracks (or what appear to be bear tracks) of a certain recognizable kind are seen in a wooded area where we would normally expect to see bears around, then these signs could be taken as indicators of the presence of a bear. However, if bear tracks were found on the ceiling of the University of Winnipeg Library, they would be taken as evidence of a student prank.

In the normal type of case, where, say, bear tracks are found in Jasper National Park on a path, then these marks can be identified by recognizable features (Rezendes, 1992). Normally we would expect that such imprints indicate the presence of some animal, and these features enable us to eliminate other hypotheses, and narrow down to the plausible hypothesis of a bear.

In the form of argument from sign, the conditional has the structure 'If sign *A* then generally (but subject to exceptions), *B* is indicated. For example, if bear tracks are found (in a context, like finding these tracks on a trail in a national park), then the presence of a bear is indicated. But is this conditional acceptable, as a plausible hypothesis used to license a *modus ponens* inference to conclude to the presence of a bear, in a particular case where the observed fact is that tracks are found? The answer is that it depends on whether the prior conditional 'If B then generally A' is true. That is, it depends on whether if a bear was present in this location and situation, bear tracks (the sign) would be left by it. If this presumption is reasonable, it can be transposed, supporting the abductive inference from sign.

Argument from sign works because certain observable characteristics: (a) form a pattern that is easily or definitely recognizable; (b) mark out the presence of one object or event as contrasted with another; and (c) work because they link contrasting patterns to contrasting characteristics of the objects or events they indicate. For example, in Rezendes (1992, p. 242), three ways of differentiating between black bear and grizzly tracks are given.

1 *Test*: 'Draw a line from the bottom of the outer (or big) toe across the front of the palm pad. In a black bear, the smaller inner toe will be mostly below the line, whereas in a grizzly, the little toe will be mostly above the line.' This test works because the toes of a black bear are arranged more in an arc than those of a grizzly.
2 *Test*: Examine the track to see whether the toe marks look pinched together or not. In a soft soil, the toes of the grizzly look pinched together. This appears so because the spaces between the toes are 'usually greater' in black bears than in grizzlies.
3 *Test*: measure the toe and nail lengths. 'If a bear track has a nail as long as or longer than the toe, there's a good chance it is a grizzly; if it has a nail shorter than the toe, it's probably a black bear.' This test works because generally the nails of the grizzly tend to be longer than those of the black bear.

It is clear from the commentary of Rezendes (1992, pp. 242–3) that these tests function as general rules or indicators only, and that they are subject to exceptions and difficulties of interpretation in certain types of cases.

In each of these instances of use of argument from sign, the observer must look at a given track or print mark to see its pattern and general characteristics. She can then apply each of these three tests, by looking for the presence of a particular sign or indicator. Then, if a sign is present, she can apply the conditional specified in the test, and draw the conclusion by inference, one way or the other (black bear or grizzly).

Notice also, in this case, how the cumulative effect of the presence of more than one of these signs would work. If two of the tests indicated 'grizzly,' then the inference to the conclusion 'grizzly, as opposed to black bear' would be more weighty than those of just the determination of a single 'grizzly' sign. If all three signs were to indicate 'grizzly' in a given case, this would give even a stronger weight of presumption towards the conclusion 'grizzly, as opposed to black bear.' On the other hand, the presence of one grizzly indicator and one black bear indicator, in a given case, would generally tend to have a cancelling-out effect.

The use of argument from sign in this type of practical, everyday case of inference has value and presumptive worth because it can rightly serve, for example, as a practical basis for taking precautions to act in a safe manner (by storing food properly, and so forth) in a case where bear tracks are observed in a park area. Of course, such an inference is best seen as a defeasible kind of reasoning to the conclusion that bears are present in this area, a hypothesis that can be verified or refuted by subsequent observations and empirical testing. But, by generating a presumptively reasonable conclusion, it functions as a basis for prudent action.

In other cases, argument from sign can function in a scientific inquiry as a way of suggesting a plausible hypothesis that can later be verified or falsified as part of a theory or explanation that is tested against other evidence. A good example is the following case from Kesterton (1994, A20), about juvenile-delinquent elephants.

Case 8.4
When conservationists at South Africa's Pilanesberg game reserve discovered a series of systematically killed rhinos, they had two clues to the culprits: tusk-shaped wounds on the corpses and elephant footprints in the vicinity. Although an elephant does not normally attack a rhinoceros, the game reserve has a number of unsupervised, adolescent males who would normally be kept in line by bulls. Without adult role models to test themselves against, the animals had become juvenile delinquents.

In this case, the wounds and footprints suggested a certain hypothesis as a conclusion of abductive inference from signs. Once the hypothesis was formulated as part of a theory, it could then be verified or falsified by further evidence collected at the later stages of the inquiry.

It is by now readily apparent how confusing abductive argument from sign with deductive argument is a basis for the committing of fallacies. Deductive reasoning is a species of necessary inference that blocks all possible exceptions to a rule or conditional warrant, whereas abductive reasoning is inherently open and defeasible.

9. Sign versus Best Explanation

Arguments from sign can be based on premises that are either prior to or posterior to the conclusion inferred. In the case of animal tracks identified as the sign of a particular animal, the sign (the tracks) we now see is posterior to the conclusion we draw – namely, that the animal had passed that way earlier. We presume that the passing of the animal caused the tracks to occur, and draw our conclusion accordingly. In the case of dark clouds that we say are a sign of rain, the sign is prior to the conclusion we draw – namely, that rain will (or might) occur.

In the animal-tracks case, it is plausible to argue that the argument from sign is based on an inference to the best explanation. But, in the clouds case, it is not so easy to do this. To say that the best explanation of the clouds is the rain, and, therefore, from the clouds we can infer the rain, does not seem appropriate.

One thing shown here is that some signs are predictive while others are retrodictive. Clouds are a predictive sign of rain, whereas tracks are a retrodictive sign of the animal identified from them. Retrodictive signs are the basis of the kind of case of argument from sign that does plausibly seem to be based on inference to the best explanation. But predictive signs, although they are associated with argumentation from sign, do not seem to be associated with an inference to the best explanation.

One might still try to preserve the parallel between the bear case and the clouds case by reconstruing the clouds case. In this case, the clouds are caused by the collection of moisturized air into a mass, and it is this mass of water that becomes the rain – or, we could say, causes the rain. Thus, there is a causal connection that could serve as an explanatory link in this case, somewhat comparable to the bear case. But the problem is that this structure of explanation is still not comparable to that of the bear case in the key respect. It still is not right to say that the rain is the best explanation of the clouds. Instead, it is a third factor – the collection of moist air – that causes the clouds, and subsequently the rain.

If our analysis of these cases is right, we should draw the conclusion that not all cases of argument from sign can be analysed as cases of inference to the best explanation. It follows that argument from sign cannot be reduced, as a distinctive type of argument, to inference to the best explanation.

It does seem to be true, however, that some, or even many, cases of argument from sign can usefully be seen as retroductive types of inference, comparable to the kind of reasoning Peirce called 'abduction' and that is called 'inference to the best explanation' in recent literature. But how useful is this connection in showing us the logical structure of this type of reasoning?

The problem is to give a useful account of the concept of an explanation. Lipton (1991) defends a causal model of explanation in his analysis of inference to the best explanation. But the problem with this approach – pointed out by Achinstein (1992, p. 352) – is that Lipton provides no analysis of the concept of causation, and admits that there is no uncontroversial analysis of this concept. Our alternative is to look to argument from sign as providing a better route to the analysis of abductive inference as a distinctive type of argument having a form or argument scheme that can be evaluated as used correctly or incorrectly in a given case. Such an evaluation is pragmatic in nature, having to do with how the argument is used in a question-reply, interactive (dialogue) sequence of exchanges at a particular stage of an inquiry or deliberation framework (see chapter 1). But this pragmatic analysis is appropriate to the presumptive and plausibilistic nature of abductive inference as a species of intelligent interrogation or 'guessing' that concludes to a provisional hypothesis. At a later verification stage of such a dialogue sequence, the hypothesis can be verified or falsified more conclusively, by appropriate use of inductive or deductive arguments.

10. Tentative Conclusions

It is our hypothesis that what Peirce called 'abduction' is, in many instances, the type of argument we are calling 'argument from sign,' especially in the cases of discovery of hypotheses or guessing stage, where Peirce was (primarily) thinking of this type of argument as used in the context of a scientific inquiry. But this type of argument from sign is also widely used in other contexts, and is familiar in argumentation used in everyday conversation and in practical undertakings. It is also a very important argument as used in legal evidence.

The reasoning used in a typical case of argument from sign has a backwards and forwards sequence. From the observed bear tracks B, we infer the presence of a bear A, for example. But the basis of this inference is a prior conditional of the form 'If A then B'; for example, 'If a bear was present in this situation, it would leave this (observed) kind of tracks.' The inference using this conditional is an affirming-the-consequent type, which infers from the existence of the tracks (B) to the presence of a bear (A). Proponents of inference to the best explanation explain this inference as an explanation – the presence of the bear is the 'best explanation' of the existence of the tracks. But, on our second interpretation of the account of Sextus (section 6, above), the inference is based on an association in common experience between A and B. We know that, in normal conditions, in a given type of situation, these tracks, of the type identified, indicate the presence of a bear. The reason is that a bear produces this type of tracks.

Similarly with the case cited by Sextus of the scar. We infer the existence of a previous wound, because a wound would normally be the sort of thing that would produce the scar. In fact, in this case, it would seem that only a wound would normally produce such a scar. What seems to be involved is an inference from effect to cause.

Similarly with the case of the smoke and the fire. The smoke is evident, so we infer the (plausible) existence of fire, because it is normally a fire that would produce smoke, in this context. The sign is an evident or visible marker of something else that is normally associated with it or connected to it.

Given the existence of the sign A, in a particular case, we then reason backwards to the resumed existence of the non-evident factor that normally produces or is associated with A – namely, B. The sequence of reasoning can be viewed as the following kind of argumentation in a dialogue:

A is evident; therefore, B must (presumably) also be present; Why?; because B normally produces or is connected with A; so, if A is evident, B is present; but A is evident; therefore, by *modus ponens*, B is present.

This sequence of reasoning is the forward-moving argument from the sign A to the non-evident factor associated with it, B.

But there is also a reverse sequence of reasoning from B to A, based on the premise that B normally produces, or is connected with A. An implicit premise, of the form 'If B then A,' is consequently involved in the chain of reasoning as well. Here the reasoning goes backwards, from the sign A, that is evident, to the non-evident associated factor, B.

This abductive type of argument, as Peirce rightly described its structure, has the form of AC, or *affirming the consequent*, a deductively invalid form of argument long featured in logic textbooks as a fallacious type of inference. And it is fallacious, or at least invalid, as far as deductive reasoning is concerned. But viewed as a presumptive, defeasible type of argument that is non-deductive in nature, it can be seen, at least generally, as a reasonable form of argument that has a distinctive structure in its own right. The fallacy, as explained in our account, is not just the failure of deductive validity. It also relates to the confusion between two types of conditionals by reversal of the conditional premise. What needs to be brought into the explanation of the fallacy is an account of why such an inference would seem to be valid, and would therefore be a potential source of deception and common error. This explanation has to do with the fact that, at least in some cases, AC in the form of argument from sign is a reasonable inference. Hence, there is a perfectly understandable reason implicit in this type of argumentation generally, why there is a tendency to get the premise turned around. The transformation of the conditional premise from a prior (reversed) conditional premise is the normal *modus operandi* of abductive reasoning.

This explanation works for many cases, but to get a more general explanation, it is necessary to observe that, in some cases, there can be considerable uncertainty about both (a) which way the conditional premise is meant to be taken and (b) what type of argument the proponent means to put forward in the given case, that is, deductive, inductive, or abductive. To take a hard case, consider this argument from Cooke (1991, p. 47):

Case 8.5
premises Only the fittest species for their biological niche survive.
Cockroaches are one of the fittest species for their biological niche.

conclusion Cockroaches survive.

Cooke reports (p. 47) that 90 per cent of third-year mathematics students at the Delft University of Technology (most of whom reportedly had taken a course in mathematical logic) regarded this argument as valid. However, as Cooke points out (p. 48), if you put the argument into a logically equivalent form, as represented below, most people would probably recognize that it is invalid.

For all species x, if x survives then x is one of the fittest for its biological niche.
Cockroaches are one of the fittest for their biological niche.

Cockroaches survive.

The difference appears to reside in the fact (or presumed fact) that most people are inclined to interpret the conditional premise of the first argument by turning it around, to get the following valid argument:

For all species x, if x is one of the fittest for its biological niche then x survives.
Cockroaches are one of the fittest for their biological niche.

Cockroaches survive.

This argument has the deductively valid form *MP*, and, moreover, the conditional premise could seem quite plausible to most people.

The problem here is that the conditional premise, having to do with evolutionary theory, is quite abstract, and it is quite hard for most of us to judge, in the case presumed to be at issue (where no further contextual clues are offered), which way this premise is perceived to be most plausible, or which way the proponent means us to take it, or even whether we are meant to take it both ways (as a biconditional). Moreover, we are given no contextual clues whether the conditional premise is meant as an exceptionless universal generalization, or as a default generalization that could be subject to exceptions in some cases. Possibly then, faced with this much uncertainty, we apply a kind of charitable interpretation and presume, without reflecting too analytically on the tricky word 'only,' that the argument has some form that either makes it deductively valid or abductively reasonable. At any rate, this could serve as one possible explanation of Cooke's reported observation on how this argument tends to be taken.

At any rate, we can see that this case suggests several complications, and shows that the fallacy of affirming the consequent is not easy to explain, in some cases. It may be that, in some cases, the respondents don't take it as a deductive argument at all, and take it as abductive, but still reverse the conditional premise. It may also be that, in some cases, owing to the absence of contextual indicators, and the opacity of the subject-matter, respondents simply lack sufficient guidance on how to interpret the argument, and therefore guess, using some criterion other than logical form, for example, try to construe the argument charitably in a way that seems to make it most plausible.

Our general conclusion is that abductive reasoning is a complex back-and-forth sequence of reasoning based on a non-explicit premise to the effect that the two propositions or factors are connected together. The paradigm type of abductive reasoning, and its most common use in everyday conversational argumentation, is argument from sign. Hence, as Peirce rightly conjectured, scientific argumentation from an observed fact to a hypothesis is a species of abductive inference. Indeed, it is our further conjecture here that scientific argumentation from an observed fact to a hypothesis, at the 'guessing' or initial stage of discovery, is based on the use of argument from sign. Positivists will not like this conjecture at all, because it makes scientific reasoning seem (to the positivists, or perhaps to the general public) too much like folk wisdom or common guesswork. Positivists will insist that scientific argumentation from an observed fact to a hypothesis must be analysed as a type of statistical or probabilistic inference, that can be quantified, that is, expressed in precise mathematical equations. No doubt this probabilistic type of inference is characteristic of the later stages of a scientific inquiry. But at the discovery stage, conjecturing to a plausible hypothesis is best viewed as what it really is – argument from sign.

Notes

Chapter One

1 At least, in the sections where the term 'argument' is defined in the textbooks, the concern is (mainly) with deductive arguments.
2 When Sextus uses the term 'true argument' (*alethon logon*), he is following Stoic terminology, as he explains just prior to the part quoted: '... they say ... a true argument is that which deduces a true conclusion from true premises' (*Outlines of Pyrrhonism*, II, 139). In modern terms, we would call this a 'sound' argument, that is, a deductively valid argument with true premises.
3 On classifying and identifying these types of dialogue, see Walton 1989, 1990b, and 1992b, and Walton and Krabbe, 1995.
4 On commitment in dialogue, see Walton and Krabbe, 1995.
5 See note 3, above.
6 Hurley, 1991, p. 1, and Fogelin and Sinnott-Armstrong, 1991, p. 4, also exclude the quarrel, squabble, or verbal fight as a meaning of 'argument' appropriate for logic.
7 Hempel, 1965.
8 See Ruben, 1990. An account of recent research in the social sciences on analysing everyday conversational explanations can be found in Antaki, 1988.
9 Ruben, 1990.
10 *NBC News*, 5:30 P.M., 29 April 1992.
11 Walton, 1989, pp. 84–93.
12 *20-20*, 1 May 1991 (segment on the Los Angeles riots).
13 Hoaglund, 1987, p. 393.
14 Walton, 1990b.
15 Barth and Krabbe, 1982.
16 Walton, 1989.

Chapter Two

1. Hempel, 1965.
2. Examples roughly similar to case 2.5 were used by Salmon (1971) to argue that explanations are not arguments.
3. Cases similar to 2.6 were used by Salmon (1978) to show that explanations are different from arguments.
4. Lipton, 1991.
5. Walton, 1990a.
6. Ibid.
7. See also Walton, 1992b.
8. See Walton, 1990b.
9. See also Ruben, 1990.
10. See also Salmon, 1971, and Ruben, 1990.

Chapter Three

1. See Johnson and Blair, 1985.
2. As shown in chapter 2, section 2, van Eemeren and Grootendorst use the term 'co-ordinative compound argument' to describe linked arguments.
3. A different convention for diagramming linked arguments (more amenable to graph theory) is proposed by Walton and Batten (1984), and used to analyse circular argumentation by Walton (1991).
4. See chapter 2, section 2, for a full list of indicator-words. See also Verbiest, 1991.
5. Walton, 1990a.
6. Van Eemeren and Grootendorst use the term 'multiple argumentation': see chapter 2, section 2.
7. Called 'subordinative compound argumentation' by van Eemeren and Grootendorst (1984, p. 93).
8. See van Ditmarsch, 1987.
9. Arthur Conan Doyle, 'A Study in Scarlet,' in *The Complete Sherlock Holmes*, vol. 1 (Garden City, NY: Doubleday, Doran & Co., 1932).
10. Ibid., p. 11.
11. Ibid., pp. 20–1.
12. This example no longer appears in the later, fourth edition (1991).
13. An analysis of this type of statement is one of the problems addressed in chapters 5 and 6.

Chapter Four

1. Meaning that both marbles are non-black, to put the conclusion another way; that is, the first marble is not black and the second marble is not black.

2 Here the assumption is made that being perfect means having all the good qualities, so that a demonstration of having even one bad quality counts decisively against the hypothesis that something is perfect.
3 Thomas (1981, p. 53) writes that all deductively valid arguments are linked, while Govier (1985, p. 259) claims only that most deductively valid arguments are linked (subject to exceptions, for example, where one premise is redundant).
4 Yanal (1991, p. 144, note 7) discusses a comparable case posed by David Hitchcock. According to Yanal (p. 143), posing odd cases like the 'bad arguments' considered here is to raise questions that are too problematic to admit of allowable answers. They are like 'those philosophical problems that Nietzsche advised us to treat like cold baths and get in and out of quickly.'
5 Snoeck Henkemans (1992, p. 92) discusses what amounts to this same ambiguity when she carefully distinguishes between the acceptability of a premise and the sufficiency of a premise for the conclusion of an argument. She points out that the language used in the textbooks to distinguish between linked and convergent arguments frequently confuses these two requirements.

Chapter Five

1 See also Blair, 1991.
2 The translation quoted is that of Sir David Ross (revised by J.L. Ackrill and J.O. Urmson), cited in the bibliography as Aristotle, 1987. The quote is from page 3 of that translation of the *Nicomachean Ethics*.
3 Much could also depend on which propositions Helen and Bob have agreed to or accepted (tacitly or explicitly) as their commitments in what is known of their previous discussion on tipping. On commitment, see Hamblin, 1970, p. 257, and Walton and Krabbe, 1995.
4 On the problem of defining the concepts of necessary and sufficient conditions in relation to practical reasoning, see Walton, 1990a, pp. 21-3.

Chapter Six

1 A currently fashionable expression of this view can be found in Fish, 1990. See the comments and criticisms in Currie, 1991.
2 See also the reply of Kneupper (1978) to Willard, and Willard's rejoinder (1978).
3 See chapters 3, 4, and 7.
4 Chapter 5, section 5.

Chapter Seven

1 A categorical syllogism is an argument with two premises and once conclusion, con-

taining three terms, each of which appears twice. The middle term appears once in each premise, and the two other terms (the so-called major and minor terms) appear once in the conclusion and one in each premise. No other argument is a categorical syllogism.
2 This, of course, is not illegitimate. It is possible to have syllogistic enthymemes and other deductive (non-syllogistic) enthymemes. Still, it leaves one wondering how enthymemes ought to be precisely defined.
3 He writes (*Prior Analytics*, 70 a 17) that the syllogism used in case 7.6 is in the first figure, and later (70 a 30) that a syllogism in the first figure cannot be refuted if it is true.
4 Aristotle, 1937, pp. 25–6.
5 Ibid., p. 25.
6 See also Hamblin, 1970.
7 According to Gough and Tindale (1985, p. 106), this example came from *Today Magazine*, 28 November 1981. It appears to be part of a letter to the editor.
8 See Jackson and Jacobs, 1980, for a discussion of the role of implicature in enthymemes.
9 See the beginning of chapter 7 (before section 1).
10 Hallie, 1967, p. 33. Peirce's notion of abduction – see Sabre, 1990 – appears to be a species of plausible reasoning, as well. This connection is analysed in chapter 8.
11 See Govier, 1989a, for a discussion of inductive enthymemes.
12 An outline of how non-explicit commitments are revealed in dialogue is given in Walton, 1993.

Chapter Eight

1 Note especially the discussions of cases 4.17, 4.18, and 4.19.
2 This meeting of the Seminar on Argumentation and Reasoning took place in Schloss Dagstuhl, Germany, 22–7 August 1993. See the seminar report by Gabbay and Ohlbach (1993).
3 It is mentioned in one of the currently most popular introductory logic textbooks, Hurley, 1991 (p. 33), where it is treated very briefly (in nine lines).
4 As Misak (1991, p. xi) notes, there is no standard way of referring to the corpus of Peirce's writings, and trying to use the existing systems is difficult and frustrating. Hence, we have followed the unusual practice of referring to the secondary works on Peirce primarily, but indicating their pagination formulas as well. The reader will find this method gives the most useful information on where citations can be found.
5 This was clearly apparent from various discussions with Dov Gabbay and Hans Jürgen Ohlbach at the Schloss meeting – see note 2, above.
6 Conditionals of the type cited by Bramer are called 'rules' in computer science.

Using Toulmin's term, they could be called 'warrants' in a way that describes their function well.
7 No measures of weighing the strength of a plausible inference are discussed or evaluated here, but the reader could consult Walton, 1992b and 1992c for further treatment of this subject.
8 Aristotle, 1955, p. 31.
9 Aristotle, in the *Rhetoric* (1357 a 14–1357 b 27), distinguished between necessary signs (*tekmeria*) that can be converted to syllogistic form, and signs that do not convert to a necessary inference: see chapter 7, section 2. And admittedly, some arguments from sign are highly conclusive. Even so, without discussing the question of how to assign weights or degrees of strength to arguments from sign, we hold to the thesis that this type of argument tends (characteristically) to be presumptive in nature.
10 See *Prior Analytics* (70 a 6–70 b 31) and *Rhetoric* (1357 b 15–1358 a 19), for example.
11 Misak, 1991, p. 17.
12 Smoke is an index (indexical type of sign) of fire, according to the classification of Peirce: see ibid.

References

Achinstein, Peter. 1992. 'Inference to the Best Explanation.' *Studies in the History and Philosophy of Science* 23, 349–64.
Acock, Malcolm. 1985. *Informal Logic Examples and Exercises*. Belmont, CA: Wadsworth.
Adams, E.M. 1954. *The Fundamentals of General Logic*. New York: Longmans, Green.
Adler, Jonathan E. 1994. 'Fallacies and Alternative Interpretations.' *Australasian Journal of Philosophy* 72, 271–82.
Antaki, Charles, ed. 1988. *Analysing Everyday Explanation*. London: Sage Publications.
Aristotle. 1937. *Rhetoric*, trans. H.J. Freese. Loeb Classical Library. Cambridge, MA: Harvard University Press.
– 1938. *Prior Analytics*, trans. Hugh Tredennick. Loeb Classical Library. Cambridge, MA: Harvard University Press.
– 1955. *On Sophistical Refutations (De Sophisticis Elenchis)*, trans. F.S. Forster. Loeb Classical Library. Cambridge, MA: Harvard University Press.
– 1987. *The Nicomachean Ethics*, trans. David Ross, revised by J.L. Ackrill and J.O. Urmson. Oxford: Oxford University Press.
Arnauld, Antoine. 1964. *The Art of Thinking (Port-Royal Logic)*, trans. James Dickoff and Patricia James. Indianapolis: Bobbs-Merrill.
Barker, Stephen F. 1965. *The Elements of Logic*. New York: McGraw-Hill.
Barth E.M., and E.C.W. Krabbe. 1982. *From Axiom to Dialogue*. New York: De Gruyter.
Beardsley, Monroe C. 1950. *Practical Logic*. Englewood Cliffs, NJ: Prentice-Hall.
Berg, Jonathan. 1987. 'Interpreting Arguments.' *Informal Logic* 9, 13–21.
Bitzer, Lloyd F. 1959. 'Aristotle's Enthymeme Revisited.' *Quarterly Journal of Speech* 45, 399–408.
– 1992. 'Whately's Distinction between Inferring and Proving.' *Philosophy and Rhetoric* 25, 311–40.

Blair, J. Anthony. 1991. 'What Is the Right Amount of Support for a Conclusion?' In *Proceedings of the Second International Conference on Argumentation*, ed. Frans H. van Eemeren, Rob Grootendorst, J. Anthony Blair, and Charles A. Willard, vol. 1A, 330–7. Amsterdam: SICSAT (Stichting International Centrum voor de Studie van Argumentatie en Taalbeheersing).

Bowles, George. 1989. 'Professor Kasachkoff on Explaining and Justifying.' *Informal Logic* 11, 107–10.

Boyce-Gibson, W.R. 1908. *The Problem of Logic*. London: Adam and Charles Black.

Bramer, M.A. 1982. 'A Survey and Critical Review of Expert Systems Research.' *Introductory Readings in Expert Systems*, ed. Donald Michie, 3–29. New York: Gordon and Breach.

Burke, Michael. 1985. 'Unstated Premises.' *Informal Logic* 7, 107–18.

Carney, James D., and Richard K. Scheer. 1964. *Fundamentals of Logic*. New York: Macmillan.

– 1974. *Fundamentals of Logic*, 2d ed. New York: Macmillan.

Castell, Alburey. 1935. *A College Logic*. New York: Macmillan.

Casullo, Albert. 1992. 'Argument.' In *A Companion to Epistemology*, ed. Jonathan Dancy and Ernest Sosa, 22. Oxford: Blackwell.

Cawsey, Alison. 1992. *Explanation and Interaction*. Cambridge, MA: MIT Press.

Clancey, William J. 1992. *Knowledge-Based Tutoring: The GUIDON Program*. London: MIT Press.

Cohen, Morris R., and Ernest Nagel. 1934. *An Introduction to Logic and Scientific Method*. New York: Harcourt, Brace & World.

Conley, Thomas E. 1984. 'The Enthymeme in Perspective.' *Quarterly Journal of Speech* 70, 168–87.

Conway, David A. 1991. 'On the Distinction between Convergent and Linked Arguments.' *Informal Logic* 13, 145–58.

Cooke, Roger M. 1991. *Experts in Uncertainty: Opinion and Subjective Probability in Science*. New York: Oxford University Press.

Copi, Irving M., and Carl Cohen. 1990. *Introduction to Logic*, 8th ed. New York: Macmillan.

Currie, Gregory. 1991. 'Text without Context: Some Errors of Stanley Fish.' *Philosophy and Literature* 15, 212–28.

Eisele, Carolyn. 1985. *Historical Perspectives on Peirce's Logic of Science*, vol. 2. Berlin: Mouton.

Ennis, Robert H. 1982. 'Identifying Implicit Assumptions.' *Synthese* 51, 61–86.

Fann, K.T. 1970. *Peirce's Theory of Abduction*. The Hague: Martinus Nijhoff.

Fish, Stanley. 1990. *Doing What Comes Naturally*. Durham, NC: Duke University Press.

Fisher, Alec. 1988. *The Logic of Real Arguments*. Cambridge: Cambridge University Press.

Fisher, Walter R. 1964. 'Uses of the Enthymeme.' *The Speech Teacher* 13, 197–203.
Fogelin, Robert. 1987. *Understanding Arguments*, 3d ed. New York: Harcourt Brace Jovanovich.
Fogelin, Robert J., and Walter Sinnott-Armstrong. 1991. *Understanding Arguments*, 4th ed. San Diego: Harcourt Brace Jovanovich.
Frankfurt, Harry G. 1958. 'Peirce's Notion of Abduction.' *The Journal of Philosophy* 55, 593–7.
Freeman, James B. 1988. *Thinking Logically*. Englewood Cliffs, NJ: Prentice-Hall.
– 1991. *Dialectics and the Macrostructure of Arguments*. Berlin: Foris.
Gabbay, Dov M., and Hans Jürgen Ohlbach. 1993. *Automated Practical Reasoning and Argumentation*. Dagstuhl Seminar Report 70. Schloss Dagstuhl, Germany.
George, Rolf. 1983. 'A Postscript on Fallacies.' *Journal of Philosophical Logic* 12, 319–25.
Gilbert, Michael A. 1991. 'The Enthymeme Buster: A Heuristic Procedure for Position Exploration in Dialogue Dispute.' *Informal Logic* 13, 159–66.
Gough, James, and Christopher Tindale. 1985. 'Hidden or Missing Premises.' *Informal Logic* 7, 99–106.
Govier, Trudy. 1985. *A Practical Study of Argument*. Belmont, CA: Wadsworth.
– 1987. *Problems in Argument Analysis and Evaluation*. Dordrecht and Providence: Foris.
– 1989a. 'Analogies and Missing Premises.' *Informal Logic* 11, 141–52.
– 1989b. 'Critical Thinking as Argument Analysis.' *Argumentation* 3, 115–26.
– 1992. *A Practical Study of Argument*, 3d ed. Belmont, CA: Wadsworth.
Grice, J. Paul. 1975. 'Logic and Conversation.' In *The Logic of Grammar*, ed. Donald Davidson and Gilbert Harman, 64–75. Encino, CA: Dickenson.
Grimaldi, William M.A. 1953. 'The Enthymeme in Aristotle.' PhD dissertation, Princeton University, Department of Classics.
Gustason, William, and Dolph E. Ulrich. 1973. *Elementary Symbolic Logic*. New York: Holt, Rinehart and Winston.
Hallie, Philip P. 1967. 'Carneades.' *Encyclopedia of Philosophy*, ed. Paul Edwards, 33–5. New York: Macmillan.
Hamblin, C.L. 1970. *Fallacies*. London: Methuen; reprt Newport News, VA: Vale Press, 1986.
Hamilton, Sir William. 1861. *Discussions on Philosophy and Literature*. New York: Harper & Brothers.
– 1874. *Lectures on Logic*, vol. 1, 3d ed. Edinburgh: William Blackwood and Sons.
Harary, Frank. 1969. *Graph Theory*. Reading, MA: Addison-Wesley.
Harary, Frank, Robert Z. Norman, and Dorwin Cartwright. 1965. *Structural Models*. New York: Wiley.

Harman, Gilbert. 1965. 'The Inference to the Best Explanation.' *Philosophical Review* 74, 88–95.
Hastings, Arthur. 1962. 'A Reformulation of the Modes of Reasoning in Argumentation,' PhD dissertation, Northwestern University.
Hempel, Carl. 1965. *Aspects of Scientific Explanation*. New York: The Free Press.
Hinderer, Drew E. 1992. *Building Arguments*. Belmont, CA: Wadsworth.
Hitchcock, David. 1985. 'Enthymematic Arguments.' *Informal Logic* 7, 83–97.
Hoaglund, John. 1987. 'Arguments and Explanations.' In *Argumentation: Across the Lines of Discipline*, vol. 3 of the Proceedings of the 1986 Conference on Argumentation, ed. Frans H. van Eemeren, Rob Grootendorst, J. Anthony Blair, and Charles A. Willard, 389–94. Dordrecht: Foris.
Hughes, William. 1992. *Critical Thinking*. Peterborough, ON: Broadview Press.
Hurley, Patrick. 1985. *A Concise Introduction to Logic*, 3d ed. Belmont, CA: Wadsworth.
– 1991. *A Concise Introduction to Logic*, 4th ed. Belmont, CA: Wadsworth.
– 1994. *A Concise Introduction to Logic*, 5th ed. Belmont, CA: Wadsworth.
Hyslop, James H. 1899. *Logic and Argument*. New York: Scribner's.
Jackson, Peter. 1986. *Introduction to Expert Systems*. Wokingham: Addison-Wesley.
Jackson, Sally, and Scott Jacobs. 1980. 'Structure of Conversational Argument: Pragmatic Bases for the Enthymeme.' *The Quarterly Journal of Speech* 66, 251–65.
Jacobs, Scott. 1989. 'Speech Acts and Arguments.' *Argumentation* 3, 345–66.
Jevons, W. Stanley. 1878. *Elementary Lessons in Logic*. London: Macmillan.
Johnson, Ralph H., and J. Anthony Blair. 1977. *Logical Self-Defence*. Toronto: McGraw-Hill Ryerson.
– 1985. 'Informal Logic: The Past Five Years 1978–1983.' *American Philosophical Quarterly* 22, 181–96.
– 1992. 'Introduction: Special Issue on Rescher's Work in Argumentation.' *Informal Logic* 14, 1–3.
Johnson, Robert M. 1992. *A Logic Book*, 2d ed., Belmont: Wadsworth.
Joseph, H.W.B. 1916. *An Introduction to Logic*. Oxford: Oxford University Press.
Josephson, John R., and Michael C. Tanner. 1994. 'Conceptual Analysis of Abduction.' *Abductive Inference*, ed. John R. Josephson and Susan G. Josephson, 5–30. New York: Cambridge University Press.
Kahane, Howard. 1978. *Logic and Philosophy: A Modern Introduction*. Belmont, CA: Wadsworth.
Kasachkoff, Tziporah. 1988. 'Explaining and Justifying.' *Informal Logic* 10, 21–30.
Kesterton, Michael. 1994. 'Social Studies.' *The Globe and Mail*, 13 October, A20.
Kienpointner, Manfred. 1987. 'Towards a Typology of Argumentative Schemes.' In *Argumentation: Across the Lines of Discipline*, vol. 3 of the Proceedings of the 1986

Conference on Argumentation, ed. Frans H. van Eemeren, Rob Grootendorst, J. Anthony Blair, and Charles A. Willard, 275–87. Dordrecht: Foris.

Kilgore, William J. 1968. *An Introductory Logic*. New York: Holt, Rinehart and Winston.

Kneupper, Charles W. 1978. 'On Argument and Diagrams.' *Journal of the American Forensic Association* 14, 181–6.

Kretzmann, Norman, and Eleonore Stump, eds. 1988. *The Cambridge Translations of Medieval Philosophical Texts*, vol. 1. Cambridge: Cambridge University Press.

Lanigan, Richard L. 1974. 'Enthymeme: The Rhetorical Species of Aristotle's Syllogism.' *The Southern Speech Communication Journal* 39, 207–22.

Latta, Robert, and Alexander MacBeath. 1956. *The Elements of Logic*. London: Macmillan.

Liddell, Henry George. 1968. *A Greek-English Lexicon*. Oxford: Oxford University Press.

Lipton, Peter. 1991. *Inference to the Best Explanation*. London: Routledge.

Little, J. Frederick, Leo A. Groarke, and Christopher W. Tindale. 1989. *Good Reasoning Matters*. Toronto: McClelland and Stewart.

McBurney, James H. 1936a. 'The Place of the Enthymeme in Rhetorical Theory.' *Speech Monographs* 3, 49–74.

– 1936b. 'Some Recent Interpretations of the Aristotelian Enthymeme.' *Papers of the Michigan Academy of Sciences, Arts and Letters* 21, 489–500.

Madden, Edward H. 1952. 'The Enthymeme: Crossroads of Logic, Rhetoric, and Metaphysics.' *The Philosophical Review* 61, 368–76.

Massie, Joseph L., and John Douglas. 1977. *Managing: A Contemporary Introduction*, 2d ed. Englewood Cliffs, NJ: Prentice-Hall.

Misak, C.J. 1991. *Truth and the End of Inquiry*. Oxford: The Clarendon Press.

Packard, Dennis J., and James E. Faulconer. 1980. *Introduction to Logic*. New York: D. van Nostrand.

Peirce, C.S. 1965. *Collected Papers of Charles Saunders Peirce*, 8 vols. Ed. Charles Hartshorne and Paul Weiss. Cambridge, MA: Harvard University Press.

Perelman, Chaim, and Lucie Olbrechts-Tyteca. 1969. *The New Rhetoric*. Notre Dame: University of Notre Dame Press.

Peter of Spain. 1988. 'Syllogisms, Topics, Fallacies (Selections).' In *The Cambridge Translations of Medieval Philosophical Texts*, vol. 1, ed. Norman Kretzmann and Eleonore Stump, 216–70. Cambridge: Cambridge University Press.

Pinto, Robert C. 1994. 'Review of Snoeck Henkemans (1992).' *Argumentation* 8, 314–18.

Quine, Willard van Orman. 1972. *Methods of Logic*, 3d ed. New York: Holt, Rinehart and Winston.

Quintilian. 1935. *Institutio Oratoria*, vol 2, trans. H.E. Butler. Loeb Library Edition. Cambridge, MA: Harvard University Press.

Reiter, Raymond. 1987. 'Nonmonotonic Reasoning.' *Annual Review of Computer Science* 2, 147–86.

Rescher, Nicholas. 1964. *Introduction to Logic*. New York: St Martin's Press.

– 1976. *Plausible Reasoning*. Assen: Van Gorcum.

Rezendes, Paul. 1992. *Tracking and the Art of Seeing*. Charlotte, VT: Camden House.

Ruben, David-Hillel. 1990. *Explaining Explanation*. London: Routledge.

Sabre, Ru Michael. 1990. 'Peirce's Abductive Argument and the Enthymeme.' *Transactions of the Charles S. Peirce Society* 26, 363–72.

Salmon, Wesley. 1971. 'A Third Dogma of Empiricism.' In *Basic Problems in Methodology and Linguistics*, ed. R. Butts and J. Hintikka, 149–66. Dordrecht: Reidel.

– 1978. 'Why Ask Why? An Inquiry Concerning Scientific Explanation.' *Proceedings and Addresses of the American Philosophical Association* 51, 683–705.

Schwartz, Thomas. *The Art of Logical Reasoning*. New York: Random House.

Scriven, Michael. 1976. *Reasoning*. New York: McGraw-Hill.

Sextus Empiricus. 1933a. *Against the Logicians*, trans. R.G. Bury. Loeb Library Edition. Cambridge, MA: Harvard University Press.

– 1933b. *Outlines of Pyrrhonism*, trans. R.G. Bury. Loeb Library Edition. Cambridge, MA: Harvard University Press.

Shoesmith, D., and T. Smiley. 1980. *Multiple-Conclusion Logic*. Cambridge: Cambridge University Press.

Sidgwick, Alfred. 1884. *Fallacies: A View of Logic from the Practical Side*. New York: D. Appleton and Co.

Snoeck Henkemans, A.F. 1992. Analyzing Complex Argumentation. PhD dissertation, University of Amsterdam, SICSAT, Amsterdam.

– 1994. 'Review of Freeman (1991).' *Argumentation* 8, 319–21.

Soccio, Douglas J., and Vincent E. Barry. 1992. *Practical Logic*. Fort Worth, TX: Harcourt Brace Jovanovich.

Spencer-Smith, Richard. 1991. *Logic and Prolog*. New York: Harvester-Wheatsheaf.

Stebbing, L. Susan. 1939. *Thinking to Some Purpose*. Harmondsworth: Penguin.

Thomas, Stephen N. 1981. *Practical Reasoning in Natural Language*, 2d ed. Englewood Cliffs, NJ: Prentice-Hall.

Toulmin, Stephen. 1958. *The Uses of Argument*. Cambridge: Cambridge University Press.

van Ditmarsch, Hans P. 1987. 'Applications of Abstraction in Argumentation.' In *Argumentation: Perspectives and Approaches*, ed. Frans H. van Eemeren, Rob Grootendorst, J. Anthony Blair, and Charles A. Willard, 162–9. Dordrecht: Foris.

van Eemeren, Frans H., and Rob Grootendorst. 1984. *Speech Acts in Argumentative Discussions*. Dordrecht and Cinnaminson: Foris.

– 1992. *Argumentation, Communication and Fallacies*. Hillsdale, NJ: Lawrence Erlbaum Associates.

van Eemeren, Frans H., Rob Grootendorst, Sally Jackson, and Scott Jacobs. 1993. *Reconstructing Argumentative Discourse*. Tuscaloosa: University of Alabama Press.

van Eemeren, Frans H., Rob Grootendorst, and Tjark Kruiger. 1984. *Argumenteren (Arguing)*. Groningen: Wolters-Noordhoff.

– 1987. *Handbook of Argumentation Theory*. Dordrecht: Foris.

van Eemeren, Frans H., and Tjark Kruiger. 1987. 'Identifying Argumentation Schemes.' In *Argumentation: Perspectives and Approaches*, ed. Frans H. van Eemeren et al., 70–81. Dordrecht and Providence: Foris.

Veitch, John. 1901. *Hamilton*. Edinburgh: William Blackwood and Sons.

Verbiest, Agnes. 1991. 'A New Supply of Argumentative Indicators?' In *Proceedings of the Second International Conference on Argumentation*, ed. Frans H. van Eemeren, Rob Grootendorst, J. Anthony Blair, and Charles A. Willard, 448–54. Amsterdam: SICSAT.

von Wright, G.H. 1971. *Explanation and Understanding*. Ithaca, NY: Cornell University Press.

Vorobej, Mark. 1992. 'Defining Deduction.' *Informal Logic* 14, 105–18.

Walton, Douglas N. 1980. '*Petitio Principii* and Argument Analysis.' In *Informal Logic: The First International Symposium*, ed. J. Anthony Blair and Ralph H. Johnson, 41–54. Inverness, CA: Edgepress.

– 1983. 'Enthymemes.' *Logique et Analyse* 103, 395–410.

– 1984. *Logical Dialogue-Games and Fallacies*. Lanham: University Press of America.

– 1987. *Informal Fallacies*. Amsterdam and Philadelphia: John Benjamins.

– 1988. 'Burden of Proof.' *Argumentation* 2, 233–54.

– 1989. *Informal Logic*. Cambridge: Cambridge University Press.

– 1990a. *Practical Reasoning*. Savage, MD: Rowman and Littlefield.

– 1990b. 'What Is Reasoning? What Is an Argument?' *The Journal of Philosophy* 87, 399–419.

– 1991. *Begging the Question: Circular Reasoning as a Tactic of Argumentation*. New York: Greenwood Press.

– 1992a. *The Place of Emotion in Argument*. University Park: Penn State Press.

– 1992b. *Plausible Argument in Everyday Conversation*. Albany: State University of New York Press.

– 1992c. 'Rules for Plausible Reasoning.' *Informal Logic* 4, 33–51.

– 1992d. *Slippery Slope Arguments*. Oxford: Oxford University Press.

– 1993. 'Commitment, Types of Dialogue, and Fallacies.' *Informal Logic* 14, 93–103.

– 1995. *A Pragmatic Theory of Fallacy*. Tuscaloosa: University of Alabama Press.

– 1996. *Argumentation Schemes for Presumptive Reasoning*. Mahwah, NJ: Lawrence Erlbaum Associates.

Walton, Douglas N., and Lynn M. Batten. 1984. 'Games, Graphs and Circular Arguments.' *Logique et Analyse* 106, 133–64.

Walton, Douglas N., and Erik C.W. Krabbe. 1995. *Commitment in Dialogue*. Albany: State University of New York Press.

Whately, Richard. 1859. *Elements of Logic*. New York: Sheldon & Co.

Willard, Charles A. 1976. 'On the Utility of Descriptive Diagrams for the Analysis and Criticism of Arguments.' *Communication Monographs* 43, 308–19.

– 1978. 'Argument as Non-discursive Symbolism.' *Journal of the American Forensic Association* 14, 187–93.

Windes, Russel R., and Arthur Hastings. 1965. *Argumentation and Advocacy*. New York: Random House.

Yanal, Robert J. 1988. *Basic Logic*. St Paul: West Publishing.

– 1991. 'Dependent and Independent Reasons.' *Informal Logic* 13, 137–44.

Index

abduction, 258, 260, 277–8; *see also* inference
abstraction, 91
absurdity, 16
Achinstein, Peter, 278
Acock, Malcolm, 125
Adams, E.M., 223
ad hominem attacks, 236
Adler, Jonathan E., 266
ambiguity, 104, 208
Amsterdam School, 9–10, 176, 180
antagonist, 114, 116, 173
appeal: to an analogy, 244; to expert opinion, 47; to pity, 75; to relevance, 113
argument, 8, 19, 40, 58, 62, 66, 72, 76, 176, 201; abductive, 39, 279; *ad hominem*, 25; affirming the consequent, 256, 279; *argumentum ad populum*, 32; bad, 170–1, 180; balance-of-considerations, 269; chain of, 120, 186, 234; characteristics of, 60; circular, 21, 185, 187; conditional evaluation of, 253; convergent, 36–7, 78–80, 95, 97–8, 118, 126, 155, 187, 196; —, defined, 87, 114–16, 147, 170–1; co-ordinative compound (*see also* argument, linked), 115, 155, 157; Copi–Cohen criterion, 23; cumulative, 158; deductive, 39, 102, 106, 211, 218, 226, 240, 249, 254, 256, 281; deductively invalid, 200, 228; deductively valid, 9, 46, 137–8, 143, 163, 171, 173–4, 233, 237, 239, 241, 271; defeasible, 244; defined, 3–4, 11, 18, 28, 40, 59, 61, 65, 176–7; —, problems with, 20; devil's advocacy, 12; diagram, 67, 79–80, 94, 197, 199, 207, 210, 218; —, primary function of, 79; diagramming, 35–6, 83–4, 93, 165, 256; —, criticisms, 198, 218; —, goal of, 218; divergent, 91, 186; *epicheirema*, 224; evaluation, 33, 81, 137, 256; evidence-accumulating, 99, 125, 150, 156–8, 273; extended, 92; fallacious, 79; forward-moving, 279; from analogy, 238–9, 246–8; from ignorance, 241, 258; from sign, 47–8, 129, 133, 227–8, 231, 245, 270–1, 273; function of, 73; goal-directed action, 39; hypothetical, 61, 97, 241; ideal, 151; identification, 33, 74, 108; inductive, 39, 240, 254, 256; invalid, 9, 238;

linked, 35–7, 67, 78–9, 91, 95, 97–8, 100, 118, 127, 177, 187, 196, 198; —, defined, 85, 110, 115, 125, 147, 170–1; meta-argument, 40; multiple (*see also* argument, convergent), 114–15, 155, 157; plausibilistic, 256; presumptive, 46, 129, 174, 215, 240–1, 244, 254, 256; probative, 21–2, 272; probative function, 21; purposes of, 9, 18; *reductio ad absurdum*, 12, 14, 38; *reductio ad falsum*, 13; semantic concept of, 37; sequence of, 93, 103, 225; serial, 84, 89, 186; single, 20, 84, 100; sorites, 224; strategy of maximally argumentative argumentation, 45; straw man, 164; subarguments, 92, 99–100; three essential characteristics of, 18; to the best explanation, 267–8; types of, 245–6; versus explanation, x, 35, 43, 48–9, 52, 57, 59, 63–4, 72–3, 79, 94–6, 202, 204, 206, 217; versus non-arguments, 14, 26–7, 43–4, 52; versus reasoning, 55; weak, 147, 265
argumentation: contra-argumentation, 9, 61, 240; counter-argumentation, 233; pro-argumentation, 9, 11, 61, 240; schemes, 28, 156, 163, 218, 239
Aristotle, 9, 24, 167–8, 202, 222, 226, 229–30, 245, 264–5, 268–70
Arnauld, Antoine, 222
Art of Thinking, 222
artificial-intelligence system, 131, 203
assumption, 8, 11, 16, 19, 249; contextual, 13; mere, 11; missing, 237

Barker, Stephen F., 225

Barry, Vincent E., 10, 211, 226
Batten, Lynn M., 94, 187
Beardsley, Monroe, 28, 85, 87, 89, 126, 159, 185
Berg, Jonathan, 212, 214, 216
bias, 198, 207
Bitzer, Lloyd F., 14, 227–8
Blair, J. Anthony, 113, 133–4, 155, 158, 201
Boethius, 230
burden of proof, 40, 119–20, 132, 147, 154–5, 167–8, 172, 177, 179, 182, 201, 215, 219, 240, 271, 273; failure of, 166; meeting the, 166, 239, 249; oblique, 177; positive, 177

Carneades, 246
Carney, James D., 7, 222
Cartwright, Dorwin, 184
Cassiodorus, 264
Castell, Alburey, 223, 231
Casullo, Albert, 6
causation, 278
Cawsey, Alison, 29
claim, 5, 7, 10, 18, 20, 22, 40, 44; first, 90; general, 90; specific, 90
Clancey, William J., 262
Cohen, Carl, 4–6, 13, 44–5, 49–54, 60–1, 82, 86–8, 95, 109–13, 120, 126, 152–3, 161–2, 202, 223, 226
commitments, 152, 203, 210, 217, 233, 243, 250–1; arguer's, 210, 214; dark-side, 203, 251; explicit, 243; propositional, 173; rules, 210, 214; set, 218; speaker's, 237; store, 173, 216
communication, speech, 27
computer science, 30, 254, 256, 260
conclusion, 3, 7–8, 11, 16–17, 20, 22, 26, 48, 58, 67, 79–80, 83, 88, 97,

146, 172, 176, 217, 219–20, 250, 270; defeasible, 245; defined, 38; multiple, 84, 92, 186; non-explicit, 41, 235, 237; one, 84, 92; reasonable, 276; subconclusion, 101; two independent, 91; ultimate, 84
conditional, 176, 263, 267–8, 270, 274–5; defeasible, 267; presumptive, 163, 261, 270, 274; prior, 278; strict, 111, 163; universal, 257
conditions: consistency, 145; plausibility, 145; relevance, 145; sufficient, 174
conflict, 162; of interests, 18; of opinions, 18, 168, 172
contradiction, 16
conversations, everyday, 152
Conway, David A., 129
Cooke, Roger M., 280–1
Copi, Irving, 4–5, 13, 44–5, 49–54, 60–1, 82, 86–8, 94, 109–13, 120, 126, 152–3, 161–2, 202, 226
counterblaming, 25
criminal trial, 215
criticism, conditional, 33

decision, practical, 55
deconstruction, 206
deductive–nomological (DN) model, 28
deductivism, 238–9, 244
deliberation, 24–5, 55, 246; personal, 65; practical, 172; prior, 45
demonstration, 24
description, 26, 94–5
De Sophisticis Elenchis, 9
dialectical shifts, 23
dialogue: advice-giving, 234; cooperative informing, 29; context of, 18, 65, 75, 96, 182, 215, 217, 240; eristic type of, 25, 61; expert-consultation, 26, 71; goal of, 27, 63; information-conveying, 71; information-seeking, 25; mixed, 23; negotiation, 23, 39, 61, 204; pedagogical, 26, 63, 70–1, 73, 204, 206; permissive persuasion (PPD), 251; persuasion, 21, 23–4, 39, 172; question-reply, 278; rigorous persuasion (RPD), 251; rules of game of, 215
Dialogues Concerning Two New Sciences, 15
digraph, 184–6; implication, 185; total implication, 185
disagreement, implied, 62
discussion: critical, 23, 25, 28, 61, 63, 152, 168, 172, 174, 179, 204, 206, 220; rule-governed, 28
distinction, linked–convergent, 114–15, 118, 145, 160, 167–8, 175, 191–2, 204, 206, 212, 218, 249
Douglas, John, 69

eikos, 229–30, 232, 269
elenchos, 9
Ennis, Robert H., 249
enthymemes, 13, 21, 80, 160, 197, 203, 206, 211, 231, 249, 269; analysis of, 185; buster, 221, 242; defined, 220, 222–3, 226, 230, 233; optimal method of completing, 221; paradigmatic, 241; ploy, 238
Euclidean geometry, 15
evidence: contextual, 205, 210; structural, 205
explanandum, 47, 60, 62, 70, 96
explanans, 47, 96
explanation, 8, 19, 22, 26, 31, 45, 57–8, 68, 72, 76; aim, 76; circular, 34;

defined, 65–6; kinds of, 59; purpose of, 60; reverse, 29
fallacy, 96, 103, 212, 214, 236, 263–4; *ad populum*, 32; affirming the consequent, 262–3; analysis of, 266; of arguing in a circle, 34, 81; of begging the question, 21, 79, 81, 151, 175, 186, 192, 195, 274; denying the antecedent, 266; of hasty generalizations, 232; of misleading precision, 128; parallel, 168; of *petitio principii*, 36–7, 175, 186; of reversing the conditional, 265; of *secundum quid*, 106, 232, 242–3; straw man, 208, 211, 214, 216–18, 221, 250, 252–3
Fann, K.T., 258–9
Faulconer, James E., 8
fight, verbal, 25
Fisher, Alec, 11, 204
Fogelin, Robert J., 28
foundationalism, 24
Freeman, James B., 6, 25, 51, 81, 112, 174

Galileo, 15–16
generalization, 253; defeasible, 248; enthymematic, 232; existential, 46; inductive, 125, 240, 247–8; premise, 241; presumptive, 248; probabilistic, 245; universal, 123, 245, 247–8, 281
Gilbert, Michael A., 220–1, 241–2
goal, 24, 55
Gough, James, 238
Govier, Trudy, 5, 10, 25, 46, 56, 71–3, 75, 113, 214, 238–9, 244, 247–8
graph, directed, 94; *see also* digraph
Grice, J. Paul, 236
Gricean: maxim of relation, 237; presumptions, 216; principle, cooperative conversational, 23, 207

Grimaldi, William M.A., 229
Groarke, Leo A., 63, 65, 211
Grootendorst, Rob, 9, 11, 23, 28, 45–6, 61, 93, 114–15, 118, 122–3, 139, 146–7, 149, 154, 157, 169, 175, 201–2, 204, 206, 210, 212
Gustason, William, 8

Hamblin, C.L., 75, 186, 210, 264
Hamilton, Sir William, 213, 223, 230
Harary, Frank, 184–5
Harman, Gilbert, 259
Hastings, Arthur, 116–18, 120, 158, 272–3
Hinderer, Drew E., 59
Hoaglund, John, 96
Hughes, William, 59
Hurley, Patrick, 8, 17, 57, 60–1, 86, 89, 105–7, 223
hypothesis, 259, 270; defeasible, 274; plausible, 276
Hyslop, James H., 223

implicature, 236
indeterminancy problem, 56
indicator-word, 19, 30, 42, 56, 58, 70, 77, 83, 86, 89–90, 96, 98, 102, 152, 157, 160–1, 170, 177–9, 181, 201, 205, 209–10, 215; conclusion, 90; contra-indicator, 245; limitation of, 52; premise, 90
indicators, 273–6, ancillary diagnostic, 167; conclusion, 49, 51; contextual, 281; premise, 49–50; suggestion, 51
inference, 4, 11, 14, 29, 53–4, 71, 196, 256, 259; abductive, 30, 176, 255–7, 258, 260, 262, 274; —, from sign, 275; backwards-directed, 259; to the best explanation, 277–8; chain of, 19, 176; deductive, 176, 257, 261; faulty,

214; goal-directed practical, 54; hypothetical, 14; hypothetical sequence of, 17; inductive, 176, 257; lack-of-knowledge, 258; *modus ponens,* 263, 275; necessary, 271; non-deductive inference structure, 173; plausible, 256; practical, 55, 92; presumptive, 269; prior, 274; rules of, 186, 254; sequence of, 41; steps, 188; —, back-and forth steps of, 189
innuendo, 236, 267
inquiry, 22, 24, 83, 179, 194–5; aim, 24; scientific, 172, 206, 258, 271, 276, 278
Institutio Oratia, 269
insufficiency, 169
intentions, speaker's, 74
interviews, 26
issue, 38; open, 38

Jackson, Sally, 262
Jacobs, Scott, 11
Jevons, W. Stanley, 231
Johnson, Robert M., 83–4, 113
Joseph, H.W.B., 224–5, 230–1
Josephson, John R., 259
justification, 31–3, 44–5, 49, 68, 113; circle-free, 193; defined, 65

Kahane, Howard, 8
Kasachkoff, Tziporah, 28, 96
knowledge-based system, 203
Krabbe, Eric, 11, 23, 210, 214, 216, 251
Kretzmann, Norman, 222
Kruiger, Tjark, 9, 45–6

language, interpretation of, 265; natural, 4, 37, 61, 107, 207–8, 218, 220–1, 225–6
Latta, Robert, 231

Lavoisier, 57
Lectures on Logic, 223
links, inferential, 84
Lipton, Peter, 277–8
Little, Frederick, 63, 65, 211
logic, 7, 27, 79, 104, 181; deductive, 225, 240, 246; formal, 16; propositional, 107; Stoic principles of, 21; syllogistic, 221–2, 225

MacBeath, Alexander, 231
margin of error, 165
Massie, Joseph L., 68
Mill, John Stuart, 213
Misak, C.J., 256, 258–9
modus ponens, 21, 87, 102, 121, 131, 138, 152, 160–1, 163, 172, 178, 186, 209–10, 252, 254–5, 261–4, 275, 279
modus tollens, 13, 15, 257

Nagel, Ernest, 223
Norman, Robert Z., 184
Nosich, Gerald, 94

Olbrechts-Tyteca, Lucie, 246
On Sophistical Refutations, 265–6
Outlines of Pyrrhonism, 21

Packard, Dennis J., 8
Peirce, C.S., 30, 245–6, 256, 270, 277–8
Perelman, Chaim, 246
Peter of Spain, 222
Pinto, Robert, 133–4, 158, 174
plausibility, 250
Port-Royal Logic, 222
positivists, 281
premise, 3, 7–8, 11–12, 16–17, 22, 26, 58, 67, 79, 83, 97, 105, 118, 146, 150,

170, 172, 176, 219–20, 227, 231; complementary, 134; conditional, 263, 280–1; defined, 38; explicit, 238; hidden, 46, 234; identification of, 41; linked, 133; missing (non-explicit), x, 95, 105–6, 211, 217–18, 220, 226, 230, 238, 244, 251; multiple, 84; non-explicit, 13, 79, 105–6, 142, 151, 221, 225, 229, 233–4, 238, 245, 248–50, 252–3, 255, 281; one, 84; pre-evident, 21; sequence of, 57; tacit, 225; three, 131; two, 111–12, 137, 169, 234

presumption, 19; basic, 144; weight of, 273

principle: of agnosticism, 216; of charity, 164, 208, 211, 213, 253; of clarity, 213; of loyalty, 213; of maximally argumentative analysis, 212; moderate, 214; of neutrality, 213; of principled preference, 213, 216; weakest-link, 120

Prior Analytics, 231

probability-values, 148

proofs: indirect, 4, 15–17; lack of definitive, 18; *reductio,* 15

proponent, 38, 172

propositions, 3, 18–19, 22, 70, 76, 92, 94, 186–7, 217; hypothetical, 61; missing, 231; sequence of, 103

protagonist, 114, 116, 173

quarrel, 25

questions, 39; critical, 246, 272; key, 248; sequence of reasoned, 274; why, 64, 75–6

Quine, Willard van Orman, 233

Quintilian, 269

reasoning, 4, 8–9, 11, 30, 38, 41, 66, 76, 96, 146, 179, 191; abductive, 197, 203, 254, 268, 274, 280; back-and-forth sequence of, 281; backward sequence of, 30, 191; backward-chaining, 260; chain of, 14–15, 35, 64, 124, 186; circular, 33, 37, 175, 189, 193–4; conversational, 270; converse structure, 191; deductive, 186, 215, 232, 245, 276; default, 229; defeasible, 32, 158, 232, 273, 276; defined, 176; forward-chaining, 260; graph, 187; hypothetical, 15, 19, 177; lack of, 189; line of, 189–90; inductive, 215, 245; inevitable circle, 193; mathematical, 167; mode of, 272; nonmonotonic, 270; out-tree, 194; pathway, 189; —, circular, 193; —, inevitable, 193; plausible, 270; practical, 26, 44–5, 53–5, 65, 87, 178, 234–5; presumptive, 47–8, 102, 158, 160, 215, 246, 257, 273; probative, 177; propositional, 249; provisional, 177; purpose of, 179; reverse sequence of, 279; scientific, 281; semicircular, 190; sequence of, 13, 18, 20, 28, 58, 76, 78, 102, 160, 187, 189–90, 219; source, 194; structure, 187; syllogistic, 229–30; tree, 194–5; vague, 205

reasons, 127

refutation, 9; strong, 22; weak, 22

relevance: probative, 113; topical, 113

Rescher, Nicholas, 25, 211, 226

requirement: falsity, 119; insufficient proof, 119; no-support, 119; suspension, 119; two conclusion, 119

respondent (opponent), 30, 38; doubt conception, 176

retraction, 24

Rezendes, Paul, 275
Rhetoric, 228–9
rules: of inference validity, 173; plausibilistic, 262; universal, 242

Scheer, Richard K., 7, 222
Schwartz, Thomas, 226
science, 11–15, 28
scientific argumentation, 281
scientific explanation, 29
scientific inquiry, 29, 39
Scriven, Michael, 96, 244–5, 252
semeion, 232
settledness, 31
Sextus Empiricus, 21, 230, 271–2, 278–9
Shoesmith, D., 81, 92, 94, 186
Sidgwick, Alfred, 265
sign, 271; predictive, 277; retrodictive, 277
situation, initial, 62
Skinner, B.F., 57
Smiley, T., 81, 92, 94, 186
Snoeck Henkemans, Francisca, 81, 133–4, 157–8, 169, 175–6, 181, 204
Soccio, Douglas J., 10, 211, 226
Stebbing, L. Susan, 264
Spencer-Smith, Richard, 260–1
Study in Scarlet, 99, 130, 158–9, 273
Stump, Eleonore, 222
sufficiency, 116, 119, 124, 143, 151, 154–6, 162, 164–6, 168–9, 171–2, 175, 201, 209, 215
supposition, 12
syllogismos, 9
syllogisms, 37, 107, 121, 138, 160, 222–3, 225–6, 232, 249–50, 264; categorical, 137–8, 223; chain of, 224; episyllogism, 224; explicit, 223; hypothetical, 138; incomplete, 224; prosyllogism, 224

tacit, 231
tactic, 212
Tanner, Michael C., 259
tests, 121, 200, 275; Copi–Cohen, 54, 60, 110–13, 162; degree support (*Degree Supp.*), 127–8, 130, 135–6, 139, 142–4, 146–50, 152, 158–9, 165–6, 168, 176, 180, 182; dialectical, 77; falsity/insufficient proof (*Fals./Insuf. Prf.*), 119; falsity/no support (*Fals./No Supp.*), 114, 119–25, 131–7, 139–44, 146–7, 153, 162, 180, 204; Freeman, James B., 112, 114, 152; Hurley, Patrick, 56–7; negative-exclusion, 58; proposition-testing method, 173; quick, 205; summing, 128–9, 132, 140, 142, 143, 149, 160–1, 165, 167; suspension/diminishment of support, 121, 125; suspension/insufficient proof (*Susp./Insuf. Prf.*), 119–22, 124–5, 132–7, 139–44, 146–57, 160–2, 164, 166–7, 171, 179, 181, 201–2, 204; suspension/no support (*Susp./No Supp.*), 113, 120, 153–4, 180; Thomas–Acock, 125–6, 159, 165; van Eemeren and Grootendorst, 156, 162, 165, 170–1, 176, 181; Yanal, 159
theorists, European, ix
thinking, critical, 94
Thomas, Stephen N., 43, 50–1, 65–9, 71, 73–4, 81, 85, 96, 125–6, 159, 206, 237
Tindale, Christopher, 63, 65, 211, 238
Toulmin, Stephen, 222
Tractatus, 222
truth, 23–4

www.ingramcontent.com/pod-product-compliance
Lightning Source LLC
Chambersburg PA
CBHW071955290426
44109CB00018B/2025